SMALL GROUP COMMUNICATION
Theory & Practice
An Anthology

Eighth Edition

Randy Y. Hirokawa
University of Iowa

Robert S. Cathcart
*Queens College of the City University
of New York, Emeritus*

Larry A. Samovar
San Diego State University

Linda D. Henman
*Psychological Associates,
St. Louis, Missouri*

New York   Oxford
OXFORD UNIVERSITY PRESS

Oxford University Press, Inc., publishes works that further Oxford University's objective of excellence in research, scholarship, and education.

Oxford New York
Auckland Cape Town Dar es Salaam Hong Kong Karachi
Kuala Lumpur Madrid Melbourne Mexico City Nairobi
New Delhi Shanghai Taipei Toronto

With offices in
Argentina Austria Brazil Chile Czech Republic France Greece
Guatemala Hungary Italy Japan Poland Portugal Singapore
South Korea Switzerland Thailand Turkey Ukraine Vietnam

Copyright © 2003 by Oxford University Press, Inc.

Published by Oxford University Press, Inc.
198 Madison Avenue, New York, New York 10016
http://www.oup.com

Oxford is a registered trademark of Oxford University Press

ISBN 978-0-19-533000-7

Contents

Part I: The Nature of Groups

Part II: Theories of Small Group Communication

*Indicates chapter new to this edition.

Part III: Organization of Groups

Part IV: Group Processes

---

*Indicates chapter new to this edition.

Part V: Groups and Teams

Part VI: Leadership in Groups

---

*Indicates chapter new to this edition.

Part VII: Diversity in Groups

Part VIII: Analyzing Group Communication

---

*Indicates chapter new to this edition.

---

*Indicates chapter new to this edition.

Preface

In the popular 1980s movie *Back to the Future*, the main characters go into the past to save the future. The Eighth Edition of *Small Group Communication* likewise draws on previous editions to produce a cutting-edge reader that should sustain the intellectual needs and pique the interest of today's students.

As in the past, we intend this anthology to serve as a general reader. Therefore, we have included materials that are broadly based and comprehensive. We avoid advocating any one particular theory or methodological approach to studying small group communication, preferring instead to give the reader a balanced sampling of the diverse philosophies and concepts that constitute the fascinating study of small group communication.

This edition continues a long-standing tradition of providing students with the most current thinking from the top scholars in the field of small group communication. Carry-over selections from previous editions have been updated, and a number of new readings have been added to make this anthology as up-to-date as possible.

Philosophy of this Book

What has not changed in this edition is our philosophy in putting this book together. We believe that group communication is a *social activity* with *consequential outcomes*. In other words, communication makes a difference in small groups. The reader will note that all selections focus on the link between communication and its group outcomes.

Organization and Content

The Eighth Edition presents an organizational structure that departs from the "mini-textbook" format of the previous edition. Here, the readings are organized into eight parts. Part I, *The Nature of Groups*, presents three chapters introducing students to the definitions and characteristics of small groups. Part II, *Theories of Small Group Communication*, provides three chapters that elaborate on major theories of group communication. Part III, *Organization of Groups*, contains two chapters that discuss how groups and their communication develop and change over time. Part IV, *Group Processes*, has three chapters that present different aspects of group communication processes as they are exhibited in small groups. Part V, *Groups and Teams*, includes four chapters that focus on communication and performance in various kinds of groups and teams. Part VI, *Leadership in Groups*, provides three chapters that review major concepts and theories relevant to an understanding of small group leadership. Part VII, *Diversity in Groups*, features three chapters focusing on diversity and intercultural issues related to small groups. Part VIII, *Analyzing Group Communication*, consists of three chapters that elaborate on different methodological approaches to analyzing and studying communication processes in small groups.

The Editors begin each part with a short introduction explaining the importance of the area and topics covered. ✦

Acknowledgments

As in the past, a great many people have helped us with this project. We especially want to thank our publisher, Claude Teweles, for giving us the freedom to develop this anthology as we thought best and to produce the best book possible.

Given the rapid changes in the field of small group communication in the last two decades, we would not have been able to keep this anthology up-to-date without the cooperation of the many scholars who contributed to this volume.

Finally, we wish to thank the many academics who graciously gave of their time to review the manuscript for the Eighth Edition. The quality of this book would not have been possible without their thoughtful guidance and advice. ◆

About the Editors

Randy Y. Hirokawa received his Ph.D. from the University of Washington and is Professor and Chair of Communication Studies and Adjunct Professor of Community and Behavioral Health, at the University of Iowa. He is known for his expertise in the area of small group communication and decision-making processes and has published more than 50 journal articles and book chapters in this area. He is the Coeditor of *Communication and Group Decision-Making*, now in its Second Edition. He was the Editor of *Communication Studies*, the scholarly journal of the Central States Communication Association, from 1991–1994, and currently serves on the editorial board of four communication journals.

Robert S. Cathcart is Professor Emeritus from Queens College of the City University of New York. He was formerly Chairman of the Department of Communication Arts and Sciences and Director of the Media Communications Research Center at Queens College. He was a member of President Lyndon Johnson's Advisory Committee on Educational Policy and Visiting Professor at Oxford University, England, and Sophia University, Japan. He is the author of six books on business communication and mass communication.

Larry A. Samovar is a Professor in the School of Communication at San Diego State University, where he has taught for 40 years. He received his Ph.D. from Purdue University and taught at that school for five years. He has authored or co-authored 13 books during the last 35 years. Many of his books have been translated and are currently being used in 11 countries. He has presented over a hundred papers at national and international conferences and has also served as a consultant in several countries.

Linda D. Henman (Ph.D.) is currently a Director of Performance Consulting at Psychological Associates in St. Louis, Missouri. Formerly, she was a communication instructor for the St. Louis Community College and Adjunct Graduate Professor in the Human Resource Development Department at Webster University. She has been a corporate consultant, trainer, and keynote speaker for more than 20 years in private, public, and government organizations. ✦

About the Contributors

J. Kevin Barge (Ph.D.) is Associate Professor of Speech Communication at the University of Georgia.

Steven A. Beebe (Ph.D.) is Professor and Chair of Communication Studies and Associate Dean of the College of Fine Arts and Communication at Southwest Texas State University.

Ernest G. Bormann (Ph.D.) is Professor Emeritus of Speech Communication at the University of Minnesota, Minneapolis.

Dale E. Brashers (Ph.D.) is Associate Professor of Speech Communication at the University of Illinois at Urbana-Champaign.

Judee K. Burgoon (Ed.D.) is Professor of Communication, Professor of Family Studies and Human Development, and Director of Human Communication Research for the Center for the Management of Information at the University of Arizona.

Robert S. Cathcart (Ph.D.) is Emeritus Professor of Communication, Queens College of the City University of New York.

Carolyn C. Clark (Ph.D.) is Professor of Communication and currently serves as the Communication Department Coordinator at Salt Lake Community College.

Kathleen M. Clauson (Ph.D.) is Vice Provost for the College of Professional Studies at Graceland University in Lamoni, Iowa.

Juliann Dahlberg (B.A.) is Facilitator for Fund Raising Events at the Levitt Center for University Advancement, University of Iowa.

Daniel H. DeGooyer, Jr. (Ph.D.) is Assistant Professor of Communication at the University of North Carolina at Greensboro.

Akiko Fukumoto (M.A.) is a doctoral candidate in the Department of Communication and Journalism at the University of New Mexico.

Connie J. G. Gersick (Ph.D.) is Visiting Scholar at the Yale University School of Management.

Dennis S. Gouran (Ph.D.) is Professor of Communication Arts and Sciences and Labor Studies and Industrial Relations at The Pennsylvania State University.

Beth Bonniwell Haslett (Ph.D.) is Professor of Communication at the University of Delaware.

Linda D. Henman (Ph.D.) is Director of Performance Consulting at Psychological Associates in St. Louis, Missouri.

Randy Y. Hirokawa (Ph.D.) is Professor and Chair of Communication Studies at the University of Iowa.

Mercilee M. Jenkins (Ph.D.) is Professor and Graduate Studies Coordinator in the Department of Speech and Communication Studies at San Francisco State University.

Joann Keyton (Ph.D.) is Professor of Communication Studies at the University of Kansas.

Mary Meares (Ph.D.) is Assistant Professor in the Edward R. Murrow School of Communication at Washington State University.

Renee A. Meyers (Ph.D.) is Professor and Chair of Communication at the University of Wisconsin-Milwaukee.

John G. Oetzel (Ph.D.) is Associate Professor of Communication and Journalism at the University of New Mexico.

John R. Ogilvie (Ph.D.) is Associate Professor of Management at the University of Hartford.

Robyn E. Parker (Ph.D.) is Assistant Professor of Communication Studies at Kent State University.

Marshall Scott Poole (Ph.D.) is Professor of Communication at Texas A&M University.

Richard E. Porter (Ph.D.) is Emeritus Professor of Speech Communication at California State University, Long Beach.

Linda L. Putnam (Ph.D.) is Professor of Communication at Texas A & M University.

Nina M. Reich (M.A.) is a doctoral candidate in the Department of Speech Communication at the University of North Carolina at Chapel Hill.

Larry A. Samovar (Ph.D.) is Professor of Communication at San Diego State University.

Craig R. Scott (Ph.D.) is Associate Professor of Communication Studies at the University of Texas at Austin.

Susan B. Shimanoff (Ph.D.) is Professor of Speech Communication at San Francisco State University.

Richard W. Sline (Ph.D.) is Assistant Professor of Communication at Weber State University in Ogden, Utah.

Kathleen S. Valde (Ph.D.) is Assistant Professor of Communication at Northern Illinois University.

Julia T. Wood (Ph.D.) is the Lineberger Distinguished Professor of Humanities at the University of North Carolina at Chapel Hill. ✦

Part I

The Nature of Groups

Most of us are pretty sure we know what a small group is. After all, small groups are all around us, and we are all members of one or more of them. However, coming up with a precise definition of a small group that everyone agrees with has proven to be a challenge for small group scholars. Because serious scholarship demands that we define our key terms and concepts clearly so others know what we are talking about, we begin this book by addressing the most basic of questions: What is a small group?

Defining Elements

A small group has been defined simply as a collection of people, few enough in number to be able to interact and communicate with each other on a regular basis in order to reach a common goal (Homans 1950, 1). There are five basic elements of a group that are embedded in such a basic definition: number, purpose, interdependence, perceptual boundary, and interaction.

First, the *number of people* is significant. To be considered a "small" group, there must be at least three, and no more than 12 to 15, people. Most group scholars would agree that three to seven people would constitute a "small group."

Second, small groups have a *shared purpose*. The success or effectiveness of a group is partially dependent upon the degree to which members of the group share a desire to achieve a commonly agreed-upon goal. This does not mean that every member of the group must want the same thing(s)—indeed, individual goals are a prominent feature of most groups. However, unless a gathering of people shares at least one common goal toward which they are all willing to contribute their individual efforts, they cannot function together as a group.

The third element that distinguishes a small group from other aggregates of people is the *interdependence* of group members. In a small group, the actions and behaviors of individual members both affect, and are affected by, the actions and behaviors of others in the collectivity. For example, a group member who fails to carry out his or her assignment could make it difficult for others in the group to carry out their assignments. Also, the absence of a group member at a meeting can hinder the progress of the entire group if that member happens to have important information that the rest of the group needs to move forward with its task. In short, the success of a small group depends on the contributions of each group member; they rely on each other to reach their shared goals.

The fourth defining property of a group is the existence of *perceived boundaries*. A small group exists when its members are able to identify themselves as part of the group and, more importantly, differentiate themselves from those outside of the group. The ability of group members to distinguish between "insiders" and "outsiders" depends on the presence of shared characteristics that help participants identify themselves as members of a particular group. For example, group members might be identified by the clothes they wear, or by the words they use, or by the geographical location where they meet and spend time together. These shared characteristics serve as perceptual markers that allow group members to separate those who belongs in the group from those who do not.

The fifth defining element of a group is the presence of *regular interaction and communication* among participants. With rare exceptions, group members are expected to communicate openly and often with one another. Interaction among group members is the basis for sharing information, providing feedback, coordinating actions, persuading others, controlling group situations, establishing rules and procedures, and so forth (Poole and Hirokawa 1986).

The advent of new communication technologies and computer-mediated electronic interactions has resulted in the emergence of new forms of small groups that challenge traditional notions of what a group is and suggest the need to expand our definition of small groups. The chapters in Part I present some current thinking about what constitutes a small group and what its defining characteristics are.

References

Homans, G. C. (1950). *The Human Group.* New York: Harcourt, World, and Brace, Inc.

Poole, M. S., and Hirokawa, R. Y. (1986). "Communication and group decision-making: A critical assessment." In R. Y. Hirokawa and M. S. Poole (eds.), *Communication and Group Decision-Making.* Beverly Hills, CA: Sage. ✦

Chapter 1
Groups as Systems

Linda D. Henman

This chapter provides us with a way of thinking about groups based on general systems theory. Henman presents the small group as an "open system" and identifies its various system-related characteristics. In doing so, she argues that viewing a small group as an open social system is the most useful way of understanding group process.

People thought for centuries that dissecting, reducing, and taking things apart was the best way to learn about something. Scientists examined an entity by analyzing each individual component, further splitting the elements until the smallest part could be scrutinized. This way of looking at the world was popular until the twentieth century. Then a new approach to understanding began to surface: the systems approach.

In 1952, Ludwig Von Bertelanffy, a theoretical biologist, identified this new approach as general systems theory. General systems theory allowed a novel way to think about and study the interactive and dynamic alterations of living phenomena (Von Bertelanffy 1952). The essence of this theory is that a system is a structure of an *organized set of interrelated and interacting parts that maintain their own balance amid the influences of the environment.*

Social scientists, psychologists, and organizational theorists began to see systems theory as a way of explaining the complicated dynamics of interpersonal relationships. In his book *The Fifth Discipline,* Peter Senge explained human endeavors as "invisible fabrics of interrelated actions." Systems thinking is a "conceptual framework, a body of knowledge and tools that has been developed over the past fifty years, to make the full patterns clearer, and to help us see how to change them effectively" (Senge 1990, 7). Applying this approach in the study of small groups was the next step to providing an awareness that groups are process-oriented, synergistic, and environmentally dependent.

Interdependence in Groups

When taken apart a system, such as a group, loses its interaction and essential properties. It loses its interdependence. Furthermore, explaining one part of the group's process without taking the entire structure into account does not give an accurate picture. In spite of this interconnectedness, the traditional analysis of small group process involved a division of the process into smaller, more manageable parts, such as roles, norms, size, and leadership. This fragmenting allowed an in-depth look at the different forces that take place within a group. But since groups are complex, ever-changing structures, reducing the process to individual elements and treating them as though they were independent, constant, and static prevented a clear understanding of how dynamic the group process is.

Viewing groups as systems, therefore, allows a deeper level of insight. Borden (1985) explained human communication systems as any dynamic set of interrelating components, at least two of which are human, functioning to achieve an objective through communication among its components. Since group members form a dynamic set of human, interrelating components that are able to reach their objectives through communication among the group's members, they are a human communication system. Applying Borden's theory for general human communication systems to small group communication provides a solid foundation for examining what happens when people form groups and interact over a period of time to achieve a goal.

Interconnected and interrelating aspects of group process cause the members to be *interdependent*. Interdependence means that group members can accomplish something as a whole that would be difficult or impossible for a single individual to achieve. However, this accomplishment can occur only when members can rely on each other to fulfill their roles and responsibilities. Moreover, only by looking at the system or group in relation to the internal and external forces affecting it can an appreciation of the complexity of group process be gained. Understanding *how* groups operate rather than merely concentrating on *what* they do gives a better picture of the wholeness of groups as systems. In other words, no one part of a system can be understood unless it is viewed within the context of the entire system.

Appreciating the complexity of a group starts with understanding the system's *input*, the combination of the raw material of the particular group and the interactions that result. Examples of raw material of the group would be the talents, education, experience, and maturity of the members. Since each individual of the group is also a separate, unique system, a group can be thought of as a system of systems, an unparalleled collection of raw material. The input of each person is changed to an *output* during the process of creating and modifying ideas in the course of the group's transformation and evolution.

Sometimes the output is concrete. For example, a committee that formulates a marketing strategy for a new product and then implements the plan for the company has produced a tangible output. Output is not always so obvious, however. The subtle and radical changes among the group's participants, their ideas, and their decisions are also examples of output. Katz and Kahn (1966) referred to the process of changing input to output as *throughput*.

Realizing that work groups make decisions is only part of appreciating what groups do, and considering output in isolation causes distortion. Taking the entire process, or throughput, into account is important also. Group norms, power, leadership, goals, roles, and a host of other variables are all interdependent, and each influences the decisions the group makes. Any one component must be analyzed in light of the whole system, the group. Only then will a particular behavior be truly understandable (Wood, Phillips, and Pedersen 1986).

The group's *purpose* also influences interaction and interdependence. A social group, whose sole purpose is to provide support for its members, will not usually need to rely on the members for financial gain or professional development. Instead, individuals form these types of groups when they want social interaction and will count on the other members to provide needed recreation and relaxation. In the case of adolescent groups, the members may even depend on each other for a large part of their identity. As Argyle (1983) pointed out, social groups in general, and adolescent groups in particular, have no specific task except to devise activities that entail the kinds of interaction that meet the needs of members. These invented activities such as dancing, eating pizza, and talking are the system's output. The parts of these groups mesh to form a system of support or maintenance.

A work group, on the other hand, has a task as its primary purpose. Work groups form when one person alone cannot achieve the task, when several types of skills are needed, or when people simply prefer the company of others (Zajonc 1963). The parts of this work system need to influence each other effectively in order to accomplish some specific goal. In short, the group members need to agree on the purpose for their working together. Then, understanding how they interact with one another can help them move ideas to action.

Another aspect of group interaction has to do with the group's *size*. As groups grow larger, the system becomes more complex. The interdependence is there but less apparent. Cohesion is often weaker, and morale tends to be lower in larger groups than in comparable smaller ones. Perhaps this is truer of groups such as social groups that have the option to meet or not to meet, but the principle is noteworthy. Since the parts of the system are interrelated and interdependent, limiting the number of parts affords more opportunity for interaction. Bostrom (1970) found that people like to talk rather than listen in a group. Smaller groups provide this opportunity to get attention and exert influence.

Group size is directly related to communication networks, a part of the overall system. As the size of a group increases, the network begins to bog down in confusion. Larger groups tend to produce lower levels of satisfaction and weaker interpersonal relations among participants because people have fewer opportunities to interact with each other, and cohesion is compromised (Tubbs 1988). Cohesion is particularly desirable in family or social groups, but its importance should not be minimized in work groups.

Synergy in Groups

Viewing any system in terms of its context is the first step to understanding the synergistic effect of the system. Simply put, this means that 1 + 1 = 3, or a system is more than the sum of its parts. Synergy occurs when the group's performance or accomplishments surpass the capabilities of the individual group members. In other words, the group's unique combination of talents, knowledge, and experience is greater than the sum of the individual contributions. The ideas of one member often trigger a response from another person that neither would have thought of independently. The vitality of one individual can spur others on when their own energy wanes.

Synergy can take either physical or mental forms. The physical presence of others is often arousing, so more work is accomplished. Even ants work harder when there is more than one of them on the job (Zajonc 1963). In the mental sense, synergy emerges when a type of collective intelligence and shared memory begins to develop as the group matures. Also, synergy can play an important role for those group members who are energized through interactions with others.

Senge described this development as a kind of aligning, during which a commonality of direction emerges and individuals' energies harmonize. He said that a resonance occurs that is "like the 'coherent' light of a laser rather than the incoherent and shattered light of a light bulb" (Senge 1990, 234). Instead of a scattering of energy, there is commonality of purpose, a shared vision, and understanding of how to complement one another's efforts.

A system is a collection of parts that interact with each other to function as a whole. If something is made up of a number of parts that do not interact and the arrangement of these parts is irrelevant, the result is a pile of materials rather than a system. For example, a pile of bricks is a pile of bricks whether we add to it or subtract from it. Cutting it in half gives two piles of bricks, and adding to it yields a bigger pile of bricks. Essentially, however, the mound of material remains a mound of material.

Conversely, a car is a system. Imagine that the best parts of each type of automobile were determined. Could the world's best car be manufactured by collecting each of these parts and putting them together? Assembling an engine from one type of car, a transmission from another model, and a carburetor from yet another would not create a working system. The parts would not be compatible, and even these best parts would not combine to make a functioning machine, much less a superlative mode of transportation.

Groups are even more complicated; they are *living* systems. Each person can be viewed as a separate segment of the system, but the effect of the interaction among people is more than the sum of the individual contributors. The energy created by the members and the outputs of the group are the result of the dynamic relationships of the members, who are constantly defining and redefining themselves, their behavior, and the functions of the group. Combined, the group members can do things that no one of them could do separately.

Each group is unique partly because each group member is unique. The group, then, becomes a system of people who bring to the experience an individualized genetic make-up, a personal life history, varying combinations of personality traits, differing values and attitudes, and a singular view of the world. Adding the input of these individuals together, however, still does not give a clear picture of what the group is or will do because each person is constantly changing as a result of association with the group, and the group is continuously reacting in response to this person's membership. The group's members will interact to create the group, a creation that will be like no other. The members' behaviors, their verbal and nonverbal interactions, their strengths and weaknesses, their insights and talents will not only separate this group from all others; they will also distinguish this particular group's interaction today from this group's interaction tomorrow.

The group's synergy, or bonding of the system's components, is a source of energy; this bonding gives structure to the system, thereby reducing *entropy,* or disorder. Without an input of energy, an open system such as a group, which is affected by other systems, will run down, and disorganization will occur.

The Domino Effect in Groups

This interconnection of the parts means that all divisions of the structure are changed when one piece of it changes. When one element alters, all others must adjust to accommodate it if the system is to survive in a healthy state (Wood et al. 1986). This "domino effect" is apparent whenever group members interact because the effects of any action will cause consequences to ripple through the system. Explaining how or why an outcome occurred is very complex because all the reasons for a result are not obvious. Often group members never find the answers to their questions because they try to look at just one aspect of the group's system, which is frequently the most recent action of an individual in the group. No one answer is likely to provide the complete story. However, looking at the patterns of causes and effects might begin to bring the situation into focus. Thinking in terms of a specific cause

for a given event in a system is futile and simplistic.

Even though groups are complex, the art of systems thinking lies in seeing *through* complexity to the underlying structures. Systems thinking does not mean ignoring complexity. Rather, it means organizing complexity into a coherent story that illuminates the causes of problems and possible remedies. Groups need ways of knowing what is important and what is not important, what variables to focus on and which to pay less attention to. Doing this helps groups or teams develop shared understanding and allows them to get at the core of the complexity (Senge 1990).

The main principle at play is that groups never do just one thing. One action causes reactions that demand an adjustment within the system and among other systems. The group accommodates the changes and responds to them, or the system fails to thrive. Since systems are dynamic, they constantly change in response to internal and external challenges. Even the degree of interconnectedness among the group members will ebb and flow during the life of the system as the members and the surrounding environment change. Successful groups learn to anticipate consequences, plan for contingencies, and think strategically.

In addition to the existence of a complex system within the group, the group is rooted in countless other systems as well. Human systems are never closed (Miller 1978). As Huse and Bowditch (1973) explained, since open systems are never completely closed off from the outside world, they are affected by the environment and, in turn, have an effect on the environment. Just as no part of the group's process can be considered in isolation, neither can the group be viewed apart from the environment, the group's *supra-system.*

Individual groups are parts of many other systems, such as the organization, the community, and the society in general. Gross (1964) identified four phenomena that characterize these open systems:

1. Entries and exits transform outsiders into members and members into outsiders.
2. Multiple memberships in groups result in members' loyalties to other groups.
3. Resources are exchanged among the groups.
4. There is mutual or reciprocal influence by both members and outsiders.

Any open system interacts with its environment in mutually influential ways. Since each group is rooted in many other systems, groups influence these larger environments and are influenced by them. Conflicts occur when incompatible demands of multiple systems clash. A work group that refuses to operate within the general policies of the company will certainly cause problems for itself and the organization. Similarly, a company that refuses to function within the prevailing ethics or norms of its society will not survive. The values of the community and the mores of the overall culture influence both individual members and the group as a whole. Ignoring culturally conditioned attitudes dooms both the work group and the organization.

Conclusions

The essence of systems theory is interdependence. Interlocking relationships among the parts of a system form to create a structure that exists among other systems. When one part of the system changes, the effect is felt within the system and throughout other systems. A constellation of factors determines whether a group will succeed in realizing its goals, but one thing is clear. The key parts of the system, the individuals, must join together in a way that harnesses the synergy of the group. A group is a living, dynamic, open system that interacts within itself and with the environment. Family, social, political, religious, military, and professional groups share a central principle:

Whatever affects one part of the system affects all its parts and many other parts of the supra-system, our world.

References

Argyle, M. (1983). "Five kinds of small social groups." In H. Blumberg, A. Hare, V. Kent, and M. Davies (eds.), *Small Groups and Social Interaction*, I. John Wiley and Sons, Ltd.

Bostrom, R. (1970). "Patterns of communication interaction in small groups." *Speech Monographs* 37: 257–263.

Borden, G. (1985). *Human Communication Systems*. Boston: American Press.

Gross, B. (1964). *Organizations and Their Managing*. New York: Free Press.

Huse, E., and Bowditch, J. (1973). *Behavior in Organizations*. Reading, MA: Addison-Wesley.

The Innovative Learning Series. (1980). *Systems One: An Introduction to Systems Thinking*. [Brochure]. S. A. Carlton, Publisher, Minneapolis, MN. Draper Kauffman, Jr.

Katz, D., and Kahn, R. (1966). *The Social Psychology of Organizations*. New York: John Wiley & Sons.

Miller, J. (1978). *Living Systems*. New York: McGraw-Hill Book Co.

Schutz, W. (1960). *The Interpersonal Underworld*. Palo Alto, CA: Science & Behavior Books Inc.

Senge, P. (1990). *The Fifth Discipline*. Doubleday, New York.

Tubbs, S. (1988). *A Systems Approach to Small Group Interaction*. New York: Random House.

Wood, J., Phillips, G., and Pedersen, D. (1986). *Group Discussion: A Practical Guide to Participation and Leadership*. Harper & Row Publishers.

Von Bertelanffy, L. (1952). *Problems of Life*. London: Watts & Co.

Zajonc, R. (1963). "Social facilitation." *Science* 149: 269–274.

Chapter 2
Rethinking the Nature of Groups

A Bona Fide Group Perspective

Linda L. Putnam

In *this chapter, the author builds off the notion of small groups as open systems and discusses four features of small groups that are themselves subsets of larger groups: (1) multiple group memberships and conflicting role identities, (2) representative roles, (3) fluctuations in group membership, and (4) group identity formation. It also explains how the very nature of a small group is affected by the way it negotiates its boundaries, identity, and relationships with other groups.*

The advent of self-regulated work teams, collaborative groups, and virtual teams has challenged the very foundation on which group communication exists. Teams perform a wide array of functions in ways that no longer reflect the original definition of small group communication. To increase productivity and fight competition with foreign markets, management and labor have joined forces on product improvement teams. To adapt to rapidly changing markets, organizations employ focus groups and evaluation teams that link internal departments to external customers, suppliers, and competitors (Ancona 1990; Hackman 1990). To work collaboratively across individual and departmental expertise, organizations have formed cross-functional teams that share task authority and that connect members across time and space. Thus, the proliferation of groups extends beyond physical location, normative cultures, and time zones as well as into arenas such as planning, policy implementation, innovation, and conflict management (Kumar and van Dissel 1996; Lipnack and Stamps 1997; Poole and Holmes 1995).

Contemporary research on organizational teams differs from the traditional views of groups in important ways. Groups are not simply three or more people who meet together in face-to-face interaction to address task and social needs (Cragan and Wright 1990). Traditional work treated groups as contained entities with fixed boundaries and no historical context. By focusing on the internal dynamics and decision-making processes of teams, these approaches typically ignored the larger social context in which groups were embedded (Frey 2003). However, during the 1990s, the study of groups in natural settings flourished, focusing on such diverse groups as youth gangs, city councils, community-volunteer teams, political action groups, health care teams, governmental commissions, and children's groups (Frey 1994; Hackman 1990). As a result, this breadth of research has led to a growing concern for how to incorporate context into researchers' ways of understanding group communication (Gouran 1999).

Organizations, as one particular context, are critical arenas for the study of groups. But organizations are not simply "a place" in which groups meet. Contemporary organizations challenge the nature, mode, and structure of groups. Groups in organizations function within shifting and flexible boundaries that extend beyond their work groups. For example, teams are sometimes composed of individuals from different countries as well as from different organizations. Moreover, organizational members often work simultaneously on five or six different project teams. Even though groups continue to interact face-to-face, they also hold electronic meetings through teleconferences and groupware that alter the mode of communication among team members. Finally, the structure of contemporary groups goes beyond a collection of individuals with a common goal. The structure of organizational teams embraces a variety of new forms, including networks, alliances, collaboratives, and cooperatives (Stohl and Walker 2002). These forms can be loosely or tightly linked and can interfuse with multiple organizational units.

Changes in the study of naturally occurring groups and teams in organizations call for new research questions and a new model of group communication. Realizing that groups exist in a larger social system, the key questions are how does communication aid in negotiating the boundaries of units in this system and how do these negotiations influence the internal and external dynamics of a team? These questions can be addressed through focusing on two elements that lay the foundation for a new model of group communication—connectivity and relationship to external context. These two features underlie a new model of group communication, the bona fide group perspective. This chapter sets forth the characteristics of this perspective and examines the way this model can be used to study organizational teams.

Connectivity: Communication as Tight and Loose Connections

Even though organizational groups exist in a web of interrelated units, linkages between groups vary in degree from loosely connected threads to tightly coupled bonds. Tight couplings between groups evolve from overlapping tasks, shared goals, a high frequency of communication, and mutual control. Tightly coupled, or *interdependent*, groups share a mutual dependency; both groups rely on one another to accomplish their respective goals. Because they are tightly connected, changes in one group alter activities in the other unit. For instance, the manufacturing group depends on the supply unit for its resources, and the supply group relies on the manufacturing department to determine what materials need to be ordered. If manufacturing changes the parts in its blueprint, supply must adapt with similar changes in acquisition of materials. In like manner, if the marketplace reveals a shortage of certain raw materials, the manufacturing group must change its product design to adapt to this problem. Both groups, then, depend on one another for their respective needs.

Loosely coupled, or *autonomous*, groups share some activities, but they conduct their work independently of the other group. The two groups may be linked through loosely connected exchanges, but they accomplish their task independently of the other group. Departments in a university setting are prime examples of autonomous groups. Even though two departments may share the same building, the two groups function as semi-autonomous units. Each department runs its own governance system and policies independent of the operations of the other. Occasionally they interact to negotiate space, to exchange students, or to settle disputes over academic turf, but for the most part, they function independently. This tradition of operating as autonomous units makes it difficult for members of academic departments to employ cross-functional and multidisciplinary teams.

Even though connectivity stems from interlocking task functions and workflow, loosely and tightly connected relationships are ultimately defined through communication. That is, interdependence varies in degree; it is not a rigid characteristic of group relationships (Weick 1979). Overlapping tasks may link the supply to the assembly departments, but the way the departments accomplish their work is a communication problem. The frequency, type, and pattern of interaction between them ultimately define their relationship and the extent of their dependency on one another. It is possible, then, for autonomous groups to become interdependent if they interact frequently and if they exert control over one another's resources and goals.

In particular, research and development groups often perform their tasks independent of other groups. They conduct market research, analyze the competition, and create a new product to enhance the company's productivity. If this process is conducted without any input from the other departments, the R & D group functions autonomously. At some point, however, the company has to implement the new product and R & D must work closely with engineering and manufacturing groups. These interactions shape relationships between the groups and lead to changes in the R & D group's process and in product design. Through communication, then, groups redefine autonomous relationships into interdependent ones.

Moreover, if the engineering group sees R & D's autonomy as a power play, they may be resentful and cautious in redefining their relationship. They might contend that major coordination problems would not have occurred if R & D had kept them informed. In essence, connectivity between groups is an ever-changing process, not a static event. It is derived, in part, from the way communication molds intergroup relationships.

The degree of interdependence between two groups also hinges on what gets imported or exported across boundaries and on how members actively shape their internal and external environments (Putnam and Stohl 1990). For instance, some groups actively influence the tasks and deadlines imposed by external organizations, while other units work strictly within the constraints set by external agents. Some groups question the authority or jurisdiction imposed by outsiders. Effective communication outside the group also impinges on the internal dynamics of the unit. In particular, members may experience a radical shift in stages of group development as a result of outside intervention that limits their choices, moves them forward, or energizes them (Gersick 1988, 1989).

This discussion underscores the need for trade-offs between internal and external communication. At various stages of a group's development, members may devote more time to communication outside the group and less attention to interaction with team members. Other contingencies such as urgency and complexity of the task and changing environmental conditions urge

members to concentrate on the internal dynamics of their group and to reduce contacts with external groups (Tushman 1978).

The Bona Fide Group Perspective

The notion that an organizational group exists within a larger context and is defined, in part, by this context supports the need for the bona fide group perspective. Drawing from notions of connectivity and relationships to external context, this perspective posits that fluid boundaries help determine the very nature of a group. Thus, a group's development, productivity, and survival hinge not only on its common purpose but also on the way it negotiates its boundaries and interdependence with other groups. Applying this notion of group development to an alternative model, two interrelated characteristics emerge to constitute the bona fide group perspective: stable yet permeable boundaries and interdependence with relevant context (Putnam 1994; Putnam and Stohl 1990, 1996; Stohl and Holmes 1993; Stohl and Putnam 1994).

The characteristic of stable yet permeable boundaries treats the borders of a group as defined, but also dynamic and fluid. Even though a group does not exist without some constructed boundary that differentiates it from its environment, this boundary is not fixed or immutable. That is, the interactions of group members through connectivity and external context open up the boundaries of a group to negotiation. Four features of group process contribute to changing group boundaries: (1) multiple group memberships and conflicting role identities, (2) representative roles, (3) fluctuation in group membership, and (4) group identity formation (Putnam and Stohl 1996). The first feature addresses the view that individuals are simultaneously members of multiple overlapping groups. An engineer may serve on a production team, a quality circle group, a task force on employee grievances, and an informal company softball team. Managers conduct their own staff meetings while serving as members of upper-level executive groups. In the university setting, a faculty member's time may be divided into service on an interdisciplinary research team, an ad hoc committee on faculty governance, a standing committee on curriculum matters, and an ongoing group on women's studies.

Multiple roles can lead to conflicting and ambiguous organizational identities. That is, membership in multiple groups may increase ambiguity about what group members should do, how much autonomy they have, and how they should coordinate their tasks with each other. As Berteotti and Seibold's (1994) study of a bona fide group illustrates, members of a hospice care team experienced role conflict and ambiguity as doctors, nurses, and volunteers sought to negotiate their relationships to their professions, the hospital, and the community-centered hospice team. Determining the roles of the volunteers, who had strong allegiances to the hospice teams, was particularly difficult since professionals viewed the volunteers as doing health care work for which they were not trained. These tensions within the team and the poor communication with external groups about team member roles affected the quality of health care delivery.

Multiple roles can also enter into the way members negotiate group boundaries through informal as well as formal interactions. For instance, in Kramer's (2002) study of community theater as a bona fide group, communication among participants flowed among task, social, and community theater roles. Boundaries of group membership were negotiated informally through discussions that recognized and prioritized group roles within the team as well as between the group members and their families, friends, and coworkers. Participants constructed and maintained their roles as fluid, their boundaries as permeable, and their memberships as multiple.

The second feature, representative role, implies that members serve as an official or unofficial representative of another group. One type of official representative role is called a boundary spanner (Tushman and Scanlan 1981). This person is a group member who links other groups, departments, and organizations. For instance, employees in marketing, public relations, advertising, and acquisition often serve as official boundary spanners to connect their units to departments in other organizations. Individuals also function as "implicit" representatives of their groups, organizations, and society at large. An implicit role is one not recognized or designated by a group. For example, a black engineer who is a member of a personnel policy group may feel compelled to speak on behalf of black members of the organization, even though his race is not directly relevant to the group's decisions. Thus, the way a representative role is enacted in a group influences, either explicitly or implicitly, different parameters of group boundaries.

The third feature that shapes the permeability of boundaries is fluctuation in group membership. Research on project teams demonstrates that over a group's lifespan, members come and go (Anderson, Riddle, and Martin 1999; Moreland and Levine 1988). Employees are reassigned to other projects; individuals leave the organization; and newcomers are added to the team. New members import new ideas to the group and former members carry a residue of the past into new groups. As membership changes, boundaries change and can alter a group's identity, goals, and even its unique niche (Conquergood 1994).

As an example, Donnellon (1994, 1996) observed in her comparison of two different corporate project teams that changes in membership hampered group deliberations. In one team, marketing members who were of high status in the organization joined the group five months after the team began. The marketing members tried to impose their agenda on the group, but the team members resisted. Analysis of the communication revealed that the group members had trouble integrating the newcomers, a pattern that led to eventual delays in product development.

The fourth characteristic, group identity formation, focuses on members' loyalty, commitment, and sense of belonging relative to each of multiple groups. Overlapping membership among different groups, then, affects the degree of allegiance and the commitment that members can give to a group. Belonging to several groups means that members are only "partially included" in any one group. If individuals have only a limited number of work hours per day, the critical test of commitment surfaces when multiple memberships create time pressures, value conflicts, and opposing commitments. For example, in a group formed of representatives from diverse departments, a strong allegiance to the "home department" may lead an individual to feel she must stand up for her department's interests rather than search for the optimal solution to realize the team's decision.

A bona fide group study of a member-owned supermarket illustrates this characteristic of group identity formation (Oetzel and Robbins 2003). Organized into overlapping teams, the members of the food cooperative exhibited three forms of identity—team identities, an organizational identity based on the values of the cooperative, and an identity linked to hierarchy or organizational position. These three types of group identity interfaced in different ways, with strong identity and upper management teams functioning more autonomously and avoiding direct confrontation with external team members. In effect, group identity formation shapes the communication patterns both within multiple and overlapping teams and with external groups.

In effect, a bona fide group perspective treats boundaries as fluid and permeable through the way multiple memberships, representative roles, fluctuations in membership, and group identity shape and reshape borders. Thus, group boundaries are not "given," or predetermined; rather, they are socially constructed as members integrate into and differentiate from the larger system.

The second distinguishing characteristic of the bona fide group perspective is interdependence with relevant context. This feature refers to the way a group draws from and relates to its organizational, cultural, or social context and the way it links its past history to its present or future actions. To illustrate, a female manager in an all-male management team knows that another woman in her lunch group is planning to file a sexual harassment charge against a male member of this management team. Since the female manager also chairs a separate affirmative action grievance committee, she knows that she may encounter her male colleague in a very different group context in the future. Awareness of this potential for future interaction serves as a barometer for gauging present interactions. In a similar example, a new member of a standing committee who is upset with the group's past actions may decide to withhold his objections when he sees that two of the group members belong to a country club that he wants to join.

Four elements comprise interdependence with relevant context: (1) coordinated actions among groups, (2) intergroup communication, (3) jurisdiction and autonomy of the group, and (4) frames for making sense of intergroup relationships. When a group coordinates with other groups for task accomplishment or information flow, it negotiates its boundaries by tightening or loosening its interdependence. When coordination outside the group is high and intergroup communication is frequent, external groups directly affect the internal dynamics of the team (Ancona and Caldwell 1988).

For instance, a bona fide group study of surgical teams in three different types of hospitals demonstrated how coordinated actions and intergroup communication affected group process (Lammers and Krikorian 1997). Different norms of communication drawn from the type of hospital affected the way that team members coordinated their tasks and the way that they interfaced with other groups. In particular, the surgical team in the private hospital exhibited a high degree of communication, a jovial atmosphere, and high coordination among team members, while the surgical groups in the teaching and the county hospitals primarily focused on task communication. Although the surgical teams relied on other groups for resources, in the operating room, these teams functioned in relative isolation and autonomy from other hospital units. In effect, surgical teams had high coordination among team members but limited their communication with other groups to issues of scheduling, surgery preparation, and use of equipment, prior to performing the surgery.

The third element, negotiation of jurisdiction and autonomy, relates to communication patterns that determine group accountability or responsibility. This feature includes internal and external interactions, seeking approval or authority to complete a task, and accountability for decisions. As an example, a dean at a university may appoint a subcommittee of department chairs to make a recommendation for how to increase graduate student stipends. Subcommittee members are part of an Executive Council composed of department chairs who represent the faculty and graduate students in 11 different units in the college (Putnam and Stohl 1996). A key stage of the decision-making process is negotiating the subcommittee's "area of freedom, its authority to collect data, its ability to represent departments, and its parameters for determining what is a feasible recommendation" (p. 169). What typically happens is that the subcommittee proceeds with its task and works out the scope and nature of its jurisdiction through a problem-solving process that entails negotiations with other units.

Finally, interdependence with the relevant context is socially constructed as members form perceptions of other groups. Members bring to the group setting divergent interests, disparate values, and specialized jargon that reflect occupational and departmental differences. Through making sense of their organizational roles, groups form stereotypes of other departments, e.g., "accountants are picky," "computer jocks are antisocial." Moreover, members of "warring factions" may take their intergroup perceptions into their team meetings in ways that construct internal dynamics similar to external stereotypes. Donnellon's (1994, 1996) research illustrates how historically rooted animosities among departments can influence

effectiveness in project teams composed of members from marketing, engineering, accounting, and manufacturing departments. Low identification with the project team and strong allegiances to organizational departments led to a win-lose style of conflict management and power plays in the group. Even communication when members digressed from the task contained snide comments about each other's departments, ones that paralleled and reinforced stereotypic perceptions brought into the group.

In a bona fide perspective, group members also construct their environments; that is, they make sense of their surroundings and interpret their task in light of perceptions of their external context. For example, Tracy and Standerfer (2003) demonstrated how a school board altered its agenda about selecting a new superintendent through directing its messages to community individuals outside the group as well as to its own board members, which reshaped its boundaries. Since communication both references and negotiates intergroup connections, team members not only function within an external context, but they also help shape the relevance and nature of that context.

In summary, since organizations consist of overlapping and interconnected groups, we need to examine the influence of communication between as well as within groups. A bona fide group perspective centers on how external and internal environments come together through the negotiation of a group's boundaries, identity, and relationships with other groups (Putnam 1994). Drawn from assumptions of connectivity and links to external contexts, the bona fide group perspective highlights the social interactions that construct the very nature of a group. Through fluid boundaries and fluctuating membership, groups may change or even dissipate as they construct links to external groups and as they alter their members' priorities and commitments.

As this chapter suggests, the two characteristics of bona fide groups, fluid and permeable boundaries and interdependence with relevant context, overlap. Some groups have only one or two elements that make them distinctive, such as fluctuating and overlapping membership. Other groups demonstrate both of these characteristics and most of the elements that comprise them. Since these characteristics are fluid and negotiable, groups may rely on some elements of bona fide groups at one time and then later make other elements more salient through their internal and external deliberations.

Based on its complexity in the external context, one type of group, a collaborative, illustrates most features of a bona fide group perspective. A collaborative is a temporary group formed from representatives of many different organizations who coordinate joint actions toward mutually accountable ends (Frey 2003; Keyton and Stallworth 2003; Stohl and Walker 2002). These groups work in temporary alliances that pool knowledge, resources, and expertise for a specific purpose. By partnering with other stakeholders, a collaborative group aims to complete difficult and complex projects in a timely fashion, pool financial resources, and increase innovation (Stohl and Walker 2002). Since no one parent organization controls the operation of these groups, they function within a different framework, one that parallels the bona fide group perspective.

To illustrate, Lange (2003) employs the bona fide group perspective to investigate the Applegate Partnership, an environmental collaboration of multiple agencies and community groups assembled to develop an ecosystem management plan for regional watersheds. The board members on the team represented all possible stakeholders and constituents, including environmentalists, timber industry personnel, federal agency personnel, ranchers, farmers, and government officials. In this type of group, communication with the larger stakeholder organizations was essential to the inner workings of the team. Lange's study revealed that this collaborative group had highly permeable and fluid boundaries, as evidenced by shifting alliances and fluctuating memberships among stakeholders. Board members represented not just one group but a web of local and national organizations. Hence, the representative role of members was continually called into question and renegotiated between the constituents and their delegates. At the level of interdependence with relevant contexts, conflicts and power disparities arose as board members had difficulty communicating with their constituents, particularly with those outside the local community. These conflicts fed into and reflected disagreements within stakeholder groups on the value of the partnership and the legality of the decision-making process. Thus, intergroup communication and coordinated actions with external groups were salient features of the collaboration and a key to its eventual success in creating a forum for mutual understanding that had the capacity to engage in genuine problem solving. Its success as a collaboration stemmed in large part from its ability to manage the complexity of a bona fide group with its multi-layered environments, shifting borders, and permeable boundaries.

Group communication is an important and vital area. Groups lie at the cornerstone of society, and teams are the primary means by which organizations do business. Consequently, the study of group communication should extend into naturally occurring contexts. But groups are not simply isolated containers that are located inside larger systems. Rather their very identity and survival hinges on their connectivity and relationships to their external context. As an alternative for understanding group communication, the bona fide group perspective calls attention to the permeable and fluid boundaries of a group and the way members negotiate interdependence with their relevant contexts. Regardless of the type of group or the mode of communication, groups navigate in a complex social world. Models of group communication need to reflect the same complexity in which this navigation and alteration of boundaries takes place.

References

Ancona, D. G. (1990). "Outward bound: Strategies for team survival in an organization." *Academy of Management Journal* 33: 334–365.

Ancona, D. G., and Caldwell, D. F. (1988). "Beyond task and maintenance: Defining external functions in groups." *Group and Organizational Studies* 13: 468–494.

Anderson, C. M., Riddle, B. L., and Martin, M. M. (1999). "Socialization processes in groups." In L. R. Frey (ed.), D. S. Gouran, and M. S. Poole (assoc. eds.), *The Handbook of Group Communication Theory and Research* (pp. 139–163). Thousand Oaks, CA: Sage.

Berteotti, C. R., and Seibold, D. R. (1994). "Coordination and role-definition problems in health-care teams: A hospice case study." In L. R. Frey (ed.), *Group Communication in Context: Studies of Natural Groups* (pp. 107–131). Hillsdale, NJ: Lawrence Erlbaum.

Conquergood, D. (1994). "Homeboys and hoods: Gang communication and cultural space." In L. R. Frey (ed.), *Group Communication in Context: Studies of Natural Groups* (pp. 23–55). Hillsdale, NJ: Lawrence Erlbaum.

Cragan, J., and Wright, D. (1990). "Small group communication research of the 1980's: A synthesis and critique." *Communication Studies* 41: 212–236.

Donnellon, A. (1994). "Team work: Linguistic models of negotiating differences." In R. J. Lewicki, B. H. Sheppard, and R. Bies (eds.), *Research on Negotiation in Organizations* (Vol. 4, pp. 71–123). Greenwich, CT: JAI Press.

——. (1996). *Team Talk: The Power of Language in Team Dynamics*. Boston, MA: Harvard Business School Press.

Frey, L. R. (ed.). (1994). *Group Communication in Context: Studies of Natural Groups*. Hillsdale, NJ: Lawrence Erlbaum.

——. (2003). *Group Communication in Context: Studies of Bona Fide Groups* (2nd ed., pp. 1–20). Hillsdale, NJ: Lawrence Erlbaum.

Gersick. C. J. G. (1988). "Time and transition in work teams: Toward a new model of group development." *Academy of Management Journal* 31: 9–41.

——. (1989). "Marking time: Predictable transitions in task groups." *Academy of Management Journal* 32: 274–309.

Gouran, D. S. (1999). "Communication in groups: The emergence and evolution of a field of study." In L. R. Frey (ed.), D. S. Gouran, and M. S. Poole (assoc. eds.), *The Handbook of Group Communication Theory and Research* (pp. 3–36). Thousand Oaks, CA: Sage.

Hackman, J. R. (ed.). (1990). *Groups That Work (and Those That Don't): Creating Conditions for Effective Teamwork*. San Francisco: Jossey-Bass.

Keyton, J., and Stallworth, V. (2003). "On the verge of collaboration: Interaction process vs. group outcomes." In L. R. Frey (ed.), *Group Communication in Context: Studies of Bona Fide Groups* (2nd ed., pp. 235–260). Hillsdale, NJ: Lawrence Erlbaum.

Kramer, M. W. (2002). "Communication in a community theater group: Managing multiple group roles." *Communication Studies* 53: 151–170.

Kumar, K., and van Dissel, H. G. (1996). "Sustainable collaboration: Managing conflict and cooperation in interorganizational systems." *MIS Quarterly* 20: 279–300.

Lammers, J. C., and Krikorian, D. H. (1997). "Theoretical extension and operationalization of the bona fide group construct with an application to surgical teams." *Journal of Applied Communication Research* 25: 17–38.

Lange, J. I. (2003). "Environmental collaboration and constituency communication." In L. R. Frey (ed.), *Group Communication in Context: Studies of Bona Fide Groups* (2nd ed., pp. 209–234). Hillsdale, NJ: Lawrence Erlbaum.

Lipnack, J., and Stamps, J. (1997). *Virtual Teams: Reaching Across Space, Time, and Organizations with Technology*. New York: John Wiley.

Moreland, R. L., and Levine, J. M. (1988). "Group dynamics over time: Development and socialization in small groups." In J. E. McGrath (ed.), *The Social Psychology of Time* (pp. 151–181). Newbury Park, CA: Sage.

Oetzel, J. G., and Robbins, J. (2003). "Multiple identities in teams in a cooperative supermarket." In L. R. Frey (ed.), *Group Communication in Context: Studies of Bona Fide Groups* (2nd ed., pp. 183–208). Hillsdale, NJ: Lawrence Erlbaum.

Poole, M. S., and Holmes, M. E. (1995). "Decision development in computer-assisted group decision making." *Human Communication Research* 22: 90–127.

Putnam, L. L. (1994). "Revitalizing small group communication: Lessons learned from a bona fide group perspective." *Communication Studies* 45: 97–102.

Putnam. L. L., and Stohl, C. (1990). "Bona fide groups: A reconceptualization of groups in context." *Communication Studies* 41: 248–265.

——. (1996). "Bona fide groups: An alternative perspective for communication and small group decision making." In R. Hirokawa and M. Poole (eds.), *Communication and Group Decision Making* (pp. 147–178). Thousand Oaks, CA: Sage.

Stohl, C., and Holmes, M. E. (1993). "A functional perspective for bona fide groups." In S. A. Deetz (ed.), *Communication Yearbook* 16 (pp. 601–614). Newbury Park, CA: Sage.

Stohl, C., and Putnam, L. L. (1994). "Group communication in context: Implications for the study of bona fide groups." In L. R. Frey (ed.), *Group Communication in Context* (pp. 285–292). Hillsdale, NJ: Lawrence Erlbaum.

Stohl, C., and Walker, K. (2002). "A bona fide perspective for the future of groups: Understanding collaborating groups." In L. R. Frey (ed.), *New Directions in Group Communication* (pp. 237–252). Thousand Oaks, CA: Sage.

Tracy, K., and Standerfer, C. (2003). "Selecting a school superintendent: Sensitivities in group deliberation." In L. R. Frey (ed.), *Group Communication in Context: Studies of Bona Fide Groups* (2nd ed., pp. 109–134). Hillsdale, NJ: Lawrence Erlbaum.

Tushman, M. L. (1978). "Technical communication in R & D Laboratories: The impact of project work characteristics." *Academy of Management Journal* 21: 624–645.

Tushman, M. L., and Scanlan, T. J. (1981). "Boundary spanning individuals: Their role in information transfer and their antecedents." *Academy of Management Journal* 24: 89–105.

Weick. K. E. (1979). *The Social Psychology of Organizing* (2nd ed.). Reading, MA: Addison-Wesley.

Chapter 3
Distinguishing Characteristics of Virtual Groups

Robyn E. Parker

Parker discusses the unique characteristics of "virtual" groups—that is, collections of individuals who interact and function as small groups without being in the same place at the same time. She argues that virtual groups are not just groups at a distance; rather, they are unique entities that differ qualitatively from collocated (face-to-face) groups. The author explains how virtual groups differ in character, conduct, and support needs from face-to-face groups. She also notes that while the functions of virtual groups are similar to those of face-to-face groups, the interaction processes used by virtual groups to achieve their goals are greatly influenced by their virtual status. This article advances the provocative claim that the communication skills and practices used in traditional face-to-face groups are likely to prove inadequate in virtual groups.

Picture in your mind a small work team engaged in a lively meeting. What does your picture look like? Perhaps you imagined group members seated around a table in a conference room. Did you picture some group members scribbling on notepads? Perhaps you imagined the walls of the room "decorated" with big sheets of paper listing the group members' ideas? In your mind's eye you may have even seen one or two members stand up and gesture wildly with their hands as they tried to persuade others to see their points of view. No matter the specific details in your picture, you probably saw the meeting occurring with all the members located in the same time at the same place. Such a picture represents the traditional, most common, format of meetings in organizations. We refer to these groups as *collocated* task groups or teams.

Now imagine you arrive at the office and find several urgent e-mails waiting for you on your computer. A colleague in your company's Australia office provided an update on the delivery of goods from Thailand as of 3:00 a.m. your time. Delivery has been delayed, again. The customer service liaison working with a major client in Japan also sends you an e-mail expressing concern about the delay. You know a group meeting would help to get things under control. But how do you do this when your work team spans four time zones and has elements in a half dozen countries? One option is to conduct an on-line, virtual meeting.

Membership in virtual groups and teams is becoming almost as common as membership in face-to-face groups and teams in organizations. The growth of transnational corporations and the increased availability of computer-based technology like the Internet have facilitated this trend. Although virtual groups are typically used in the same way, and for the same purposes, as traditional collocated groups and teams, it is important to understand that virtual groups have unique properties and characteristics that differentiate them from traditional collocated groups. This chapter focuses on the unique properties and qualities of virtual groups.

Characteristics of Virtual Groups

What is a "virtual" group? Very simply, a *virtual* group is a collection of individuals who interact and function as a group without being in the same place at the same time. Virtual groups are frequently created to complete a task. The task may be to solve a problem, make an important decision or set of decisions, or formulate a plan to accomplish a desired objective. Virtual groups also serve social functions. A great deal of information sharing occurs in groups organized via the Internet. Additionally, and perhaps even more importantly, Internet-based groups (a.k.a. cyber groups) also provide social support for their members. Some virtual groups are organized with support as their primary purpose. Alcoholics Anonymous, for example, holds weekly virtual meetings, "Staying Cyber," where members can read and post messages at will.

Virtual groups are unique. They have several characteristics that distinguish them from traditional collocated small groups.

Geographic Dispersion

The most obvious distinction between traditional groups and virtual groups is that the latter are not collocated. They tend to be geographically dispersed, perhaps never coming together in the same physical location. The earlier example of a geographically dispersed team depicted global membership, but geographic dispersion may involve only cross-town or cross-department separation. According to the traditional rule of proximity, collaboration is unlikely to occur between individuals who are more than 50 feet apart (Allen 1976). Virtuality bridges the physical divide that once stymied opportunities for cooperative activity.

Take, for example, a geographically dispersed recruiting team for a major employer. Once handled as an independent task with mixed results, recruiting is now conducted by a dispersed group of recruiters, each with his or her own area of specialization. By moving away from regional hiring and taking a collaborative approach to initial screenings of applicants, a larger pool of potential hires is accessed for each job opening. The large applicant pool allows for implementation of more stringent screening standards. Collaboration occurs through e-mailing of applicant information to all team members for review, followed by a teleconference to discuss job matches.

Asynchronism

Geographic dispersion also infers time differentials. Virtual groups often function asynchronously, or not at the same time. Members may contribute to group activity at various moments in time, sending messages that other members will later retrieve and respond to at their discretion. Virtual groups *meet* through the use of electronic bulletin boards, e-mails, and other electronic means of communication where members access, read, and respond to messages from other group members at different times of the day. Because the members of virtual groups are not collocated in space and time, they are often fully dependent on asynchronous communication.

Conference calling is a popular option for overcoming geographic dispersion, but its usefulness is limited when there is little or no overlap in working hours, as with the transnational team described earlier. New computer-based communication technologies help to bridge time gaps. For example, multi-shift operations once negated collaboration between individuals working for the same company, in the same department, with similar job functions, but not in the building at the same time. Groups working the "first shift," without active input from alternate "shifts," made operational decisions. Decision quality and commitment to implementation were therefore not what they might have been if all shifts had been directly involved in the decision-making process. Developments in computer conferencing software now enable shift workers to log into an electronic meeting from home and actively participate in group problem solving.

Porous Boundaries

Another distinction between virtual and traditional groups is the lack of clear group boundaries that characterize virtual groups. In traditional groups, boundaries are more or less fixed, albeit by subjective and largely arbitrary means (McCollom 1990). Artifacts such as uniforms, work implements (tools, stationery), office locale or decor, as well as shared language and normative behavior all serve as observable signs and demarcations of group membership. In contrast, membership boundaries in virtual groups tend to be porous. Membership tends to wax and wane as participants' levels of interest dictate (Lipnack and Stamps 1999). Porous boundaries fundamentally distinguish traditional small groups from virtual groups.

An example of porous boundaries is the cross-functional project team brought together to implement a changeover in the company retirement plan following a proposed company merger. All employees must be switched from the present plan to the new company's plan on the day the merger closes. A group consisting of representatives from the finance, legal, human resources, and accounting units from both companies is created to produce this change-over plan.

As the project moves forward there are moments when the accountants are critically interested in what the team is doing. For instance, they would be very involved in initial plans to ensure that the proposed changes would not have tax consequences for employees or the company. Once their concerns are addressed, however, their involvement in the project would be minimal unless information was requested from them or a problem arose requiring their input. The same would also be true for the legal representatives. At the same time, the involvement of the finance and human resources representatives would likely last throughout the implementation of the plan and beyond. Determining precisely who is involved in the project at any given time challenges observers of virtual groups.

Network Composition

A final characteristic unique to virtual groups is their networked nature. Virtual groups comprise patterns of relations; hence, they are unbounded by proximity or organizational membership. They are primarily social networks best understood when examined in terms of "who exchanges what resources with whom" (Haythornthwaite, Wellman, and Garton 1998). More specifically, virtual groups are computer-supported social networks (CSSNs), with members communicating largely via computer networks. Computer support mitigates proximity as a discriminator for collaboration, allowing group members to interact without leaving their desks. Group membership evolves through pre-existing and new relationships with individuals who, for traditional groups, would be external to the pool of potential members. Moreover, the networked nature of virtual groups prompts cross-boundary collaboration. CSSNs enable cross-functional, cross-cultural, multi-organizational, and transnational groups to evolve around a common purpose.

Research and development have traditionally operated in a virtual context. In mapping the history of the Internet, ARPANET originated in the 1960s to support military communication in the event that more centralized communication channels were knocked out. Universities with defense contracts began to collaborate over ARPANET, eventually driving the military to another network (Gackenbach and Ellerman 1998). Virtual groups are unique in that they routinely cross boundaries (Lipnack and Stamps 1999).

Interaction Challenges in Virtual Contexts

Virtual group interaction takes place through a variety of channels (e.g., telephone, voicemail, electronic mail, and real-time chat). Paradoxically, the communication modes that make virtual group status possible are the same modes that make group interaction difficult. Misunderstandings abound in virtual contexts. One explanation is the limited bandwidth of computer-mediated communication (CMC), the mode upon which virtual groups most depend. CMC is synchronous or asynchronous electronic mail and computer conferencing by which senders relay text-encoded messages (Walther 1992). Electronic mail is perceived as the most prevalent form of CMC (Walther 1996; Garton and Wellman

1995; Sproull and Kiesler 1986), and it has been found to increase communication and productivity by increasing the frequency of communication between interactants (Trevino and Webster 1992).

Communicating in Virtuality

CMC plays a major role in the life of virtual groups. In fact, most of the resources, training, and support that virtual group members receive are within the realm of CMC. While several researchers have described the character of electronic communication similarly, media users do not uniformly experience CMC. For instance, Walther (1994) found CMC to be more interpersonally positive when interactants believe there is some longevity to their association with the other interactants. King and Xia (1997) contend that experience with the media will influence individual perceptions of media appropriateness. Also, these perceptions may not be stable over time, which adds further complexity.

The agreed-upon characteristics of CMC that distinguish it from more traditional forms of communication are: (1) reduced social cues, (2) anonymity, (3) limited interaction venue, and (4) orientation toward technology.

Reduced Social Cues. CMC, regardless of its form, contains fewer social cues than conventional face-to-face interaction. As Bordia (1997) puts it, "Preoccupation with receiving, composing, and sending messages leads to a lack of awareness of social context" (p. 108). By and large, CMC lacks nonverbal information (e.g., proxemics, kinesics, and paralanguage). Reduced social cues leave group members vulnerable to misunderstandings and reduce the influence of social norms and constraints in virtual groups (Kiesler, Siegal, and McGuire 1984).

Anonymity. Social and contextual clues are further diminished by CMC's predisposition toward anonymity. The use of personas or pseudonyms is prevalent in CMC. Individuals have come to expect a level of anonymity not available in face-to-face contexts. Cherny (as cited in Reid 1998) describes online social interaction as operating on the basis of WYSIWIS (What You See Is What I Say). Individuals can intentionally manipulate interactions through inaccurate projection of personal attributes. The presumption of anonymity in on-line interactions does not exist in comparable settings off-line.

Take, for example, a recent set of focus groups conducted with virtual team members for the purpose of exploring the effects of virtuality on group identification. Teams that were geographically proximate came together for focus-group interviews, with participants speaking freely with one another while an audio tape documented all that was said. Teams that could not collocate participated in "virtual" focus groups. They were provided with the URL to an electronic bulletin board that they accessed via a university server. Only the researcher and focus group participants (fellow virtual work team members) were provided access.

Sessions were conducted asynchronously over a two-week period. Members were asked to log in daily and encouraged to post responses both to researcher questions and team member responses. Surprisingly, subjects created user names that masked identity (e.g., "Spring3," "Tetris," and "Jangles"); however the site software compiled a list of user names coupled with their e-mail addresses. This roster was available to all focus group members. Obviously, the connection of the user name to an e-mail address, which tended to contain users' real names (e.g., *bob.jones@xyz.com*) made it easy to determine user identity. The researcher received a flurry of off-line messages from team members complaining about a lack of anonymity. One wrote, "I thought we wouldn't know who said what." Another wrote, "I thought this was confidential." Confidentiality had been assured; anonymity, however, had not been discussed but was clearly presumed by participants. Interaction at the sites was minimal.

Paradoxically, a lack of anonymity may impede interaction, but so too might the existence of anonymity. Studies comparing levels of unconstrained behavior in face-to-face groups and computer conferencing groups found a greater preponderance for hostile interaction—cursing, name calling, and insults—among those groups using computers to communicate. The highest level was among anonymous users (Siegal, Dubrovsky, Kiesler, and McGuire 1986). Anonymity increases participation, enhances idea generation and encourages freer exchange of ideas. Unfortunately, it also leads to disinhibited behavior such as flaming, excessive self-disclosure, manipulation of other group members through deceitful disclosure, intentional violation of group behavioral norms, and disindividuation—behavior occurring in a group context that runs contrary to behavior one would engage in as an individual (Haythornthwaite et. al. 1998).

Limited Interaction Venue. CMC occurs within a finite interaction environment. In other words, incidental communication, such as unexpectedly meeting a colleague in the cafeteria or at the copy machine, does not occur in virtuality. When workers are not proximate, they lose opportunities for casual conversation that enable members to expand their contact with other people (Sarbaugh-Thompson and Feldman 1998). Casual conversations support formal communication by keeping the channels of contact open (March and Savon 1984). Unscheduled communication plays a vital role in the processes of feedback and socialization (Hage 1974). Virtual team members miss out on these "water cooler" interactions because they are not co-present and lack the means, even electronically, to "bump into" each other.

The finite interaction venue provided by CMC may partially explain why virtual group dynamics are unpredictable, while traditional group dynamics, being similar across groups, are more predictable (Oravec 1996). The inherent uncertainty of virtual group interactions necessitates that members pay attention to the social aspects of the group process. Sometimes called "group maintenance behaviors" (e.g., supporting, harmonizing, compromising, encouraging), they serve to ease tensions, build trust, increase solidarity, and facilitate teamwork (Brilhart 1982).

Orientation Toward Technology. The reliance on computer-supported interaction that virtual groups require makes it necessary that group members become proficient in the use of communication technology. Technology consists of the specific tools, machines, and techniques that enable tangible work processes (Barley 1990). There are a variety of technology-related interaction challenges faced by virtual groups. Members may lack the knowledge and skills required to use computer-supported communication hardware and software (e.g., groupware, audio-video conferencing tools, media spaces). Moreover, teams may lack the technical support needed to configure and utilize network operating systems. Members may be technophobic (irrationally fearful of technology), hence unable or unwilling to fully utilize available communication media. Members may also be uncertain about which computer-supported media to use (Jude-York, Davis, and Wise 2000).

Understanding computer-supported media use in virtual groups is important because selection decisions can influence group effectiveness and efficiency, as well as dictate how work is performed. The general consensus among researchers is that the answer to the question "which medium is most appropriate in a given circumstance?" cannot be reduced to location or cost criteria. Media selection research is beginning to evolve from isolated media choices made by individuals to studies of how pairs negotiate choices and how groups develop media use norms (Haythornthwaite et. al. 1998).

Summary and Conclusions

At this point it should be clear that virtual groups are not just groups at a distance; rather, they are unique entities that are qualitatively different from traditional groups. Virtual groups differ in character, conduct, and support needs. While the functions of virtual groups are similar to those of traditional groups, the interaction processes used by virtual groups to achieve their goals are greatly influenced by their virtual status. Communication skills and practices used in traditional group settings are likely to prove inadequate in virtual contexts.

Four characteristics that distinguish virtual groups from traditional groups are (1) geographic dispersion, (2) asynchronism, (3) porous boundaries, and (4) network composition. These characteristics limit the modes of communication available to virtual groups, which, in turn, present interaction challenges to members.

Given the increase in organizational dependency on collaborative, information-based work along with a corresponding increase in alternate work arrangements such as telecommuting, understanding virtual group processes and how best to support them is of critical concern to individuals, groups, and organizations alike. This chapter does not present solutions; however, identification of the issues is an important first step in the search for understanding.

References

Alderfer, C. P., and Smith, K. K. (1982). "Studying intergroup relations embedded in organizations." *Administrative Sciences Quarterly* 27: 35–65.

Allen, T. (1977). *Managing the Flow of Technology: Technology Transfer and the Dissemination of Technological Information Within the R & D Organization.* Cambridge, MA: MIT Press.

Balint, L. (1999). "Computer-mediated communication: the HCHI approach." In D. L. Day and D. K. Kovacs (eds.), *Computers, Communication, and Mental Models* (pp. 28–35). London: Francis and Taylor.

Barley, S. (1990). "The alignment of technology and structure through roles and networks." *Administrative Science Quarterly*, 35, 61–103.

Baym, N. (1997). "Interpreting soap operas and creating community: Inside an electronic fan culture." In S. Kiesler (ed.), *Culture of the Internet* (pp. 103–120). Mahwah, NJ: Lawrence Erlbaum.

Bordia, P. (1997). "Face-to-face versus computer-mediated communication: A synthesis of experimental literature." *Journal of Business Communication*, 34, 99–119.

Brilhart, J. K. (1982). *Effective Group Discussion* (4th ed.). Dubuque, IA: Wm. C. Brown Company.

Carnevale, P. J., and Probst, T. M. (1997). "Conflict on the Internet." In S. Kiesler (ed.), *Culture of the Internet* (pp. 233–255). Mahwah, New Jersey: Lawrence Erlbaum Associates.

Chadwick, S. A. (1996). Optimizing the communication effectiveness of telecommuters. Paper presented at Telecommuting Conference, April 1996.

Davison, R. M., and Briggs, R. O. (2000). "GSS for presentation support." *Communications of the ACM* 43(9): 91–97.

Day, D. L., and Kovacs, D. K. (1999). *Computers, Communication, and Mental Models.* London: Francis and Taylor.

Fuller, R. (1999). "Human-computer-human interaction: How computers affect interpersonal communication." In D. L. Day and D. K. Kovacs (eds.), *Computers, Communication, and Mental Models* (pp. 11–14). London: Francis and Taylor.

Gackenbach, J., and Ellerman, E. (1998). "Introduction to the psychological aspects of Internet use." In J. Gackenbach (ed.), *Psychology and the Internet: Intrapersonal, Interpersonal and Transpersonal Implications* (pp. 1–28). San Diego, CA: Academic Press.

Garton, L., and Wellman, B. (1995). "Social impacts of electronic mail in organizations: A review of research literature." *Communication Yearbook* 18: 434–453.

Hage, J. (1974). *Communication and Organizational Control: Cybernetics in Health and Welfare Settings.* New York: Wiley.

Haythornthwaite, C., Wellman, B., and Garton, L. (1998). "Work and community via computer-mediated communication." In J. Gackenbach (ed.), *Psychology of the Internet* (pp. 199–226). San Diego, CA: Academic Press.

Herring, S. (1996). "Posting in a different voice: Gender and ethics in computer-mediated communication." In C. Ess (ed.), *Philosophical Approaches to Computer-Mediated Communication* (pp. 115–145). Albany: SUNY Press.

Hiltz, S. R., and Wellman, B. (1997). "Asynchronous learning networks as a virtual classroom." *Communications of the ACM* 40(9): 44–49.

Joinson, A. (1998). "Causes and implications of disinhibited behavior on the Internet." In J. Gackenbach (ed.), *Psychology of the Internet* (pp. 43–60). San Diego, CA: Academic Press.

Joinson, C. (1999). "Teams at work." *HR Magazine* 44: 30.

Jude-York, D., Davis, L. D., and Wise, S. L. (2000). *Virtual Teaming: Breaking the Boundaries of Time and Place.* Menlo Park, CA: AISP.

Kell, C. L. and Corts, P. R. (1980). *Fundamentals of Effective Group Communication.* New York: Macmillan.

Kiesler, S., Siegal, J., and McGuire, T. W. (1984). "Social psychological aspects of computer mediated communication." *American Psychologist* 39: 1123–1134.

King, R. C., and Xia, W. (1997). "Media appropriateness: Effects of experience on communication media choice." *Decision Sciences* 28: 877–910.

Lea, M., and Spears, R. (1991). "Computer-mediated communication, de-individuation and group decision making." *International Journal of Man-Machine Studies* 39: 283–301.

Lipnack, J. and Stamps, J. (1997). *Virtual Teams: Reaching Across Space, Time, and Organizations with Technology.* New York: Wiley.

MacDonald, M. (1999). Using technology to assist facilitation. Paper presented at the International Association of Facilitators Annual Meeting, Williamsburg, Virginia, January, 1999.

Mandviwalla, M. (1999). "The world view of collaborative tools." In D. L. Day and D. K. Kovacs (eds.), *Computers, Communication, and Mental Models* (pp. 57–66). London: Taylor and Francis.

March, J. G., and Savon, G. (1984). "Gossip, information, and decision making." In L. Sproull and P. D. Larkey (eds.), *Advances in Information Processing in Organizations.* (Vol. 1). Greenwich, CT: JAI.

McCollom, M. (1990). "Group formation: Boundaries, leadership and culture." In J. Gillette and M. McCollom (eds.), *Groups in Context* (pp. 34–48). Reading, MA: Addison-Wesley.

Mills, T. M. (1984). *The Sociology of Small Groups* (2nd ed.). Englewood Cliffs, NJ: Prentice-Hall.

Oravec, J. (1996). *Virtual Individuals, Virtual Groups: Human Dimensions of Groupware and Computer Networking.* New York: Cambridge University Press.

Palmer, M. T. (1995). "Interpersonal communication and virtual reality: Mediating interpersonal relationships." In F. Biocca and M. Levy (eds.), *Communication in the Age of Virtual Reality* (pp. 277–299). Hillsdale, NJ: Lawrence Erlbaum.

Poole, M. S., and DeSanctis, G. (1990). "Understanding the use of group decision support systems: The theory of adaptive structuration." In J. Fulk and C. Steinfield (eds.), *Organizations and Communication Technology* (pp. 173–191). Newbury Park, CA: Sage.

Pratt, L., Wiseman, R., Cody, M., and Wendt, P. (1998). Interrogative strategies, relationship development, and computer-mediated communication. Paper presented at the National Communication Association, New York, November 1998, 1–32.

Reid, E. (1998). "The self and the Internet: Variations of the illusion of one self." In J. Gackenbach (ed.), *Psychology of the Internet* (pp. 29–42). San Diego, CA: Academic Press.

Sarbaugh-Thompson, M., and Feldman, M. S. (1998). "Electronic mail and organizational communication: Does saying 'Hi' really matter?" *Organization Science* 9: 685–698.

Scott, C. R. (1999). "Communication technology and group communication." In L. R. Frey (ed.), *Handbook of Group Communication Theory and Research* (pp. 432–472). Thousand Oaks, CA: Sage.

Shaw, M. E. (1976). *Group Dynamics: The Psychology of Small Group Behavior* (2nd ed.). New York: McGraw-Hill.

Siegal, J., Dubrovsky, V., Kiesler, S., and McGuire, T. (1986). "Group processes in computer-mediated communication." *Organizational Behavior and Human Decision Processes* 37: 157–187.

Sproull, L., and Kiesler, S. (1986). "Reducing social context cues: Electronic mail in organizational communication." *Management Science* 32: 1492–1512.

Stone, A. R. (1995). "In novel conditions: The cross-dressing psychiatrist." *The War of Desire and Technology at the Close of the Mechanical Age* (pp. 65–81). Cambridge, MA: MIT.

Trevino, L. K., and Webster, J. (1992). "Flow in computer-mediated communication." *Communication Research* 19: 539–573.

Walther, J. B. (1992). "Interpersonal effects in computer-mediated interaction: A relational perspective." *Communication Research* 19: 1992.

——. (1994). "Anticipated ongoing interaction versus channel effects on relational communication in computer-mediated interaction." *Human Communication Research* 20: 473–501.

——. (1995). "Relational aspects of computer-mediated communication: Experimental observations over time." *Organization Science* 6(2): 186–203.

——. (1996). "Computer-mediated communication: Impersonal, interpersonal, and hyperpersonal." *Communication Research* 23: 3–43.

Webster's New Universal Unabridged Dictionary. (1996). New York: Barnes and Noble.

Wellman, B., Salaff, J., and Dimitrova, D. (1996). "Computer networks as social networks: Collaborative work, telework, and virtual community." *Annual Review of Sociology* 22: 213–238.

Part II

Theories of Small Group Communication

According to Thomas Kuhn (1970), all scholarly disciplines experience periods of intellectual discontent. For the study of small group communication, that period was the 1970s (Frey 1996). Essays by Bormann (1970), Gouran (1970, 1973), Mortensen (1970), Fisher (1971), Larson (1971), Bochner (1974), and others criticized small group communication research on the grounds that it lacked solid theoretical underpinnings (Mortensen 1970, 304). In short, critics in the 1970s concluded that the study of small group communication to date had not been guided by a clear understanding of how various aspects of group communication fit together, and, as a result, researchers were merely producing "piles of isolated facts" (Poole 1999, 37).

Small group communication scholars responded to the criticisms of the 1970s by developing theories of group communication and filling the theoretical vacuum noted by critics. By the end of the 1980s, group communication research had "moved out of the more or less exploratory, atheoretical, unfocused mode [of earlier research] and . . . exhibited the influence of . . . reasonably clear, well-developed, and theoretically grounded orientations" (Gouran, Hirokawa, McGee, and Miller 1994, 258). Three theories in particular provided much of the theoretical grounding for small group communication research in the 1980s and 1990s:

Functional Theory, Symbolic Convergence Theory, and *Structuration Theory.*

Part II presents chapters on these three important theories of small group communication by their principal architects.

References

Bochner, A. P. (1974). "Task and instrumentation variables as factors jeopardizing the validity of published group communication research, 1970–1971." *Communication Monographs*, 41: 169–178.

Bormann, E. G. (1970). "The paradox and promise of small group research." *Speech Monographs*, 41: 169–178.

Fisher, B. A. (1971). "Communication research and the task-oriented group." *Journal of Communication*, 21: 136–149.

Frey, L. R. (1996). "Remembering and re-membering: A history of theory and research on communication and group decision-making." In R. Y. Hirokawa and M. S. Poole (eds.), *Communication and Group Decision-Making* 2nd Edition (pp. 19–51). Thousand Oaks, CA: Sage.

Gouran, D. S. (1970). "Response to 'The paradox and promise of small group research.'" *Speech Monographs*, 37: 217–218.

Gouran, D. S. (1973). "Group communication: Perspectives and priorities for future research." *Quarterly Journal of Speech*, 58: 22–29.

Gouran, D. S., Hirokawa, R. Y., McGee, M. C., and Miller, L. (1994). "Communication in groups: Research trends and theoretical perspectives." In F. L. Casmir (ed.), *Build-*

ing *Communication Theories: A Socio/Cultural Approach* (pp. 241–268). Hillsdale, NJ: Lawrence Erlbaum Associates.

Kuhn, T. (1970). *The Structure of Scientific Revolutions*. Chicago: University of Chicago Press.

Larson, C. E. (1971). "Speech communication and research on small groups." *Speech Teacher*, 20: 89–107.

Mortensen, C. D. (1970). "The state of small group research." *Quarterly Journal of Speech*, 56: 304–309.

Poole, M. A. (1999). "Small group communication theories." In L. R. Frey, M. S. Poole, and D. S. Gouran (eds.), *Handbook of Group Communication*. Thousand Oaks, CA: Sage. ✦

Chapter 4
Effective Decision Making and Problem Solving in Groups

A Functional Perspective

Dennis S. Gouran
Randy Y. Hirokawa

This chapter presents a general overview of Functional Theory. This theory was developed to explain how group communication contributes to, and inhibits, group decision-making and problem-solving effectiveness. In short, Functional Theory posits that the performance level of decision-making and problem-solving groups can be traced to the extent to which communication among group members contributes to the fulfillment of particular requirements of their task. If group interaction does not lead to the adequate fulfillment of task requirements, the chances of a group's making a good decision or identifying an effective solution to a problem are greatly diminished. Functional Theory has evolved over two decades, and this chapter summarizes the theory at its most recent level of sophistication.

Much of what we experience on a daily basis in contemporary life is the outcome of countless decision-making and problem-solving discussions in which groups of various sorts, backgrounds, and composition have engaged. Often, these groups perform effectively and, in so doing, better our lives. On other occasions, however, they do not perform well and, in the process, complicate our lives. In some instances, they may even do considerable harm (Janis 1982, 1989).

The reasons for faulty performance in decision-making and problem-solving groups are many and varied, and not fully identified or completely understood. Because of the pervasiveness and importance of such groups, they undoubtedly will continue to receive the attention of interested scholars from the different disciplines, such as political science, psychology, sociology, management science, and communication, in which studies of decision making and problem solving in groups are common. Enough is presently known, however, to take steps to reduce the likelihood of a group's making a poor decision or generating ineffective solutions to problems.

Over the last 20 years, research on communication in decision-making and problem-solving groups[1] has contributed to the development of the Functional Theory of Communication in Decision-Making and Problem-Solving Groups (Gouran and Hirokawa 1983, 1996). This theory, often referred to as the *Functional Perspective*, was developed to explain how group communication contributes to, and inhibits, group decision-making and problem-solving effectiveness. From this perspective, successful decision making and problem solving in groups can be traced to the extent to which communication among group members ensures that particular requirements for their task are properly fulfilled. If group interaction does not lead to the adequate fulfillment of task requirements, the chances of a group's making a good decision or identifying an effective solution to a problem are greatly diminished. This chapter provides a general, but necessarily incomplete, overview of this theory.[2]

Background for the Theory

Although the Functional Perspective is relatively new as a formal theory, its origins date well back into the twentieth century (Gouran, Hirokawa, Julian, and Leatham 1993). One origin was the appropriation and adaptation of American philosopher John Dewey's (1910/1997) method of reflective thinking for use in the teaching of group discussion. Dewey characterized the method as consisting of five steps:

> (1) a felt difficulty; (2) its location and definition; (3) suggestion of possible solution; (4) development by reasoning of the bearings of the suggestion; (5) further observation and experiment leading to its acceptance or rejection; that is, the conclusion of belief or disbelief. (p. 72)

For teachers of communication interested in group process, these steps provided a useful standard agenda for conducting decision-making and problem-solving discussions and represented a scientific approach to making choices in group situations that cast the activity as one of inquiry rather than advocacy and fostered a spirit of cooperation rather than competition (see, for example, Ewbank and Auer 1951).

A second major origin was the study of problem-solving groups by sociologist Robert Freed Bales (1950) that began in the 1940s and continued throughout the remainder of the century. Among his many contributions to the study of groups, Bales developed a method he called Interaction Process Analysis for use in the study of group performance. IPA requires that one classify all communicative acts (verbal and nonverbal) into 12 categories, three of which capture positive reactions, three negative reactions, three questions related to the task, and the final three responses to questions (see Keyton 1997). Bales held that groups strive for equilibrium (or a balance in satisfying the demands of the task and in maintaining the type of relational climate that enables members to perform as a unit). Acts of the sorts mentioned above are the means by which the members of groups both become aware of imbalances and achieve equilibrium; hence, they have functional value. In other words, communicative acts have consequences that determine, in part, how well

or inadequately the members of groups go about their work.

Drawing on these separate strands of scholarly thought, as well as some work by Irving Janis (1972) on the causes for faulty American foreign policy decisions made by various governmental groups, we produced and published an early version of the Functional Perspective in the early 1980s (Gouran and Hirokawa 1983). Since its initial introduction, the theory has become the object of considerable research and has achieved both recognition and standing among communication-based theories of group process (Gouran 1999; Poole 1999).

Overview of the Theory

The Functional Perspective accounts for group decision-making and problem-solving performance in terms of the communicative actions of group members. In so doing, the theory also specifies how group members should, and should not, interact to maximize their chances of arriving at high-quality decisions or solutions.

Assumptions

The Functional Perspective is based on some general assumptions about the nature of group decision making and problem solving. We discuss four here.

1. *Group members are motivated to make the best choice(s) possible.* The Functional Perspective assumes that the members of a group want to make a good decision or arrive at an effective solution. If the group members are not motivated to make the best choice possible, their performance will likely be attributable to factors other than the communication they engaged in to arrive at a choice, and the claims of the Functional Perspective will therefore not likely hold true.

2. *The choice to be made is nonobvious.* Many group choices do not require careful reflection or thought. Either they have precedents that dictate the

choice to be made (e.g., mandatory sentencing for a given class of crime), or the level of uncertainty associated with making a particular choice is so small that the choice to be made is obvious (e.g., deciding which of two children got into the cookie jar when only one of them was at home). A systematic, reflective approach to choice making becomes necessary when the issue of concern is consequential (that is, when the costs of being wrong can be high), and there is some degree of uncertainty as to which among a set of alternatives represents the appropriate choice. The claims of the Functional Perspective apply to such nonobvious choices.

3. *Group members have access to information and other resources necessary for successful task completion.* Simply put, a group cannot be expected to arrive at an appropriate decision or effective solution unless it is privy to important information and data. Likewise, a group cannot be expected to arrive at a good decision or effective solution unless it has other necessary resources, such as a sufficient amount of time to arrive at a high-quality choice. The claims of the Functional Perspective are therefore assumed to apply to situations in which the informational and other resources that a group needs to arrive at a high-quality decision or solution are available to its members or can be realistically acquired by them.

4. *Group members collectively possess the cognitive and communicative skills necessary for dealing with various facets of the decision-making or problem-solving process.* If the task presented to a group is so difficult or complex that group members do not know how to go about trying to arrive at a decision or solution, the group cannot be expected to perform well on that task. Likewise, if group members do not possess the skills necessary to communicate effectively with each other (e.g., they don't all speak the same language), they cannot be expected to arrive at a high-quality

decision or solution. Hence the claims of the Functional Perspective are based on the assumption that group members have the requisite skills to properly complete their task.

In short, the Functional Perspective assumes that the members of a decision-making or problem-solving group must (1) want to make an appropriate choice, (2) understand their task and its requirements, (3) have access to necessary resources like information and time, and (4) possess the capabilities and skills needed to deal with various facets of the task and the process required to successfully complete it. If these basic conditions are not met, the Functional Perspective is likely to be ineffective in accounting for the decision-making or problem-solving performance of groups.

Propositions

When the aforementioned conditions are present, the Functional Perspective posits that successful group decision making and problem solving is most likely to occur when members' interaction results in the fulfillment of the particular requirements of the task. If the requirements are not adequately addressed, the chances of a group's making a good decision or identifying an effective solution are diminished. More precisely, three of the Functional Perspective's key propositions posit that effective group decision making and problem solving are most likely to occur when group members:

1. Attempt to satisfy five fundamental task requirements: (a) show a correct understanding of the issue to be resolved, (b) determine the minimal characteristics any acceptable alternative must possess, (c) identify a relevant and realistic set of alternatives, (d) examine carefully the alternatives in relationship to each previously agreed-upon characteristic of an acceptable choice, and (e) select the alternative that analysis reveals to be most likely to have the desired characteristics.

2. Employ appropriate interventions for overcoming cognitive, affiliative, and egocentric constraints that are interfering with the satisfaction of fundamental task requirements.

3. Review the process by which the group comes to a decision and, if necessary, reconsider judgments reached (even to the point of starting over). (Gouran and Hirokawa 1996, 76–77)

Proposition 1 has five elements, each of which represents a particular requirement that ordinarily must be satisfied if a decision-making or problem-solving group is to have reasonable assurance of choosing appropriately. For the first element, Proposition 1 links showing a correct understanding of what is at issue to effective decision making and problem solving. In most instances, this entails making sure, by communicative means, that all of the members of a decision-making or problem-solving group know what type of question is to be resolved—*fact, conjecture, value,* or *policy* (Gouran 1982/1990)—and that they be aware of what each type of question obligates them to do.

In dealing with a *question of fact*, a group attempts to determine what is true, as in the case of the controversy concerning who received the most votes in the 2000 presidential election in Florida. *Questions of conjecture* involve the determination of what is probable or likely under some set of conditions that do not exist at the time a group is dealing with the issue of concern; for instance, "Will an increase in the prime interest rate prevent an inflationary spiral in the economy?" When a group discusses a *question of value*, its aim is to make a judgment about what constitutes acceptable beliefs, attitudes, and behavior, usually in a moral or ethical sense. One example is the question, "Under what circumstances, if any, is sentencing a person to death for the commission of any crime justifiable?" Finally, a *question of policy* is one for which the answer suggests a course of action; for instance, "What can be done to increase the safety of sport-utility vehicles?"

Each of these four types of question presents those involved in their resolution with a somewhat different set of specific requirements (Gouran 1982/1990). For instance, the applicable criteria for a decision-making or problem-solving group discussing a *question of policy* would consist of standards for which there are such indicators as feasibility, cost, and practicality, all of which make possible more meaningful comparisons among alternative courses of action with respect to their merits and potential consequences. In discussing a *question of value*, however, a group would have to use other values not in dispute as criteria for determining which position concerning the value in dispute is appropriate (Hempel 1965). Hence, unlike a *question of policy*, consistency with other fundamental values would be the most, and possibly only, relevant consideration for assessing what constitutes an appropriate choice. Space does not permit us to consider all of the variations here, but one can find relevant discussions in any of several different sources, including Barge (1994), Gouran (1982/1990), and Hirokawa and Salazar (1997).

Of greater importance for the purposes of this essay is recognizing that understanding what is at issue has a considerable bearing on how a decision-making or problem-solving group performs its task. Irving Janis (1989), for example, has noted that problem analysis is an aspect of choice making at which many individuals and groups are not especially good and at which unsuccessful groups are the least adept.

This deficiency can easily begin with a failure to understand the requirements unique to the matter a group is attempting to resolve. In effective decision-making and problem-solving groups, however, one or more of the members will have minimized this possibility by asking such questions as, "Do we all understand what is at issue and what we have to do to reach an appropriate conclusion?," or possibly even making a direct observation, such as, "As I see it, to be able to conclude that . . . , we will have to establish that. . . ." Moreover, one would expect such an individual or individuals to persist in the effort until it becomes apparent that everyone in the group understands what is at issue and what he or she must do to dispose of the issue(s) satisfactorily.

The second element, or subtask, included in Proposition 1 has to do with the standards against which the members of a decision-making or problem-solving group determine the merits of alternatives they are considering. One can think of this aspect of the process as the identification of criteria. For some questions, the number of criteria (minimal characteristics any alternative must possess to be endorsable) might be relatively small, as in the case of a jury that is trying to determine whether a verdict of guilty is appropriate in the case of someone accused of first-degree murder (*question of fact*). The only relevant criteria might be motive, opportunity, means, and presence at the scene of a crime. In other situations, say, the decision to purchase a new home, a fairly large number of criteria might pertain, for example, price, square footage, appearance, condition, property tax, landscaping, location, quality of area schools, safety, friendliness of neighbors, and so on.

The members of most decision-making and problem-solving groups have criteria that they apply implicitly in judging the merits of alternatives. A problem is that the criteria may not be the same for everyone. More important, unless the criteria are explicit, others can only infer which ones any given individual is using and the importance he or she attaches to them. It may even be the case on occasion that one selects a particular criterion after the fact to justify a preference for a particular alternative.

In effective groups (that is, you will recall, ones that make appropriate choices), members take time to set criteria in advance of the consideration of alternatives. In so doing, they openly discuss the criteria that are relevant to the matter under consideration—which ones are most applicable and how they wish to weight them in assessing alternatives. A failure to engage in this sort of interaction is to invite possible discord at later stages, even to the point of a group's being unable to make a choice at all, let alone the most appropriate one.

The third subtask that Proposition 1 includes is the identification of pertinent and realistic alternatives. Occasionally, these will be both obvious and limited in number. As an illustration, in considering the possible impact of an advertising campaign promoting the sale of a product (*question of conjecture*), the number of possibilities is limited. Sales could improve, they could decline, or they could stay about the same. On the other hand, considering what type of campaign would most likely have a desired effect (again a *question of conjecture*), a very large number of possibilities might be germane.

A defect that groups often display is to err on the side of identifying too few alternatives rather than too many. From one perspective called Image Theory, both individuals and groups are prone to accept a choice option if it in no conspicuous way violates core values and beliefs they possess (Beach and Mitchell 1996). We are in that sense given to expediency rather than deliberation and prefer to exert no more cognitive effort than, on the surface, appears to be necessary. Choosing between two alternatives, one of which appears to satisfy criteria reasonably well, for instance, requires far less cognitive effort than considering, say, five alternatives (Beach 1997). Consequently, given human nature, many groups would be inclined to follow the lines of least resistance and settle on only a few alternatives rather than assess the merits of all that might be pertinent.

Recognizing this tendency among members of his firm, advertising executive Alex F. Osborn (1957) many years ago devised a set of procedures to stimulate creative thinking, which he subsequently referred to as "brainstorming." Brainstorming involves having the members of a group think of and verbalize as many different solutions to a problem or alternatives as possible in a restricted period of time without any attempt to evaluate the output until after the allotted time has expired. Although research findings are mixed concerning the value of brainstorming and its variants (Seibold and

Krikorian 1997), there is sufficient evidence to suggest that, when possible, having more rather than fewer alternatives increases the statistical odds for a group's making good choices, especially when the identification of alternatives is subsequently followed by careful analysis (Herek, Janis, and Huth 1987).

The preceding reference to the study by Herek, Janis, and Huth provides a bridge to the next element in Proposition 1, examining all alternatives in relation to all criteria. This may seem to be an obvious move in the sequence suggested by the order of items in Proposition 1 and the other models discussed earlier. However, it is not always the case that members of decision-making and problem-solving groups perform this aspect of their overall task in a consistent, systematic, or rigorous fashion. A common temptation is to apply criteria selectively and focus on those for which initially preferred alternatives appear to achieve a minimally acceptable level of satisfaction. For example, Bazerman (2002) has summarized a good deal of research showing that in making choices based on anticipated payoffs, individuals may overestimate or underestimate costs and benefits of the alternatives they are considering, discount one or the other altogether, and possibly ignore the probability of occurrence of various outcomes associated with the alternatives.

In group situations, members may find themselves embroiled in controversy because the application of criteria to alternatives has been idiosyncratic. It is also possible that selectivity will have caused the group as a whole to overlook what might be the most important of the criteria for choosing among alternatives. In either event, the prospects for making the most appropriate choice are not very bright.

These deficiencies are far less likely to surface when at least one member of the group plays the role of reminder and offers comments that reinstate what the group is supposed to be doing at this stage of its deliberations (Schultz, Ketrow, and Urban 1995); for instance, "Remember, we are supposed to consider every alternative in relation to every criterion," or, "I think we have been underestimating, if not ignoring altogether, the importance of public reaction and acceptance of the proposals we have been considering."

The final subtask embraced by Proposition 1, reduced to its simplest form, has the members of a decision-making or problem-solving group selecting the alternative that best satisfies the established criteria. If the members have performed the other four subtasks in the manner called for, this one should almost be *pro forma*. However, addressing this requirement may take place at a time during which members whose preferred alternatives have not survived the choice-making process become antagonistic and introduce new sources of conflict into the proceedings (Fisher 1970). Participants also become highly defensive under such circumstances (Gibb 1961). Another possibility, especially if the group has considered a reasonably large number of alternatives and criteria, is that the members will experience some sort of selective recall that results in distortion of which alternative actually best satisfied the criteria.

In the performance of the five subtasks just reviewed, communication plays a vital role in effective groups. However, other problems may arise in the course of a group's interaction that complicate the satisfactory completion of decision-making and problem-solving tasks and may require different sorts of interventions from those we have examined in relation to the fundamental requirements imposed by the task. These additional complications arise from three types of constraints indirectly alluded to in the section dealing with the assumptions underlying the Functional Theory of Communication in Decision-Making and Problem-Solving Groups. Proposition 2 concerns the role of communication in overcoming these constraints, and it is to that proposition that we now direct our attention.

Proposition 2 posits an increased likelihood of a decision-making or problem-solving group's choosing appropriately when communication functions to help members overcome the obstacles posed by *cognitive, affiliative,* and *egocentric constraints.* Cognitive constraints involve feelings of pressure deriving from limited time or information. Affiliative constraints arise when concerns about maintaining relationships surpass those relating to successful task performance. Egocentric constraints are those involving dominance tendencies and other forms of self-serving interaction. (See Chapter 16 of this book for a more detailed discussion.)

When any of these three types of constraints takes hold, the members of a decision-making or problem-solving group are apt to resort to shortcuts of various sorts that do not serve the interests of making informed and judicious choices. Even if the members are equipped to recognize and accurately interpret the signs of these constraints and have anticipated their possible emergence, to prevent their having undue influence on how the group performs its task and goes about successfully satisfying the underlying requirements, one or more of the members must intervene.

Janis (1989) has formulated 17 hypotheses concerning the factors that give rise to and foster the dominance of the three types of constraints. These can be very useful in recognizing when and what type of constraint has taken hold. Janis has also generated 20 additional hypotheses and identified even more specific practices dealing with leadership that, in principle, can assist a group in overcoming the negative influence of such constraints. The practices that Janis recommends are largely communication-based and, with the types mentioned in conjunction with the first proposition as well as those discussed elsewhere (Gouran and Hirokawa 1996), provide groups with reasonably good prospects for being able to respond effectively to the difficulties that *cognitive, affiliative,* and *egocentric constraints* present.

Unfortunately, as in the case of requirements specific to each of the four types of questions with which decision-making and problem-solving groups contend, space does not allow us to provide a complete overview of the practices available. A representative sampling, however, suggests what communicative means group members have available for counteracting unwanted sources of influence.

Among the practices Janis recommends are: (1) actively encouraging all group members to adopt a vigilant approach to choice making; (2) generating disagreement if consensus is being too easily achieved; (3) denying that problems the group may be facing are insurmountable and insisting that the group continue to rely on high-quality procedures when time considerations appear to be driving the interaction; (4) adopting a posture of openness to potentially repugnant ideas; and (5) remaining appropriately skeptical of both ideas and evidence, especially when they come from sources of dubious reputation and contain extraordinary claims. We (Gouran and Hirokawa 1996) have identified and would add to the list such practices as: (1) making clear that one is questioning ideas, not attacking the person presenting them; (2) making salient problems associated with seemingly easily adopted alternatives through cost-benefit analysis; (3) shifting the focus of conflict from personalities to issues; (4) heightening awareness that some members are dominating by calling for input from less active ones; and (5) asking for elaboration of the bases for positions on issues when more powerful group members appear to be pressuring others to adopt their position.

The third proposition of the Functional Perspective concerns a step groups should take but typically do not take after the members have reached a decision or adopted a solution to a problem they have been discussing. This proposition holds that the likelihood of an appropriate choice is greater if the members of a decision-making or problem-solving group review the process by which they have arrived at their choice and, if necessary, reconsider the choice. The basis for this practice resides in the fact that while engaged in a process, people are not always able to attend to its dynamics and, hence, may overlook or otherwise be unaware of problems that are interfering with their performance. Doing a post mortem of the choice-making process can give members of decision-making and problem-solving groups the distance necessary to reflect in a reasonably objective fashion on what they have done, as well as the opportunity to change their minds if warranted in light of the review and reconsideration. This step in the choice-making process is one that Janis (1982) especially recommends.

The primary communicative activities associated with this aspect of a decision-making or problem-solving discussion are: (1) to remind the members of the importance of reviewing the process and (2) to enforce even-handedness in making the assessment. For a review to be useful, members must take a frank look at how they have performed their task, acknowledge weaknesses and unwanted sources of influence, and be prepared to reconsider their judgments, even if that necessitates starting over. Knowing that an honest and open review carries with it such a prospect also may lead the members from the outset to be more careful in how they perform their task. It can also prepare the members of groups to avoid certain types of difficulties on future occasions, as well as reinforce what they have done well.

Current Status of the Functional Perspective

The Functional Perspective can be viewed as *normative*, that is, as stipulating how members of decision-making and problem-solving groups *should* rather than how they *do* behave. To the extent that we feel that groups would perform more effectively if they were to behave in accordance with the propositions comprising the theory, the characterization appears to be apt, and we do, in fact, recommend that members of decision-making and problem-solving groups, whenever possible, attempt to behave in accordance with the essential aspects of the theory. As to the most suitable designation for the theory we have developed and reviewed herein, however, we prefer to think of it as *descriptive* in some respects and *predictive* in others, rather than as *normative*. We

take this view because there is a reasonable body of evidence providing direct or indirect support for most of the propositions that comprise the theory, and which, when considered properly, establishes the appropriateness of referring to the theory as both *descriptive* and *predictive*. The basis for that judgment should become evident in the remarks that follow.

It is clear that the Functional Perspective is not *descriptive* in the commonly understood sense of that term. We have no basis for arguing that all, or even most, individuals and groups confronted with the need to choose do so in a manner consistent with basic tenets of the theory. On the contrary, evidence dating to the pioneering work of Nobel Laureate in Economics Herbert A. Simon (1955) suggests quite the opposite (see also Beach 1997; Frey 1994; Janis 1989; Zey 1998). That reality, however, does not obviate the possibility that when individuals and groups, in fact, do behave in accordance with the theory, they improve their chances for making appropriate choices. We contend that the *descriptive/predictive* character of the theory resides in, and is demonstrated by, research evidence indicating that: (1) effective decision-making and problem-solving groups behave in greater conformity with the propositions comprising the Functional Perspective than do ineffective groups (*descriptive*), and (2) when group-member behavior has been manipulated along lines suggested by the theory, expected differences in performance have been the result more frequently than not (*predictive*).

In addition to research we have cited in reviewing the propositions comprising the Functional Perspective, there are a number of laboratory studies one would do well to consult (e.g., Cragan and Wright 1993; Hirokawa 1982, 1983a, 1983b, 1985, 1987, 1988; Hirokawa, Ice, and Cook 1988; Hirokawa and McLeod 1993; Papa and Graham 1990; Propp and Nelson 1994) and several case studies as well (e.g., Gouran 1984, 1987, 1990; Gouran, Hirokawa, and Martz 1986; Hirokawa, Gouran, and Martz 1986, 1988;

McKinney 1985). Most of this research has been supportive of the theory in one or more respects. For a more comprehensive overview and discussion of the pertinent research, we also refer the reader to a recently published and comprehensive summary by Hirokawa and Salazar (1999).

Despite its general supportiveness, the evidence assembled thus far is by no means conclusive, as not all of the propositions have been tested directly, either in isolation or in combination. Certainly, there has been no test of the set of propositions as whole. Until all of the propositions derived from the Functional Perspective have been tested directly and as a collective, as well as verified, its validity will, to some extent, be open to question.

In addition to less-than-complete tests of the theory, the content of communicative acts serving various functions related to task requirements in decision-making and problem-solving groups has not been examined at a qualitative level, for the most part. The accent in research to date has been on the categories particular acts best fit and the relative frequency with which given acts represent the categories, not on how well such acts serve the functions indicated by the categories to which they have been assigned. A communicative act can serve a function, such as attempting to focus a group's attention on the need to generate criteria, but not do so especially well in respect to its intended or desired consequence. This deficiency in how communicative acts have been studied may account for data that do not consistently affirm various propositions, as when a group whose members' communicative behavior shows attention to fundamental task requirements performs no better than one whose members' communicative behavior does not. Determining how well communication serves the functions related to satisfying task requirements should either take the theory to the next level in precision and, thereby, enhance its pragmatic value or possibly suggest a need for rethinking and revising some aspects of the theory.

Circumstantial factors may also partially account for apparent inconsistencies in the fit of data to the theory. For example, a group that is performing exceptionally well may show a lower incidence of the of the types of functional communicative behavior we have illustrated than a group in serious difficulty. In the latter case, repeated attempts at assuring that task requirements are fulfilled may be symptomatic of an exercise in futility or counterproductive perseverance. Such possibilities must also be examined in subsequent inquiries if we are to increase our confidence in the validity of the theory, or make necessary alterations in it.

Conclusion

Even though the Functional Perspective has not been fully supported by research and is in need of further refinement and development, on the whole, the evidence backing it is far greater than that which would lead one to question its validity. The fact that case studies, experimental research, and descriptive laboratory investigations all offer similar indications as to the reasons why some decision-making and problem-solving groups succeed and others fail, moreover, gives us greater confidence in extolling the virtue and value of the theory for the practitioner. Although we are not prepared to argue that groups whose members use communication in the ways suggested by the theory will succeed in all instances, or even in any given case, we are of the firm conviction that behaving communicatively in accordance with the propositions we have reviewed, under the conditions the theory assumes, will increase the likelihood of a group's performing effectively and, as a result, making appropriate choices. If nothing else, we trust that we have made the bases for such a conviction apparent in the material here and hope that you, at least, will be willing to try out some of what you have learned in future decision-making and problem-solving discussions.

Notes

1. Throughout this essay, the terms *decision making* and *problem solving* are used inter-

changeably. In a strict sense, *decision making* refers to the act of choice among predetermined alternatives, whereas *problem solving* entails the generation of alternatives aimed at movement from an existing state to a preferred state (Brilhart, Galanes, and Adams 2001). In either case, however, the process culminates in an act of choice, even if the act is, ironically, not to make a choice. In our work, we have found nothing in the distinction between the two terms that alters the structure of the theory and, hence, treat both decision making and problem solving as specific forms of choice making.

2. For a more extensive and detailed discussion of the Functional Perspective, the reader is encouraged to consult Gouran and Hirokawa (1996) and/or Gouran, Hirokawa, Julian, and Leatham (1993).

References

Bales, R. F. (1950). *Interaction Profile Analysis: A Method for the Study of Small Groups*. New York: Free Press.

Barge, J. K. (1994). *Leadership: Communication Skills for Organizations and Groups*. New York: St. Martin's Press.

Bazerman, M. (2002). *Judgment in Managerial Decision Making* (5th ed.). New York: John Wiley and Sons.

Beach, L. R. (1997). *The Psychology of Decision Making: People in Organizations*. Thousand Oaks, CA: Sage.

Beach, L. R., and Mitchell, T. R. (1996). "Image theory, the unifying perspective." In L. R. Beach (ed.), *Decision Making in the Workplace: A Unified Perspective* (pp. 1–20). Mahwah, NJ: Lawrence Erlbaum.

Brilhart, J. K., Galanes, G. J., and Adams, K. (2001). *Effective Group Discussion: Theory and Practice* (10th ed.). New York: McGraw-Hill.

Cragan, J. F., and Wright, D. W. (1993). "The functional theory of small group decision making: A replication." *Journal of Social Behavior and Personality* 8: 165–174.

Dewey, J. (1910/1997). *How We Think*. Mineola, NY: Dover.

Ewbank, H. L., and Auer, J. J. (1951). *Discussion and Debate: Tools of a Democracy* (2nd ed.). New York: Appleton-Century-Crofts.

Fisher, B. A. (1970). "Decision emergence: Phases in group decision-making." *Speech Monographs* 37: 53–66.

Frey, L. R. (1994). "The naturalistic paradigm: Studying groups in the postmodern era." *Small Group Research* 25: 551–577.

Gibb, J. R. (1961). "Defensive communication." *Journal of Communication* 11: 141–148.

Gouran, D. S. (1982/1990). *Making Decisions in Groups: Choices and Consequences*. Prospect Heights, IL: Waveland Press.

——. (1984). "Communicative influences related to the Watergate coverup: The failure of collective judgment." *Central States Speech Journal* 35: 260–268.

——. (1987). "The failure of argument in decisions leading to the 'Challenger disaster': A two-level analysis." In J. W. Wenzel (ed.), *Argument and Critical Practices: Proceedings of the Fifth SCA/AFA Conference on Argumentation* (pp. 439–448). Annandale, VA: Speech Communication Association.

——. (1990). "Factors affecting the decision-making process in the Attorney General's Commission on Pornography: A case study of unwarranted collective judgment." In R. S. Rodgers (ed.), *Free Speech Yearbook 28* (pp. 104–119). Carbondale: Southern Illinois University Press.

——. (1999). "Communication in groups: The emergence and evolution of a field of study." In L. R. Frey, D. S. Gouran, and M. S. Poole (eds.), *The Handbook of Group Communication Theory and Research* (pp. 3–36). Thousand Oaks, CA: Sage.

Gouran, D. S., and Hirokawa, R. Y. (1983). "The role of communication in decision-making groups: A functional perspective." In M. S. Mander (ed.), *Communications in Transition: Issues and Debates in Current Research* (pp. 168–185). New York: Praeger.

——. (1996). "Functional theory and communication in decision-making and problem-solving groups: An expanded view." In R. Y. Hirokawa and M. S. Poole (eds.), *Communication and Group Decision Making* (pp. 55–80). Thousand Oaks, CA: Sage.

Gouran, D. S., Hirokawa, R. Y., Julian, K. M., and Leatham, G. B. (1993). "The evolution and current status of the functional perspective on communication in decision-making and problem-solving groups." In S. A. Deetz (ed.), *Communication Yearbook 16* (pp. 573–600). Newbury Park, CA: Sage.

Gouran, D. S., Hirokawa, R. Y., and Martz, A. E. (1986). "A critical analysis of factors related to decisional processes involved in the Challenger disaster." *Central States Speech Journal* 37: 119–135.

Hempel, C. G. (1965). *Aspects of Scientific Explanation and Other Essays in the Philosophy of Science.* New York: Free Press.

Herek, G., Janis, I. L., and Huth, P. (1987). "Decisionmaking during international crises: Is quality of process related to outcome?" *Journal of Conflict Resolution* 31: 203–226.

Hirokawa, R. Y. (1982). "Group communication and problem-solving effectiveness I: A critical review of inconsistent findings." *Communication Quarterly* 30: 134–141.

——. (1983a). "Communication and problem-solving effectiveness II: An exploratory investigation of procedural functions." *Western Journal of Speech Communication* 47: 59–74.

——. (1983b). "A descriptive investigation of the possible communication-based reasons for effective and ineffective group decision making." *Communication Monographs* 50: 363–379.

——. (1985). "Discussion procedures and decision-making performance: A test of a functional perspective." *Human Communication Research* 12: 203–224.

——. (1987). "Why informed groups make faulty decisions: An investigation of possible interaction-based explanations." *Small Group Behavior* 18: 3–29.

——. (1988). "Group communication and decision-making performance: A continued test of the functional perspective." *Human Communication Research* 14: 487–515.

Hirokawa, R. Y., Gouran, D. S., Martz, A. E. (1988). "Understanding the sources of faulty group decision making: A lesson from the Challenger disaster." *Small Group Behavior* 19: 411–433.

Hirokawa, R. Y., Ice, R., and Cook, J. (1988). "Preference for procedural order, discussion structure, and group decision performance." *Communication Quarterly* 36: 217–226.

Hirokawa, R. Y., and McLeod, P. L. (1993, November). Communication, decision development, and decision quality in small groups: An integration of two approaches. Paper presented at the annual meeting of the Speech Communication Association, Miami Beach, FL.

Hirokawa, R. Y., and Salazar, A. J. (1997). "An integrated approach to communication and group decision making." In L. R. Frey and J. K. Barge (eds.), *Managing Group Life: Communicating in Decision-Making Groups* (pp. 156–181). Boston: Houghton Mifflin.

——. (1999). "Task-group communication and decision-making performance." In L. R. Frey, D. S. Gouran, and M. S. Poole (eds.), *Handbook of Group Communication Theory and Research* (pp. 167–191). Thousand Oaks, CA: Sage.

Janis, I. L, (1972). *Victims of Groupthink: A Psychological Study of Foreign-Policy Decisions and Fiascoes.* Boston: Houghton Mifflin.

——. (1982). *Groupthink: Psychological Studies of Policy Decisions and Fiascoes* (2nd ed.). Boston: Houghton Mifflin.

——. (1989). *Crucial Decisions: Leadership in Policymaking and Crisis Management.* New York: Free Press.

Keyton, J. (1997). "Coding communication in decision-making groups." In L. R. Frey and J. K. Barge (Eds.), *Managing Group Life: Communicating in Decision-Making Groups* (pp. 236–269). Boston: Houghton Mifflin.

Martz, A. E. (1986). An investigation of the functions of communication in the production and acceptance of unwarranted inferences by members of decision-making groups. Unpublished master's thesis, The Pennsylvania State University, University Park.

McKinney, B. C. (1985). Decision-making in the President's Commission on the Assassination of President Kennedy: A descriptive analysis employing Irving Janis's groupthink hypothesis. Unpublished doctoral dissertation, The Pennsylvania State University, University Park.

Osborn, A. F. (1957). *Applied Imagination: Principles and Procedures of Creative Problem-Solving.* New York: Scribner.

Papa, M. J., and Graham, E. E. (1990, November). A test of the ecological validity of the functional communicative perspective of small group decision-making. Paper presented at the annual meeting of the Speech Communication Association, Chicago.

Poole, M. S. (1999). "Group communication theory." In L. R. Frey, D. S. Gouran, and M. S. Poole (eds.), *The Handbook of Group Communication Theory and Research* (pp. 37–70). Thousand Oaks, CA: Sage.

Propp, K. M., and Nelson, D. (1994, April). Decision-making performance in naturalistic groups: A test of the ecological validity of the functional perspective. Paper presented at the annual meeting of the Central States Communication Association, Oklahoma City.

Schultz, B., Ketrow, S. M., and Urban, D. M. (1995). "Improving decision quality in the small group: The role of the reminder." *Small Group Research* 26: 521–541.

Seibold, D. R., and Krikorian, D. H. (1997). "Planning and facilitating group meetings." In L. R. Frey and J. K. Barge (eds.), *Managing Group Life: Communicating in Decision-Making Groups* (pp. 270–305). Boston: Houghton Mifflin.

Simon, H. A. (1955). "A behavioral model of rational choice." *Quarterly Journal of Economics* 69: 99–118.

Zey, M. (1998). *Rational Choice Theory and Organizational Theory: A Critique.* Thousand Oaks, CA: Sage.

Chapter 5
Symbolic Convergence Theory

Ernest G. Bormann

In this very readable essay, Bormann explains how and why group members come to share a common understanding for symbols and their accompanying meanings. He shows how the "dramatizing message" of a single group member can lead to a series of dramatizing messages by multiple group members, each building on the others before it, producing what the author calls a "fantasy chain." Bormann goes on to explain how, by participating in the creation of a fantasy chain, group members "create a common ground of meanings" that enables them not only to communicate effectively with each other but also to achieve a "meeting of the minds."

Although the small task-oriented group participates in the culture of its environment, it also develops a subculture of its own.... The styles are essentially a result of a given group's process of acculturation.

Some small groups have an unruly, boisterous style, and others are quiet and reserved. Some use scapegoats and refuse to face difficult internal and external problems. Some are prone to take flight or to fight whenever they face a crisis. Some are warm and emotional and member-oriented, while others are preoccupied with manipulating the external environment. In some groups, concepts are combined and language is used with considerable skill. Members of these groups deal with abstractions and reason

fluently and consistently. Participants in other groups typically mobilize their resources largely with gestures and monosyllables and grunts. In yet other groups, members go through long, involved rationalizations before and after making decisions.

This chapter elaborates on a communication theory that explains how a group's culture is formed. The theory is called Symbolic Convergence Theory.

Symbolic Convergence and Group Culture

The basic communicative dynamic of the theory is the sharing of group fantasies, which brings about symbolic convergence for the participants.

Investigators in small group communication laboratories discovered the process of sharing fantasies when they investigated dramatizing messages and their effect on the group culture. Bales (1950, 1970) and his associates originally developed 12 categories to use in making a content analysis of communication in small groups. One of the categories was "Shows Tension Release," but over the years investigators changed the category to "Dramatizes." Continued work in which observers investigated the communication episodes associated with dramatizing led to the discovery of group fantasy events.

The Minnesota studies replicated the work of Bales and his associates beginning in the early 1970s. The preliminary results of these investigations were reported in the previous edition of this book, and the results of the small group studies since that edition was published, culminating with the formulation of the symbolic convergence theory, are summarized in this edition.

Dramatizing Messages

A dramatizing message is one that contains one or more of the following: a pun or other word play, a double entendre, a figure of speech, analogy, anecdote, parable, allegory, fable, or narrative. . . . In symbolic convergence theory . . . *figures of speech* refer to short, direct or implied comparisons as well as to the important figure of personification, in which a nonhuman object or life form is portrayed as having human features and characteristics. *Analogies* are defined as longer comparisons that extend the similarities through the discourse.

A number of scholars have suggested that it is useful to view the process of a communication episode as dramatic action. Thus, even everyday behavior can be interpreted as role playing or self-monitoring and self-presentation. All the world becomes a stage and we are all actors at all times. Portraying everyday life as drama does provide some useful insights into human communication, but the analogy ought not be pushed too far. After all, a small group meeting such as a jury deliberation portrayed in a motion picture is not the same as a jury deliberation over the fate of a defendant in a court of law.

The studies of dramatizing messages, therefore, have led to the conclusion that it is useful to distinguish between the ongoing unfolding of experience and the messages that discuss events in other than the here and now.

If in the middle of a group discussion several members come into conflict, the situation would be dramatic; but because the action is unfolding in the immediate experience of the group, it would not qualify as the basis for the sharing of a group fantasy. Immediate experience is often confusing and contradictory. We may not know for sure what happened or whom to blame or praise for their actions during the event. If, however, the group members begin talking about a conflict some of them had in the past, or if they envision a future conflict, of if they dramatize a current conflict taking place somewhere else, these comments would be dramatizing messages. Such messages make sense out of our confusing experiences and provide an explanation and interpretation of what happened.

The Communicative Process of Sharing a Fantasy

As they studied these messages, the Minnesota investigators found, as did Bales and his associates, that some seemed to fall on deaf ears: The group members did not pay much attention to certain comments. Other dramatizing messages, however, caused a symbolic explosion in the form of a chain reaction. The tempo of the conversation picked up. People grew excited, interrupted one another, blushed, laughed, lost self-consciousness. The tone of the meeting, which was often quiet and tense immediately prior to the dramatizing, became animated and boisterous. In the chaining process, both verbal and nonverbal communication indicated participation in the drama. Then, as abruptly as it started, the episode was broken off by a member who changed the subject, often by pulling the group back to work. The people who shared the fantasy did so with the appropriate responses. In short, the replications at Minnesota found the same processes of apathy or chaining when group members dramatized as did other investigators.

In addition, the Minnesota studies found that not all dramatizing messages result in a group's sharing a fantasy or in a group's ignoring the message or responding with a "ho hum" attitude. Some dramatizing messages are actively rejected. Members express disapproval or groan when they should laugh, or laugh when they should feel sadness. Further study of the active rejection of dramatizing messages found that such messages also provide important evidence for the analysis of group culture by indicating the symbols, meanings, and emotions toward which the members do not converge.

Group fantasy chains are those moments of dramatization in which all or most of the members participate. You should not get the impression that the term *fantasy* as used here means that the communication is bizarre like science fiction, or unrealistic like a cartoon, or make-believe like a fairy tale. A group fantasy may and often does deal with real-life situations and people.

Figure 5.1 presents the nature of dramatizing messages and the possible responses of members of a group. Note that if the dramatizing message results in

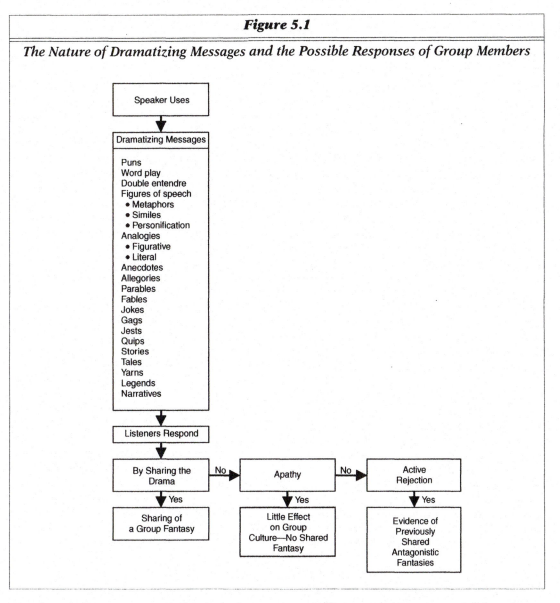

Figure 5.1

The Nature of Dramatizing Messages and the Possible Responses of Group Members

member participation and sharing, the result is a group fantasy.

In symbolic convergence, the term *fantasy* means the creative and imaginative shared interpretation of events that fulfills a group's psychological or rhetorical need to make sense of its experience and to anticipate its future. Rhetorical fantasies often deal with things that have actually happened to group members or that are reported in works of history, the news media, or the oral history and folklore of groups and communities.

Bales argues persuasively that fantasies are not usually developed entirely out of the mind. Most often, fantasies are formed in context, and the internal fantasy life of group members is full of images that are produced as a result of the "furniture" of the world. Members are likely to perceive objects of the environment in similar ways. The fantasy chain is, thus, seldom a case of mind over matter. Stressing the subjective aspects of human response to experience or the effects of individual differences is likely to miss substantial similarities. It is better to assume that the dramatizing messages that result in fantasy chains are, in Bales's words, traceable to *"some 'original facts.'"*

If symbol systems stood in a one-to-one relationship with experience, then it might be argued that group communication mirrored the facts. A sign relationship is one in which the sign is invariably related to the experience. Thus, lightning is a sign of thunder and thunder inevitably follows. Symbols, however, open the way for embroidering the facts. The symbol for lightning can denote the flash of light in the sky and signify the sound of thunder, but the symbol may also be placed on a military uniform to denote an elite corps or on a bottle to denote a potent kind of "white lightning." In short, objects of the real world when dramatized symbolically are, in Bales's words, "selected, remade, smoothed out, and bent to some semblance of consistency with the existing mental world of the particular individual or group."

When group members respond emotionally to a dramatic message, they publicly proclaim some commitment to an attitude. They also have evidence that a new meaning has been shared by others for a symbol that has been singled out and made important. A fantasy chain brings the participants who share it into symbolic convergence and creates a common ground of meaning and culture that enables group members to achieve empathic communion as well as a "meeting of the minds."

A fantasy chain is symbolic because it deals with the human tendency to interpret signs, signals, current experience, and action and invest them with meaning. When we share a fantasy, we attribute events to human action and thus make sense out of what may have previously been a confusing state of affairs. We do so in common with others who share the fantasy with us. Thus, we come to symbolic convergence on the matter and we envision that part of our world in similar ways. We have created common villains and heroes and celebrated certain basic dramatic actions as laudable and pictured others as despicable. We have created some

symbolic common ground and we can talk with one another about that shared interpretation with code words or brief allusions. . . .

Convergence refers to the way in which, during certain processes of communication, two or more private symbolic worlds incline toward each other, come more closely together, or even overlap. When members placed in a new group participate in fantasy chains, their private symbolic worlds begin to overlap as a result of symbolic convergence. Having experienced symbolic convergence, they share a common group consciousness. They have the basis for communication with one another to raise the consciousness of new members, to sustain the consciousness of group members when challenged, to discuss their common concerns and experiences as group members, and to agree on how to make decisions.

The members of a new group may all have previously come to symbolic convergence in other groups so that they bring the same symbolic common ground, the same heroes and villains, with them to the group. Case studies indicate that such luck or accident is extremely rare, however; and although members often bring some commonalities with them, they usually must share new fantasies in order to build a unique group consciousness. The creation of such a common consciousness is essential to the development of a group culture and cohesiveness.

Fantasy Themes

The content of the dramatizing message that sparks the fantasy chain is called a *fantasy theme*. The fantasy theme is the pun, figure, or analogy that characterizes the event, or it is a narrative that tells the story in terms of specific characters going through a particular line of action.

When someone characterizes an event with a figure of speech or dramatizes what happened, he or she must select certain people to be the focus of the story and present them in a favorable light while selecting others to be portrayed in a more negative fashion. Without protagonists (heroes) and antagonists (villains), there is little drama.

Shared fantasies are coherent accounts of past experiences or those envisioned in the future that simplify, organize, and form the social reality of the participants. The group's shared dreams of the future, no matter how apocalyptic or utopian, provide artistic and comprehensive forms for thinking about and experiencing the future. Fantasy themes always put a spin on the facts, which are thus slanted, ordered, and interpreted. By sharing different fantasy themes, members of different groups have the rhetorical means to account for and explain the same experiences or events in different ways. For example, often the classroom groups that received a grade of A to be shared by all members will participate in fantasy chains that account for and explain what happened in terms of their innate excellence and superior work, whereas the groups that received a grade of C or D might explain the results in terms of unfair teacher evaluations.

Symbolic Cues

The Minnesota studies revealed another important communication phenomenon in the workings of *symbolic cues* or triggers. The communication phenomenon of the inside joke is an example of such a trigger. The studies showed that only those who have shared the fantasy theme that the inside joke refers to will respond in an appropriate fashion.

Of course, the symbolic cue need not be an inside joke. The allusion to a previously shared fantasy may arouse tears or evoke anger, hatred, love, or affection as well as laughter and humor. The symbolic cue may be a code word, phrase, slogan, or nonverbal sign or gesture. Using symbolic cues to trigger previously shared emotions and meanings is a sure sign that participants have shared fantasies and that they have, at least, the beginnings of a group culture.

Fantasy Types

The symbolic cue is an induction which allows members to symbolize an entire fantasy chain with a brief allusion to it. Such inductions provide the basis for further clusterings of similar dramatizations. When the similar clusters deal with stories, the way is open for outside observers and group members to generalize to another communicative feature of small groups: the use of *fantasy types*. When a number of similar themes, including particulars of scene, characters, and situations, have been shared, members often move to a more abstract level of making a general description of a fantasy type that refers to all similar dramatizations.

A fantasy type is a stock scenario repeated again and again by the same or similar characters. For example, the Minnesota study of zero-history leaderless natural groups in the classroom revealed several groups in which members shared personal-experience stories about parties they had recently attended. Often these stories began to fall into a stock scenario of what the members should do on such occasions to have a good time, what they celebrated as laudable, and what they portrayed as bad. When these stories began to have a similar form, observers could classify them as forming a type.

Participants, too, make typal classifications of fantasy themes, and after they have created a group culture they tend to use the more abstract and general fantasy type in their communication. Rather than dramatizing a fantasy theme with specific characters in a specific setting, they present only the general plot line. A participant might say, "What really makes me angry is trying to find a professor to talk to during registration. You know how professors are. They're never around when you really need to talk to them. Why is it that there's never anyone in the office and the answering machine is all you get when you telephone?"

Whenever a participant casts a generalized persona—such as a teacher, a student, a worker, a bureaucrat, a banker, or a farmer—as part of an anecdote, the result is likely to be a fantasy type. Of course, if the group has shared a number of similar stories about the same character, a fantasy type might be about that individual. "Joe got in trouble again last night. He went out partying, and as usual he ended up in a hassle with the police. And you can guess the end of the story. Janet went down to the stationhouse and got him out again."

Group members can also use a fantasy type as a way of fitting their unfolding experiences into their shared consciousness. Thus, classroom participants might share a utopian fantasy portraying themselves as a cohesive and effective group of problem solvers who fail only when some outside person (such as the class instructor) frustrates them. Should they fail to make a good group grade on a class assignment, they may portray the experience as an instance of the fantasy type. ("It's our instructor's fault that we did not get an A.")

By using the fantasy type as a script to explain and evaluate new events, the members bring these events into line with the overall values and emotions of their group culture. They also sustain a key element of their consciousness: their utopian group fantasy. Since the utopian drama is often a non-coping fantasy, it tends to make the group ineffective in dealing with changing circumstances and the environment. In this way, the sharing of group fantasies can lend an emotional tone to the group experience and affect overall decision-making effectiveness.

Figure 5.2 charts the relationships among fantasy themes, inside cues, fantasy types, and group culture. Note that symbolic convergence provides an explanation for how the communication (what a member says) is responded to by the listeners in order to create cohesiveness and the common ground required for productive discussion.

Reasons for Fantasy Sharing

Why do group members share some fantasies, respond to others in a ho-hum fashion, and actively reject still others? Three promising factors explain why people share or reject fantasies: (1) the members' past hang-ups and their current baggage of personal and previously shared fantasies; (2) the common concerns that group members have because of their experiences in the group; and (3) the rhetori-

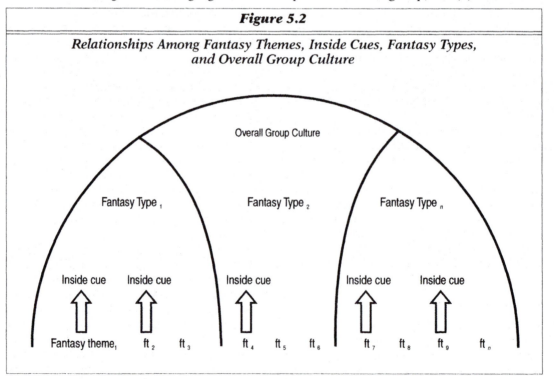

Figure 5.2

Relationships Among Fantasy Themes, Inside Cues, Fantasy Types, and Overall Group Culture

cal skill with which participants dramatize during the group meetings.

Bales provided a psychoanalytic accounting that was heavily Freudian. However, the importance of the chaining out of dramas to the group's culture can be explained without such heavy reliance on Freudian concepts. A rhetorician, for example, might argue that the chaining out of the drama was a result of the skill with which the original drama was presented.

Bales distinguished three dimensions of the communication events coded into the "Dramatizes" category. The first dimension related to the content of the messages: What do the group members say? The second dimension of a shared fantasy was the drama as a mirror of the group's here-and-now experience and its relationship to the external environment. The drama played out somewhere else or in some other time often symbolized a role collision or ambiguity, a leadership conflict, or a problem related to the task dimension of the group. Just as an individual's repressed problems might surface in dream fantasies, so a group's hidden agenda might surface in a fantasy chain, and a critic might interpret the surface content with an eye to discovering the hidden agenda.

The third dimension of the dramatizing message, which manifested itself in some groups, was an expression in a given social field of the individual psychodynamics of the participants.

Bales argued that the past history of each individual affects the personal hang-ups that individual brings to a zero-history group. In this view, members bring concerns to the meeting only some of which they have in common. In a given group, for example, all members might have problems with their relationships with their fathers. Dramatizing messages that tap the participants' psychological problems with the male parent would then be shared, whereas if several members have had good relations with their mothers they would reject a dramatization that portrayed a mother in an unsavory light.

Individuals also bring to the group their personal fantasy lives and their past experiences in sharing fantasies in other groups. Suppose all the group members have previously, in other groups, shared dramas about the ineptness of the current President of the United States. When someone dramatizes a story about the President's ineptness, the members are likely to share it. When they do, they have publicly demonstrated how they stand on the persona of the President and that persona becomes a common symbol in the group's culture.

One of the more intriguing questions that has emerged from the study of group fantasies is the extent to which the chaining is inevitable or accidental or the result of a deliberate effort on the part of one or more members to generate a certain kind of symbolic world for the group.

Evidence from the Minnesota case studies suggests that the artistry with which the drama is presented is a factor in whether it chains through the group. One can never be sure whether a play will be a success, but if the playwright is talented and knows the craft, the play is more likely to be successful than if the writer is untalented and inexperienced; something analogous to the playwright's success seems to be operating in the case of chaining fantasies in a small group.

Timing, too, appears to be a factor in whether a fantasy chains out once it is introduced. In much the same way that group decisions cannot be forced on a group before it is ready to make them, so the group members must be predisposed to respond by a common attitude or problem before they chain out a particular fantasy. Fantasies that are unsuccessfully introduced early in a group's life sometimes chain out when reintroduced later. Thus, proper timing, as well as the artistry of the manner of presentation, appears to be a factor in the success or failure of a fantasy to chain through a group.

In one case study, a woman had written up a fantasy for her diary on her group experience which took the form of a fable. She had depicted each member as an animal or bird. She was reading some of her diary to another member in a low voice while the others were going on about the group's business; the other person became intrigued and called the group's attention to the fable. He urged her to read it to the entire group. She was reluctant at first, but with some urging she started. She caught the group's attention, and they began to respond, at first tentatively, then with greater enthusiasm until, finally, all the others were actively participating, injecting comments, and roaring with laughter. She had not written her diary with an eye to the audience or with the conscious intent to persuade others to adopt a certain position or attitude. In other words, she did not have a rhetorical purpose. She had simply written the sketch for her own amusement. Her skill in writing it, however, contributed to the chaining of the fantasy. Moreover, the group had reached a state of tension because of interpersonal conflicts that it had not been able to handle in a direct way, and the fantasy personality analysis in her fable was presented to the group when all its members were at least intellectually aware that personality problems were crippling the group's effectiveness in the task area and were ready for her oblique analysis of their conflicts.

The fact that a person has more chance of having a drama chain through the group if it is presented skillfully makes a rhetorical approach to introducing fantasy themes into a new group possible. Indeed, some people do use group methods for persuasive ends, and they often use fantasies for their own purposes. Organizers of consciousness-raising sessions and other groups designed for conversion purposes frequently rely on dramas for their persuasive ends. The planners of groups used for rhetorical purposes usually arrange for a majority of the group to consist of people already committed to the position. Usually, the meeting will include only one or two potential converts. A person being rushed for a fraternity or sorority may find himself or herself closeted with four or five "actives." The woman attending a women's consciousness-raising session may find herself in a group in which the vocal and articulate members are committed to the movement.

Once a meeting gets under way, the insiders begin to introduce important dramas from their community's culture, and the committed then chain into them with the appropriate nuances and emotional responses. Under the pressure of the group, the potential convert often begins to participate in appropriate ways in the fantasies. Neophytes are particularly susceptible if their previous experiences have been similar to those of the already committed. One of the studies at Minnesota was of consciousness-raising groups associated with gay liberation. The pattern of fantasy themes in the sessions began with dramas that were widely disseminated nationally through underground presses and the gay liberation grapevine. Most of the committed knew the national rhetoric, although some of them were not personally acquainted with one another. When they had formed some common ground by participating in the nationally known dramas, they moved to the narration of personal experiences about the repressions they had suffered. All the dramas, however, were on themes related to the subculture of the gay liberation movement.

Although a conscious rhetorical effort to cause fantasies to chain through a group can succeed in igniting a chain reaction, the results are not always what was hoped for or intended. The fantasy often begins to take on a life of its own, and the member who first introduced the theme may well lose control of its development. When the fantasy gets out of hand in a rhetorical group, the organizers will judge that it was a bad session. As the others participate, they add new directions and new emphases to the drama. The originator may be astonished and frightened by the way the chain develops. The final fantasy event, viewed in retrospect, is the joint effort of all the members who contributed to it.

The fact that a person has more chance to have a drama chain through the group if it is presented skillfully makes possible a rhetorical approach to inducing fantasy sharing in a new group. Indeed, value-shift groups use fantasy sharing for persuasive purposes in just this way.

Of course, good storytellers, clever punsters, and imaginative users of figures of speech may do a lot of dramatizing in group meetings for the enjoyment they get from being the center of attention. After all, rhetorical skill marks a group member and draws both positive and negative attention. But when a person dramatizes only for the immediate effect of gaining attention, the group may accidentally create a culture that is more or less coping and enjoyable.

References

Bales, Robert F. (1950). *Interaction Process Analysis.* Reading, MA: Addison-Wesley.

Bales, Robert F. (1970). *Personality and Interpersonal Behavior.* New York: Holt, Rinehart and Winston.

Dunphy, Dexter C. (1966). "Social change in self-analytic groups." In P. J. Stone et al. (eds.), *The General Inquirer: A Computer Approach to Content Analysis* (pp. 287–340). Cambridge, MA: MIT Press.

Gibbard, G. S., J. J. Hartman, and R. D. Mann. (1974). *Analysis of Groups.* San Francisco: Jossey-Bass.

Bormann, Ernest G., Linda L. Putnam, and Jerie M. Pratt. (1978). "Power, authority, and sex: Male response to female dominance." *Communication Monographs* 45: 119–155.

Chapter 6
Group Communication and the Structuring Process

Marshall Scott Poole

Arguably the most difficult of the three theories to understand, Structuration Theory is concerned with how people create relational and behavioral patterns and regularities ("structure") in their groups by making use of social rules and resources. The author does a masterful job of not only presenting and explaining the major concepts and propositions of the theory, but illustrating how they account for the emergence of structure in small groups. He concludes his article with a discussion of why it is useful to study structuration processes in small groups.

Most social scientific research paints a picture of group members as passive, reactive creatures. Members' behavior is said to be determined by communication networks, group norms, status structures, peer pressure, feedback, and numerous other forces. Members are pictured as though all they do is react to these factors. They are pawns, moved about by forces beyond their control. And the picture of the group as a whole is no less passive. Its effectiveness is explained in terms of the influences of groupthink and other social fallacies, by its level of cohesiveness, its collective motivations, by "necessary" stages of problem solving, and many other factors. If all an alien from another planet knew about people was what he or she read in the social scientific journals, he or she would be highly likely to conclude that they are robots, driven by external and internal forces and with no minds of their own.

We all know that this is not a true picture. Certainly, we are subject to forces beyond our control. Certainly, dynamics like groupthink can take over as though they had a life of their own and lead a group into remarkably bad decisions. But we do have freedom to act as we wish to make choices that shape our lives. If the group has a norm that we do not agree with, we can choose to break the norm, and we may persist even in the face of severe pressure from other members. If we understand how groupthink works, we can try to prevent it from occurring and, when it does occur, we can inform our group and take measures to counteract its effect. In short, we can control our actions and the actions our groups take. Any social scientific research must take this into account, or it will produce an inaccurate explanation of human behavior.

Now this is not to say that people have total control over their behavior or over how their interactions with others will go. We live in a world not of our own making. Outside forces intrude and shape how we can act. A small architectural firm may suddenly hear that it is in danger of running behind on a project and, therefore, may lose its biggest customer. Group members must drop whatever they are doing and work until this threat to group survival is conquered. Practices and traditions internal to our groups constrain what we can do. If a committee has a 10-year tradition of electing a new chair every six months, a new member, no matter how motivated or well-intentioned, is unlikely to be able to convince the group to change the term to two years. The member is better advised to accept the tradition until the group accepts him or her. Then there is a chance of changing it (unless the new member has come to believe that a six-month term really is the best for this group!). We cannot exert absolute control over other group members, and we are affected by their activities. If a member starts to cry for no apparent reason at all, we might feel constrained to disregard other business for a while and comfort him or her. Interaction is a give and take that no one, no matter how forceful and determined, can control.

So, people can actively control their behavior, but they do so within constraints of external forces, internal group structures, and other members' behavior. For instance, in a very cohesive secretarial group, which is normally pretty productive, members may decide to take the afternoon off and go on an extended lunch. In this case, high cohesiveness does not cause high productivity; it actually works against it. And whether cohesiveness increases or decreases productivity depends on what the group members choose to do. This does not mean that there are no causal forces acting on groups. Productivity will in general be facilitated by higher levels of cohesiveness. But because level of productivity depends on how the members choose to respond to the task, there will be cases where this relationship does not hold.

It is hard to describe and explain the influence of free will on behavior, because there are so many possible ways in which the group could go. Simple cause-effect patterns are no longer possible. To be realistic in our thinking about group behavior forces us to adopt much more complex and less definite explanations. The advantage of this is that our theories of group behavior will be based on much more realistic assumptions than are simple cause-effect theories.

A Theory of Structuration

What would this type of theory be like? It would have to recognize that people in groups actively control their behavior. It would also have to recognize that behavior is shaped and constrained by forces not totally under the control of the members. The influence of these forces is channeled by members' choices about how to react to them.

One theory of social behavior that accepts this challenge is the *theory of structuration*. This theory is concerned with how people structure their groups by making active use of social rules and resources. As the word structuration suggests, the process in which members structure groups is ongoing and continuous. It happens throughout the life of the group and is never finished. According to this theory, members are always structuring their groups. They do so with every act. If the structure of the group changes, it is because members have done something that has changed it. If the structure of the group stays the same, it is because members are acting in such a way that the same structure is created and maintained with every act. According to this theory, nothing is ever completely accomplished. The group is never finished or static. Instead, groups are always in the process of creation and re-creation. Nothing ever stops. Even if the group looks very stable and conservative, it is because members are acting in such a way to create the same group structure over and over, creating an appearance of sameness and stability. However, underlying this is a constant process of change.

Definitions

So far we have not defined several terms—*structure, rules,* and *resources*. First we will do that and explain a few of the basic assumptions of the theory of structuration. Then we will give an example of structuration in groups. After that we will discuss the theory in more detail.

One of the basic distinctions in the theory of structuration is the distinction between system and structure. A *system* is an observable pattern of relationships among people. A *structure* is a set of rules and resources used to generate the system. These rules and resources are unobservable and must be deduced from how the system operates. Often people are aware of rules and resources that they use. *Rules* are propositions that indicate how something ought to be done or what is good or bad. For example, a norm is a rule that tells members what the group expects of them if they are to remain in good standing. Another example is the communication rules that define the meanings of terms and what various behaviors mean. *Resources* are materials, possessions, or attributes that can be used to influence or control the actions of the group or its members. Examples of resources include money, special knowledge in an area important to the group, status outside the group, and a formal leadership position.

The final important term, structuration, has a very complex definition, but one that can be understood, if we take it apart. *Structuration* can be defined as the *production and reproduction of the social systems through members' use of rules and resources in interaction*. This is a very complex statement that contains a number of ideas.

First, the notion of structuration implies that the primary constituents of the group system are interaction and relationships among members. The very existence of a group depends on members' interactions. If members stopped interacting and broke off their relationships with one another, the group would cease to exist. This is true even of formal groups, such as organizational work groups, where members are assigned and expected to show up. If members decide to work individually and never meet or interact as a group, there really is no group. It is a group in name only, and members do not identify with the group or feel accountable to each other.

Second, the definition implies that rules and resources (structures) are the "tools" members use to interact. Hence rules and resources are the "tools" that create and maintain the group system. As we noted above, a group system is composed of patterns of relationships and interaction among members. These patterns are created and maintained by members' use of rules and resources. For example, if one norm (rule) is that members of the group must all be good friends, then members will try to get to know each other. They guide their interaction by the rule. In following this rule, members employ various resources—such as their social skills and their status outside the group—to

get others to like them. If they are successful at getting to know one another, their interaction will create and maintain a dense communication network. This in turn will make the group more cohesive. The two properties of the group—high cohesiveness and a dense network—are direct results of members using rules and resources. The properties will exist only as long as group members continue to apply the rules and resources just mentioned. If members choose not to follow the norm or if they decide to use resources like social skills to control each other rather than to build friendships, the group system will change. The group will have a different character.

So far we have emphasized rules and resources as tools for action. However, they are equally important as tools for interpreting what is occurring in group interaction. For example, consider the group system in the previous paragraph. If a member teases another member for always being late for meetings, the teasing will probably be interpreted as friendly chiding. However, in another group in which there has been considerable tension and in which there is a strong norm favoring punctuality, the same teasing may be construed as a rather "catty" personal attack. Rules are tools for interpreting others' behavior. We think about their behavior in light of related rules. The same is true of resources. If members regularly use their special expert knowledge to influence the group, then making a suggestion is likely to be interpreted as an attempt to be seen as an expert.

A third point is one that makes structurational theory quite different from many other points of view: Structures—rules and resources—are produced and reproduced along with the system. As Anthony Giddens wrote: "Structures are both the medium and the outcome of action." To illustrate what this means, think about rules and resources in groups you have been in. In every group there are somewhat different rules. Even for very common rules, groups develop their own versions and special interpretations. For example, majority voting is often used to make decisions, but this rule differs in different groups. In some groups "majority" really means "the two most important members," while in others it is actually "more than half the members." In some groups a majority vote is interpreted as an expression of democracy; in other groups it is viewed as a power move by which the majority can force the minority to do what it does not want to do. Resources, too, vary from group to group. A college degree is a source of influence in a group of teachers. In a group of steel workers it may actually be a disadvantage.

So each group has, in effect, its own rules and resources. The group's particular structure of rules and resources is created and maintained by members' interaction. For example, a few members might become friends and decide this helped their work. They would then encourage others to build friendships, creating a norm favoring close relationships among group members. As this norm continues to be followed, it becomes a permanent, prominent feature of the group. At some point, however, members may begin to believe that maintaining close friendships saps their energy and prevents the group from functioning as well as it could. If they begin to place less emphasis on building relationships, the norm will become less important. At the extreme, members may stop using the norm altogether, and it will no longer be part of the group's structure. And so it is with every group. The group copies its own versions of some rules and resources and develops others on its own. And, knowingly or unconsciously, it may change or eliminate rules and resources.

Rules and resources do not exist independent of an interaction system. They only continue to exist in a group if members use them. So systems and structures have a reciprocal relationship. Members use rules and resources to create the group system, but rules and resources can only exist by virtue of being used in the system. In producing and reproducing the group system, people are producing and reproducing rules and resources.

As we have noted, a group can change, reinterpret, and even eliminate rules and resources. Sometimes this is done by conscious choices of members. A member might, for example, argue that majority voting procedures are unfair to the minority and convince the group to adopt motions only if all members favor them. More often, structural change comes about without planning or awareness. Members may just gradually drop or reinterpret a norm, without realizing they are doing so. A major interest of research into structuration is how members initiate, maintain, and change rules and resources. We will discuss this in more detail below.

A fourth and final point is needed to qualify what has been said up to here: Members do not totally control the process of structuration. Members' activities are influenced by external forces that limit what they can do. For example, if the group is assigned a very difficult task, members cannot organize their work in any way they please. To be successful, they must structure their work so it is appropriate for the task. The task places limits on their choices. External factors, including the nature of group tasks or goals, the group's general environment (including the larger organization the group is part of), and members' level of competence are limits. Members' actions can "restructure" these external forces. For example, the group may break the difficult task into smaller, easier subtasks. This redefinition changes the task to some extent. Yet the task still exerts a powerful defining force on group interaction.

Another limitation on members' control over structuration processes is the actions of other members. Interaction, by definition, is beyond the control of any single actor. Members' actions often blend together so that interaction unfolds in unexpected directions. For example, in a conflict one member might make an attempt at reconciliation. If another member attacks the response, it may make the first counterattack, resulting in an escalating conflict no one wanted in the first place. External forces and uncontrollable interaction dynamics can result in *unanticipated consequences* of structuration.

So, according to the theory of structuration, the groups that appear so "real" and stable to us are actually continuously in flux. They are continuously being produced and reproduced by members' interactions. It is the job of researchers to explain how this process of production and reproduction leads to stability or change in groups. An example of structuration processes will serve to illustrate many of the points we have just made.

A Case

The group in question was dedicated to teaching newly graduated methods of diagnosing psychological ailments. It was composed of three psychiatrists who had MD degrees, a psychologist, and two social workers. The group's leader, Jerry, was a "take-charge" person who fully intended to create a democratically run group, but ended up as the head of a small clique, which made decisions in an authoritarian manner.

All of the members of the group were very competent in their areas. When the medical school created the group, the deans handpicked strong, competent people who had shown exceptional teaching ability. The deans told the group it was free to develop the program as it saw best, provided members could get grants from public and private agencies to support their operations. Jerry had numerous contacts and was able to get a very large grant to support the project for its first two years.

When the group first met to plan the program, it was decided that all decisions would be made "rationally." That is, a decision would be accepted only if *all* members were satisfied it was sound. Jerry was appointed "leader" of the group, but there was an understanding that he would encourage participation and equalize influence over the decision. And Jerry made an active effort to do this. He strongly believed that the best decisions were those with the most member input. He read books on group communica-

tion, and did everything he could to facilitate group interaction.

However, there were forces working against democratic control of the group. All members had worked extensively in medical settings and had great respect for people with MD degrees. This gave the three members of the group with MD degrees more clout than those without them. Further, members knew that continuation of their program depended on garnering funds. This gave Jerry something of an advantage, because he was the primary source of funds for the project.

As a result of these two forces, the psychologist and social workers (the non-MDs) tended to give in to the psychiatrists (the MDs). The non-MDs did not speak as often or as long as the MDs. They were also more tentative than the MDs and let their ideas "die" or be swept aside more easily than did the MDs. These were not large effects, but they did result in a less democratic group than was originally envisioned. And the non-MDs felt they had less influence than the MDs. They were frustrated, and often talked with one another about their lack of influence. In meetings they exchanged meaningful glances that implied "here we go again!" when MDs expressed their opinions.

Jerry noticed that non-MDs contributed less than MDs. He also spoke with one of the social workers, and she expressed her dissatisfaction. He attempted to involve the non-MDs by calling on them, and setting aside special periods for "brainstorming." But this undermined democracy still further because Jerry was, in effect, directing members to contribute. The non-MDs came to depend on Jerry as an advocate. Ironically, this contributed to his power in the group.

Jerry's manner of running meetings also contributed to the development of a pecking order in the group. He was a rather forceful participant, and talked more than other members. The more a member talks, the more influence he or she has. Jerry also attempted to "help" the group by rephrasing and redefining ideas in order to improve them. Despite his good intentions, Jerry rephrased other members' contributions in line with his own thinking. Without realizing it, he influenced decision making. And members (especially non-MDs) came to value and count on his rephrasings, reinforcing Jerry's influence. The MDs began to change non-MD ideas, to talk longer and more confidently, and to interrupt non-MDs more frequently.

The end result was movement toward a more authoritarian leadership style. The group developed a "pecking order," in which MDs were accorded higher status than non-MDs. The non-MDs lost the confidence necessary for maintaining equal democratic participation. Non-MDs were dissatisfied with the group. Conflict increased and was not handled well, resulting in a tense climate. An outside observer would see a divided group, with clear differentiations in status and power. In spite of its members' best intentions, this group structured an authoritarian climate.

In the psychological training group the following elements can be discerned: The *system* is the pattern of interaction among members, specifically the "pecking order" and communication network. The *structures* in this case are (a) *rules* related to "rational" decision making, the communication and phrasing of proposals and ideas, and contributions of "superior" members, and (b) *resources*, including medical degrees, access to funding, and Jerry's interaction skills. *External forces* that influenced group interaction include the task set for the group by the deans and the need to garner funds to keep the project going.

Structuration processes reinforced and reproduced the rules and resources related to authoritarian group structures. Rules relating to preference for contributions of "superior" members and resources such as medical degrees were supported and validated in the group. At the same time other rules and resources that would support democratic decision making were not emphasized or reproduced. So, norms like those favoring equal time for each member to talk did not evolve and resources such as the amount of energy and commitment members have were not valued as much as those favoring evolution of status orders.

Structuration led to a group quite different from what members hoped for. Their interaction "got away" from them, producing unintended consequences. In part this was due to the pressure of external forces, particularly the need to get funds to continue the project. This pressure encouraged members to turn to Jerry who could, they thought, "get the job done." The structure also "got away" from members because changes happened very gradually. The shift from a democratic to an authoritarian group did not occur all at once. It emerged slowly, as rules and resources favoring authoritarian operations were used more and more (and therefore reproduced), while rules favoring democracy were used less. And when democratic structures were employed, they were often justified on the grounds that proposals had to be put in "rational" format so that all proposals would be given equal weight. A democratic veneer was put on an autocratic move. The effects of structuration often "sneak up" on groups, because they are so gradual.

Structure Development

Where do structures come from and why do groups choose the structures they do? Occasionally groups create their own rules and resources. For example, some groups develop unique code words for sensitive topics. One group developed a code word for its higher level supervisor. Group members called her "Waldo" when outsiders were present, so the outsiders wouldn't know members were talking about her.

But these instances are relatively rare. Usually, groups borrow or adopt rules and resources from other groups or social institutions. Members draw on their own experiences and on what they have learned. They try to do things as they have seen them done in other groups. As a result, we encounter different versions of the same rules and resources in many groups. For example, various interpretations and adaptations of majority voting are found in many groups. The same is true of education as a resource. It is a widely respected source of influence, although it is interpreted differently and has different weight in various groups. When rules and resources are widely accepted and used, they become *institutions* in their own right. Majority rule, for example, is often equated with democracy.

So an important part of structuration is the *groups' appropriation* of social institutions for its own uses. Groups fashion themselves after other groups and after their members' ideas about institutions. In doing this the group creates its own version of these institutions. The strength of a social institution—determined by how widespread it is and how much a part of the culture it is—has an important influence on how likely it is to be reproduced. A structure drawn from an institution has a clear reference point, and will be relatively long-lived, even if it is seldom used. Structures created uniquely by the group must be used quite often or they will die out. The more "institutionalized" the structure is, the less it must be used if it is to survive in the group.

But what are institutions anyway? Although the majority-rule procedure is very common, there is no such thing as a "general" or "abstract" majority-rule principle. Majority rule only exists in the groups that use it. The reason majority rule seems to be an abstraction is that it is widely used and that it is taught and talked about in the abstract. However, this is only an illusion. The majority-rule procedure exists only insofar as it is used in our society. And survival of majority rule and other institutions depends on their structuration by groups. If groups (and other social organizations) stopped using majority rule altogether, it would pass out of existence. So groups reproduce social institutions as they produce and reproduce themselves.

Why do groups choose the particular structures they do? There are at least three reasons. In some cases rules and resources are used because the group gives members negative reinforcement if they "deviate." For example, in a group that employed majority rule, a member who attempted to seize control would likely meet with disapproval from the group, and perhaps would be asked to leave. Another reason members use rules and resources is that they are traditions in the group. Often we follow traditions without thinking. They are second nature, used by habit. For example, if a group has always taken a vote to confirm important decisions, members will often continue to do so without really thinking. A final, and probably the most important reason members use rules and resources is because they are useful—they enable members to achieve their goals and build the group. Resources like status, a leadership position, or special knowledge are also useful for members, and so they form an important part of the group system.

Influences on Structuration

What factors influence structuration? Three types of influences on structuration can be identified:

Member Characteristics and Orientations

Members' motivations in the group influence which structures they use and how they use them. Members who are primarily concerned with the group and with getting the job done will use structures in very different ways than will members whose goal is to realize their own individual interests or to control the group. Group-oriented members will generally use structures in "the spirit" of the rule or resource. Members concerned primarily with themselves or with controlling the group often turn structures in very different directions, as Jerry did in the psychological diagnostic group.

Members' characteristic interaction styles also influence structuration. An autocratic leader will use majority voting procedures very differently than will a democratic leader. Other stylistic differences, such as differences in group conflict-management styles, will also influence how structures are used.

Members' degree of knowledge and experience with structures also affect structuration. For example, groups that have had a lot of training in decision-making procedures will incorporate techniques like nominal group procedure into their structures with more success than will less knowledgeable groups.

External Factors

As mentioned above, forces beyond members' control also influence structuration. Factors such as the nature of group task, the effects of larger organizations on the group, and the talents of personnel assigned to the group limit what the group can do.

Structural Dynamics

A third influence on structuration are the relationships between different rules and resources. Two main types of relationships can be discerned:

1. *Mediation* occurs when one structure influences the operation or interpretation of another. In effect, the first structure controls the second. For example, because business is such an important part of American culture, it is common for groups to use an economic cost return metaphor to guide their behavior. Alternatives are rated with respect to gains or losses they promise, and decisions are made with formal or informal calculations. This even affects how value-related decisions are made. Often groups faced with value choices do not debate ethics or higher ends. Instead they decide which values are important, rate each alternative on the values, and calculate a "utility" score for the alternatives. That alternative with the highest score is chosen. This converts an ethical choice into a "rational" calculation. Economic thinking mediates and controls ethical thinking.

2. *Contradiction* occurs when two structures, each of which is important to the operation of the group, work against each other. Contradictions in structures create conflicts

and dilemmas in groups. Sometimes these take some time to show up, but when they do, they can disrupt the group and often stimulate change. There was a contradiction in the psychological diagnosis group discussed above. Democratic principles were very important to members, and they used these to justify their actions and as behavioral ideals. However, the group operated according to an autocratic structure. The contradiction between democratic values and autocratic operations set up tensions in the group. The members who were left out of decisions resented it, and over time this developed into a major split in the group. Eventually there was a prolonged conflict and the two social workers quit. Contradictions fueled change in the group.

Member characteristics, external forces, and structural dynamics combine to influence how groups structure themselves. To explain structuration it is necessary to account for the influence of these forces on members' actions.

Studying Structuration

Why is it useful to study structuration? There are three reasons to study structuration. First, it gives a more accurate picture of group processes than traditional social scientific theories. The theory of structuration accepts the fact that group members actively control their behavior but it also recognizes limitations and constraints on members' activities. The theory attempts to show how action influences the operation of "deterministic" forces and how external forces constrain action. This can produce important insights into group behavior, as the case of the psychological diagnosis group shows. Many of the points raised there could only have been uncovered through analysis of structuration.

A second advantage of the structurational model is its recognition of the importance of gradual change and unintended consequences of members' behavior. Because of its emphasis on the continuous production and reproduction of social systems and structures, the theory of structuration makes us aware of how small, incremental changes can mount up to a major change in the system. It is well-equipped to study these gradual developments. In addition, the theory explains how structuring processes can lead to outcomes completely different from those intended by the members. These surprises often mark turning points in group development.

Third, and perhaps most important, the theory of structuration suggests ways for members—especially those with little power—to change their groups. The theory points out how members can effect change by altering their behavior in what appear to be small ways. If persistent, these small changes can alter the group's directions. This strategy is often particularly effective (for members with little or no power) because small moves are less noticeable to powerful members who might squelch attempts at change. In the psychological diagnosis group, the group was temporarily turned in a more democratic direction with this strategy. One of the social workers decided that she would stop allowing Jerry to rephrase her ideas. She insisted that they be stated as she said them. This made Jerry more conscientious of preserving other members' ideas, and for a while the group operated in a more democratic fashion. Eventually, however, a crisis arose and members (without meaning to) again fell back into their old habits. Jerry was a key figure in handling the crisis, and members continued to turn to him for help after it had passed. As a result, the social worker was unable to sustain her initiative. If changes such as this could have been reproduced, the group could have changed. However, forces operating in the autocratic direction were stronger.

Decision-making methods like Nominal Group Technique, brainstorming, and Reflective Thinking are often employed to structure group interaction and change how groups make decisions. However, their effectiveness depends on how these structures are produced and reproduced in the group. If used as designed, these techniques can equalize power and contribute to more rational decision making. However, they can also be used to control the group. On one occasion Jerry decided to use brainstorming in the psychological diagnosis group. However, since he ran the session himself, non-MDs were hesitant to contribute and censored their ideas. Although the group believed it was increasing participation by using brainstorming, the end result was a reproduction of the same autocratic patterns.

The theory of structuration has the potential to help members understand and control the forces that influence group interaction. Its goal is to make people aware of the part they play in the creation and maintenance of structures they would otherwise take for granted.

References

Folger, Joseph P., and Poole, Marshall Scott (1983). *Working Through Conflict.* Glenview, IL: Scott Foresman.

Giddens, Anthony (1976). *New Rules of Sociological Method.* New York: Basic Books.

Giddens, Anthony (1979). *Central Problems in Social Theory.* Berkeley, CA: University of California Press.

Poole, Marshall Scott, Seibold, David R., and McPhee, Robert D. (1985). "Group decision-making as a structurational process," *Quarterly Journal of Speech* 71: 74–102.

Poole, Marshall Scott, Seibold, David R., and McPhee, Robert D. (1986). "A structurational approach to theory building in decision-making research." In R. Y. Hirokawa and M. S. Poole (eds.), *Communication and Group Decision-Making.* Beverly Hills: Sage.

Part III

Organization of Groups

No two groups are alike. Groups differ in terms of the characteristics of their members, their leadership structure, and the ways they go about doing things. In Part III, we focus on how the interaction and communication in a group change and develop over time.

The Phase Hypothesis

In 1951, Robert Bales and Fred Strodtbeck published a descriptive study that provided empirical support for the "phase hypothesis." This hypothesis posited that *all* groups move through the same sequence of phases (or stages) in the process of reaching a decision (pp. 485–487). Subsequent work by Bennis and Shepard (1956), Tuckman (1965), and Fisher (1970) supported and further validated the phase hypothesis. By the mid-1970s, the idea that all groups display the same sequence of phases was firmly established in the small group literature and was taught in virtually every small group communication course.

In 1981, Marshall Scott Poole published a landmark article in which he challenged the validity of the phase hypothesis. Poole pointed to earlier research by Scheidel and Crowell (1964) and Mintzberg, Raisinghani, and Theoret (1976) that found evidence for complex cycles in group decision making that could not be reduced to a small set of unified phasic units. Scheidel and Crowell (1964) found evidence to suggest the existence of a "spiral" process in group decision making, whereby group members revisit and rediscuss ideas as they move toward a final group decision. Mintzberg et al. (1976) likewise found that "unstructured" group decision making displays distinct, but not necessarily sequential, phases of interaction. In short, Poole (1983) concluded that "extensive qualifications are necessary to maintain [the phase hypothesis] because it can no longer encompass what we know about decision development" (p. 325).

Today, virtually no one believes that all groups go through the same sequence of phases in reaching a decision. Instead, most small group communication scholars accept the notion that groups display uniquely different sequences of phases or activities in reaching a decision or solution. This idea is referred to as the "multiple sequence model" of group development. The two chapters in Part III present what we currently know about the multiple sequence perspective. These are, in fact, two of the most important essays written on multiple sequence models of group development.

References

Bales, R. F., and Strodtbeck, F. L. (1951). "Phases in group problem-solving." *Jour-

nal of Abnormal and Social Psychology, 46: 485–495.

Bennis, W. G., and Shepard, H. A. (1956). "A theory of group development." *Human Relations,* 9: 415–437.

Fisher, B. A. (1970). "Decision emergence: Phases in group decision-making." *Communication Monographs,* 37: 53–66.

Mintzberg, H., Raisinghani, D., and Theoret, A. (1976). "The structure of 'unstructured' decision processes." *Administrative Science Quarterly,* 21: 246–275.

Poole, M. S. (1981). "Decision development in small groups I: A comparison of two models." *Communication Monographs,* 48: 1–24.

——. (1983). "Decision development in small groups III: A multiple sequence model of group development." *Communication Monographs,* 50: 321–341.

Scheidel, T. M., and Crowell, L. (1964). "Idea development in small groups." *Quarterly Journal of Speech,* 50: 140–145.

Tuckman, B. (1965). "Developmental sequence in small groups." *Psychological Bulletin,* 63: 384–399. ✦

Chapter 7
Time and Transition in Work Teams

Toward a New Model of Group Development

Connie J. G. Gersick

Following is an abridged version of a critically acclaimed essay that introduced readers to Gersick's now well-known "Punctuated Equilibrium Model" of group development. This model characterizes the group development process as periods of stable or habitual routines that are disrupted by transition periods, where abrupt and often dramatic changes in behaviors and focus occur. During these radical transition periods, patterns of interaction observed during stable times disappear and are replaced by new ways of interacting and working together to complete the task. Ironically, once the group adjusts to these new patterns of interaction, its members settle into another routine or stable period that in time will be disrupted by another transition period. In short, Gersick's Punctuated Equilibrium Model presents the group-development process as a sequence of stable and disruptive periods of interaction among group members.

Groups are essential management tools. Organizations use teams to put novel combinations of people to work on novel problems and use committees to deal with especially critical decisions; indeed, organizations largely consist of permanent and temporary groups (Huse and Cummings 1985). Given

the importance of group management, there is a curious gap in researchers' use of existing knowledge. For years, researchers studying group development — the path a group takes over its life span toward the accomplishment of its main tasks—have reported that groups change predictably over time. This information suggests that, to understand what makes groups work effectively, both theorists and managers ought to take change over time into account. However, little group-effectiveness research has done so (McGrath 1986).

One reason for the gap may lie in what is unknown about group development. Traditional models shed little light on the triggers or mechanisms of change or on the role of a group's environment in its development. Both areas are of key importance to group effectiveness (Gladstein 1984; Goodstein and Dovico 1979; McGrath 1986). This hypothesis generating proposed a new way to conceptualize group development. It is based on a different paradigm of change than that which underlies traditional models, and it addresses the timing and mechanisms of change and groups' dynamic relations with their environments.

Traditional Models of Group Development

There have been two main streams of research and theory about group development. The first stream deals with group dynamics, the other with phases in group problem solving. Group dynamics research on development began in the late 1940s, with a focus on the psychosocial and emotional aspects of group life. Working primarily with therapy groups, T-groups, and self-study groups, researchers originally saw a group's task in terms of the achievement of personal and interpersonal goals like insight, learning, or honest communication (Mills 1979). They explored development as the progress, over a group's life span, of members' ability to handle issues seen as critical to their ability to work, such as dependency, control, and intimacy (Bennis and Shepard 1956; Bion 1961; Mann, Gibbard, and Hartman 1967; Slater 1966).

In 1965, Tuckman synthesized this literature in a model of group development as a unitary sequence that is frequently cited today. The sequence, theoretically the same for every group, consists of forming, storming, norming, and performing. Tuckman and Jensen's 1977 update of the literature on groups left this model in place, except for the addition of a final stage, adjourning. Models offered subsequently have also kept the same pattern. Proposed sequences include: define the situation, develop new skills, develop appropriate roles, carry out the work (Hare 1976); orientation, dissatisfaction, resolution, production, termination (LaCoursiere 1980); and generate plans, ideas, and goals; choose/agree on alternatives, goals, and policies; resolve conflicts and develop norms; perform action tasks and maintain cohesion (McGrath 1984).

The second stream of research on group development concerns phases in group problem solving, or decision development. Researchers have typically worked with groups with short life spans, usually minutes or hours, and studied them in a laboratory as they performed a limited task of solving a specific problem. Studies have focused on discovering the sequences of activities through which groups empirically reach solutions—or should reach solutions—and have used various systems of categories to analyze results. By abstracting the rhetorical form of group members' talk from its content and recording percentages of statements made in categories like "agree" and "gives orientation," researchers have portrayed the structure of group discussion. The classic study in this tradition is Bales and Strodtbeck's (1951) unitary sequence model of three phases in groups' movement toward goals: orientation, evaluation, and control.

Though they differ somewhat in the particulars, models from both streams of research have important similarities. Indeed, Poole asserted that "for thirty years, researchers on group development have been conducting the same study with minor alterations" (1983b: 341). The resultant models

are deeply grounded in the paradigm of group development as an inevitable progression: a group cannot get to stage four without first going through stages one, two, and three. For this reason, researchers construe development as movement in a forward direction and expect every group to follow the same historical path. In this paradigm, an environment may constrain systems' ability to develop, but it cannot alter the developmental stages or their sequence.

Some theorists have criticized the validity of such models. Research by Fisher (1970) and by Scheidel and Crowell (1964) suggested that group discussion proceeds in iterative cycles, not in linear order. Bell (1982) and Seeger (1983) questioned Bales and Strodtbeck's methodology. Poole (1981, 1983a, 1983b) raised the most serious challenge to the problem-solving models by demonstrating that there are many possible sequences through which decisions can develop in groups, not just one. Despite these critiques, however, the classic research continues to be widely cited, and the traditional models continue to be widely presented in management texts as the facts of group development (Hellriegel, Slocum, and Woodman 1986; Szilagy and Wallace 1987; Tosi, Rizzo, and Carroll 1986).

Apart from the question of validity, there are gaps in all the extant models, including those of the critics, that seriously limit their contribution to broader research and theory about groups and group effectiveness. First, as Tuckman pointed out in 1965 and others have noted up to the present (Hare 1976; McGrath 1986; Poole 1983b), they offer snapshots of groups at different points in their life spans but say little about the mechanisms of change, what triggers it, or how long a group will remain in any one stage. Second, existing models have treated groups as closed systems (Goodstein and Dovico 1979). Without guidance on the interplay between groups' development and environmental contingencies, the models are particularly limited in their utility for task groups in organizations. Not only do organizational task groups' assignments, resources, and requirements for success usually emanate from outside the groups (Gladstein 1984; Hackman 1985), such groups' communications with their environments are often pivotal to their effectiveness (Katz 1982; Katz and Tushman 1979).

The Approach of This Study

The ideas presented here originated during a field study of how task forces—naturally occurring teams brought together specifically to do projects in a limited time period—actually get work done. The question that drove the research was, what does a group in an organization do, from the moment it convenes to the end of its life span, to create the specific product that exists at the conclusion of its last meeting?

Because this study was somewhat unconventional, it may help to start with an overview. I observed four groups (A, B, C, and D in Table 7.1) between winter 1980 and spring 1981, attending every meeting of every group and generating complete transcripts for each. This observation was done as part of a larger study of group effectiveness (Gersick 1982; Hackman 1990). Four additional groups (E, F, G, and H in Table 7.1) were studied in 1983.

Several features distinguish the groups included in the domain of this research. They were real groups—members had interdependent relations with one another and developed differentiated roles over time, and the groups were perceived as such both by members and nonmembers (Alderfer 1977). Each group was convened specifically to develop a concrete piece of work; the groups' lives began and ended with the initiation and completion of special projects. Members had collective responsibility for the work. They were not merely working side by side or carrying out preset orders; they had to make interdependent decisions about what to cre-

Table 7.1

The Groups Observed

Teams[a]	Task	Time-Span	Number of Meetings
A. Graduate management students: 3 men	Analyze a live management case.	11 days	8
B. Graduate management students: 2 men, 3 women	Analyze a live management case.	15 days	7
C. Graduate management students: 3 men, 1 woman	Analyze a live management case.	7 days	7
D. Community fundraising agency committee: 4 men, 2 women	Design a procedure to evaluate recipient agencies.	3 months	4
E. Bank task force: 4 men	Design a new bank account.	34 days	4
F. Hospital administrators: 3 men, 2 women	Plan a one-day management retreat.	12 weeks	10
G. Psychiatrists and social workers: 8 men, 4 women[b]	Reorganize two units of a treatment facility.	9 weeks[c]	7
H. University faculty members and administrators: 6 men	Design a new academic institute for computer sciences.	6 months[c]	25

[a] The three student groups were from one large, private university. Team H was from a small university.
[b] Two other members attended only once; one other member attended two meetings.
[c] The actual time span (shown) differed from the initially expected span (see Table 7.2).

ate and how to proceed. The groups all worked within ongoing organizations, had external managers or supervisors, and produced their products for outsiders' use or evaluation. Finally, every group had to complete its work by a deadline.

The eight groups in the study (see Table 7.1) came from six different organizations in the Northeast; the three student groups came from the same university. Their life spans varied from seven days to six months. [For a full description of research methods, see the original article.]

An Overview of the Model

The data revealed that teams used widely diverse behaviors to do their work; however, the timing of when groups formed, maintained, and changed the way they worked was highly congruent. If the groups had fit the traditional models, not only would they have gone through the same sequence of activities, they would also have begun with an open-ended exploration period. Instead, every group exhibited a distinctive approach to its task as soon as it commenced and stayed with that approach through a period of momentum or inertia[1] that lasted for half its allotted time. Every group then underwent a major transition. In a concentrated burst of changes, groups dropped old patterns, re-engaged with outside supervisors, adopted new perspectives on their work, and made dramatic progress. The events that occurred during those transitions, especially groups' interactions with their environments, shaped a new approach to its task for each group. Those approaches carried groups through a second major phase of inertial activity, in which they executed plans created at their transitions. An especially interesting discovery was that each group experienced its transition at the same point in its calendar—precisely halfway between its first meeting and its official deadline—despite wide variation in the amounts of time the eight teams were allotted for their projects.

This pattern of findings did not simply suggest a different stage theory, with new names for the stages. The term "stage" connotes hierarchical progress from one step to another (Levinson 1986), and the search for

stages is an effort to "validly distinguish . . . types of behavior" (Poole 1981: 6–7), each of which is indicative of a different stage. "Stage X" includes the same behavior in every group. This study's findings identified temporal periods, which I termed phases, that emerged as bounded eras within each group, without being composed of identical activities across groups and without necessarily progressing hierarchically. It was like seeing the game of football as progressing through a structure of quarters (phases) with a major half-time break versus seeing the game as progressing in a characteristic sequence of distinguishable styles of play (stages). A different paradigm of development appeared to be needed.

The paradigm through which I came to interpret the findings resembles a relatively new concept from the field of natural history that has not heretofore been applied to groups: *punctuated equilibrium* (Eldredge and Gould 1972). In this paradigm, systems progress through an alternation of stasis and sudden appearance—long periods of inertia, punctuated by concentrated, revolutionary periods of quantum change. Systems' histories are expected to vary because situational contingencies are expected to influence significantly the path a system takes at its inception and during periods of revolutionary change, when systems' directions are formed and reformed.

In sum, the proposed model described groups' development as a punctuated equilibrium. *Phase 1*, the first half of groups' calendar time, is an initial period of inertial movement whose direction is set by the end of the group's first meeting. At the midpoint of their allotted calendar time, groups undergo a transition, which sets a revised direction for *phase 2*, a second period of inertial movement. Within this phase 1—transition—phase 2 pattern, two additional points are of special interest: the first meeting, because it displays the patterns of phase 1; and the last meeting, or completion, because it is a period when groups markedly accelerate and finish off work generated during phase 2.

Special Aspects of the Model

The importance of the first meeting was its power to display the behaviors (process) and themes (content) that dominated the first half of each group's life. Each group appears to have formed almost immediately a framework of givens from which the group operated throughout phase 1. Teams seldom formulated their frameworks through explicit deliberation. Instead, frameworks were established implicitly, by what was said and done repeatedly in the group.

Central approaches and behavior patterns that appeared during first meetings and persisted during phase 1 disappeared at the halfway point as groups explicitly dropped old approaches and searched for new ones. They revised their frameworks. The clearest sign of transition was the major jump in progress that each group made on its project at the temporal midpoint of its calendar. . . . [Examples from one of the student groups illustrate each part of the model. See the original article for more examples.]

Illustration of the Model

First Meeting and Phase 1

Excerpt 1 (E1). A team of three graduate management students start their first, five-minute encounter to plan work on a group case assignment, defined by the professor as an organizational design problem.[2]

1. Jack: We should try to read the [assigned] material.

2. Rajeev: But this isn't an organizational design problem, it's a strategic planning problem.

3. (Jack and Bert agree.)

4. Rajeev: I think what we have to do is prepare a way of growth [for the client].

5. (Nods, "yes" from Jack and Bert.)

Excerpt 1, representing less than one minute from the very start of a team's life, gives a clear view of the opening framework. The team's approach toward its organizational context (the professor and his requirements)

is plain. The members are not going to read the material; they disagree with the professor's definition of the task and will define their project to suit themselves.

Their pattern of internal interaction is equally visible. When Rajeev made three consequential proposals—about the definition of the task, the team's lack of obligations to the professor, and the goal they should aim for—everyone concurred. There was no initial "storming" (Tuckman 1965; Tuckman and Jensen 1977) in this group. The clip also shows this team's starting approach toward its task: confidence about what the problem is, what the goal ought to be, and how to get to work on it. The team's stated performance strategy was to use strategic planning techniques to "prepare a way of growth." [The team worked within this framework for two full meetings. Rajeev led the group through a structured set of strategic planning questions. At this point, the team had a complete draft outline of a growth plan for its client.]

Table 7.2 summarizes the findings about the first meetings and phase 1. Column 1 presents each team's starting approach toward its task, and column 2 summarizes the central task activity of phase 1, including first meetings.

Each group immediately established an integrated framework of performance strategies, interaction patterns, and approaches toward its task and outside context. The most concise illustration of this finding comes from the student group, whose (1) easy agreement on (2) a specific plan for its work represented (3) a decision to ignore the outside requirements of its task—all within the same minute of group discussion. Such frameworks embodied the central themes that dominated all through the first half of groups' calendar time, even for teams that were frustrated with the paths they were following. This finding contradicts traditional models, which pose teams' beginnings as a discrete stage of indeterminate duration during which teams orient themselves to their situation, explicitly debating and choosing what to do.

	Teams	First Meeting	Phase 1	Transition	Phase 2	Completion
A.	Student team A	Agreements on a plan.	Details of plan worked out; client's "growth options."	First draft revised; second draft planned.	Detail of second plan worked out; organization design.	Homework compiled into paper, finished, and edited.
B.	Student team B	Disagreement on task definition.	Argument over how to define task; challenge vs. follow client's problem statement.	Task defined; case analysis rough-outlined.	Details of outline worked out; affirmative action plan, following client's request.	Paper (drafted by one member) finished; edited.
C.	Student team C	One member proposes concrete plan; others oppose it.	Argument over details of competing plans ("structured" vs. "minimal") but no discussion of goals.	Goals chosen; case analysis outlined.	Details of outline worked out; "minimalist" U.S. trade policy.	Homework compiled into paper, finished, and edited.
D.	Community fundraising agency committee	Agreement on a plan.	Details of plan worked out; "nonthreatening" self-evaluation for member agencies.	First draft revised; second draft planned.	Details for second plan worked out; explicitly allocations-related evaluation plan.	Report (drafted by two members) edited.
E.	Bank task force	Uncertainty about new product; federal regulations unclear.	Team "answers questions"; maps possible account features.	Account completely outlined.	Members work throughout bank on systems, supplies for account.	Account finalized for advertising; bank-wide training planned.
F.	Hospital adminis-trators	Team fixes on "trust" theme; uncertain what to do with it for program.	Unstructured trial and rejection of program possibilities; disagreement about goals.	Complete program outlined.	Consultant hired to plan program; team arranges housekeeping details.	Responsibility for final preparations delegated.
G.	Psychia-trists and social workers	Leader presents "the givens"; team opposes project.	Subgroup reports presented; members object to all plans; leader rebuts objections.	Disagreement persists; leader picks one plan; redelegates task; dissolves team.		
H.	University faculty members and admin-istrators	Team divided on whether to accept project; leader proposes diagnosis as first step.	Structured exploration; diagnosis of situation.	Team redefines task; commits to project.	Computer institute designed (original task) plus system for university computer facilities planning.	Report (written by leader from members' drafts) edited and approved.

Table 7.2

An Overview of the Groups' Life Cycles

Though each team began with the formation of a framework, each framework was unique. . . . Some teams began with harmonious interaction patterns; others with internal storms. Teams took very different approaches to authority figures. . . . These findings contradict the typical stage theory paradigm which assumes that all teams essentially begin with the same approach toward their task (e.g., orientation), their team (e.g., forming then storming), and toward authority (e.g., dependency).

The Midpoint Transition

As each group approached the midpoint between the time it started work and its deadline, it underwent great change. [Members' awareness of time and their behavior toward outside supervisors were particularly noteworthy.]

Excerpt 5 (E5). [On the sixth day of the 11 days they had for their project, things changed. This is how that meeting began:]

1. Rajeev: I think, what he said today in class—I have, already, lots of criticism on our outline. What we've done now is OK, but we need a lot more emphasis on organization design than what we—I've been doing up to now.

2. Jack: I think you're right. We've already been talking about [X]. We should be talking more about [Y].

3. Rajeev: We've done it—and it's super—but we need to do other things, too.

4. (Bert agrees.)

5. Jack: After hearing today's discussion—we need to say [X] more directly. And we want to say more explicitly that. . . .

6. Rajeev: . . . should we be . . . organized and look at the outline? We should know where we're going.

(The group goes quickly through the outline members had prepared for the meeting, noting changes and additions they want to make.)

7. Rajeev: The problem is, we're very short on time.

The students came to this meeting having just finished the outline of the strategic plan they had set out to do at their opening encounter (see E1). At their midpoint, they stopped barreling along on their first task. They marked the completion of that work, evaluated it, and generated a fresh, significantly revised agenda. The team's change in outlook on its task coincided with a change in stance toward the professor. Revisions were made that were based on "what he said today in class" and "hearing today's discussion." Having reaffirmed the value of their first approach to the case, members reversed their original conviction that it was "not an organizational design problem."

This was the first time members allowed their work to be influenced by the professor, and at this point, they accepted his influence enthusiastically.

It is significant that Rajeev's remark, "we're very short on time," was only the second comment about the adequacy of the time the group had for the project, and it marked a switch from Jack's early sentiment that "we've got some more time" (E2, Line 6). A new sense of urgency marked this meeting.

The structure of the transition period was similar for all the teams, even though the specific details differed widely. Table 7.3 shows the timing of each team's transition meeting, describes the changes that occurred in the work at that point, and documents those changes in members' words. Five major indicators, or earmarks, of the transition are reviewed below.[3]

First, teams entered transition meetings at different stages in their work, but for each, progress began with the completion or abandonment of phase 1 agendas. For example, groups A and D entered transition meetings with complete drafts of plans that had been hatched when they started, and team H finished a system diagnosis just before its midpoint (see Table 7.2). The hospital administrators dropped key premises that the program they were designing would be about trust and run by themselves. Team G's leader unexpectedly pronounced the group's task complete at its midpoint (G, 2),[4] but interviews indicated that members, too, felt it was time to move dramatically: "At that point . . . there was a need to go up. But instead of going up, we stopped."

Second, team members expressed urgency about finishing on time. At this time—and no other—members expressed explicit concern about the pace and timeliness of their work: "We ought to be conscious of deadlines" (team H, transition meeting). Group G, dissolved with no prior warning (or protest) at its midpoint, was the only team that did not fit this pattern.

Table 7.3

Transition Meetings in the Eight Groups

A. Student team A: Day 6 of 11-day span
Team revises first draft of case analysis; plans final draft.

Opening	(1)	I think what he said today in class—I have . . . lots of criticism on our outline. . . . We've done it—and it's super—but we need to do other things too.
Closing	(2)	The problem is, we're very short on time.

B. Student team B: Day 7 of 15-day span
Team progresses from argument over how its task should be defined to rough outline of case analysis.

Opening	(1)	This is due next Monday, right?
	(2)	Right. Time to roll.
Later	(3)	Not bad! We spent one hour on one topic, and an hour on another! . . . We're moving along here, too. I feel a lot better at this meeting than I have—
	(4)	Well . . . we're also making decisions to be task-oriented, and take the problem at its face value—

C. Student team C: Day 4 of 7-day span
Team progresses from argument over details of competing plans, with no discussion of overall goals, to goal clarification and complete outline of product.

Opening	(1)	This morning I redesigned the whole presentation! I don't know what the *content* is, but—
Later	(2)	[Surveying the blackboard] OK—we've got goals! Those are the U.S. goals for [X topic]. . . . The [outline for the paper is] the lead-in, the goals, and the strategy.
	(3)	That makes sense! . . .
	(4)	I like it!

D. Community fundraising agency committee: Meeting 3 of 4 preset meetings
Team revises first plan for evaluation procedure; agrees on final plan.

Opening	(1)	Does anyone have problems with the . . . evaluation draft?
	(2)	Let's be realistic—we don't have the staff time to sit down with each [recipient] agency every year.
	(3)	What are we accomplishing, then? We need to know [X]. Otherwise I say, "Don't bother!"
Later	(4)	[Summing up a revised version of the plan] If you tell [member agencies] they *will* be evaluated . . . and these are questions you'll be asked, so—get your baloney swinging. . . ! [Laughter from team] OK. Let's move on, otherwise we're going to get behind.

E. Bank task force: Day 17 of 34-day span
Team progresses from "answering questions" to designing complete outline of new bank account.

Opening	(1)	I just hope we don't get stuck, toward the end, without—
	(2)	What are we gonna do—just—answer a lot of questions today?—or—
	(3)	. . . basically, we're gonna lay out the characteristics of the account.
Closing	(4)	Oh, I think that's super!
	(5)	I think we got a good product!

F. Hospital administrators: Week 6 of 12-week span
Team progresses from uncertainty and disagreement about goal to a complete program plan.

Opening	(1)	. . . we need to . . . come up with [something to] bounce off Tom next time.
Closing	(2)	We are making progress! I was afraid we weren't moving fast enough!
	(3)	We've made progress, folks!

G. Psychiatrists and social workers: Week 9 of 17-week plan
Leader chooses one of three reorganization plans to break stalemate; dissolves team.

Opening	(1)	Is [plan A] a reasonable way to go? *That's* the question.
Closing	(2)	We are nearing the completion of our task . . . the next step is turning [the work] over [to Dr. C]. . . . There is disagreement in here, [but] I think . . . we have to come *down* . . . [on one plan]. . . . Then we are—dissolved. . . . Thank you.

H. University faculty members and administrators: Week 7 of 14-week plan
Team redefines task; progresses from skepticism to commitment.

Opening	(1)	. . . the task force reached a crossroads last meeting . . . and decided it [must choose] whether it should [continue with original task] or consider the overall needs. For that reason, we've asked two people at the vice-presidential level to . . . help us deliberate that question.

Table 7.3 *(continued)*

Transition Meetings in the Eight Groups

Closing (2) I think we've . . . reached a conclusion today, and that is, we need to include the administrative end [in our task].

(3) Hey. I think we're finally giving Connie some good stuff here! Isn't this typical? You go through, you roll along, and then all of a sudden you say, "What are we doing?" Then we go back and *reconstitute* ourselves! Anyway, processes are taking place!

Third, teams' transitions all occurred at the midpoints of their official calendars, regardless of the number or length of meetings teams had before or after that.

Fourth, new contact between teams and their organizational contexts played important roles in their transitions. Most often, this contact was between the team and its task delegator. Sometimes it was initiated by the team (E and F), sometimes by both at once (A, D, and H), and sometimes by the task delegators (B and C).

These contacts both fostered decision making and outcomes. Five groups showed explicit new interest in the match between their product and outside resources and requirements. Excerpts A and D and the bank's work with computer experts show how groups shaped their products specifically to contextual resources and requirements. The bank group also illustrates the other side of the coin—a team member took his new assessment of the project out to the organization to request more resources. The importance of this contact is highlighted by the exception, team G, whose lack of information about outside requirements exacerbated its inability to choose. A member stated during its pretransition meeting: "If we are expected [to do X] then there is no [way to support plan A over plan B, but] . . . that may not be the demand. Obviously, there's a lot of politics outside this room that are going to define what [we] have to do."

Finally, transitions yielded specific new agreements on the ultimate directions teams' work should take. Regardless of how much or how little members argued during phase 1, every team that completed its task agreed at transition on plans that formed the basis for the completion of the work. In teams with easy phase 1 interaction, the agreeableness itself was not a change. But for teams where phase 1 had been conflictful, transition meetings were high points in collaboration. Indeed, in the one team whose members still disagreed at this point, the leader dissolved the group, chose a plan unilaterally, and moved the work forward by shifting it into other hands (G, 2).

Overall, the changes in teams' work tended to be dialectical. Teams that had started fast, with quick decisions and unhesitating construction of their products, paused at their transitions to evaluate finished work and address shortcomings (A and D). For teams that started slowly, unsure or disagreeing about what to do, transitions were exhilarating periods of structuring, making choices, and pulling together (B, C, E, F, and H). In either case, transitional advances depended on the combination of phase 1 learning and fresh ideas. For example, the bankers' transitional raw materials were ideas generated during phase 1, refined and integrated with the help of expertise newly infused into the team. The hospital administrators, newly open to an alternative format, found use for a theme they had discussed but not developed earlier.

Traditional models of group development do not predict a midpoint transition. They present groups as progressing forward if and whenever they accumulate enough work on specific developmental issues—not at a predictable moment, catalyzed by team members' awareness of time limits. Traditional group development models are silent about team-context relations and the influence of such relations on teams' progress. The findings reported here suggest that there is a predictable time in groups' life cycles when members are particularly influenceable by, and interested in, communication with outsiders. Cases in which task delegators contacted teams at this point suggest this interest might be mutual.

Phase 2

Teams' lives were different after the midpoint transition. In all seven surviving teams, members' approaches toward their tasks clearly changed and advanced (Table 7.2). All seven executed their transitional plans during this period. Post-transitional changes in teams' internal interaction patterns and approaches toward their outside contexts were not so simple. Transitions did not advance every team in these areas, nor did every team use its transition equally well. Internal troubles that went unaddressed during transition sometimes worsened during phase 2, and teams that were lax in matching their work to outside requirements during the transition showed lasting effects.

The student group, which developed strategic "growth options" for its client in phase 1, spent phase 2 building the organizational design, planned at the transitional meeting, to support those options. As the task approach shifted from strategic planning to organizational design, one element of the team's interaction pattern changed. Jack took over from Rajeev as lead questioner. Other than that, the team continued the easy, orderly agreement of its phase 1 interaction style. The team sustained its new perspective on its context, formed at transition, by maintaining attentiveness to the professor's requirements throughout phase 2.

Phase 2 was a second period of inertia in teams' lives, shaped powerfully by the events of their transitions. Teams did not alter their basic approaches toward their tasks within this phase. As one hospital team member stated, "We decided what we were going to do [at the midpoint meeting] . . . and the rest was just mechanics."

Since all teams were doing construction work on their projects during phase 2, similar to "performing" in Tuckman's (1965) synthesis, it was a time when teams were more similar both to each other and to the traditional model than they were in phase 1. However, progress was not so much like traditional models in other respects, since it was not so linear. Some teams started performing earlier than others, without previous conflict; other teams returned to internal conflict after their transition and during phase 2 performance. In every team, transitional work centered explicitly on solving task problems, not on solving internal interaction problems; it is not surprising, then, that some teams' internal processes worsened after the major need for collaborative decision making was past.

Completion

Completion was the phase of teams' lives in which their activities were the most similar to each others'. Three patterns characterized final meetings: (1) groups' task activity changed from generating new materials to editing and preparing existing materials for external use; (2) as part of this preparation, their explicit attention toward outside requirements and expectations rose sharply; and (3) groups expressed more positive or negative feeling about their work and each other. At this point, the major differences among the groups involved not what they were doing but how easily their were doing it. Not surprisingly, groups that had checked outside requirements early on and groups that had paced themselves well all along had easier, shorter final meetings.

The last distinct change in the student team's life occurred the day before the paper was due. This meeting was considerably longer than any other; the team now had to keep working until the case analysis was finished. Members' work activities changed from generating ideas to editing what they had into the form required by the instructor. A sample from that meeting is "I'm not disagreeing with anything you're saying. But I think you got 'em in the wrong section." Though the long hours and the need to edit each others' work made the meeting more difficult than usual, by the time the team was ready to give its presentation, members were expressing their feelings that the project had gone well. The presentation went smoothly and the team received a good grade.

In every team, discussion of outsiders' expectations was prominent at the last meeting. As teams anticipated releasing their work into outside hands, they scrutinized it freshly, through outsiders' eyes: "We'll be judged poorly if we . . ."; "You can't promise [X] and then do [Y]." Since phase 2 actions carried out, but did not alter, plans made at transition, teams that entered phase 2 with a poor match between product and requirements had an especially hard time confronting outside expectations at completion. But even teams that discovered in last-day meetings that they had major gaps to fill framed their remaining work as rearranging or fixing what they already had, as these excerpts indicate: "I think our content . . . is good . . . it's just a matter of reorganizing it . . ." (team B) and "I think we have all the ideas. . . . The main task is how to arrange them" (team A). Though teams' attention to outside requirements was high at last meetings, completion activities did not undo the basic product revisions established at transition.

Discussion

The traditional paradigm portrays group development as a series of stages or activities through which groups gradually and explicitly get ready to perform, and then perform, their tasks. All groups are expected to follow the same historical path. Proponents of existing models specify neither the mechanisms of change nor the role of a group's environment. In contrast, the paradigm suggested by the current findings indicates that groups develop through the sudden formation, maintenance, and sudden revision of a framework for performance; the developmental process is a punctuated equilibrium. The proposed model highlights the processes through which frameworks are formed and revised and predicts both the timing of progress and when and how in

their development groups are likely, or unlikely, to be influenced by their environments. The specific issues and activities that dominate groups' work are left unspecified in the model, since groups' historical paths are expected to vary.

The proposed model works in the following way: A framework of behavioral patterns and assumptions through which a group approaches its project emerges in its first meeting, and the group stays with that framework through the first half of its life. Teams may show little visible progress during this time because members may be unable to perceive a use for the information they are generating until they revise the initial framework. At their calendar midpoints, groups experience transitions—paradigmatic shifts in their approaches to their work—enabling them to capitalize on the gradual learning they have done and make significant advances. The transition is a powerful opportunity for a group to alter the course of its life midstream. But the transition must be used well, for once it is past a team is unlikely to alter its basic plans again. Phase 2, a second period of inertial movement, takes its direction from plans crystallized during the transition. At completion, when a team makes a final effort to satisfy outside expectations, it experiences the positive and negative consequences of past choices.

The components of this model raise an interesting set of theoretical questions. Why do lasting patterns form so early and persist through long periods of inertia? Why do teams' behavior patterns and product designs undergo dramatic change precisely halfway through their project calendars? What is the role of a team's context in its development? This exploratory study did not test or prove any prior hypotheses; nonetheless, it is appropriate to ask whether established theory provides any basis for understanding the observed results, to help formulate hypotheses and questions for future testing.

Early Patterns

Why do lasting patterns form so early and persist through long periods of inertia? The present findings show that lasting patterns can appear as early as the first few seconds of a group's life. This finding was unexpected, but it is not unheard of. Reports from the psychoanalytic literature show the power of the first minutes of a therapeutic interview to predict the central issues of the session (Ginnette 1986; Pittenger, Hockett, and Danehy 1960, 22b). Quite recently, Bettenhausen and Murnighan found that "unique norms formed in each [of several bargaining groups], typically during their very first agreements" (1985: 359).

The sheer speed with which recurring patterns appear suggests they are influenced by material established before a group convenes. Such material includes members' expectations about the task, each other, and the context and their repertoires of behavioral routines and performance strategies. The presence of these factors would circumscribe the influence of the interaction process that occurs in the first meeting but not rule it out. Bettenhausen and Murnighan (1985) discussed norm formation in terms of what happens when team members encounter the scripts (Abelson 1976) each has brought to a group's first meeting. Pittenger, Hockett, and Danehy (1960: 16–24) described the opening of a therapeutic interview as the interaction of "rehearsed" material brought in by the patient with the therapist's opening gambit. This construction of first meetings suggests that peoples' earliest responses to each other set lasting precedents about how a team is going to handle the issues, ideas, questions, and performance strategies that members have brought in.

In phase 1, groups define most of the parameters of their situation quickly and examine them no further, concentrating their work and attention on only a few factors. The contrast between this model and the traditional idea that groups take time to generate, evaluate, and choose alternative views before getting to work parallels Simon's (1976) contrast between bounded and perfect rationality, and it may be understood through his argument that people must make simplifying assumptions in order to take any action at all.

The Halfway Point

Why do teams' behavior patterns and product designs undergo dramatic change exactly halfway through their project calendars? The transition can be understood through a combination of two concepts: problemistic search (March and Simon 1958) and pacing. The idea of problemistic search simply extends the theory of bounded rationality. Its proponents posit that innovation is the result of search and that people do not initiate search unless they believe they have a problem. New perspectives appear to enter a group at transition because team members find old perspectives are no longer viable and initiate a fresh search for ideas.

The problem that stimulates search and stimulates it at a consistent moment in groups' calendars may be explained with the construct of pacing. Groups must pace their use of a limited resource, time, in order to finish by their deadlines. The midpoint appears to work like an alarm clock, heightening members' awareness that their time is limited, stimulating them to compare where they are with where they need to be and to adjust their progress accordingly: it is "time to roll." Since the groups in this research are charged with creating novel products, perspectives created quickly at the first meeting are likely to be found wanting in some way. For example, it may be perfectly suitable to begin with the approach "we're mapping out the task," but that approach must change at some time if there is to be a product. Even groups that started with a plan they liked learned by working on it to see flaws that were not visible when the plan was just an idea.

This model has some important qualifications. If the midpoint is primarily a moment of alarm, when groups feel "we need to move forward now," then the transition is an opportunity for, not a guarantee of, progress. This allows for the possibility that a group, like an individual, might feel strongly that it is time to move ahead, yet be unable to do so. Similarly, to hypothesize that transitions are catalyzed by groups' comparison of their actual progress with their desired progress leaves room for the chance that a group may—correctly or incorrectly—be largely satisfied and proceed with little visible change. These qualifications are consistent with the observation that groups' historical paths vary, and they provoke further research by posing the question, what factors affect the success of groups' transitions?

Why the consistent midpoint timing? Halfway is a natural milestone, since teams have the same amount of time remaining as they have already used, and they can readily calibrate their progress. Adult development research offers analogous findings. At midlife, people shift their focus from how much time has passed to how much time is left (Jaques 1955). Levinson found a major transition at midlife, characterized by "a heightened awareness of mortality and a desire to use the remaining time more wisely" (1978: 192). Nonetheless, it would be premature to base the entire weight of these findings on the midpoint timing of the transition. Some groups may work on schedules that make times other than the midpoint highly salient. Ultimately, the midpoint itself is not as important as the finding that groups use temporal milestones to pace their work and that the event of reaching those milestones pushes groups into transitions. This study raises, but cannot answer, the question of what sets the alarm to go off when it does and precisely how it works in groups.

Context

What is the role of a team's context in its development? Traditional group development theory leaves little room for environmental influence on the course of development; all groups are predicted to go through the same steps, and all are predicted to suspend opinions of what they are about until they have thrashed that issue out through their own internal processes. Neither do these theories comment about development-linked changes in interaction between a group and its context. In contrast, the current findings suggest that the outside context may play a particularly important role in a group's developmental path at three points: the design of the group and two well-defined critical periods.

As noted, the speed with which distinctive patterns appear suggests the influence of materials imported into the group. The finding is congruent with, but does not test, a viewpoint from the group-performance research tradition. In that view, the *design* of a group—the composition of the team, the structure of the task, the contextual supports and circumstances under which the team is formed—precedes and conditions the interaction that transpires among members (Hackman 1986). In terms of the current model, the pool of materials from which a team fashions its first framework is set by the design and designer of the group.

A critical period is a time in an organism's life within which a particular formative experience will take and after which it will not (Etkin 1967). Though the analogy is imperfect, there appear to be two critical periods when groups are much more open to fundamental influence than they are at other times. The first is the initial meeting. As a time when the interaction in the group sets lasting precedents, it holds special potential to influence a team's basic approach toward its project.

The transition is the second chance. Not only did teams open up to outside influence at this point, they actively used outside resources and requirements as a basis for recharting the course of their work. The transition appears to be a unique time in groups' lives. It is the only period when the following three conditions are true at once: members are experienced enough with the work to understand the meaning of contextual requirements and resources, have used up enough of their time that they feel they must get on with the task, and still have enough time left that they can make significant changes in the design of their products.

In contrast, teams did not make fundamental changes of course in response to information from their contexts during phase 1 and phase 2, when ideas that did not fit with their approach to the task did not appear to register. That observation does not suggest that teams universally ignore or cut off environmental communication during phases 1 and 2, but it suggests that outsiders are unlikely to turn teams around during those times.

The . . . example teams showed how groups may insulate themselves from environmental input at some times yet seek it during transitions—partly to get help limiting their own choices and moving forward, partly to increase the chances that their product will succeed in their environment. That pattern has interesting implications for the theoretical debate between population ecologists, who argue that environments "select," and advocates of resource dependency, who argue that systems "adapt." Researchers have already observed that organizations change through alternating periods of momentum and revolution (Miller and Friesen 1984; Tushman and Romanelli 1985). Further, organizations commonly construct time-related goals for productivity and growth, such as monthly, annual, and five-year plans, as well as possibly much longer-term objectives for their ultimate growth schedules. It appears worth investigating (1) whether pacing or life cycle issues affect the timing or success of organizational revolutions and (2) how organization environment communication, or lack of it, during revolutionary periods particularly affects outcomes. Interaction with an environment may be very likely to foster and shape adaptation at certain predictable times in a system's life cycle and unlikely to do so at other times. If its environment changes dramatically when an organization is also entering a change phase, that organization may be more likely to adapt. Organizations that are instead in a phase of inertia will be less able to respond and may be selected out. Since this study did not include interviews with external stakeholders or observation of them outside teams' meetings, more research is needed to study the effects of environmental influence attempts during phases 1 and 2, versus during transition.

Implications for Action

The results reported here have many implications for managers working with groups. Although traditional theory implies that group leaders have plenty of time at a project's beginning before the group will choose its norms and get to work, this model implies that a group's first meeting will set lasting precedents for how the group will use the first half of its time. That finding suggests that group leaders prepare carefully for the first meeting, and it identifies a key point of intersection between group-development and group-effectiveness research on team design. According to traditional theory, a group must also expect an inevitable storming stage. In contrast, the proposed model suggests that groups use the first meeting to diagnose the unique issues that will preoccupy them during phase 1.

The proposed model also suggests that a group does not necessarily need to make visible progress with a steady stream of decisions during phase 1 but does need to generate the raw material to make a successful transition. For example, groups that begin with a clear plan may do best to use phase 1 to flesh out a draft of that plan fully enough to see its strong and weak points at the transition. Groups that begin with a deep disagreement may do best to pursue the argument fully enough to understand by transition what is and is not negotiable for compromise. A leader who discovers at the first meeting that the group adamantly opposes the task may do best to decide whether to restart the project or help the group use phase 1 to explore the issues enough to determine, at transition, whether it can reach an acceptable formulation of the task. In such a case, a leader might want to redefine a group's task as a preliminary diagnostic project, with a shorter deadline. Once past the first meeting, phase 1 interventions aimed at fundamentally altering a group, rather than at helping it pursue its first framework more productively, may be unsuccessful because of members' resistance to perceiving truly different approaches as relevant to the concerns that preoccupy them.

The next new implication of the present model is that the midpoint is a particularly important opportunity for groups and external managers to renew communication. Again, note that the teams and supervisors studied did not all automatically do this or do it uniformly well. The special challenge of the transition is to use a group's increased information, together with fresh input from its environment, to revise its framework knowledgeably and to adjust the match between its work and environmental resources and requirements. This is another point of special intersection between group development and group-effectiveness research, since that research should be especially helpful in evaluating and revising a group's situation (Hackman and Walton 1986). Further research is needed to explore ways to manage the transition process productively.

Once the transition is past, the major outlines of a group's project design are likely to be set; the most helpful interventions are likely to be aimed at helping the group execute its work smoothly. For external managers, this may be an especially important time to insure a group's access to needed resources.

Author's Note

I am grateful to Richard Hackman, Kelin Gersick, David Berg, Lee Clarke, Barbara Lawrence, William McKelvey, and several anonymous journal reviewers for their helpful comments on earlier drafts of this work. This research was supported in part by the Organizational Effectiveness Research Program, Office of Naval Research, under contract to Yale University.

Notes

1. This paper uses the dictionary definition of inertia as the tendency of a body to remain in a condition: if standing still, to remain so; if moving, to keep on the same course.

2. All names used in this report are pseudonyms.

3. Two additional indicators of transition, a pretransition low point and a change in groups' routines, are not covered here because of space limitations. A discussion of all seven indicators is available in Gersick (1984).

4. In the discussion of indicators, letters (e.g., A, B, C) identify teams, and numbers (e.g., 1, 2, 3) identify lines of dialogue in Table 7.3.

References

Abelson, R. P. (1976). "Script processing in attitude formation and decision making." In J. Carroll and J. Payne (eds.), *Cognition and Social Behavior* (pp. 33–45). Hillsdale, NJ: Lawrence Erlbaum Associates.

Abernathy, W., and Utterback, L. (1982). "Patterns of industrial innovation." In M. Tushman and W. Moore (eds.), *Readings in the Management of Innovation* (pp. 97–108). Boston, MA: Pitman Publishing.

Alderfer, C. P. (1977). "Group and intergroup relations." In J. R. Hackman and J. L. Suttle (eds.), *Improving Life at Work* (pp. 227–296). Santa Monica, CA: Goodyear Publishing.

Bales, R. F., and Strodtbeck, F. L. (1951). "Phases in group problem solving." *Journal of Abnormal and Social Psychology* 46: 485–495.

Bell, M. A. (1982). "Phases in group problem solving." *Small Group Behavior* 13: 475–495.

Bennis, W., and Shepard, H. (1956). "A theory of group development." *Human Relations* 9: 415–437.

Bettenhausen, K., and Murnighan, J. K. (1985). "The emergence of norms in competitive decisionmaking groups." *Administrative Science Quarterly* 30: 350–372.

Bion, W. R. 1961. *Experiences in Groups*. New York: Basic Books.

Donnellon, A., Gray, B., and Bougon, M. (1986). "Communication, meaning, and organized action." *Administrative Science Quarterly* 31: 43–55.

Eldrege, N., and Gould, S. J. (1972). "Punctuated equilibria: An alternative to phyletic gradualism." In T. J. Schopf (ed.), *Models in Paleobiology* (pp. 82–115). San Francisco: Freeman, Cooper and Co.

Etkin, W. (1967). *Social Behavior from Fish to Man*. London: University of Chicago Press.

Fisher, B. A. (1970). "Decision emergence: Phases in group decision-making." *Speech Monographs* 37: 53–66.

Gersick, C. G. (1982). "Manual for group observations." In J. R. Hackman (ed.), *A Set of Methodologies for Research on Task Performing Groups.* Technical report no. 1, Research Program on Group Effectiveness, Yale School of Organization and Management, New Haven, CT.

——. (1983). *Life Cycles of Ad Hoc Task Groups.* Technical report no. 3, Research Program on Group Effectiveness, Yale School of Organization and Management, New Haven, CT.

——. (1984). The life cycles of ad hoc task groups: Time, transitions, and learning in teams. Unpublished doctoral dissertation, Yale University, New Haven, CT.

Ginette, R. (1986). OK, let's brief real quick. Paper presented at the 1986 meeting of the Academy of Management, Chicago, IL.

Gladstein, D. (1984). "Groups in context: A model of task group effectiveness." *Administrative Science Quarterly* 29: 499–517.

Glaser, B., and Strauss, A. (1967). *The Discovery of Grounded Theory: Strategies for Qualitative Research.* London: Wiedenfeld and Nicholson.

Goodstein, L. D., and Dovico, M. (1979). "The decline and fall of the small group." *Journal of Applied Behavioral Science* 15: 320–328.

Hackman, J. R. (1985). "Doing research that makes a difference." In E. Lawler, A. Mohrman, S. Mohrman, G. Ledford, and T. Cummings (eds.), *Doing Research That Is Useful for Theory and Practice* (pp. 126–148). San Francisco: Jossey-Bass.

——. (1986). "The design of work teams." In J. Lorsch (ed.), *Handbook of Organizational Behavior* (pp. 315–342). Englewood Cliffs, NJ: Prentice-Hall.

—— (ed.). (1990). *Groups That Work.* San Francisco: Jossey-Bass.

Hackman, J. R., and Walton, R. E. (1986). "Leading groups in organizations." In P. S. Goodman and Associates (eds.), *Designing Effective Work Groups* (pp. 72–119). San Francisco: Jossey-Bass.

Hare, A. P. (1976). *Handbook of Small Group Research* (2nd ed.). New York: Free Press.

Harris, S., and Sutton, R. (1986). "Functions of parting ceremonies in dying organizations." *Academy of Management Journal* 29: 5–30.

Hellriegel, D., Slocum, J., and Woodman, R. (1986). *Organizational Behavior* (4th ed.). St. Paul: West Publishing Co.

Huse, E., and Cummings, T. (1985). *Organization Development and Change* (3rd ed.). St. Paul: West Publishing Co.

Jaques, E. (1955). "Death and the mid-life crisis." *International Journal of Psychoanalysis* 46: 502–514.

Katz, R. (1982). "The effects of group longevity on project communication and performance." *Administrative Science Quarterly* 27: 81–104.

Katz, R., and Tushman, M. (1979). "Communication patterns, project performance, and task characteristics: An empirical evaluation and integration in an R & D setting." *Organizational Behavior and Human Performance* 23: 139–162.

Kuhn, T. S. (1962). *The Structure of Scientific Revolutions.* Chicago: University of Chicago Press.

Labov, W., and Fanshel, D. (1977). *Therapeutic Discourse.* New York: Academic Press.

LaCoursiere, R. B. (1980). *The Life Cycle of Groups: Group Developmental Stage Theory.* New York: Human Sciences Press.

Levinson, D. J. (1978). *The Seasons of a Man's Life.* New York: Alfred A. Knopf.

——. (1986). "A conception of adult development." *American Psychologist* 41: 3–14.

Mann, R., Gibbard, G., and Hartman, J. (1967). *Interpersonal Styles and Group Development.* New York: John Wiley and Sons.

March, J., and Simon, H. (1978). *Organizations.* New York: John Wiley and Sons.

McGrath, J. E. (1984). *Groups: Interaction and Performance.* Englewood Cliffs, NJ: Prentice Hall.

——. (1986). "Studying groups at work; Ten critical needs for theory and practice." In P. S. Goodman and Associates (eds.), *Designing Effective Work Groups* (pp. 363–392). San Francisco: Jossey-Bass.

Miller, D., and Friesen, P. (1984). *Organizations: A Quantum View.* Englewood Cliffs, NJ: Prentice-Hall.

Mills, T. (1979). "Changing paradigms for studying human groups." *Journal of Applied Behavioral Science* 15: 407–423.

Mintzberg, H. (1981). "Organization design, fashion or fit?" *Harvard Business Review* 59(1): 103–116.

Pittenger. R., Hockett, C., and Danehy, J. (1960). *The First Five Minutes: A Sample of Microscopic Interview Analysis.* Ithaca, NY: Paul Martineau.

Poole, M. S. (1981). "Decision development in small groups I: A comparison of two models." *Communication Monographs* 48: 1–24.

——. (1983a). "Decision development in small groups II: A study of multiple sequences of decision making." *Communication Monographs* 50: 206–232.

——. (1983b). "Decision development in small groups III: A multiple sequence model of group decision development." *Communication Monographs* 50: 321–341.

Scheidel, T., and Crowell, L. (1964). "Idea development in small discussion groups." *Quarterly Journal of Speech* 50: 140–145.

Schutz, W. C. (1958). *FIRO: A Three-Dimensional Theory of Interpersonal Behavior.* New York: Rinehart and Winston.

Seeger, J. A. (1983). "No innate phases in group problem solving." *Academy of Management Review* 8: 683–689.

Simon, H. A. (1976). *Administrative Behavior* (3rd ed.). New York: Free Press.

Slater, P. E. (1966). *Microcosm: Structural, Psychological, and Religious Evolution in Groups.* New York: John Wiley and Sons.

Szilagy, A., and Wallace, M. (1987). *Organizational Behavior and Performance* (4th ed.). Glenview, IL.: Scott, Foresman and Co.

Tosi, H., Rizzo, J., and Carroll, S. (1986). *Managing Organizational Behavior.* Marshfield, MA: Pitman Publishing.

Tuckman, B. (1965). "Developmental sequence in small groups." *Psychological Bulletin* 63: 384–399.

Tuckman, B., and Jensen, M. (1977). "Stages of small-group development." *Group and Organizational Studies* 2: 419–427.

Tushman, M. L., and Romanelli, E. (1985). "Organizational evolution: A metamorphosis model of convergence and reorientation." In L. Cummings and B. Staw (eds.), *Research in Organizational Behavior*, Vol. 7: 171–222. Greenwich, CT.: JAI Press.

Walton, R. E., and Hackman, J. R. (1986). "Groups under contrasting management strategies." In P. Goodman and Associates (eds.), *Designing Effective Work Groups* (pp. 168–201). San Francisco: Jossey-Bass.

Chapter 8
A Multiple Sequence Model of Group Decision Development

Marshall Scott Poole

This chapter is an abridged version of the author's landmark essay that eventually changed the way scholars conceptualize development in small groups. He begins by explaining why traditional unitary sequence models are inadequate for understanding group development. He then proposes a more complex model that presents the group development process as continuously evolving tracks or threads of group activities that intertwine over time. Poole concludes his article by pointing out the advantages of his multiple sequence model of group development over traditional unitary sequence models.

That groups pass through a definite sequence of developmental stages has become a truism in basic and advanced textbooks in communication, management, social psychology and sociology. Widespread acceptance of this proposition stems from two sources—support garnered from dozens of studies and, perhaps more important, repetition of the same simple idea in dozens of summaries. Simplicity is one of the hallmarks of good science. However, simplicity and elegance can also hide important details. In the case of group development, simple summary statements have omitted careful qualifications concerning scope-condi-

tions and departures from the rule that earlier researchers placed on their results (Bales and Strodtbeck 1951; Bennis and Shepard 1956). A growing body of evidence suggests developmental processes in groups are considerably more complex than has hitherto been supposed. This evidence warrants a reexamination of previous developmental models not only in terms of their particular propositions but in terms of the basic model underlying them—the analysis of development as a series of phases.

Description of Developmental Sequences

Phasic Descriptions and Their Problems

The "phase" or "stage" is the traditional unit of analysis in the study of group development. The dictionary defines stage as "a presumably natural or non-arbitrary division of a changing process" and phase as "a recurrent state in something that exhibits a series of changes; for example, the several phases of the moon" (Webster 1961). Both terms connote a period of more or less unified activity that fulfills some function necessary to completion of the group's task—for example, the orientation phase of Bales and Strodtbeck's model, in which the group defines its problems, decides how to attack it, and shares relevant information (Bales and Strodtbeck, 1951).

The phasic model is the dominant archetype for developmental studies of group communication: as such, it exerts a subtle pressure on researchers to utilize a certain type of description and conform to a single theoretical form. In the ideal case, a phasic model would be composed of a small, manageable number of phases which can be easily identified via empirical operations and which occur in a definite order (or a small set of different orderings). The phases would be applicable to a wide range of groups and, in the best of all possible worlds, would support generalizations about all group experiences. The model generally explains group behavior in terms of necessary structural conditions that require a certain set of phases to occur in a definite temporal order, such as Bales and Strodtbeck's logical sequence for problem-solving, Fisher's four-step conflict resolution pattern, or Lacoursiere's life-cycle model (Bales and Strodtbeck 1951; Fisher 1970; Lacoursiere 1980). While contingencies may require limited departures from the sequence, phases are presumed to exist and to occur in a definite order due to the practical prerequisites of completing a task, coming to consensus, living in a group, etc. With a few exceptions, previous research has operated within this ideal and has strained to realize it at the expense of attention to other forms of description or explanation.

Without question, the phasic model has led to great advances in our understanding of group processes. Research employing this model has generated a strong foundation of knowledge. However, progress in the social sciences requires a continuing critique of prevalent ideas with an eye to improving our representations and explanations of social processes. Several developments in recent research suggest that it is time to move beyond the phasic model.

We should begin with the observation that the great majority of studies in the phasic tradition identify developmental phases *ex post facto*. This process usually consists of tracking trends in indicators of group activity and deducing phases from observed activity. Fisher (1970), for example, identified decision-making phases by dividing discussions into four parts and comparing the relative levels of occurrence of various acts across parts. He labeled his first segment the orientation phase because it contained more acts and interacts characteristic of orientation (e.g., ambiguity, clarification, tentative evaluation of opinions) than the other three parts. Other studies using this method include those by Bennis and Shepard (1956), Hirokawa (1983), Mintzberg et al. (1976), and Poole (1983). Summaries that attempt to present "general" models, such as Tuckman's (1965) widely-cited review and Lacoursiere's (1980) book, rely on *ex post*

facto studies as their primary source of evidence.

There is, of course, nothing inherently wrong with *ex post facto* methods. They serve the valuable function of disclosing new phenomena and offer patterns for interpretive understanding which are often superior to that permitted by deductive designs. However, when *ex post facto* patterns become common knowledge, there is a danger they will lead to the assimilation of observations to expectations, to the sharpening of some occurrences and the neglect of others in service of a coherent story. They can quite easily become self-fulfilling and blind the researcher to the "marvelous particularity" of the object of study. When most support for a theory stems from *ex post facto* studies, we should be wary of accepting it wholeheartedly. As Tudor (1976) has observed, *discovery* of patterns is only one aspect of research; researchers must also *confirm* their existence via empirical tests.

Several studies have explicitly attempted to fulfill this requirement by testing *a priori* hypotheses about developmental phases. Unfortunately, the imprint of the phasic model of these studies is so strong that their results, though favorable, are inconclusive and equivocal. In some cases researchers have posited vague and indefinite hypotheses, which are partially confirmed, then rescued and revamped in the discussion (see, e.g., Ivancevich 1974; Morris 1970). Those studies which carefully specify clear, definite hypotheses are hindered by problems of design and analysis that bias them in favor of finding a unitary sequence of phases (see, e.g., Bales and Strodtbeck 1951; Mabry 1975; Runkell et al. 1971). These problems include (a) dividing discussions into the same number of segments as expected phases, thereby hiding developmental complexities that might refute the hypotheses and (b) combining data across groups, thereby eliding between-group developmental differences (Poole 1981).

Moreover, the *a priori* tests, as well as a large proportion of the *ex post facto* analyses, use only a few types of behavior categories to identify phases or confirm phasic sequences. Bales and Strodtbeck (1951), for example, relied on trends in four categories—information, opinions, solutions, and socioemotional acts—to test their model. Focusing on such a small sample of functions may ignore others which would qualify conclusions about phases. An ambiguous and aimless period at the beginning of discussion seems to be quite different from a quick, well-planned orientation by the leader, yet they would both be classified as orientation phases if information-giving and [information]-asking were the functions used to identify periods. This problem is likely to be even worse in cases where only a selective sample of acts is used (i.e., where the coding system has an "other" category or only a few categories from a system are used). Those acts not sampled may play a critical role in the discussion and lend a flavor to group activities not indicated by the restricted sample of phasic markers.

Studies examining the detailed local structure of group activities have revealed a much more complex picture of group behavior than simple phasic schemes can encompass. Poole (1981) isolated clusters of associated behaviors from 30 interact segments of discussions for a sample of student groups and a sample of physician groups. He found 19 distinct activity clusters for students and 17 for physicians, suggesting considerable diversity of behavior throughout the discussions. In a study of member-to-leader behavior in classroom groups, Mann (1966) found six dimensions that combined in complex ways as the group interaction unfolded. Considering that both studies focused on only a small range of group behaviors, they reveal a high degree of complexity and suggest things are not as simple as they may seem.

The results of previous research also suggest that decision development is considerably more complex than the phasic model envisions. Although reviews generally stress convergence in the findings of *ex post facto* studies, a closer look uncovers notable differences. For example, five studies of task-oriented groups by Bales and Strodtbeck (1951), Cronin and Thomas (1971), Fisher (1970), Tuckman (1965), and Zurcher (1969) report developmental sequences that follow the form of the unitary phasic model. When we look at specifics, however, each study reports a different set of phases and posits somewhat different explanatory mechanisms for movement through the sequence. . . .

Of course, these differences can be interpreted as the result of "noise" from different research designs and group situations. . . . However, given the conceptual and methodological biases raised earlier, another interpretation is possible: differences in findings may reflect actual differences in development, differences which are attenuated by efforts to accommodate our observations to an overly restrictive conception of developmental processes.

Recent studies of multiple sequences and cycles in group decisions support the latter interpretation. Several studies have tested the assumption of a simple unitary sequence of phases and found it untenable (Chandler 1981; Poole 1981). This and other research indicate that phases can occur in many possible orders, depending on various factors (Hirokawa 1983; Mintzberg et al. 1976). One such factor is the nature of the group's task: studies of phasic development in bargaining have shown an ordering of phases quite different from that obtained for problem-solving groups (Putnam and Jones 1982).

The complex nature of group activity types and the extreme variability of phases and phasic sequences suggests that there is a much wider range of group activities than has formerly been assumed and reinforces the notion that the traditional phases may be too restrictive. This certainly does not mean that group research is now in a period of "crisis." Rather it is what should be expected in an advancing discipline: existing concepts and models are used as stepping stones toward more accurate and encompassing positions (Toulmin 1972).

To summarize the thrust of the argument thus far, traditional phasic definitions—which emphasize isolating a simple set of periods of unified activity—are too general and too vague to encompass the diversity of group activities. Studies of group development show a far greater variety of activities than can be covered by any simple set of phases; they also suggest that prolonged, unified periods of activity may not always occur in groups. These conclusions imply that we should move away from the traditional conception of phases toward a more dynamic and flexible model.

Multiple Sequence Model of Decision Development

The model developed here attempts to avoid the oversimplifications of the phasic conception, yet at the same time account for the observable unity of much group activity. Rather than picturing group decision making as a series of phasic "blocks" dropped one after another into sequence, it portrays development as a set of parallel strands or tracks of activity which evolve simultaneously and interlock in different patterns over time.[1] Each track represents a separate aspect or mode of group activity—for example, task process or topic focus—and the various tracks are assumed to develop unevenly. For this reason, coherent, unified phases do

not exist at all points in a discussion. When the development of the tracks converges in a coherent pattern, phases similar to those in the classic research may be found. However, at other points there may be no relationship among the tracks and therefore no recognizable phases.

Activity Tracks. The group activity tracks form the core of the multiple sequence model. Previous research suggests that a minimal description of group decision making requires at least three activity tracks:

1. Task process activities: those activities the group enacts to manage its task.

2. Relational activities: those activities that reflect or manage relationships among group members as these relate to the group's work.

3. Topical focus: the substantive issues and arguments of concern to the group at a given point in the discussion.[2] Table 8.1 displays examples of categories for task process and relational activities.

Table 8.1

Classifications for Two Activity Types*

Task Process Activities	Relational Activities
Problem Activity T1. Problem Analysis	**Work-Focused Relationships** R1. Focused Work (no criticism; extended idea development and analysis) R2. Critical Work (idea development through criticism and repartee)
Executive Activity T2a. Orientation T2b. Process Reflection	
Solution Activity T3a. Establish Solution Guidelines T3b. Solution Design T3c. Solution Evaluation T3d. Solution Confirmation and Selection	**Conflict** R3a. Opposition R3b. Resolution-Accommodation R3c. Resolution-Avoidance/Smoothing R3d. Resolution-Integration (Bargaining/Consensus Building/Problem-Solving) **Integration** R4. Integration **Ambiguous Relationships** R5. Expression of Ambiguity

*Note: Both classifications represent the major distinctions in coding systems presently under development. The distinctions are based on previous research, notably Fisher, "Decision Emergence," Hirokawa, Mintzberg et al., and Poole, "Decision Development, II." Finer distinctions within some classifications are also being developed.

Even a cursory look at Table 8.1 indicates that other activity tracks could have been included in the model. Especially promising are the control strategies outlined by relational researchers (Rogers and Farace 1975; Folger and Poole 1981) and various conflict-management activities (Sillars 1980). Clearly, these could be incorporated into the model in future refinements. The three tracks outlined here represent a minimal model that clearly reflects the role of the decision task as a generative mechanism for developmental processes.

The three activity tracks enter into the multiple sequence model differently than they would in the phasic model. Phases would require coordinated sets of the three activity types, as when Tuckman characterizes his "forming" stage as a period in which the group is concerned with problem definition on the task level and defining relationships on the socioemotional level (Tuckman 1965). This implies that there would be a fairly restricted set of combinations available and when one combination (phase) came to a conclusion all elements in it would terminate—a given type of relational behavior could not continue once its corresponding task activity had ceased.

Breakpoints. Breakpoints are of key importance to an understanding of the developmental process because they represent developmental transitions. Breakpoints govern the group's pacing and serve as a good indicator of linkages among threads of activities. When breakpoints only interrupt a single track, this suggests that the track is operating somewhat independently of the others. When, on the other hand, the breakpoint interrupts all three tracks, the tracks are likely to be coordinated and the rupture may presage major, recognizable shifts in activity.

At least three types of breakpoints, each with very different implications for developmental processes, can be distinguished: (1) *Normal breakpoints* relate to the pacing of the discussion. The most common normal breakpoint is the topic shift, which may occur dozens of times as a group repeatedly doubles back to various topics (Scheidel and Crowell 1964). Two other normal break-points are natural breaks in activities such as adjournment or quitting time, and planning periods, in which one or more members attempt to organize the group. Normal breakpoints are more or less expected or sanctioned by the group; they are nothing unusual and the group copes with them as a matter of normal procedure. (2) *Delays* are a second type of breakpoint. Mintzberg et al. (1972) observed "comprehension cycles" in organizational decisions—periods when the decision process halted as the group worked out a problem by recycling through the same analysis or development process repeatedly. The point at which a group enters such a cycle is an important breakpoint because it signals a shift in the tenor of discussion. For all practical purposes the group is in a holding pattern until it makes a transition to another type of activity. Members do not ordinarily anticipate delays; depending on the nature of the delay and the mood of the group, this breakpoint can signal the start of a difficult or a highly creative period. (3) *Disruptions* are the third genre of breakpoints. At least two sorts of disruptions can be distinguished. First, a major disagreement or conflict may occur. When this happens in a very definite and salient manner, the group's activity is redirected and disrupted, and a major reorientation may be required for the group to proceed. Second, the group may fail—the strategies or solutions employed by the group may not be sufficient to its task. The importance of this breakpoint should be evident as should the fact that both disruptive breakpoints require considerable adjustment on the part of the group.

Summary: Advantages of the Multiple Sequence Model

The description of developmental processes elaborated here is based on a view of group process as a set of interlocking tracks of activities oriented toward task or goal accomplishment. The elements of the description are a set of three activity types, breakpoints signaling changes in group activity, and an objective for decision activity—the accumulation of structural components for task accomplishment. This description presents several advantages and also raises several questions.

One advantage of the model is the greater accuracy and finer resolution its descriptions promise. The model proposes an intertwining, multiple-sequence developmental process which is disrupted at a number of breakpoints that require reorganization of group effort. Together these three elements provide a description more accurately and finely attuned to the picture of group work emerging in recent years than does the phasic model.

A second advantage of the model is its greater flexibility relative to the phasic model. More and more varied combinations of activities can be observed, and this permits researchers to distinguish periods of unified activity (i.e., periods where phases exist) from periods which lack coherency or represent transitions in group activity.

A third advantage of the model stems from its inclusion of critical events in the developmental description. Through identifying breakpoints such as comprehension cycles or disruptions, the model enables the researcher to pinpoint an important class of critical incidents or turning points in group activity. This provides a valuable counterbalance to the standard methods of interaction analysis, which tend to assign equal weight to every act in group discussions.

Notes

1. This model is presaged in Scheidel and Crowell's "spiral model" of idea development, which has been elaborated considerably in B. Aubrey Fisher, *Small Group Decision-Making*, 2nd. ed. (New York: McGraw-Hill 1980).

2. Before proceeding any further, it is necessary to acknowledge that all descriptions are theory-laden (although the quality and explicitness of the theory differs from case to case). Rather than being a weakness, this is an advantage because it provides a link between present description and previous theoretical advances. The descriptive matrix derived here draws on the work of dozens of previous researchers and would not be possible without it. It is also necessary to acknowledge that

a "full description" is impossible if by this we mean a timeless, absolutely adequate picture. The best we can do is incorporate what we know of the culture's categories for understanding and acting in interaction. These categories emerge in participants' attempts to channel their discussions and in their reflections about their own activities, as well as in researchers' reports; over the years they appear repeatedly in studies from many different areas of research and form a bedrock for understanding group processes.

References

Bales, R. F. (1950). *Interaction Process Analysis: A Method for the Study of Small Groups.* Cambridge, MA: Addison-Wesley.

Bales, R. F., and Strodtbeck, F. L. (1951). "Phases in group problem solving." *Journal of Abnormal and Social Psychology* 46: 485–95

Bennis, W. G., and Shepard, H. A. (1956). "A theory of group development." *Human Relations* 9: 415–437.

Chandler, T. A. (1981). Decision-making in small groups: A comparison of two models. Unpublished master's thesis, Cleveland State University.

Cronin, T. E., and Thomas, N. C. (1971). "Federal advisory processes: Advice and discontent." *Science* 171: 771–779

Fisher, B. A. (1970). "Decision emergence: Phases in group decision-making." *Communication Monographs* 37: 53–66.

Folger, J. P., and Poole, M. S. (1981). "Relational coding schemes: The question of validity." In M. Burgoon (ed.), *Communication Yearbook 5.* New Brunswick, NJ: Transaction Press.

Hirokawa, R. Y. (1983). "Group communication and problem-solving effectiveness: An investigation of group phases." *Human Communication Research* 9: 291–305.

Ivancevich, J. M. (1974). "A study of a cognitive training program: Trainer styles and group development." *Academy of Management Journal* 17: 428–439.

Lacoursiere, R. (1980). *The Lifecycle of Groups.* New York: Human Sciences Press.

Mabry, E. A. (1975). "Exploratory analysis of a developmental model for task-oriented small groups." *Human Communication Research* 2, 66–74.

Mann, R. D. (1966). "The development of member-trainer relationships." *Human Relations* 19: 84–117.

Mintzberg, H., Raisinghani, D., and Theoret, A. (1976). "The structure of 'unstructured' decision processes." *Administrative Science Quarterly* 21: 246–275.

Morris, C. G. (1970). "Changes in group interaction during problem solving." *Journal of Social Psychology* 81: 157–165.

Poole, M. S. (1981). "Decision development in small groups, I: A comparison of two models." *Communication Monographs* 48: 1–24.

——. (1983). "Decision development in small groups, II: A study of multiple sequences in group development." *Communication Monographs* 50: 206–232.

Putnam, L. L. and Jones, T. S. (1982). "The role of communication in bargaining." *Human Communication Research* 8: 262–280.

Rogers, E. L., and Farace, R. V. (1975). "Analysis of relational communication in dyads: New measurement procedures." *Human Communication Research* 1: 222–239.

Runkell, P. J., Lawrence, M., Oldfield, S., Rider, M., and Clark, C. (1971). "Stages of group development: An empirical test of Tuckman's hypothesis." *Journal of Applied Behavioral Science* 7: 180–189.

Scheidel, T. M., and Crowell, L. (1964). "Idea development in small groups." *Quarterly Journal of Speech* 50: 140–145.

Sillars, A. (1980). "Attributions and communication in roommate conflicts." *Communication Monographs* 47: 180–200.

Toulmin, S. (1972). *Human Understanding.* Princeton, NJ: Princeton University Press.

Tudor, A. (1976). "Misunderstanding everyday life." *Sociological Review* 24: 479–503.

Webster's Third New International Dictionary (1961). Springfield, MA: G. C. Merriam.

Zurcher, L. A. (1969). "Stages of development in poverty program neighborhood action committees." *Journal of Applied Behavioral Science* 15: 223–258.

Abridged and edited from: Marshall Scott Poole, "Multiple Sequence Theory of Group Development." *Communication Monographs*, 50(4), December, 1983, pp. 321–341. Reprinted by permission of the National Communication Association. ✦

Part IV

Group Processes

Communication is a pervasive aspect of all groups. Whether we choose to work together or are forced into the company of others, group activity necessitates communication. The link between group activity and communication is so strong that studying one without the other is virtually impossible. This link is why many scholars believe that the study of small groups must invariably address the complexities of social interaction and group communication (Poole 1999).

Dimensions of Group Communication

What makes the study of small group communication so interesting—but at the same time so challenging—is that there are so many different facets of group communication to be concerned about. At a minimum, group communication scholars must differentiate between *verbal* and *nonverbal* communication.

Verbal communication is the creation of shared meaning among group members through the use of words. Words, spoken or written, gives group members a means for sharing ideas, influencing attitudes, and expressing emotion, but words can also build barriers and serve as a source of conflicts in groups. In contrast, *nonverbal communication* is the process of creating shared meaning through the use of nonlinguistic symbols. Nonlinguistic symbols include gestures, objects, actions, posture, facial expressions, eye contact, vocal qualities, and everything else not specifically identified as a word. Nonverbal symbols provide scholars information about the climate and culture of the group, as well as the personality and personal preferences of its individual members (Birdwhistle 1970).

In addition to differentiating between verbal and nonverbal communication, group communication scholars often need to distinguish between the *micro* and *macro* aspects of group communication. *Micro* aspects of group communication refer to the communication behaviors of individual group members. For example, a group communication researcher might be interested in discovering how information flows in a group by examining who talks to whom in the group, how often they talk to each other, and what they talk about. *Macro* aspects of group communication, on the other hand, are concerned with more general aspects of group communication. For example, instead of focusing on the types of communicative behaviors produced by individual group members, a researcher might be more interested in looking at larger aspects of group communication, such as the "metaphorical language" used by group members (Bormann 1996) or the "rhetorical functions" of group interaction (Poole and Hirokawa 1996).

Part IV examines the complexity of communication in small groups.

References

Birdwhistle, R. L. (1970). *Kinesics and Context.* Philadelphia: University of Pennsylvania Press.

Bormann, E. G. (1996). "Symbolic convergence theory and communication in group decision-making." In R. Y. Hirokawa and M. S. Poole (eds.), *Communication and Group Decision-Making* (pp. 81–113). Thousand Oaks, CA: Sage.

Poole, M. S. (1999). "Group communication theory." In L. R. Frey, M. S. Poole, and D. S. Gouran (eds.), *The Handbook of Group Communication Theory and Research* (pp. 37–70). Thousand Oaks, CA: Sage.

Poole, M. S., and Hirokawa, R. Y. (1996). "Introduction: Communication and group decision-making." In R. Y. Hirokawa and M. S. Poole (eds.), *Communication and Group Decision-Making* (pp. 3–18). Thousand Oaks, CA: Sage. ✦

Chapter 9
Spatial Relationships in Small Groups

Judee K. Burgoon

Burgoon focuses on an important dimension of nonverbal communication in small groups—spatial relationships. She explains how informal space and fixed feature and semi-fixed feature space relate to and influence comfort, status, leadership, interaction patterns, relational communication, and spatial deviancy in small groups.

An old German fable has it that one fall night, the porcupines came together in the forest for a little socializing. Finding the night air to be quite cold, they tried to move close together for warmth but found they kept pricking each other with their quills. So they moved farther apart but once again became cold. They continued moving back and forth until they finally arrived at a distance that afforded them both warmth and comfort. Henceforth, that distance became known as good manners.

Like the porcupines, we humans also seek optimal spacing arrangements when in groups. Our *proxemic* patterns—the ways in which we perceive, utilize, and arrange our spatial environment—seem to be governed by two competing needs. One is the *need for affiliation.* We are social creatures who desire to associate with other people and to form bonds of attachment with them. Close proximity both signals that desire and permits those social bonds to develop.

The other requirement is a *need for privacy.* There are times when we wish to distance ourselves from the group to achieve greater physical security, to escape stimulation and stress, to gain a greater sense of personal control, or to permit greater psychological freedom and self-reflection. Greater distance provides a form of insulation, a cushion against intrusions from others.

These two conflicting needs sometimes lead us to approach the group and sometimes to avoid it. Typically, group spacing behavior reflects an equilibrium state in which these approach-avoidance tendencies are brought into balance within individual members and among members of the group. Because our proxemic patterns relate to some of our most fundamental human needs, proxemic behaviors, and especially deviations from the equilibrium or expected spatial arrangement, can convey some very powerful albeit subtle messages.

The Organization of Space

There are two perspectives from which group spacing behavior can be examined. One is to consider the nature of the people involved and the purposes of the interaction factors that dictate how individuals choose to distance themselves from one another. This aspect of spacing is what the anthropologist Edward T. Hall has called *informal space.*[1] The second is to consider what constraints on spacing are imposed by the environment, or the arrangement of what Hall calls *fixed feature* and *semi-fixed feature* space.[2] At any point in time, the proxemic patterns of a group will be influenced by both considerations.

Informal Space

This facet of proxemic behavior concerns how we orient toward and distance ourselves from other members of the group. Whether that group be our family, a circle of friends at a social gathering, a committee working on a task, or a department within an organization, we will have characteristic distances that we adopt and characteristic means of insuring that those distances are maintained. These spacing patterns usually operate outside our conscious awareness but are of great importance. As Hall has said,

"... informal spatial patterns have distinct bounds, and such deep, if unvoiced, significance that they form an essential part of the culture. To misunderstand this significance may invite disaster."[3]

There are three levels at which informal space can be analyzed. One is *territoriality*. A territory is a fixed, geographically identifiable space to which an individual or group has laid claim. An obvious example is one's home or neighborhood. These often have *territorial markers* such as fences, signs, or locks that clearly signal boundaries and degree of accessibility to "outsiders."

There are also other kinds of territories to which we lay claim, however, ones for which the right of possession may be more ambiguous. Have you ever noticed that in a classroom, many people gravitate to the same seat time after time? They come to feel it is "their" seat. If someone else then sits in it, they feel their territory has been violated. At public beaches, we claim a space for ourselves and attempt to ward off intrusions by spreading out towels and other personal possessions as territorial markers, even though the space actually belongs not to us but the public at large.

This territorial urge seems to be deep-seated and possibly innate. By demarcating a tangible geographic area under our personal control we apparently gain a greater sense of security and autonomy. In times past, the ability to secure and defend a territory undoubtedly had survival value. Today, one's physical survival may not be at stake (street gangs defending their turf being one exception), but the ability to maintain a territory provides greater protection and privacy for the individual and for the group. Consequently, when our territory is violated, even when the violation seems unintended or inconsequential, we react strongly. Archie Bunker's vitriolic reactions to people sitting in "his" chair are a prime example. Because territorial invasions provoke such strong emotional reactions and may lead to physical aggression, it is important to understand how individuals within groups express their territorial proclivities and how groups in turn operate on these territorial imperatives.

The instincts that give rise to territorial behavior also shape a second level of informal spacing behavior that has been identified: *personal space*. In contrast to the visible and fixed nature of territory, personal space is an invisible, flexible, and portable "bubble" of space that surrounds us. It expands and contracts according to our needs and the situation. It may be very large when we are interacting with a hostile stranger and may temporarily disappear entirely in an intimate situation. As with territorial invasions, personal space invasions arouse and distress us. We will therefore want to consider how groups can recognize these distress signals and can arrange themselves in ways to minimize such stress.

Our personal space needs in turn determine the third level of informal spacing: *conversational distance*. This is the distance at which we normally conduct face-to-face interactions. This may coincide with or exceed the personal space needs of the individual participants. It permits a measure of spatial insulation and comfort, and is largely governed by cultural norms. Hall attempted to identify four categories of interpersonal distance that correspond to different sensory experiences and different interaction purposes. His widely accepted categories are as follows:

1. *Intimate distance* (0–18 inches)—a distance reserved for physical contact or intimate encounters and entailing high sensory involvement.

2. *Personal distance* (1½–4 feet)—a distance used for close interpersonal relationships or more private discussion topics; it entails a high degree of kinesthetic involvement but doesn't have the same impact on cutaneous, visual, olfactory, auditory, and thermal receptors as does intimate distance.

3. *Social distance* (4–12 feet)—a range of distances used for informal social activity, business consultations, and other relatively impersonal encounters; this distance category is outside the range of touch and involves less sensory impact.

4. *Public distance* (12 feet and beyond)—a distance reserved for highly formal encounters, platform presentations, and interactions with public figures; this distance minimizes kinesthetic involvement and requires a louder speaking voice than normal.[4]

While these distance categories have proven useful in elevating awareness that people adjust distances according to the intimacy level of their interpersonal relationships and conversational topics, some social science research (to be discussed shortly) indicates that these categories fail to capture the complexity of the norms governing spacing behavior. For example, gender, age, degree of acquaintance, social status, and personality, among other factors, will all dictate the normative distance for a given interaction.[5] If groups are to maximize their effectiveness, they must recognize how these various factors influence the behaviors and desires of individual members.

Fixed Feature and Semi-Fixed Feature Space

This facet of proxemic behavior encompasses the ways in which architecture, interior design, furniture arrangement, and the like influence spacing behavior. Fixed feature space, as the name implies, concerns the spacing patterns resulting from permanent structures such as walls, doorways, and the configuration or use of those spaces. For example, in this culture we divide homes into a number of smaller compartments, some of which become individual bedrooms, some of which are designated for private and personal hygiene activities (bathrooms), and some of which are available for multiple functions (e.g., family rooms).

Fixed features of the environment may dictate what proxemic patterns people establish among themselves. The volume of space available is one major influence. Take the case of a committee assembling to plan campaign strategy. If they meet in a large hall, they may adopt rather close seating positions in the center of the room but distribute themselves evenly within the space. This permits an audible conversation while giving everyone a "share" of the space around the perimeter of the group. If, instead, the committee meets in a small conference room, members may distribute themselves unevenly and closer to the walls to maximize their spatial freedom.

The normal functions of the environment may also constrain behavior. If the committee meets in the family room of someone's home, the informality associated with the room may encourage more informal seating arrangements. On the other hand, if the committee is forced to meet in the sanctuary of a church, the normal reverent behavior elicited in this environment, coupled with the large volume of space, may cause people to cluster close together so that they can speak in hushed tones.

Semi-fixed feature space refers to the proxemic arrangements resulting from movable environmental structures such as partitions and furniture. As with fixed feature space, the configuration of these elements at a given point in time will affect how people distance themselves from one another. A formal conference table, for example, specifies one kind of spacing pattern; sofas in a lounge necessitate another.

Environmental psychologists have identified two different arrangements of semi-fixed feature space that produce very different kinds of interaction. One is a *sociopetal* arrangement. This pattern, as exemplified in Figure 9.1, brings people together. Well-designed restaurants, bars, or living rooms use a sociopetal spatial pattern to facilitate interaction among people. By contrast, *sociofugal* patterns turn people away from one another and discourage interaction. These types of arrangements, as illustrated in Figure 9.1, are commonly found in public places such as hotel lobbies or airports, where social interaction and loitering are intentionally discouraged. Psychologist Robert Som-

Figure 9.1

Top, *Examples of Sociopetal Arrangements;*
Bottom, *Examples of Sociofugal Arrangements*

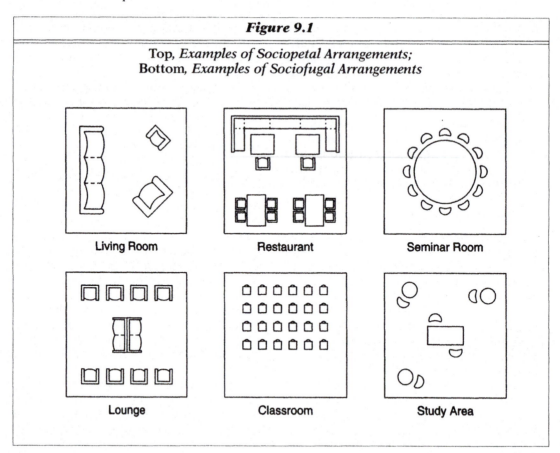

| Living Room | Restaurant | Seminar Room |
| Lounge | Classroom | Study Area |

mer also found this pattern in state institutions such as hospitals. Often chairs lined the walls of lounges so as to ease the work of custodians and orderlies. Sommer found that after he rearranged the chairs to create a sociopetal space, previously depressed and noncommunicative patients showed significant improvement in their mental health and their ability to relate to others.[6] His observations confirmed the profound effects that environmentally imposed spacing can have on our emotional states, our behavior, and our relationships with other people.

Having identified the various perspectives from which the organization of space can be analyzed, we are now ready to consider in greater specificity how proxemic patterns relate to small group communication. Of interest will be how proxemics regulate our interactions and what messages are implied by various spatial behaviors.

Comfort

Underlying all of the effects of proxemics on human behavior is how comfortable people are with the amount of space provided them. If we were to trust Hall's distance categories as a guide, we would assume that anything closer than eighteen inches would typically be an uncomfortable interaction distance because it is an intimate distance and therefore reserved for only the most personal and arousing interchanges. In fact, a classmate of mine and I set out to demonstrate this in a study we conducted as graduate students. However, we got some unexpected results.[7]

Our primary interest was in discovering what kinds of classroom seating arrangements are most conducive to comfort, attention, learning, and participation. We hypothesized that students, given the opportunity to voluntarily arrange their classroom, would select distances apart that exceeded eighteen inches. (We also had some expectations about what pattern they would choose in which to arrange the chairs.) We selected some classrooms that had movable chairs and prior to the students arriving for class, pushed all of the chairs into a jumble in the center of the room. After the students had arrived and created their own arrangement, we entered the room, measured the distances between chairs, recorded the arrangement, and gave students a grid on which to record their preferred classroom arrangement.

The unexpected result from the study was that students voluntarily placed themselves an average of seventeen inches apart. This was greater than the average distance of thirteen inches that we found in comparable, undisturbed classrooms, but still less than we had anticipated. We concluded that people are able to tolerate relatively close distances without becoming uncomfortable and in fact may prefer some degree of closeness. The results also made us aware that the four distance categories alone do not give us enough information; a number of other factors need to be taken into account in ascertaining at what distances people are most likely to be comfortable.

Research suggests that there are three kinds of considerations that will determine what the normative, and presumably most comfortable, distance is for a given interaction. These considerations include the nature of the people in the group, the nature of the interaction itself, and the environmental constraints. Regarding people characteristics, the following have all been identified as important:[8]

1. *Gender:* Females sit and stand closer to other females than do males interacting with one another. The research is mixed on whether opposite-sex pairs adopt closer distances than female-female pairs. Specifically, in a group setting females tolerate crowding far better than males and may respond in a more intimate, pleasant way to close proximity, while males may respond with aggressive, unpleasant reactions.

2. *Cultural background:* Some cultures interact at closer distances than others. Those who are accustomed to close proximity during face-to-face encounters are called contact cultures. Those that display more distant interaction patterns are called noncontact cultures. The United States in general is considered a noncontact culture, although many subcultural groups (such as those from southern Europe, the Middle East or Central America) would qualify as contact groups.

3. *Race:* The research here is very mixed but there is some evidence that black males in the United States adopt the greatest distances and black females adopt the closest, compared to white males and females. Blacks also appear to have a more fluid approach to distancing, as compared to the more static (fixed) pattern exhibited by whites.

4. *Age:* People maintain closer distances with people who are the same age than with those who are younger or older than they are, even if the older person is a parent.

5. *Status:* Like age, the greater the differential between interactants, the greater the distance.

6. *Degree of acquaintance:* Not surprisingly, people adopt the closest distances with close friends, adopt intermediate distances with acquaintances, and maintain the greatest distance from strangers.

7. *Personality:* Different personality types have characteristic distances they adopt from others. For example, introverts and highly anxious individuals require more space than their extroverted or less anxious counterparts. Some research with violent prisoners has documented that they require as much as twice the space that nonviolent prisoners need, suggesting that the discomfort they experience in close proximity to others

may be a factor in their aggressive tendencies.

Other people factors no doubt also play a role. In addition, the nature of the interaction itself influences how comfortable people are likely to feel. For example, if the group is gathering for a social purpose, people will expect and be comfortable at closer distances. If the purpose is a formal meeting or a task-oriented discussion, they may be more comfortable at greater distances.

The environment plays a role by setting limits on the options available to people. In a living room situation, if people have a choice they will usually opt for across seating. This is particularly true if the available side-by-side seating is one to three feet. However, if the across seating exceeds three and one-half feet, and especially if it is farther away than an alternative side-by-side seat that is at a reasonable distance, people will choose to sit alongside another. This implies that the "arc for comfortable conversation" is about a five and one-half foot distance nose-to-nose.

If the available seating arrangement forces people into close proximity, such as in an auditorium, a classroom, or a small meeting room, people may adapt temporarily, recognizing that the proximity between themselves and their neighbors has been imposed upon them rather than being a matter of choice. One way that people adapt is to develop a *nonperson orientation*. This means essentially acting as if the other person were not present or were merely an object. This is exactly how people adjust to being confined in an elevator with a group of strangers. They look straight ahead, avoid contact with the other riders, and pretend that they are unbothered by the closeness of the others.

Collectively, all research on proxemic norms indicates that the process of arriving at a comfortable distance is a rather complex one. It is governed by a large number of factors that must all be brought into balance. This becomes particularly complicated in a group situation, where there is a mix of individual characteristics and preferences that must be accommodated. Fortunately, the research also reveals that we are adaptable creatures who can tolerate deviations from our preferred spacing for short periods of time.

Nevertheless, we have strong physiological reactions to inappropriate spacing and over a period of time will display evidence of our discomfort. Studies have shown that, compared to being in close physical proximity to a paper figure or an object (such as a hat rack), people manifest much greater physical arousal (as measured by galvanic skin response) when their personal space is invaded by another person.[9] Other reactions to spatial invasions that have been documented include: (1) displaying anxiety through such behaviors as restless leg and foot movements, fidgeting with objects, scratching the head, and touching oneself; (2) sometimes staring hostilely at the intruder but more often avoiding eye contact; (3) erecting barriers with personal possessions such as books or coats; (4) erecting "body blocks"—shading the eyes or putting arms and elbows between oneself and the intruder; (5) increasing distance by leaning away, moving farther apart, or reorienting the body away from the intruder; and (6) if the invasion is prolonged, taking flight (i.e., actually leaving the situation altogether). It is interesting to note that people rarely respond to an invasion or experience of crowding verbally. Rather, they rely on nonverbal signals to reveal their discomfort and to ward off continued intrusion.

If it can be assumed that discomfort reduces a group member's satisfaction and the quality of his or her contributions to group process, then groups would be wise to watch for these symptoms of spatial inadequacy and attempt to compensate for them. As a minimum it might mean making adjustments between members within a location. As a maximum it might mean finding a different location in which to interact.

Status and Leadership

As noted earlier, status confers the privilege of greater spatial insularity. Politicians, celebrities, and corporate presidents are always accorded greater distances from those of lesser status. The story is told that when John F. Kennedy became president, friends with whom he had formerly socialized suddenly began observing an invisible threshold some thirty feet from him that they would not cross until he first breached the distance. It served as eloquent recognition of the significant change in status he had achieved.

People in positions of status and power enjoy other proxemic privileges. They are permitted to initiate whatever seating arrangement or distance is going to be observed, they are free to violate spatial norms, they have access to more and better territory, and they are accorded more privacy.[10]

In the context of small group communication, individuals of power and status often emerge as group leaders, or the person designated as leader takes on status and power by virtue of his or her position. Therefore, these proxemic power relations should and do have analogues in the group setting.

The high-status individual and/or group leader typically occupies the best position in the group. Selecting the best position, in turn, confers status on its occupant and the expectation that the individual will demonstrate leadership. Research has shown that leaders, high-status members, and dominant individuals gravitate toward the end positions of a rectangular table; that is, they take the head of the table, or they choose to sit opposite the most other people. In unacquainted groups, the people who select these positions will more often be perceived as the leader, and people placed in these positions will be induced to become more dominant in the ensuing interactions.[11]

For those wishing to have influence in a group, the implications are clear: Choose a spot that places you at the symbolic head of the group or across from the most other people. If your goal is to elicit more leadership from a particular member, place him or her in one of those positions. If your goal is merely to identify who in a group is most likely serving as its leader, look for the individual around whom the spatial arrangement revolves, who is accorded more space, and who occupies a central position within the group.

Interaction Patterns

Just as group proxemics affect leadership emergence and vice versa, so do proxemic patterns influence the ways in which the group communicates. Proximity in itself encourages interaction. The act of bringing people together usually impels them to speak to one another. Even a group of strangers will often strike up a conversation if placed in close proximity long enough. In a classroom, unacquainted individuals seated next to one another will often develop a friendship before the term is over. There is even a high rate of marriages among people who live within six blocks of each other!

Physical closeness alone is a powerful force determining to whom we will talk. The "who" and "how" of small group communication also depend on the existing furniture arrangement and the purposes of interaction.

One type of group context that has been frequently studied is the classroom. It will be recalled that in my study with Pat Garner, we observed what spatial arrangements students adopted and asked them what arrangement they would prefer so as to maximize participation, learning, and attention. Overwhelmingly, students expressed a preference for a U-shaped or circular arrangement and tended to approximate such an arrangement when they placed their own chairs in the room. This preference seems to be based on two considerations: the proximity and visual access to one another and to the instructor that this arrangement affords to students.

Other classroom research supports the importance of the twin elements of proximity and eye contact. Classrooms with straight-row seating tend to produce the greatest interaction from the front and center seats, creating almost a "triangle of participation." It should be obvious that such seats, by virtue of their spatial and visual access to the instructor, make it easier to see the teacher and gain his or her attention. Similarly, classrooms with laboratory seating (i.e., everyone seated around small lab tables) produce the greatest amount of total participation, presumably because students are close to one another and can maintain a high degree of eye contact with one another. Proximity alone, however, apparently is not sufficient to induce equal participation. In seminar seating arrangements (i.e., everyone seated around one large table), the most participation comes from those opposite the instructor and the least comes from those seated at the instructor's side. So long as the instructor takes an active role in leading the group, most interaction comes from those who can maintain eye contact with the instructor.[12]

In small group discussions, the same principle holds: Whoever is in the most central position or has visual access to the most other people is likely to participate the most. This conclusion must be tempered somewhat by the nature of the interaction and the presence or absence of a strong leader. There is some evidence that task discussions produce more "across" interaction, while social discussions produce more "alongside" interaction. However, the presence of a directive leader may also encourage more conversation among people seated next to one another.[13]

The nature of the task also affects people's preferences for a seating arrangement. A number of studies have demonstrated that people prefer corner-to-corner or side-by-side seating for cooperative and conversational activities. They prefer opposite seating for competitive activities. One study even suggests that competitors prefer some degree of distance which pemits surveillance of one's opponent. When people are engaged in coaction (i.e., they are engaged in simultaneous, noninteracting activities) they prefer greater separation and less opportunity for direct eye contact.[14] These preferences suggest that when planning seating arrangements for group activities, one could facilitate cooperative and social interchange by placing people close together but with some ability to make eye contact with one another (as in a circular or "catty-corner" arrangement). If the activities require competition,

somewhat greater distance is desirable with a concomitant increase in the ability to make direct eye contact with one's competitors.

Relational Communication

An aspect of proxemic behavior that is gaining recognition is the relational messages that are conveyed by distance and seating selection. Relational messages are statements that help define the nature of a relationship: whether people like each other, how involved they are in the relationship, who is controlling the relationship, and so forth. Usually such messages are expressed nonverbally, and one of the chief nonverbal channels through which they are communicated is proxemics.

One of the more obvious relational messages signalled proxemically is liking and attraction. Musical lyrics speak of being "close to you," of "getting together," and "the nearness of you." We show our attraction and favorable regard for others by moving closer to them physically and we show our dislike by distancing ourselves. If people choose to sit near us in a group meeting, we take that as a sign of their affection or positive regard for us. Conversely, if they elect to sit at the opposite end of the room, we may interpret that as a message that we are being rejected.

In a similar vein, we interpret distance as a message of involvement. If someone sits very close, orients himself or herself so as to face us directly and/or leans forward, we take that as an indication that this person is very interested in what we have to say, that he or she is involved in our relationship. Certainly that kind of closeness insures high-sensory involvement. If, on the other hand, someone takes a more distal position, orients himself or herself more indirectly (that is, faces away to some degree), or leans away from us, we are likely to read detachment into such behavior. We think that the individual is uninterested in us personally, in our conversation, or in our total relationship; however, the person may simply be expressing a desire for greater privacy.

Another kind of message we may read into a person's distancing behavior is how aroused and uncomfortable, or relaxed and composed, that person is in our presence. Because people in a rage or a high state of emotional arousal often move extremely close to others, sometimes even putting their noses in others' faces, we tend to equate extreme proximity with more arousal and less self-control. By contrast, someone who is very relaxed may lean sideways or backward (if in a chair), thereby increasing the distance to some degree. This creates some difficulty for us in the interpretation of proxemic relational messages because we could interpret backward leaning as having either the negative connotations of lack of interest and disregard or the positive connotation of relaxation. We could likewise construe close proximity as a sign of affection and attraction, or as a sign of hostile emotional activation. In other words, the meaning of the proxemic message may be ambiguous by itself. In practice, we rely on other nonverbal cues and the verbal content to decide which interpretation to select.

One final set of meanings associated with spatial behavior further compounds our interpretation task; these concern dominance and control. We have already noted that high-status individuals and group leaders maintain greater distances between themselves and others, and in group meetings tend to occupy the most central, controlling position. The selection of distance or seating position by such individuals not only is instrumental in their gaining control of the group, it also conveys the relational message that they are dominant. By contrast, those adopting subordinate or submissive roles wait for more dominant individuals to dictate the pattern to be observed and may find their personal space violated by the more powerful individuals.

The knowledge that proxemic choices carry relational meaning can be used to your advantage. If you wish to make a group member feel better liked and accepted, you can place him or her in closer proximity to others. If you instead want to communicate rejection and exclusion, you can symbolically convey that message by placing the person at the periphery of the group. If you wish to elicit greater participation on someone's part, you can convey your own interest in what this person has to say by moving closer, facing him or her more directly, and leaning forward. Finally, you can assert power and dominance by violating another's territory or distancing yourself (both of which are ploys that have been recommended for people seriously engaged in power games). If you wish to communicate submissiveness or deference, you may do so by waiting for another's proxemic initiative and then conforming to the pattern that person establishes.[15]

Effects of Spatial Deviancy

Some of the recommendations in the last section may have struck you as unorthodox because most writers in the area of nonverbal communication tell you to conform to the norms if you want to be successful. At least that is the dictum in most popular literature. For some time I have felt that conformity to the norms may not always be the best strategy. Therefore, my colleagues, students, and I undertook a series of experiments to test this thesis.

The initial research began with the premise that deviations from the normative or expected distance may have positive or negative communication consequences, depending on who engages in the distance violation. After some false starts, my cohorts and I arrived at the following predictions: People who are "rewarding," that is, who are high status, attractive, givers of positive feedback, controllers of tangible rewards, or favorably regarded for some other reason, have the freedom to violate distancing expectations with impunity. In small group language, they have idiosyncratic credits; they are allowed to be deviants at no or little cost. Moreover, when they engage in a violation, they arouse the "victim," making him or her more attentive to the relationship between violator and victim. In the process of searching out explanations for the arousal, they become more conscious of the violator's rewarding characteristics and therefore choose to select positive connotations for the violator's proxemic behavior. The final result is that the violator gains even better communication outcomes than if he or she had conformed to the norm.

In the case of a less rewarding person, for example, someone who is unattractive, who is unpleasant to be around, who is always criticizing, or who is of low status, exactly the opposite predictions are made. Violations of the expected distance—moving closer or farther away—has negative consequences because the aroused victim is more sensitized to the violator's negative characteristics and ascribes more unfavorable meanings to the violator's proxemic behavior. For example, a "close" violation is seen as pushy or threatening; a "far" violation is seen as dislike or lack of interest. People who enter a situation with few rewards to offer the recipients, then, are better off conforming to the norms.

A series of experiments has largely supported these predictions. What is of special interest here is one study we conducted using small groups. We wanted to see whether violations would still be effective for a "high-reward" person when in the presence of another rewarding individual who did not deviate. We wanted to see how it would affect ability to influence others and how it would affect the individual's credibility and attraction. At the same time, we were interested in whether the negative consequences for a "low-reward" person would become even worse if that individual engaged in deviant behavior in the presence of another nonrewarding individual who did not deviate.

In brief, this is how we designed the experiment: We told subjects that they were going to participate in a small group activity intended to test the effects of different sizes of juries on decision making. They were told they had been assigned to a three-person group. Unknown to them, the other two members of the group were our confederates who were dressed to be physically attractive and given more prestigious background in their introductions (high-reward condition) or were made to look unattractive and given

less prestigious background (low-reward). One confederate presented defense arguments from an actual murder trial and one presented prosecution arguments. The subject was asked to serve as an undecided member. In the process of presenting their arguments, the confederates either maintained their initial distance (normative condition) or one of them engaged in a violation, moving eighteen inches closer (close violation) or eighteen inches farther (far violation) than the initial distance.

The results were intriguing and have real implications for actual group processes. In the high-reward discussions, the deviating confederate was more persuasive and rated as more attractive, competent, and of good character when he or she engaged in a distance violation—particularly a far violation. This was true both when compared to his or her own results in the normative condition and when compared to the other, non-deviating confederate. In other words, deviant behavior improved the person's influence and interpersonal evaluations relative to conforming to the norm and relative to another rewarding group member. In the low-reward discussions, distance violations lowered the confederate's perceived persuasiveness and caused him or her to lose ground on persuasiveness, sociability, and attraction, as compared to the other nondeviating confederate. In other words, the nonrewarding person's deviant behavior tended to confer greater credibility and persuasiveness on his or her opponent. These results thus strongly suggest that deviant proxemic behavior may pay off for people who are well-regarded by the rest of the group. For those who are less well-regarded, the main beneficiaries of their deviant behavior are their opponents.[16]

Summary

It should be clear from this brief review that proxemic patterns play a subtle but powerful role in human interactions. People's proxemic behavior reflects competing needs between desires for affiliation and desires for privacy. Usually, the distance or seating position they adopt will indicate at what distance they feel comfortable in that context with those participants. The voluntarily selected or environmentally imposed spatial relationships may signal or influence who exercises leadership, may affect who talks to whom on what kinds of topics, and may convey messages about the interpersonal relationships among group members. Finally, contrary to popular opinion, spatial deviancy may sometimes prove profitable in gaining greater control over the group and/or improving others' evaluations of one's credibility and attractiveness.

Notes

1. Edward T. Hall, "The Anthropology of Space: An Organizing Model," in H. M. Proshansky, W. H. Ittelson, and L. G. Rivlin (eds.), *Environmental Psychology: Man and His Physical Setting* (New York: Holt, Rinehart & Winston, 1970), 16–27.

2. Ibid.

3. Ibid., 20.

4. Edward T. Hall, *The Silent Language* (Garden City, NJ: Doubleday, 1959).

5. Judee K. Burgoon and Stephen B. Jones, "Toward a Theory of Personal Space Expectations and Their Violations," *Human Communication Research*, (1976), 131–146.

6. Robert Sommer, *Personal Space: The Behavioral Basis of Design* (Englewood Cliffs, NJ: Prentice-Hall, 1969).

7. Judee K. Heston and Patrick Garner, "A Study of Personal Spacing and Desk Arrangement in the Learning Environment," Paper presented to the International Communication Association convention, Atlanta, April 1972.

8. For a review of research on norms, see Burgoon and Jones, op. cit., and Judee K. Burgoon and Thomas Saine, *The Unspoken Dialogue: An Introduction to Nonverbal Communication* (Boston: Houghton Mifflin, 1978), 93–96.

9. Ibid. Also see Judee K. Heston, "Effects of Anomia and Personal Space Invasion on Anxiety, Non-Person Orientation and Source Credibility," *Central States Speech Journal* 25 (1974), 19–27.

10. For a comprehensive summary of proxemic correlates of status and power, see Nancy M. Henley, *Body Politics* (Englewood Cliffs, NJ: Prentice-Hall, 1977).

11. For some of the classic research in this area, see A. Paul Hare and Robert F. Bales, "Seating Pattern and Small Group Interaction," *Sociometry* 26 (1963), 480–486; L. T. Howells and S. W. Becker, "Seating Arrangement and Leadership Emergence," *Journal of Abnormal and Social Psychology* 64 (1962), 148–150; D. F. Lott and Robert Sommer, "Seating Arrangements and Status," *Journal of Personality and Social Psychology* 7 (1967), 90–95; F. L. Strodtbeck and L. H. Hook, "The Social Dimensions of a Twelve Man Jury Table," *Sociometry* 24 (1961), 397–415; Robert Sommer, "Leadership and Group Geography," *Sociometry* 24 (1961), 499–510; Charles D. Ward, "Seating Arrangement and Leadership Emergence in Small Discussion Groups," *Journal of Social Psychology* 74 (1968), 83–90. See also Marvin E. Shaw, *Group Dynamics: The Psychology of Small Group Behavior* (New York: McGraw-Hill, 1971), 117–154.

12. For a review of this literature, see Heston and Garner; Sommer, 1969.

13. Some of the original research in this area includes Hare and Bales; G. Hearn, "Leadership and the Spatial Factor in Small Groups," *Journal of Abnormal and Social Psychology* 54 (1957), 269–272; Bernard Steinzor, "The Spatial Factor in Face to Face Discussion Groups," *Journal of Abnormal and Social Psychology* 45 (1950), 552–555; Strodtbeck and Hook.

14. M. Cook, "Experiments on Orientation and Proxemics," *Human Relations* 23 (1970), 61–76; Gary A. Norum, Nancy Jo Russo, and Robert Sommer, "Seating Patterns and Group Task," *Psychology of the Schools* 4 (1967), 276–280; Robert Sommer, "Studies of Small Group Ecology" in R. S. Cathcart and L.A. Samovar (eds.), *Small Group Communication: A Reader* 2d ed. (Dubuque, IA: Wm. C. Brown, 1974), 283–293.

15. For reviews of relevant literature and a report of one experiment on relational communication, see Judee K. Burgoon, "Privacy and Communication," in M. Burgoon (ed.), *Communication Yearbook* 6 (Beverly Hills, CA: Sage Publications, 1982), 206–249; Judee K. Burgoon, David B. Buller, Jerold L. Hale, and Mark deTurck, "Relational Messages Associated with Immedi-

acy Behaviors," paper presented to the International Communication Association convention, Boston, May 1982.

16. For the details of this particular study, see Judee K. Burgoon, Don W. Stacks, and Steven A. Burch, "The Role of Interpersonal Rewards and Violations of Distancing Expectations in Achieving Influence in Small Groups," *Communication: Journal of the Association of the Pacific* 11 (1982), 114–128. For a review of research on proxemic violations of expectations, see Judee K. Burgoon, "Nonverbal Violations of Expectations," in J. Wiemann and R. Harrison (eds.), *Nonverbal Interaction* 11, Sage Annual Reviews of Communication, (Beverly Hills, CA: Sage, 1983).

Chapter 10
Feedback Processes in Task Groups

Beth Bonniwell Haslett
John R. Ogilvie

This chapters focuses on feedback in small groups—that is, the messages that group members send each other regarding events and processes in the group. The authors elaborate on the dimensions of feedback, review what is known about the relationship between feedback and group performance, and conclude with a discussion of feedback as a communication process. They also examine some of the major factors that influence feedback in small groups, such as trustworthiness, power and status, and communication style.

Human communication involves dialogue between at least two people. An essential part of this dialogue is *feedback*, the response listeners give to others about their behavior. Both communicators give feedback—they respond to each other's behavior. Feedback from others enables us to understand how our behavior affects them, and allows us to modify our behavior to achieve desired goals. Finally, feedback is essential for personal growth and development since others' responses to our behavior help us define our identities.

The setting in which feedback occurs is also important. Task groups, like any work context, are rich in information (Hanser and Muchinsky 1978). Considerable research suggests that individuals actively seek information about themselves and their role in the group (Ashford and Cummings 1983; Larson 1984). A key motivator for this search is uncertainty. It is this uncertainty that gives feedback its value (Ashford and Cummings 1983). When uncertain, individuals feel a tension or uneasiness and seek to reduce those feelings through feedback from others. Early stages of group development are fraught with uncertainty; members are tentative and reluctant to take action. Thus, in task-oriented groups, feedback is a primary means of reducing uncertainty and moving the group along to productive ends.

The function of feedback in systems and cybernetics has long been recognized. Negative feedback acts to correct deviations in the performance of a system that serves to stabilize and maintain it. An example will help to clarify this point. A thermostat in a house controls the furnace by giving the furnace feedback. When the temperature in the house falls below a certain point, say 60 degrees for the brave and energy conscious, the thermostat signals this drop to the furnace, which then starts up. When the temperature rises to a certain level, the thermostat signals a shutdown and the furnace no longer runs. This is an example of a closed loop system, using negative feedback. The thermostat uses only one type of information, which serves to maintain a relatively steady state of room temperature.

Positive feedback in systems terminology is not "good news." It is the amplification of deviations that act to destabilize a system. A manager may at times amplify a disagreement for constructive ends. The disagreement serves as a basis for making changes, which are temporarily destabilizing but beneficial in the long run. Humans, however, do not function as *closed systems* restricted to only limited forms of information. Interpersonal feedback occurs in an open system setting, using negative and positive feedback features. As such, it is varied, flexible, and gathered from a variety of sources.

This article will focus on feedback processes in small task groups. Task groups are a collection of individuals who work interdependently on a task to accomplish a goal. They are different from informal or friendship groups in that they have a specific purpose to achieve or accomplish. Task groups could include a group of four students required to make a presentation on the dangers of acid rain or a task force in a corporation deciding on which configuration of computer technology to acquire. We all belong to task groups, whether they are in work organizations or social clubs. Groups interact over time to reach goals and satisfy needs (Palazzolo 1981). They also evolve a structure for individual roles and norms to guide behavior. For the group, feedback provides important information on group interaction and group performance. Feedback can improve the effectiveness of group performance since it provides information about how successful the group has been and gives specific suggestions for improvement.

Our research has tried to understand what makes some feedback work more effectively than others. In this paper we will draw on the results of a recently completed study (Ogilvie and Haslett 1985), in which we videotaped a group of students who had to complete several tasks. They were also required to meet and exchange feedback with one another. We then played the videotape of the feedback session to other students several semesters later and asked them to evaluate the way in which feedback was exchanged. Thus, our conclusions are based on our research of task groups, and our suggestions for giving feedback effectively are based on our own personal experiences with groups. In what follows, we will present a discussion of the nature of the feedback process, and the factors influencing the feedback process, and we will offer suggestions for giving feedback effectively.

The Nature of Feedback

Given the important functions of feedback for group performance, it seems crucial that a clear understanding of feedback be developed. However, feedback as a concept and as a process is poorly understood. Scholars analyzing feedback have attempted to conceptualize the underlying dimensions of feedback in order to better understand how feedback works.

Dimensions of Feedback

Dimensions reflect the distinct underlying features of feedback that are evaluated by people. A number of studies have detailed different aspects of feedback. Falcione (1974) had workers fill out a questionnaire on the feedback that they received from their supervisors. He found that workers were sensitive to the reciprocity, perceptiveness, responsiveness, and permissiveness of the feedback. O'Reilley and Anderson (1980) found that managers rated three dimensions of feedback as important: its perceived accuracy and relevance, its developmental nature, and the quantity of feedback. They judged the relevance and accuracy of the feedback as more important than the amount of feedback. Herold and Greller (1977) asked people in a variety of settings how often they received feedback on many different topics. From analysis of these responses, they identified five dimensions of feedback: negative feedback, positive feedback from persons higher in authority, positive feedback from peers, internal (or self-determined) criteria, and work flow feedback. Since each study asked people to evaluate different aspects of feedback in different contexts, these underlying dimensions appear quite diverse.

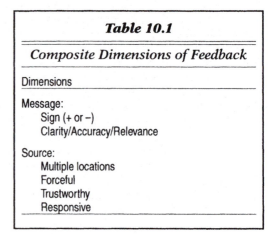

Table 10.1

Composite Dimensions of Feedback

Dimensions

Message:
    Sign (+ or −)
    Clarity/Accuracy/Relevance

Source:
    Multiple locations
    Forceful
    Trustworthy
    Responsive

To address this diversity, we (Ogilvie and Haslett 1985) had students observe and assess feedback with a set of descriptive adjectives compiled from other studies. In our study, the critical dimensions in the feedback process were its dynamism, trustworthiness, clarity, mood or general tone, and critical nature. This study identified some of the same feedback features as previous studies, establishing the critical nature of feedback.

Several conclusions can be drawn from these studies. (See Table 10.1 for a set of general underlying dimensions.) The positiveness or critical nature of the feedback appears to be very important. This feature reflects the valence (positive or negative) of the feedback. Another important feature is the clarity, accuracy, or relevance of the message. Other important dimensions of feedback involve the *source* of the feedback. Feedback comes from multiple sources, and those sources are judged on the basis of their trustworthiness, forcefulness, and responsiveness.

Feedback and Group Performance

Since we have defined task groups in terms of accomplishing goals, we will present a model that discusses group productivity and performance. Hackman and Morris (1975) developed a model of group performance, emphasizing the interaction processes among group members. Across groups, performance can vary widely; some groups perform well with little apparent difficulty. Others struggle constantly and still barely reach mediocrity. According to Hackman and Morris

> The challenge is to identify, measure and change those aspects of group interaction process that contribute to such obvious differences in group effectiveness (1975, 46).

To this end, they identified three determinants of performance. First, group members need relevant skills and knowledge. If those skills are absent, group performance will be hurt, and goals cannot be attained. Second, sufficient motivation must be present to coordinate activities with fellow group members and complete tasks. The third determinant is the selection of appropriate task performance strategies. Groups can have the necessary knowledge and effort, but may not be effective because of inappropriate ap-

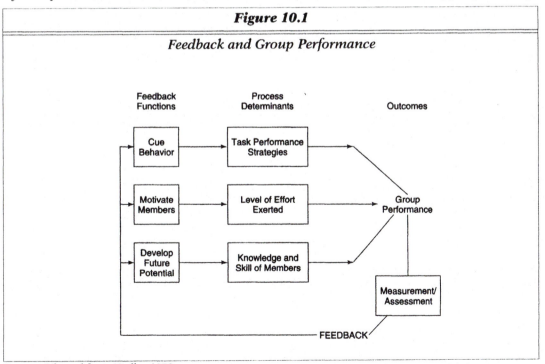

Figure 10.1

Feedback and Group Performance

Source: Adapted from Nadler 1979.

proaches to completing the task. (See Figure 10.1 for a model of this process.)

This model can also be used to understand the functions of feedback, its influence on performance, and its influence on the attitudes of group members (Nadler 1979). One important function of feedback is to correct inappropriate behavior of members. This corrective effect is often called *cueing*. It signals that the task behavior is not desired and has the effect of correcting inappropriate strategies. Feedback can also function to set goals and *motivate* members, addressing the effort determinant. Individuals may receive feedback judging their efforts to be below the group's standard (i.e., norms) or that more cooperation is needed to accomplish goals. Supervisory appraisals often establish specific goals to motivate future performance. These appraisals may also suggest areas for skill improvement or enhancement. Similarly, other group members may suggest specific areas of knowledge or skill development through feedback, which can improve performance. This type of feedback functions to develop members' *potential* for future activities. By developing new skills and acquiring knowledge, feedback functions to help individuals to acquire some degree of mastery over their environment (Ashford and Cummings 1983). Thus, feedback appears relevant for all aspects of group performance. To be effective, performance must be measured or assessed and feedback sought from multiple sources. In short, groups cannot be effective without feedback.

Feedback as a Communicative Process

While the underlying dimensions of feedback are useful in revealing the complexity of feedback, additional insight into feedback can be gained when feedback is viewed as a communicative process (Ilgen, Fisher and Taylor 1979). That is, while feedback is an essential component of any communication model, feedback itself can be studied as communication. As suggested by dimensional studies and other research, we can assess feedback by examining the *source* of the feedback, the feedback *message* itself (e.g., is the feedback positive or negative, is it task-oriented or process-oriented, etc.?), and the

receiver of the feedback (e.g., an individual, group, or organization).

Ilgen, Fisher, and Taylor (1979) attempted to understand how and why individuals respond to feedback. They identified four important processes in feedback. First, individuals must *perceive* the feedback. Second, they must *accept* it. Third, they must then develop the *intentions to respond*, and finally must set specific, moderately difficult *goals for improvement*.

They concluded that the perception of feedback is a function of the source, message, and recipient. In addition, they suggested that the perception and acceptance of feedback are critical elements in determining the receiver's response to feedback. Generally, the source of the feedback has the greatest impact on its acceptance, although other research has indicated that the influence of the source and message interact with one another (Ilgen, Mitchell and Fredrickson 1981; Ogilvie and Haslett 1985).

Viewing feedback as a communicative process allows us to look more specifically at the different aspects of feedback. We now turn to an examination of factors influencing the giving and receiving of feedback. These factors will be examined as source characteristics, message characteristics, and recipient characteristics.

Factors Influencing Feedback

Source Characteristics

We receive feedback from a variety of sources. In task groups and in work organizations, there are generally five sources of feedback: self (intrinsic), the task, peers, supervisors, and the organization itself. Task and self-generated sources are psychologically closer to the individual and are seen as more valuable (Greller and Herold 1975). More external, distant sources of feedback require more scrutiny because they cannot be trusted as automatically as intrinsic sources. If feedback from some of these sources is blocked, other problems arise. Obstruction of task and supervisory sources of feedback results in higher levels of anxiety among workers. Blockage of supervisory sources is also strongly related to job satisfaction and intention to leave the company (Walsh, Ashford and Hill 1985).

A number of other characteristics of these sources have been found to influence the feedback process. Among the influential variables are the trustworthiness of the source, the power and status of the source, the relationship between the source and recipient, and the communicative style of the source.

1. Trustworthiness. A source's trustworthiness and credibility (believability) are major influences on the acceptance of feedback (O'Reilly and Anderson 1980). These two issues—trustworthiness and credibility—cannot be discussed separately since we tend to believe those we trust, and trust those whom we believe. Feedback from credible, trustworthy sources receives more attention as well as acceptance from recipients. Those giving positive feedback to others are also perceived as being more trustworthy and credible. Leaders' feedback is also perceived as being more accurate, trustworthy, and credible than that of peers, although peers and leaders show high agreement on their feedback of others.

In our study, trust was an important dimension of giving feedback. Trusted feedback was also viewed as being credible and fair. When comparing the trustworthiness of feedback to other variables, we found that it was associated with perceptions of how effectively the feedback was given. Feedback that was communicated in a responsive and relaxed manner was also more trusted. Trust seems linked to reciprocity. If the person believes that you are fair in giving feedback, you should be relaxed and responsive to them. If you are defensive and nervous, then the feedback will not be trusted. Clearly, trust is an important feature; it may be the "golden rule" of feedback. If you trust the feedback, you assume that the motives and intentions of the source are fair.

2. Power and Status of the Source. In general, the more powerful the source, the more attention and acceptance the recipients give the feedback. Power can be measured in a number of ways. A supervisor who has direct control over his or her employees will exert a powerful influence over the people she or he supervises. This influence may also explain the strong effect that the obstruction of supervisory feedback has on employees. The absence of information causes anxiety and uncertainty. Thus, leaders generally are perceived as giving more accurate, credible feedback.

Power could also be measured in terms of expertise. We are not likely to accept feedback from a source we consider inexperienced or unknowledgeable about a particular area. Generally, it appears that for feedback to be readily accepted the source of the feedback must have some competency with respect to the type of feedback being given.

Our research suggests that in many groups where there is no formally designated leader, the manner in which feedback is given can also have much influence on the receiver. In our research, dynamism (a combination of activity and strength) accounted for much of the variation in perceptions of feedback. Dynamism was most strongly related to the overall impression group members leave and accounted for most of the individual differences in the way that feedback was given. Similarly, a communication style that was verbally assertive was strongly related to dynamism and to perceptions of the effectiveness with which the feedback was given.

3. Communicator Style. Communicator style refers to the *manner* in which feedback is given. The more consideration and influence a leader has, the greater perceived relevance for that leader's feedback. Ogilvie and Haslett (1985) found significant communicative differences across group members in their styles of giving feedback. Group members varied in the dynamism, clarity, mood, and criticalness of their feedback. Effectiveness of feedback was significantly related to the source's verbally assertive style, dynamism, responsiveness, and being relaxed. Dynamism and clarity of feedback were also positively related to the impression group members made. Feedback style has been positively related to a recipient's job satisfaction and acceptance of feedback as well.

Message Characteristics

1. Content. A message can contain several types of information. One type of information refers to behaviors which help to attain a desired goal. This type of information is referred to as referent information and is similar to the cueing function described above. Thus, a feedback message containing *referent* information should improve group productivity. Another type of information is more subjective—it tells a person how their behavior is perceived and evaluated. This type of message contains *appraisal* information and is actually more useful to the individual in reducing their uncertainty about their role in the group.

2. Timing. A number of studies have demonstrated that effective feedback is more effective when closer in time to the occurrence. That is, feedback should be given relatively close to the behaviors or job being done. Delays may reduce the impact and relevance of the feedback.

3. Channel. Feedback can be given across a number of different modes or channels: feedback can be written or oral, verbal or nonverbal. Zajonc (1980) found that important affective/evaluative information is given nonverbally, while cognitive information is presented verbally. The evaluative content delivered through nonverbal channels is similar to the appraisal content mentioned above. Thus, some channels may be used more for some types of content than others. Both effect and cognitions are important aspects of giving feedback (Larson 1984).

Furnham (1982) investigated the effect of message content and channel on giving messages. He found that people preferred to give messages face-to-face, rather than by writing or the telephone. In general, "the nature of the communication to be made determines the choice of situation in which to communicate." Subjects preferred to communicate most messages in a one-on-one situation, especially for messages that were situation-specific (e.g., giving bad news or disclosing some personal information).

Daft and Lengel (1984) have noted that the channels or media used to communicate vary in terms of their information richness. Face-to-face communication is the most rich while data on a computer printout are relatively low in richness. Very rich media, like oral communication, allow for more rapid, timely feedback and are more useful in solving complex problems in which more feedback is needed.

4. Message Valence. Perhaps the most important message characteristic influencing feedback is whether it is positive or negative (i.e., its sign or valence). In general, positive messages are more accepted than negative, while negative messages seem to be rejected unless they are from high-status sources. Positive messages produce higher trust among individuals as well as enhance group cohesion. Generally, individuals also find positive messages more believable and acceptable. Gordon (1985) also found a significant correlation between individuals giving positive information and receiving positive comments. The more a group member was perceived as giving conducive feedback, the more she or he received in turn.

In contrast, negative messages are often not transmitted to the intended recipient. People are reluctant to give negative information to others, even while they acknowledge that the intended recipients have a right to know, and a greater desire and interest to know than others. This generalization has been documented in a wide variety of situations, across different communicators and recipients, and across different channels. Tesser and Rosen (1975) found that pleasantness of a message was significantly correlated with the likelihood of its being transmitted ($r = 0.73$). If there is a negative message to be transmitted, frequently a subordinate is asked to do it. They suggest that people are reluctant to transmit negative messages because they fear being negatively evaluated themselves; they are concerned about the mood created for the intended recipient, and they experience guilt and anxiety over transmitting the message. Tesser and Rosen also suggest that negative messages are threatening to the self-image of the intended recipient and thus would negatively influence the relationship between the source and intended recipient. However, negative messages have the greatest potential for improving performance. The manner in which these messages are delivered is most critical so that one avoids eliciting defensive reactions and/or damaging the relationship. (See the last section of this article for more suggestions on giving feedback.)

Recipient Characteristics

The characteristics of the intended recipient also influence the feedback process. People send messages to accomplish specific goals that are designed for a specific target audience. It seems reasonable to assume that individuals design their feedback with specific purposes and specific recipients in mind. Since feedback is designed to give an individual information about his or her behavior, obviously those messages will vary as a function of the particular intended recipient. While some studies have explored the recipient's characteristics and their impact on the feedback process, more research needs to be done in this area.

1. Recipient's Mind-Set. One of the most influential factors in determining the recipient's response to feedback is his or her mind-set or frame-of-reference when feedback is received. This temporary frame-of-reference influences the recipient's perception, acceptance, and response to feedback. If an employee has just had a difficult time with a customer, he or she will not be receptive to a co-worker providing critical feedback about her or his work habits. Expectations can also influence a recipient's mind-set and be a major factor in his or her perception of feedback (Ilgen et al. 1979). We tend to see and hear what we expect, distorting the feedback received.

2. Personal Qualities. Several more stable enduring characteristics of the recipient also influence the feedback process. Self-esteem and social anxiety were two personality variables that have been studied in this context (Ilgen et al. 1979). People who have varying degrees of self-esteem interpret feedback differently. Individuals with high *self-esteem* interpret negative feedback in an ambiguous way and thus do not respond as strongly to it. In contrast, people with high *social anxiety* anticipate receiving more negative feedback than those having less social anxiousness and consequently tend to interpret feedback as being more negative.

Varca and Levy (1984) examined several related variables in the way that people respond to feedback. They noted that critical feedback represents a threat to an individual's self-esteem. However, people may cope differently with these threats. Some choose to ignore or deny the threat posed by critical feedback. These people are *repressors*. Repressors tend to have high self-esteem since the feedback is not seen as relevant. An alternative means of coping is to amplify the threat and its consequences by an excessive expression of anxious feelings. These individuals are *sensitizers*. The exaggeration by sensitizers helps them cope by reducing the possibility of consequences from negative events. Such exaggerated expectations of consequences are rarely met and the sensitizer is much relieved. Again, sensitizers are similar to those with high social anxiety in that they interpret feedback more negatively.

Source, message, and recipient characteristics are summarized in Table 10.2.

How to Give Feedback

Giving and receiving feedback is an integral part of interpersonal communication. Many interactions will occur in a small group setting, whether it be a sorority or a task force recommending changes in organization structure. Within organizations, feedback is critical because employees need to perform their tasks adequately so the organization continues to survive. For every organizational member, then, understanding feedback is important. However, we also need to know how to give feedback effectively in order

> ### Table 10.2
>
> #### Summary of Communication Features in Feedback
>
> | Source Characteristics | Message Characteristics | Recipient Characteristics |
> |---|---|---|
> | Trustworthiness | Content | Mind-Set |
> | | Referent | |
> | Power and Status | Appraisal | Expectations |
> | Communication Style | Timing | Personality |
> | Assertive | | Repressors/ |
> | Dynamic | Channel | Self-Esteem |
> | Relaxed | | Sensitizers/ |
> | Responsive | Sign or Valence | Social Anxiety |

to maximize our performance and the performance of others. Giving feedback effectively is, of course, particularly important for those in managerial positions. In what follows, we suggest some general strategies for giving feedback effectively and deal particularly with the problems of giving negative feedback.

General Communicative Strategies

The best general suggestions for effective communication in small groups have been succinctly expressed by Gouran and Fisher (1984).

> In general, those communicative behaviors that are task oriented, that serve to keep energy focused on the group's goals, and that show a concern with maintaining workable interpersonal relations have correspondingly positive effects on the quality of interaction, the ease with which a task is completed, members' acceptance of group positions, and the satisfaction of the participants (630).

Generally, then, maintaining good working relationships with others requires that we communicate as constructively as possible.

Some communicative strategies for giving feedback (and receiving it as well) that facilitate a constructive working environment are outlined below. First, in order for feedback to be effective, it needs to be fairly *direct* and *specific*. A general remark such as "That's the wrong way to do that" is so vague and general as to be of no value in changing how the task is done. In contrast, a specific, direct message such as "The water pressure

must always be maintained at 100 pounds by adjusting this valve" details the necessary activities for successful task completion. An example from the small group that was videotaped in our study makes this point quite succinctly:

> C: I put ___ as a dominator because he asserts authority and especially I think over ___ umm I think that the group impact I think, you know, I also put you as task and socially oriented but—I think it's a little annoying sometimes how—I don't know—it seems—like you ummmmmmm.
>
> D: Say it.

In this situation, C is struggling for words, and D, who is receiving this feedback, quite clearly wants C to spit it out! Contrast this with the following example of specific, direct feedback:

> A: I put ___ as a harmonizer, um, when we have a lot of tension in the group she tends to try and break it down. . . .

Second, effective feedback needs to be *supported by evidence.* Generally people are much more responsive and accepting of comments when some rationale has been given. This can be seen in the following comment made in the small group feedback session.

> B: I see you in a very dominant role because of your personality. You're aggressive, you're assertive, and you have your own ideas and you display them. Impact on the group as far as

that's concerned I find very good for one thing because you provide direction and you also push the group to achieve. . . .

In this example, a judgment was made, but B gave reasons for his judgment and the effect of these behaviors. In addition, providing reasons for actions may forestall or defuse critical reactions, as well as giving the appearance of thoughtful deliberation behind the recommendations.

Finally, feedback should clearly *separate the issue under discussion from the personalities* involved. That is, as Gouran and Fisher suggest, messages should be focused on the task to be accomplished. Both sources and targets of feedback messages should maintain a careful distinction between task and personality.

While these general strategies are useful in giving feedback to others, negative messages represent a situation that deserves special consideration. It deserves separate discussion because of people's general tendency to avoid sending negative messages, and the guilt and anxiety produced by giving negative messages. However, there are situations in which negative assessments must be given and our concern here is how they might be conveyed most effectively. (See Table 10.3 for a summary of suggestions for giving feedback.)

Giving Feedback Containing Negative Messages

While a voluminous literature on feedback has noted the reluctance to transmit negative messages, very little research has addressed the issue of how such negative information can be transmitted. One study (Davies and Jacobs 1985) looked at the effect of combining negative (N) and positive (P) messages and assessing the effectiveness of various combinations. Specifically, chains of feedback (PNP, PPN, NPN, and NNP) were examined. It was found that the PNP chain (positive message, negative message, and a final positive comment) was the most effective format for giving feedback. PNP sequences were rated as significantly more accurate, credible, desirable, and had the most positive emotional responses. In addition, PNP sequences contributed most to group

> ### *Table 10.3*
>
> ### *Summary of Suggestions for Giving Feedback*
>
> 1. Be specific and direct.
> 2. Support comments with evidence.
> 3. Separate the issue from the person.
> 4. "Sandwich" negative messages between positive ones.
> 5. Pose the situation as a mutual problem.
> 6. Mitigate or soften negative messages to avoid overload.
> 7. Timing: Deliver feedback close to occurrence.
> 8. Manner of delivery:
>   a. Assertive, dynamic;
>   b. Trustworthy, fair and credible;
>   c. Relaxed and responsive;
>   d. Preserve public image of recipient.

cohesiveness and a positive group experience. Interestingly, NPN sequences were viewed most negatively and PPN sequences were not superior to NNP sequences except in desirability. This study suggests that when it is necessary to give negative information, it is most effective to "sandwich" the negative message between two positive comments. For example, "Our engineering division has been doing exceptionally well. Although your group has had the lowest performance, the latest figures show some improvement." The negative comment about low performance has been surrounded by positive comments.

Beyond "sandwiching" the negative feedback, another communicative strategy is to approach the problem area from a collective or collaborative perspective. That is, rather than saying what the problem with the target's group or behavior is, it is more effective to approach the situation as a *problem* that affects both of us. For example, instead of saying "Your group is really performing poorly," a supervisor might say, "We seem to have a problem with the group's decreasing productivity. What do you think might be done about it?" The latter comments invite the subordinate to think constructively about an issue that admittedly affects both of them, rather than blaming the subordinate and creating resentment and hostility.

Another strategy might be to *mitigate* or *soften* the force of the negative message through the use of disclaimers or qualifications. Phrases of uncertainty, such as "I'm really not sure about this but I think that . . . ," or the use of tag questions such as "don't you think so, too?" soften the force of a negative comment. In the videotape data collected by Ogilvie and Haslett (1985), group members frequently used disclaimers or tag questions to soften the force of their remarks and thus preserve all participants' positive public image. Below are some examples of this from our data.

> A: I also put, um, gatekeeper down for myself because I feel that I encourage others and facilitate participation, and I'm always interested in what other people have to say within the group.
>
> *And I guess that's, I don't know,* a positive impact. I'm sure there are negative things about what I do *but I'm not quite sure* what they are.

In this example, the italicized portion reflects A's qualifications about what the effects of her actions are and thus weakens her self-criticism. Another member of the group, a male, uses the same qualifying strategy in giving feedback to other group members on their performances.

> B: *I think, I find that I don't know,* I see us struggling to be dominating, a dominant role, we seem like we're trying to compete with one another at times for either attention or even impact and input into the group.

The uncertainty projected through these comments softens the impact of the negative comment and lessens the likelihood of a negative response to the initial negative comments. Such qualifiers help preserve good working relationships when difficult evaluative comments must be made—and all groups will experience moments when negative comments must be made.

Finally, the *language* used in giving feedback is important. Generally, group members should be descriptive in their language, rather than being evaluative. The American Management Association, in its pamphlet on supervisory management, suggests that supervisors focus on describing the problem, rather than blaming employees for the problem. For example, instead of stating "Bill, you are arrogant and domineering," rephrase that and say, "Bill, many colleagues perceive your attitude as being arrogant and domineering." With that rephrasing, attention is focused on the behavior rather than the person: this lessens the likelihood of a negative, defensive response on the part of Bill.

Generally, then, although negative messages are difficult to give and receive, it can be done when attention is given to *how* such feedback can be constructively given. We suggest that the most important consideration is to maintain everyone's positive public image. By maintaining all participants' public images, the group, as a whole, preserves good working relationships among its members. This, in turn, enables the group to be productive, efficient, and cohesive. When negative feedback must be given, members can: (1) sandwich the negative comment with positive comments; (2) frame the problem or issue as one that involves both of you; (3) use qualifiers to soften the force of the negative feedback; (4) give reasons for the negative feedback; and (5) use descriptive rather than evaluative language.

Conclusions and Implications

Throughout this article, we have suggested that feedback is a central component of human communication. Feedback is a complex, multifaceted process that is critical to interpersonal and group effectiveness since it enables communicators to understand the effects of their behavior.

Feedback itself, as a process, may also be analyzed as a separate communicative activity. We have analyzed feedback as a communicative process and assessed the impact of source, message, and recipient on the feedback process. The most influential source characteristics are the source's power and status, trustworthiness, credibility, forcefulness, and responsiveness. It is also important to keep in mind that feedback comes from many different sources, and that each source may be valued for a different type of feedback. The feedback message, to be effective, should be clear, accurate, relevant, and positive. Negative feedback is generally avoided by both source and recipient, and anxiety and guilt are associated with negative feedback. Finally, recipients of feedback perceive feedback differently as a function of self-esteem and other personal characteristics. While these general findings provide insight into the feedback process, feedback processes are still in need of further study. We have little understanding, for example, of the complex interactions among the various dimensions of feedback: What occurs when a trusted source gives very negative feedback? What are the effects of that negative feedback on the source's perceived trustworthiness and his or her subsequent relationship with the recipient?

Given the complexity of feedback and its importance, we have suggested some strategies to follow in order to enhance the effectiveness of feedback offered to others. Generally, sources need to be constructive, clear, direct, and specific. In addition, a source's remarks should clearly separate the issue from the recipient's personality: critique the behavior at issue rather than the person.

Negative feedback, as already pointed out, creates special difficulties because of the general avoidance of negative messages. However, at times, negative feedback must be given, and we suggested a number of strategies by which this could be done to maximize the feedback's effectiveness. In particular, we suggested trying to "sandwich" the negative comments among positive comments; to use descriptive rather than evaluative language; and to maintain all participants' positive public images.

To effectively communicate, we believe it is particularly important to communicate in such a way that all participants have positive attitudes about themselves and others in that group. Even very difficult, negative comments can be given *if sufficient attention has been paid to how to express those comments as constructively as possible*. This, we

submit, is especially important in giving feedback to others and the most challenging part of the communicative process. With the information provided in this article, hopefully both sources and recipients will have a better understanding of the feedback process and how to give/receive feedback with maximum effectiveness.

References

Ashford, S. J., and Cummings, L. L. (1983). "Feedback as an Individual Resource: Personal Strategies of Creating Information." *Organizational Behavior and Human Performance* 32: 370–398.

Daft, R. L., and Lengel, R. H. (1984). "Information Richness: A New Approach Managing Information Processing and Organizational Design." In B. Shaw and L. L. Cummings (eds.), *Research in Organizational Behavior* 6: 118–133.

Davies, D., and Jacobs, A. (1985). " 'Sandwiching' Complex Interpersonal Feedback." *Small Group Behavior* 16: 387–396.

Falcione, R. (1974). "Communication Climate and Satisfaction with Immediate Supervision." *Journal of Applied Communication Research* 2: 13–20.

Furnham, A. (1982). "The Message, the Context and the Medium." *Language and Communication* 2: 33–47.

Gordon R. (1985). "Self-Disclosure of Interpersonal Feedback." *Small Group Behavior* 16: 411–413.

Gouran, D., and Fisher, B. A. (1984). "The Function of Human Communication in the Formation, Maintenance, and Performance of Small Groups." In G. Miller and M. Knapp, (eds.), *The Handbook of Interpersonal Communication.* Sage: Beverly Hills, CA.

Greller, M. M., and Herold, D. M. (1975). "Sources of Feedback: A Preliminary Investigation." *Organizational Behavior and Human Performance* 13: 244–256.

Hackman, J. R., and Morris, C. G. (1975). "Group Tasks, Group Interaction Process and Group Performance Effectiveness: A Review and Proposed Integration." In L. Berkowitz (ed.), *Advances in Experimental Social Psychology* 8. New York: Academic Press.

Hanser, L. and Muchinsky, D. (1978). "Work as an Information Environment." *Organizational Behavior and Human Performance* 21: 47–60.

Herold, D. M., and Greller, M. M. (1977). "Feedback: The Definition of a Construct." *Academy of Management* 20(1): 142–147.

Ilgen, D. R., Fisher, C. D., and Taylor, M. S. (1979). "Consequences of Individual Feedback on Behavior in Organizations." *Journal of Applied Psychology* 64(4): 349–371.

Ilgen, D. R., Mitchell, T. R. and Frederickson, J. W. (1981). "Poor Performers: Supervisors and Subordinates Responses." *Organizational Behavior and Human Performance* 27: 386–410.

Larson, J. M., Jr. (1984). "Performance Feedback Processes: A Preliminary Model." *Organizational Behavior and Human Performance* 34: 42–76.

Nadler, D. A. (1979). "The Effects of Feedback on Task Group Behavior: A Review of Experimental Research." *Organizational Behavior and Human Performance* 23: 309–338.

Ogilvie, J. R., and Haslett, B. (1985). "Communicating Peer Feedback in a Task Group." *Human Communication Research* 12(1): 79–98.

O'Reilly, C., and Anderson, J. (1980). "Trust and Communication of Performance Appraisal Information: The Effect of Feedback on Performance and Job Satisfaction." *Human Communication Research* 6: 290–298.

Palazzolo, C. S. (1981). *Small Groups, an Introduction*. Belmont, CA: Wadsworth Publishing.

Tesser, A., and Rosen, S. (1975). "Reluctance to Transmit Bad News." In L. Berkowitz (ed.), *Advances in Experimental Social Psychology* 8: 193–232. New York: Academic Press.

Varca, P. E., and Levy, J. C. (1984). "Individual Differences in Response to Unfavorable Group Feedback." *Organizational Behavior and Human Performance* 33: 100–111.

Walsh, J. P., Ashford, S. J., and Hill, T. E. (1985). "Feedback Obstruction: The Influence of the Information Environment on Employee Turnover Intentions." *Human Relations* 38(1): 23–46

Zajonc, R. (1980). "Feeling and Thinking: Preferences Need No Inferences." *American Psychologist* 35(2): 151–175.

Chapter 11
Influencing Others in Group Interactions

Individual, Subgroup, Group, and Intergroup Processes

Renee A. Meyers
Dale E. Brashers

The authors provide an overview of prominent theories, models, and research studies concerning influence processes in small groups. As the title of the chapter implies, they explain how influence in groups can occur at individual, subgroup, group, and intergroup levels. Meyers and Brashers use the activist group PETA (People for the Ethical Treatment of Animals) as an example of a successful persuasive campaign that employed all four levels of social influence. This chapter clearly demonstrates the importance of understanding group communication at each level of social influence. This type of multilevel analysis is important because it helps both researchers of small groups and practitioners to better understand the complexities and intricacies of group communication and social influence processes.

Every day, in many places in the world, the activist group PETA (People for the Ethical Treatment of Animals) tirelessly works to persuade others to treat animals more humanely. PETA is the largest animal rights group in the world. More than seven hundred thousand people subscribe to its ideals and practices. PETA operates under "the simple principle that animals are not ours to eat, wear, experiment on, or use for entertainment" (PETA 2000).

PETA members have developed a well-organized influence campaign that includes at least four levels of action: (a) individual-level action, (b) subgroup-level action, (c) group-level action, and (d) intergroup-level action. Each of these levels of influence is persuasive in its own right, but when combined, they produce a holistic influence campaign that is both widespread and effective.

At the individual level, PETA asks members to generate letters to the editors of local newspapers, to contact legislators in person and in writing, and to visit targeted companies to complain about inhumane practices. On their website, for example, PETA urged members to write the owner of a retail store in Ohio and request that he cancel his upcoming fur show. They encouraged members to contact *The Rosie O'Donnell Show* and complain about her Friday "Wear Leather Day." Members of PETA believe that individuals can have an impact. They state that "as an individual you can educate hundreds of people in your community and affect their often unwittingly exploitative attitudes and lifestyles" (PETA 2000).

At the subgroup level, PETA encourages interested community members to form collectivities to exert local-level influence. PETA encourages local community subgroups to pursue public education (leafletting, library displays, and collective letters to the editors of local newspapers), to target seasonal events (demonstrations when a circus or rodeo comes to town, picketing fur stores, caroling at the zoo during the holidays), and to undertake long-term campaigns (shut down a lab, puppy mill, or zoo). Above all, PETA urges subgroups to "be visible. Get into the public eye often, and always try to get media coverage for your events" (PETA 2000).

At the broader group level, PETA itself functions as an influential resource, consultant, and information provider. PETA tells its members that "we want you to know that you can call on us for anything, anytime, and we'll be there to help." Their website states that "whether you're working as an individual or with a group, whether you're a veteran activist or just getting started with animal rights, PETA can help you speak out for animals in your area!" (PETA 2000). The larger PETA group makes available to its members abundant information on the current campaigns sponsored by PETA, up-to-date resources on animal rights issues, campaign materials, and an online publication of PETA's grassroots campaign handbook, *Guide to Becoming an Activist*. In addition, primary organizers of PETA often appear on national news programs and talk shows to persuade national audiences of the importance of their cause.

At the intergroup level, PETA encourages members to link up with other groups in their communities to produce more widespread influence. PETA advocates that subgroups approach scientists, veterinarians, doctors or other experts who will lend credibility to the campaign. PETA also urges members to get support from related national and local groups (civic associations, the League of Women Voters, Rotary Clubs, Humane Society, and other political clubs). The more that intergroup cooperation is fostered, the greater the potential for widespread influence.

PETA has developed a sophisticated and elaborate hierarchical influence network that begins with the individual, supports the formation of subgroups, provides resources and information at the group level, and finally fosters intergroup connections. Such a multifaceted approach allows PETA's persuasive messages to be broadcast to all levels of society.

Past research on group influence also has concentrated on these four levels of persuasion. In this chapter, we review some of the most prominent theories and research traditions that describe how group influence is produced on each of these four levels. Most of the research we review in this chapter has been conducted on *decision-making* groups rather than relationally oriented groups (friendship groups, family, support groups)

because most research on group communication, in general, investigates decision-making groups (see Frey 1994, 1996). In addition, the research we review investigates *verbal* communication rather than nonverbal communication, since little research has been conducted on the nonverbal elements of influence in groups (but see Ketrow 2000 for a recent review of nonverbal communication research in groups). Finally, since we cannot possibly overview all the research on group communicative influence in one book chapter, we have had to exclude many deserving investigative efforts (for a more comprehensive review, see Meyers and Brashers 2000). Nevertheless, we believe this review highlights some of the most prominent scholarship on group influence.

Group Influence Theories, Models, and Research Traditions

Influence at the Individual Level

Social Comparison Theory. One of the most extensively tested theories of individual influence in groups is Social Comparison Theory (SCT) (see Myers 1982). Proponents of SCT assert that prior to group discussion, individuals guess where others might stand on an issue and then choose an initial decision based on their perceptions of those members' positions. The main function of group discussion is to allow members to reveal their positions toward the decision choices so that comparisons can be made amongst members. It is during the comparison process that social influence occurs, with the result that some members may change their opinions.

How does this theory work in practice? Suppose you were attending the first class of the semester. The instructor arrives and reviews the syllabus with the class. At one point, she indicates that the class can choose whether they would like to do a group presentation or a group paper for one of their final assignments. She asks each person to think about which of these two assignments would be preferable.

You look around the room at the other group members and try to discern whether your classmates would prefer to do a presentation or a paper. Then you choose the option that you think would be most similar to other class members' positions. Let's assume that you decide that option is the presentation. The teacher then asks people to raise their hands if they prefer the paper option. You notice that a good friend of yours raises her hand to support the paper. As a result, you may decide to change your opinion toward the choice of your friend (i.e., the paper), and so you raise your hand in support of that option.

As you can see in this example, SCT assumes that just by knowing others' choices, and comparing your choice to others' choices, you may be influenced to change your mind. There is much scholarly debate over whether information about others' choices alone is sufficient to produce influence (e.g., Sanders and Baron, 1977). As Latane and Liu (1996) recently noted, social comparison processes are probably sufficient in some situations (such as the case described above) but are insufficient in others where more complex choices are being discussed and participants are interested in hearing the communicative arguments for both sides of the issue. As they stated:

> For many aspects of our lives, social comparison may be more influential than conversation, and it does not take much discussion with the other people in a classical music hall to realize that our Bermuda shorts are out of place. For cognitively elaborated attitudes, however, influence may depend on persuasive arguments delivered through conversation. (p. 30)

Persuasive Arguments Theory. A second prominent theory of group influence at the individual level is Persuasive Arguments Theory (PAT). According to this theory, there exists in any social community a standard set of arguments for any given decision option, and each individual knows some or all of these arguments. As a result of ignorance or lack of recall, however, the same arguments may not be equally available to all participants in a particular group decision-mak-

ing situation (Burnstein 1982). PAT scholars predict that *novel* arguments (i.e., arguments that were not considered by group members prior to discussion and that are stimulated by, or created in, group discussion) cause members to reconsider their initial decision choices (Burnstein 1982). As members become convinced of the merits of the novel arguments, they change their opinions in the direction of the decision choice supported by those novel arguments (Burnstein, Vinokur, and Pichevin 1974).

How does Persuasive Arguments Theory work in practice? Suppose you are involved in a discussion with other group members about which topic to choose for a final group presentation. The assignment involves teaching the class a concept related to group communication. Several topics are suggested by the group members: conflict in groups, leadership in groups, group cohesion, and group decision making. Members start to discuss the topic "group cohesion" and offer arguments for ways that the group might teach this topic. One person suggests that each group member take one aspect of group cohesion and write an individual report. All of these individual reports can then be compiled into a group presentation. This group member argues that such a strategy will lead to the most thorough and complete presentation. Another group member argues that the group should do something more interesting such as a skit showing a cohesive and a noncohesive group. The group continues to offer suggestions and arguments. Suppose, however, that none of the ideas or arguments offered in support of these topics is novel to any of the group members. Instead they are all part of that "standard set" of arguments that PAT suggests are available for this decision option, and all of the group members possess, and can recall, these arguments.

Suddenly, one of the quietest members of the group suggests that instead of the usual "tried and true" formats for teaching group cohesion, this time the group members should go out into the community, locate a group for whom cohesion is vital, and hold the class at this community location. The student suggests a fire-fighting team and argues that the presentation should take place at the fire station. Prior to the presentation, the group members would interview a set of fire fighters about the role of cohesion in their fire-fighting team. During the presentation at the fire station, the group members would provide information from those interviews. Then the class would be allowed to ask the fire fighters any questions they wanted about cohesion issues as they pertained to the fire-fighting team. The final part of the class would involve a ride on the fire truck.

Now the group comes alive! This student has presented both a novel idea and novel arguments to support his idea. No one in the group has thought about this idea or these arguments before. According to Persuasive Arguments Theory, these novel arguments should be very influential, and cause many group members to reconsider their earlier opinions, and to change their minds about the presentation plan.

Both SCT and PAT describe influence at the individual level, but with very different explanations. In most persuasion situations, both SCT and PAT are likely viable accounts of influence. In many situations, we probably begin by trying to "guess" others' opinions on a given proposal and then choose a stance fairly closely aligned to others in the group (SCT). But we probably do not always make our final decision based just on others' opinions. We are interested in hearing the arguments (pro and con) for each idea, and then we make a decision based on those arguments. If those arguments are novel, PAT suggests we are more likely to be persuaded. In short, it is likely that SCT and PAT are both viable individual-level explanations of successful group influence.

Individual-level influence is vitally important to achieve an effective group outcome. As is evident in PETA's campaign, they rely on interested and committed individuals to write letters, complain to local legislators, and to educate people in the community. Such individual-level influence is often the foundation of a successful persuasion effort.

However, individual-level influence is not the only form of influence in groups. Another important source of persuasion is subgroup influence. Most research in this area has focused on the roles of majority and minority subgroups to influence the group's final decision. Research shows that both subgroups' influence is integral to achieving an effective group outcome.

Influence at the Subgroup Level

Distributed Valence Model. The Distributed Valence Model (DVM) is a prominent explanation of group influence at the subgroup level (McPhee, Poole, and Seibold 1982). This model predicts final decision choices by counting each group member's positive and negative comments for each decision option. Using majority rule, the option favored by the largest subgroup is the predicted group choice.

How does this model predict an actual group decision? Suppose that you are in a group of five friends trying to decide between three restaurants to attend for dinner one evening. One of the restaurants is a Chinese place, one is a Russian place, and one is McDonald's. As you and your friends discuss these three options, all the members of the group express both positive and negative comments about each choice. According to the numbers on the following table, two of the five people favor the Chinese restaurant (i.e., two people have more positive comments than negative comments regarding the Chinese restaurant), four of the five friends favor the Russian restaurant (i.e., four members have more positive comments than negative comments for the Russian restaurant), and only one person has more positive than negative comments for McDonald's. (See Table 11.1.)

If the DVM was used to predict the final group decision, it would count up the positive and negative comments for each group member for each restaurant choice. According to the DVM, the group would choose the Russian restaurant because more members of the group (4 out of 5) favor that restaurant (according to the ratio

Table 11.1

Friends	Chinese restaurant		Russian restaurant		McDonald's	
	Positive	Negative	Positive	Negative	Positive	Negative
Shelly	4	8	8	2	1	10
Mark	9	2	5	1	1	3
Kerry	6	3	2	6	6	4
Tim	2	4	7	2	3	8
You	3	7	8	1	2	9

of their positive versus negative comments) than favor either the Chinese restaurant (2 out of 5) or McDonald's (1 out of 5).

Tests of the DVM have shown it to be a fairly accurate predictor of group choices. In an investigation of 10 four-person groups whose task was to decide on a topic of study, McPhee et al. (1982) found that the DVM was an accurate predictor much of the time. Meyers and Brashers (1998) utilized the DVM to investigate the role that subgroups' arguments play in group decision choices. They found that the DVM accurately predicted 88.9 percent of the group choices.

The DVM model utilizes majority rule as its primary selection rule. Research findings stemming from the DVM model support a large body of research on the influential role of the majority in group decision-making contexts.

Majority/Minority Influence. The majority subgroup generally exerts more influence than minority subgroups (Zaleska 1976), and its strategies of influence can include social pressure, ridicule, and even derision (Nemeth and Wachtler 1983). Research on mock juries reveals that the side the majority favors before group discussion becomes the verdict about 90 percent of the time (Davis 1973; Nemeth 1986).

A number of researchers have advanced explanations of how majority influence works in group discussion. Moscovici, Lage, and Naffrechoux (1969) were among the earliest researchers to suggest that the cause of majority influence was not the sheer number of majority members or the social pressure they exerted per se, but the *consistency* of the subgroup's comments. That is, those sub-

groups who did not sway from their initial position and consistently stayed committed to a single choice were more likely to be persuasive. In a later study, Moscovici and Faucheux (1972) found that when majority members were inconsistent in presenting their proposals, they were less likely to influence minority members.

Although majority influence appears to have considerable impact on group deliberation and outcomes, minority subgroups also can exert influence under various conditions (see Meyers, Brashers, and Hanner 2000; Wood, Lundgren, Ouellette, Busceme, and Blackstone 1994). As with majority influence, one important determinant of minority subgroup success is consistency in comments. Nemeth (1982) pointed out that early in group deliberation, minority subgroup members are likely to encounter resistance, even outright derision, from the majority. However, if the minority subgroup persists, is consistent in its comments toward a decision choice, and resists influence attempts from the majority, members of the majority may begin to show doubt in their position and may even convert to the minority viewpoint. Additionally, Alderton and Frey (1983, 1986) reported that if group members offer favorable reactions to minority positions, the minority is more likely to exert influence than if the group members show only unfavorable reactions toward the minority subgroup's comments. Finally, Garlick and Mongeau (1993) suggested that a minority subgroup will have even greater impact if its members produce arguments of high quality as well as remain behaviorally consistent.

Besides consistency and quality, another determinant of minority influence that has received attention is the relative size of the minority and majority (Haslett and Ruebush 2000). Empirical research in which the size of a minority varies while holding the majority constant suggests that a single-member minority is less influential than a minority of two or three (Arbuthnot and Wagner 1982). More recently, Clark and Maass (1990) showed that as the size of the majority increased (from 4 to 8 to 12), minority influence declined.

Minority influence has been associated with higher-quality group decisions (Peterson and Nemeth 1996). Participants exposed to a minority viewpoint are more likely to find correct, novel, and creative solutions than those exposed only to the majority view (Van Dyne and Saavedra 1996; Wood et al. 1994). Exposure to minority views also leads to more private acceptance (internalization) of ideas by all group members (Nemeth 1986), as well as more accurate recall of information (Nemeth, Mayseless, Sherman, and Brown 1990).

Although much research shows that the majority subgroup typically is the victor in group decision-making situations, this does not mean that minority influence should be discounted. If a minority presents its comments in a consistent and confident manner, if the majority size is not overwhelming, and if the other members' responses are favorable, it also can influence the final group choice. Moreover, such influence is often vital to the accomplishment of an effective group decision.

Tag-Team Argument. One way that both majority and minority subgroups can be particularly persuasive is through the use of tag-team argument. Tag-team argument is a set of claims, evidence, warrants, justifications, and agreements that is co-constructed in group interaction by two or more members of a subgroup (see Brashers and Meyers 1989; Canary, Brossmann, and Seibold 1987; Meyers, Seibold, and Brashers 1991). In short, subgroup members supply evidence for each others' claims or justifications for each others' conclusions and thereby provide a complete argument of claim and evidence. In addition, Brashers and Meyers (1989) found that tag-team arguments in subgroups are maintained by means of consistent support for each others' statements and repetitive agreement among tag-team members. Agreement among tag-team subgroup members appears to function as a connective tool that allows members favoring the same decision proposal to come together in interaction.

How exactly does tag-team argument work in a group discussion? Suppose that your group is discussing which one of two topics your group should research for a final group paper due at the end of the term. Notice how in the excerpt below, Tom, June, and Liz team up to form a single, persuasive argument for the topic, "group leadership."

Group Discussion Excerpt

Tom: I think group leadership would be the most interesting topic for us to pursue.

June: I agree. I think everyone is interested in leadership and since we have to present this paper to the class, I think the class would like to hear more about this topic.

Liz: I agree too. I think leadership is a very timely topic.

Tom: Also, there is a lot of literature on group leadership. It wouldn't be hard to find sources to read.

John: I would really rather do "nonverbal communication in groups" than "group leadership." I think the topic of group leadership is too broad and overwhelming.

Liz: Yes, John, but wouldn't you rather have too many resources than not enough? Our instructor has already said there isn't much available research on nonverbal communication in groups.

June: I agree with Liz. I think we are better off going with a well-researched topic. Besides, as was already stated, I think group leadership would be more interesting for most class members.

Tom: I agree too.

Tony: I don't know, I think John may have a point.

Tom: C'mon Tony, leadership would a much easier topic to cover. Remember, you even did a paper last semester on organizational leadership. I'll bet you could use some of those sources for this paper.

Tony: Oh, that's right. Maybe the leadership topic is a better choice. What do you think John?

As you can see in this excerpt, Tom, June, and Liz all work together in interaction to argue persuasively for their topic choice. They provide joint evidence for the "leadership" topic, agree with each others' comments, and remain consistent throughout the discussion. In the end, they will probably be successful in convincing John that the group should choose "leadership" as its paper topic.

Although research on tag-team argument is still in its infancy, results suggest that this form of argument both promotes cohesion among subgroup members and influences opposing factions. This form of argument is persuasive because it "presents a unified view of what supporters consider reasonable" (Canary et al. 1987, 33).

Coalition Formation. Related to research on majority and minority influence and tag-team influence are investigative efforts to understand coalition formation in groups (e.g., Putnam 1986). Past research has demonstrated that group members perceive the forming and maintaining of coalitions to be a powerful influence strategy in group decision-making discussions.

As Brashers and Meyers (1989) noted, research has shown that coalitions form when individuals with few resources (Gamson 1961) and/or little power (Gamson 1964) "seek alignment with other members in an effort to increase their share of expected payoffs" (543). Segal (1979) observed that coalitions form in response to group members' perceptions that one of them has more power in the group. Often, group members in that study were willing to sacrifice their own gain to defeat the "top dog," perhaps because of a sense of "commonality" that exists among members relatively low in power. Similarly, ambiguity about who has the power and resources might lead to coalition formation. Mannix and White (1992) discovered that coalitions were more likely to form when a group lacked an established distribution rule for resources, even when coalition formation was detrimental to the group. Finally, others have suggested that coalitions may form (1) on the basis of the popularity of a group member (Norton 1979), (2) when subgroup members identify more with the subgroup than with the group (Gresson 1978), or (3) when communication among group members is restricted (Vinacke, Mogy, Powers, Langan, and Beck 1974).

Although coalitions can serve a facilitative function for subgroup influence attempts, they also may be detrimental to the overall health of a group. Vitz and Kite (1970) found that groups with coalitions were more likely to engage in risky behavior than were groups low in coalitions, resulting in these groups being more vulnerable to threats from outside groups Coalitions can also decrease communication among group members. Buchli and Pearce (1975) noted that when coalitions form in three-person groups, communication between members of the coalition and the excluded person is reduced. In addition, members of coalitions might reduce communication with other group members because they view them as different or deviants (Pendell 1990).

Thus, coalitions form when subgroups perceive the need to influence other subgroups. Coalitions can facilitate subgroup influence attempts but may harm the overall health of the group if communication is reduced. However, coalitions may not last forever in groups. Ellis and Fisher (1975) argued that competing coalitions begin to disintegrate when "members of both coalitions realize they must come to some common ground of agreement" (p. 209).

As is evident by this review, subgroup influence plays an important role in group persuasion practices. Clearly, the activist group PETA also recognizes the impact that subgroups can play in an influence campaign. PETA knows that subgroups can often be more visible than individuals and so relies on collectivities to get media coverage and keep PETA in the public eye. Meanwhile, and simultaneously, PETA is also engaging in group-level influence efforts. This form of influence also has important contributions to make to a persuasive campaign.

Influence at the Group Level

Group Valence Model. The Group Valence Model (GVM), developed by Hoffman and colleagues (Hoffman 1979; Hoffman and Kleinman 1994), is an excellent example of influence produced at the group level. The GVM predicts final group outcomes from the total number of comments (positive and negative) made by the whole group for a given decision proposal.

How does this model predict final group decisions? Consider the restaurant example (Table 11.1) used previously to illustrate the DVM model. The GVM counts up all the positive comments made by all the group members and all the negative comments made by all the group members for each restaurant. Then for each choice, the group's negative comments are subtracted from the group's positive comments for that option. The restaurant option with the largest positive number of comments is the group's predicted final choice.

There are 24 positive group comments and 26 negative comments (-2) for the Chinese restaurant. There are 36 positive group comments and 12 negative group comments (+24) for the Russian restaurant. For McDonald's, there are 13 positive group comments and 34 negative group comments (-21). Given these results, the GVM would predict that the group would choose the Russian restaurant (which has the most positive total number of comments).

Hoffman (1979) noted that in about 85 percent of the decision-making groups he studied, the GVM accurately predicted the final group choice. To date, both the GVM and DVM have been shown to be accurate predictors of group decisions. Only in those cases in which the minority is more vocal than the majority does the GVM sometimes fail to predict as accurately as the DVM model. How can this happen? Given the scenario described in the chart, suppose that the numbers for the Russian restaurant fall out differently. That is, imagine that four of the five people are in favor of the Russian restaurant and produce more positive comments than negative comments but do not produce a large number of comments overall between them. But the fifth group member really does not want to go to the Russian restaurant and makes lots of negative comments against the Russian restaurant. If this person makes more negative comments than the other four group members' positive comments combined, the GVM (which calculates the final choice from the difference between the *total* number of positive and negative group comments) would predict that the Russian restaurant would *not* be the final group choice. However, the DVM, which predicts according to individual preferences would still pick the correct winner (the Russian restaurant) because there are four of five members who make more positive than negative comments for the Russian restaurant (even if the quantity of comments is small).

Group Argument. Another group-level influence strategy is argument constructed by the entire group (Meyers and Brashers 2000). To date, research on group argument has produced important findings about the structure and character of argument in groups. For example, Canary et al. (1987) identified four broad categories of argument structures in decision-making groups: simple arguments (one, and only one, point is developed), compound arguments (extending an argument or using two parallel arguments), eroded arguments (arguments that are never fully developed), and convergent arguments (arguments created by two or more people). In addition, Meyers, Seibold, and Brashers (1991) provided an initial picture of the distribution of argument acts in 45 decision-making group discussions, finding that argument was characterized primarily—and almost exclusively—by Assertions (claims), Elaborations (evidence), and Agreement.

Most recently, Meyers and Brashers (1998) tested a model of group argument that showed that three of four argument message types (claims, reasoning statements, and agreements) were accurate predictors of final group decision outcomes. Disagreement statements (perhaps due to the lack of disagreement found in many groups' decision-making discussions) were less accurate predictors of decision outcomes. Meyers and Brashers (1998) concluded that group argument has an impact on the final group decision because it stimulates more complex reasoning and/or helps to forge agreement among group members.

Clearly, group-level influence is another vital source of persuasion in group practices. As noted in the introduction to this chapter, PETA is deeply committed to group-level influence. It provides resources, information, and help from the group level for all types of persuasion efforts. Members of the larger PETA group also are activist spokespersons for PETA values on national television news and talk show programs. PETA obviously views group-level influence as integral to its persuasion campaign for animal rights.

In addition, PETA advocates the use of intergroup influence. Such influence is especially important if any type of bargaining or negotiation must take place (unions and management, warring countries, hostage situations, activist groups, and the law, etc.). These situations sometimes set up in-groups and out-groups who differentiate themselves from each other, and typically have great difficulty reaching any kind of final consensus. The next section addresses these intergroup influence strategies.

Influence at the Intergroup Level

Bargaining and Negotiation. Intergroup influence situations involve group members working together to confront or challenge an opposing group; individuals may be designated by groups to act as their representatives in bargaining and negotiation contexts (Putnam and Jones 1982). Bargaining and negotiation, according to Putnam, Van Hoeven, and Bullis (1991), is "a process in which two or more parties who hold incompatible goals engage in a give-and-take process to reach a mutually acceptable solution" (p. 86).

In research on communication, bargaining and negotiation has been studied as a form of argument (see Keough 1987; Putnam, Wilson, Waltman, and Turner 1986). Putnam et al. (1986) maintained that parties in negotiation interactions create arguments in which they "exchange, defend, and modify proposals and counterproposals as ways of developing a mutually acceptable solution" (p. 63). Moreover, Putnam and Geist (1985) found that arguments in bargaining and negotiation were constructed more often with analogy, cause, and hypothetical examples than with "hard facts" or "data" (p. 243).

One situation in which bargaining and negotiation occurs is in intergroup decision making between a labor union and representatives of an organization's management. These kind of negotiations often involve discussion of topics such as pay, benefits, and working conditions. For example, Putnam et al. (1991) investigated negotiations between teachers' unions and schools in two different areas, finding that different bargaining rites and rituals characterized negotiations in the two school districts. In one district, "negotiators engaged in the collective development of a legal document, complete with written proposals, ongoing deliberations at the table, and judgments of precedent cases" (p. 98). In the other district, "bargaining rituals . . . resembled shuttle diplomacy between two top secret teams who sent ambassadors to work behind closed doors" (p. 98). Putnam et al. (1991) speculate that these differences in how participants approach the task may be due, in part, to differences in perceptions of goals that negotiation and bargaining can achieve (e.g., reducing conflict, facilitating communication, enhancing solidarity, and balancing power).

In-group/Out-group Differentiation. Another line of research on intergroup influence has focused on communication strategies that increase or decrease in-group/out-group differentiation (e.g., Pittam and Gallois 1997). In-group/out-group differentiation occurs when individuals use social categories (e.g., gender or race) to distinguish members of their own category (in-group) from members of another category (out-group) (Wilder 1986). One strategy for managing in-group/out-group differentiation is to minimize real or perceived resource differences between the groups. For example, Brashers and Jackson (1991) argued that the activist group AIDS Coalition to Unleash Power (ACT UP) was able to influence government and medical scientific groups about drug-testing procedures because they educated themselves about governmental and medical-scientific methods of drug testing. In short, they reduced the differences between the in-group (government and the medical establishment) and the out-group (AIDS activists) on the resource of expertise and then were better able to exert influence that facilitated mutually acceptable solutions.

Another strategy to minimize differences between in-groups and out-groups might involve the verbal and nonverbal communication style choices made by group members. Communication Accommodation Theory (see Giles, Mulac, Bradac, and Johnson 1987) posits that individuals use converging or diverging communication styles to decrease or increase differentiation between themselves and members of other groups. Converging communication styles are characteristic of speakers who desire "social approval" or desire a "high level of communication efficiency" (Giles et al. 1987, 36–37). Diverging communication styles, in contrast, characterize speakers who desire "to communicate a contrastive self-image" or desire "to dissociate personally from the recipients or the recipients' definition of the situation" (37). Hence, using a convergent style will decrease differentiation between in-groups and out-groups, whereas a divergent style will increase differentiation.

Increasing communication between groups also may decrease in-group/out-group tensions. Bornstein, Rapoport, Terpel, and Katz (1989) concluded that if communication was restricted to within-group discussions, then in-group/out-group bias was increased. However, if between-group discussion was allowed, such discussion blurred the in-group/out-group distinctions and led group members to be more committed to between-group agreements.

Intergroup influence can be very effective, especially if in-group/out-group distinctions can be overcome. As can be seen by PETA's actions, intergroup influence that involves linkages between PETA advocates and other groups (e.g., scientists, veterinarians, doctors, or political groups) is especially persuasive. Such connections lend credibility to the influence campaign and create the potential for greater impact.

Conclusion

In this chapter, we provided an overview of prominent theories, models, and research programs concerning influence processes in groups. As is evident, influence in groups can occur at the individual, subgroup, group, and intergroup level. As illustrated by the example of PETA described at the beginning of this chapter, some of the most successful influence campaigns employ all of these levels of influence. Ideas from Persuasive Arguments Theory and Social Comparison Theory demonstrate how individuals might be a source of influence in groups, either because the individual serves as a source of novel arguments (i.e., PAT) or as a basis for comparison (i.e., SCT). At the level of the subgroup, The Distributed Valence Model predicts that the "will of the majority" determines most group decisions, whereas the research on majority-minority influence demonstrates that, despite the fact that the majority subgroup often is the most successful, minorities can succeed when they are consistent, persistent, and produce high-quality arguments. Research on tag-team argument and coalition formation further explores communicative strategies for subgroup influence. At the group level of influence, the Group Valence Model predicts the choices of groups based on the total number of arguments for and against proposals; the group argument model focuses on *how* arguments are constructed and how that might influence group decisions. Finally, intergroup influence has been investigated in research on bargaining and negotiation settings (e.g., between a labor union and the management of an organization) and in situations in which in-group/out-group differentiation is high (e.g., between activists and experts such as scientists). Taken together, these theories demonstrate the importance of understanding group communication at each level of influence. This type of multi-level analysis is important because it can help researchers, as well as group managers and members, to better understand the complexities and intricacies of group influence.

References

Alderton, S. M., and Frey, L. R. (1983). "Effects of reactions to arguments on group outcome: The case of group polarization." *Central States Speech Journal* 34: 88–95.

Alderton, S. M., and Frey, L. R. (1986). "Argumentation in small group decision-making." In R. Y. Hirokawa and M. S. Poole (eds.), *Communication and Group Decision-Making* (pp. 157–173). Beverly Hills, CA: Sage.

Arbuthnot, J., and Wagner, M. (1982). "Minority influence: Effects of size, conversion, and sex." *Journal of Psychology* 111: 285–295.

Bornstein, G., Rapoport, A., Terpel, L., and Katz, T. (1989). "Within- and between-group communication in intergroup competition for public goods." *Journal of Experimental Social Psychology* 25: 422–436.

Brashers, D. E., and Jackson, S. (1991). " 'Politically savvy sick people': Public penetration of the technical sphere." In D. W. Parson (ed.), *Argument in Controversy: Proceedings of the Seventh Speech Communication Association/American Forensic Association Conference on Argumentation* (pp. 284–288). Annandale, VA: Speech Communication Association.

Brashers, D. E., and Meyers, R. A. (1989). "Tag-team argument and group decision-making: A preliminary investigation." In B. E. Gronbeck (ed.), *Spheres of Argument: Proceedings of the Sixth Speech Communication Association/American Forensics Association Conference on Argumentation* (pp. 542–550). Annandale, VA: Speech Communication Association.

Buchli, R. D., and Pearce, W. B. (1975). "Coalition and communication." *Human Communication Research* 1: 213–221.

Burnstein, E. (1982). "Persuasion as argument processing." In H. Brandstatter, J. H. Davis, and G. Stocker-Kreichgauer (eds.), *Group Decision Making* (pp. 103–124). New York: Academic Press.

Burnstein, E., Vinokur, A., and Pichevin, M. F. (1974). "What do differences between own, admired, and attributed choices have to do with group induced shifts in choice?" *Journal of Experimental Social Psychology* 10: 428–443.

Canary, D. J., Brossmann, B. G., and Seibold, D. R. (1987). "Argument structures in decision-making groups." *Southern Speech Communication Journal* 53: 18–37.

Clark, R. D., III, and Maass, A. (1990). "The effects of majority size on minority influence." *European Journal of Social Psychology* 20: 99–117.

Davis, J. H. (1973). "Group decision and social interaction: A theory of social decision schemes." *Psychological Review* 80: 97–125.

Ellis, D. G., and Fisher, B. A. (1975). "Phases of conflict in small group development." *Human Communication Research* 1: 195–212.

Frey, L. R. (1994). "The naturalistic paradigm: Studying small groups in the postmodern era." *Small Group Research* 25: 551–577.

Frey, L. R. (1996). "Remembering and 're-membering': A history of theory and research on communication and group decision making." In R. Y. Hirokawa and M. S. Poole (eds.), *Communication and Group Decision Making* (pp. 19–51). Thousand Oaks, CA: Sage.

Gamson, W. A. (1961). "A theory of coalition formation." *American Sociological Review* 26: 373–382.

Gamson, W. A. (1964). "Experimental studies in coalition formation." In L. Berkowitz (ed.), *Advances in Experimental Social Psychology* Vol. 1 (pp. 81–110). New York: Academic Press.

Garlick, R., and Mongeau, P. A. (1993). "Argument quality and group member status as determinants of attitudinal minority influence." *Western Journal of Speech Communication* 57: 289–308.

Giles, H., Mulac, A., Bradac, J. J., and Johnson, P. (1987). "Speech accommodation theory: The next decade and beyond." In M. McLaughlin (ed.), *Communication Yearbook 10* (pp. 13–48). Thousand Oaks, CA: Sage.

Gresson, A. D. (1978). "Phenomenology and the rhetoric of identification: A neglected dimension of coalition communication inquiry." *Communication Quarterly* 26: 14–23.

Haslett, B. B., and Ruebush, J. (2000). "What differences do individual differences in groups make? The effects of individuals, culture, and group composition." In L. R. Frey, D. S. Gouran, and M. S. Poole (eds.), *The Handbook of Group Communication Theory and Research* (pp. 115–138). Thousand Oaks, CA: Sage.

Hoffman, L. R. (Ed.). (1979). *The Group Problem Solving Process: Studies of a Valence Model.* New York: Praeger.

Hoffman, L. R., and Kleinman, G. B. (1994). "Individual and group in group problem solving: The Valence Model redressed." *Human Communication Research* 21: 36–59.

Keough, C. M. (1987). "The nature and function of argument in organizational bargaining research." *Southern Speech Communication Journal* 53: 1–17.

Ketrow, S. M. (2000). "Nonverbal aspects of group communication." In L. R. Frey, D. S. Gouran, and M. S. Poole (eds.), *The Handbook of Group Communication Theory and Research* (pp. 192–222). Thousand Oaks, CA: Sage.

Latane, B., and Liu, J. H. (1996). "The intersubjective geometry of social space." *Journal of Communication* 46(4): 26–34.

Mannix, E. A., and White, S. B. (1992). "The effect of distributive uncertainty on coalition formation in organizations." *Organizational Behavior and Human Decision Processes* 51: 198–219.

McPhee, R. D., Poole, M. S., and Seibold, D. R. (1982). "The valence model unveiled: Critique and alternative formulation." In M. Burgoon (ed.), *Communication Yearbook 5* (pp. 259–278). New Brunswick, NJ: Transaction Books.

Meyers, R. A., and Brashers, D. E. (1998). "Argument in group decision-making: Explicating a process model and investigating the argument-outcome link." *Communication Monographs* 65: 261–281.

Meyers, R. A., and Brashers, D. E. (2000). "Influence processes in group interaction." In L. R. Frey, D. S. Gouran, and M. S. Poole (eds.), *The Handbook of Group Communication Theory and Research* (pp. 288–312). Thousand Oaks, CA: Sage.

Meyers, R. A., Brashers, D. E., and Hanner, J. (2000). "Majority-minority influence: Identifying argumentative patterns and predicting argument-outcome links." *Journal of Communication* 50(4): 3–30.

Meyers, R. A., Seibold, D. R., and Brashers, D. E. (1991). "Argument in initial group decision-making discussions: Refinement of a coding scheme and a descriptive quantitative analysis." *Western Journal of Speech Communication* 55: 47–68.

Moscovici, S., and Faucheux, C. (1972). "Social influence, conformity bias, and the study of active minorities." In L. Berkowitz (ed.), *Advances in Experimental Social Psychology* Vol. 6 (pp. 149–202). New York: Academic Press.

Moscovici, S., Lage, E., and Naffrechoux, M. (1969). "Influence of a consistent minority on the responses of a majority in a color perception task." *Sociometry* 32: 365–380.

Myers, D. G. (1982). "Polarizing effects of social interaction." In H. Brandstatter, J. H. Davis, and G. Stocker-Kreichgauer (eds.), *Group Decision Making* (pp. 125–161). New York: Academic Press.

Nemeth, C. (1982). "Stability of faction position and influence." In G. H. Brandstatter, J. H. Davis, and G. Stocker-Kriechgauer (eds.), *Group Decision Making* (pp. 185–213). New York: Academic Press.

Nemeth, C. (1986). "Differential contributions of majority and minority influence." *Psychological Review* 93: 23–32.

Nemeth, C. J., Mayseless, O., Sherman, J., and Brown, Y. (1990). "Exposure to dissent and recall of information." *Journal of Personality and Social Psychology* 58: 429–437.

Nemeth, C., and Wachtler, J. (1974). "Creating the perceptions of consistency and confidence: A necessary condition for minority influence." *Sociometry* 37: 529–540.

——. (1983). "Creative problem solving as a result of majority vs. minority influence." *European Journal of Social Psychology* 13: 45–55.

Norton, R. W. (1979). "Identifying coalitions: Generating units of analysis." *Small Group Behavior* 10: 343–354.

People for the Ethical Treatment of Animals (PETA). (2000). Website available at *www.peta.org*. New York: Author.

Pendell, S. D. (1990). "Deviance and conflict in small group decision making: An exploratory study." *Small Group Research* 21: 393–403.

Peterson, R. S., and Nemeth, C. J. (1996). "Focus versus flexibility: Majority and minority influence can both improve performance." *Personality and Social Psychology Bulletin* 22: 14–23.

Pittam, J., and Gallois, C. (1997). "Language strategies in the attribution of blame for HIV and AIDS." *Communication Monographs* 64: 201–218.

Putnam, L. L. (1986). "Conflict in group decision making." In R. Y. Hirokawa and M. S. Poole (eds.), *Communication and Group Decision-Making* (pp. 135–155). Thousand Oaks, CA: Sage.

Putnam, L. L., and Geist, P. (1985). "Argument in bargaining: An analysis of the reasoning process." *Southern Speech Communication Journal* 50: 225–245.

Putnam, L. L., and Jones, T. S. (1982). "Reciprocity in negotiations: An analysis of bargaining interaction." *Communication Monographs* 49: 171–191.

Putnam, L. L., Van Hoeven, S. A., and Bullis, C. A. (1991). "The role of rituals and fantasy themes in teachers' bargaining." *Western Journal of Speech Communication* 55: 85–103.

Putnam, L. L., Wilson, S., Waltman, M. S., and Turner, D. (1986). "The evolution of case arguments in teachers' bargaining." *Journal of the American Forensic Association* 23: 63–81.

Sanders, G. S., and Baron, R. S. (1977). "Is social comparison irrelevant for producing choice shifts?" *Journal of Experimental Social Psychology* 13: 303–314.

Segal, J. (1979). "Coalition formation in tetrads: A critical test of four theories." *Journal of Psychology* 103: 209–219.

Van Dyne, L., and Saavedra, R. (1996). "A naturalistic minority influence experiment: Effects of divergent thinking, conflict and originality in work-groups." *British Journal of Social Psychology* 35: 151–167.

Vinacke, W. E., Mogy, R., Powers, W., Langan, C., and Beck, R. (1974). "Accommodative strategy and communication in a three person matrix game." *Journal of Personality and Social Psychology* 29: 509–525.

Vitz, P. C., and Kite, W. R. (1970). "Factors affecting conflict and negotiation within an alliance." *Journal of Experimental Social Psychology* 6: 233–247.

Wilder, D. A. (1986). "Social categorization: Implications for creation and reduction of intergroup conflict." In L . Berkowitz (ed.), *Advances in Experimental Social Psychology* Vol. 19: 291–355). New York: Academic Press.

Wood, W., Lundgren, S., Ouellette, J. A., Busceme, S., and Blackstone, T. (1994). "Minority influence: A meta-analytic review of social influence processes." *Psychological Bulletin* 115: 323–345.

Zaleska, M. (1976). "Majority influence on group choices among bets." *Journal of Personality and Social Psychology* 33: 8–17.

Part V

Groups and Teams

Groups and teams are pervasive aspects of everyday life and, in fact, appear to be functional necessities in contemporary American society (Hirokawa, DeGooyer, and Valde 2000). From work to play, almost everything we do seems to involve groups and teams.

Sayings like "two heads are better than one" express a folk wisdom reflecting the belief that when individuals join together to solve problems and reach decisions, they usually produce better decisions and solutions to problems than individuals working alone. At the same time, other sayings like "a camel is a horse designed by a committee" attest to the fact that groups often do not perform as well as they should. To be sure, there is nothing magical about groups and teams—they can do a "bad" job as easily as they can do a "good" one.

The question of why some groups perform well while others do not is an important one to ask—especially given our heavy reliance on groups and teams in contemporary American society. Over the years, much research has addressed the group effectiveness question (Bettenhausen 1991; Cohen, Ledford, and Spreitzer 1996; Hirokawa 1996; Larson and LaFasto 1989; McGrath 1997). The results of decades of research indicate that the performance of task-oriented groups and teams is attributable to many different factors that "do not come in separate, easily distinguishable packages" (Hackman 1990, 8).

Defining Group Effectiveness

What is an "effective" group or team? Group communication research is generally concerned with the "bottom line"— that is, the impact of communication processes on outcomes such as decision quality, member satisfaction, member motivation, and so forth. However, incorporating such outcomes into a viable measure of group "effectiveness" is difficult.

To illustrate this difficulty, let us take decision quality as a measure for group effectiveness. In most real-world tasks, decisions and solutions to problems cannot be proven to be "good" or "bad" on absolute grounds. A solution judged to be effective in the short run may turn out to be a total failure in the long run, and vice versa. A decision judged to be a "good" one from the perspective of one party may be seen as a "terrible" decision for other parties.

Assessing group effectiveness has an additional complication. We generally treat outcomes as though they happen at the end of the group process. But outcomes like member satisfaction and motivation do not necessarily form at the end of a group's deliberations. In fact, such outcomes are "produced" and "reproduced" over time in groups (see Chapter 6 in Part II of this book). For example, the outcomes of a group's prior decision may affect the level of motivation among group members in the current decision situation, which, in turn, could change in future decision episodes, depending on the outcome of the current instance. In other words, a group outcome, and hence group effectiveness, is a dynamic entity—constantly changing and shifting over time. An "effective" group or team today could be an "ineffective" group or team tomorrow.

Despite the difficulties of assessing group effectiveness, group communication scholars have persevered in their attempts to confront the group effectiveness challenge. Part V provides a collection of essays that address the question: What are the factors that influence the performance of groups and teams?

References

Bettenhausen, K. L. (1991). "Five years of group research: What have we learned and what needs to be addressed." *Journal of Management,* 17: 345–381.

Cohen, S. G., Ledford, G. E. J., and Spreitzer, G. M. (1996). "A predictive model of self-managing work team effectiveness." *Human Relations,* 49: 643–676.

Hackman, J. R. (ed.). (1990). *Groups That Work (and Those That Don't).* San Francisco: Jossey-Bass.

Hirokawa, R. Y. (1996). "Communication and group decision-making effectiveness." In R. Y. Hirokawa and M. S. Poole (eds.), *Communication and Group Decision-Making* 2nd Edition, (pp. 269–297). Thousand Oaks, CA: Sage.

Hirokawa, R. Y., DeGooyer, D., and Valde, K. (2000). "Using narratives to study task group effectiveness." *Small Group Research,* 31: 573–591.

Larson, C. E., and LaFasto, F. M. J. (1989). *Teamwork: What Must Go Right/What Can Go Wrong.* Newbury Park, CA: Sage.

McGrath, J. E. (1997). "Small group research: That once and future field." *Group Dynamics: Theory, Research, and Practice,* 1: 1–36. ✦

Chapter 12
Communication and Group Decision-Making Efficacy

Randy Y. Hirokawa

The role that communication plays in group decision-making effectiveness is the focus of this chapter. Hirokawa argues that groups do not reach good or bad decisions by accident. Rather, a group is able to make a high-quality decision because its final choice is characterized by (a) a proper understanding of the problem, (b) appropriate choice-making objectives, and (c) an accurate evaluation of the positive and negative qualities of available choices. It follows that errors occurring in one or more of those areas are likely to lead to a regrettable group decision. The author concludes by identifying a set of cognitive, affiliative, and egocentric constraints that, if left unchecked, can lead to major breakdowns in a group's deliberations.

Benjamin Franklin once wrote, "in this world nothing is certain but death and taxes." If Franklin were alive today, he would probably revise his statement to include group decision participation.

It is safe to say groups pervade virtually all facets of our everyday lives. From work teams to church committees, whatever we do seems to involve group work. Consider the following facts about group work in the United States.

- Over 90 percent of Fortune "500" companies have reported using groups in their daily operations (Lawler and Mohrman 1985).
- Studies of managers show that they spend between 30 and 80 percent of their time in meetings (Poole 1991).
- The average executive spends almost two out of every five working days in small group meetings (Tubbs 1995).
- Between 40 and 50 percent of the U.S. workforce uses work teams to manage businesses, produce products, and provide services (Engleberg and Wynn 1997).
- The average tenured university professor serves on six committees simultaneously and spends eleven hours per week in meetings of various kinds (Brilhart and Galanes 1989).

Our reliance on groups, however, must be tempered by the realization that groups are *not* "magic bullets." Asking groups to solve problems or make decisions involves risk. Humorous folklore sayings like, "A camel is a horse designed by a committee," or "Any problem can be made unsolvable by a committee" attest to the fact that groups frequently do not work as they should. Groups can make dreadfully "bad" decisions as easily as they can make wonderfully "good" ones (Hackman 1990; Janis 1982). This is perhaps why scholars from a variety of academic disciplines have been captivated by the question: "Why do some groups make better decisions than others?"

Why Groups Succeed or Fail

The fact that groups often fail to perform as they should has prompted many small group researchers to investigate the question of what contributes to effective group decision-making performance. The results of these studies have identified several different factors that contribute to a group's ability to reach a high-quality decision. One important factor is the *informational resources* available to the group. In general, researchers have found that the better informed group members are about the problem they are required to solve, as well as the positive and negative qualities of optional choices available to it, the better able it is to reach a high-quality decision. In fact, numerous authors have indicated that the ability of a group to gather and retain a wide range of information is the single most important determinant of high-quality decision making (Kelley and Thibaut 1969).

A second factor that appears to make a difference in group decision-making efficacy is the *quality of effort* group members put forth in trying to reach a decision. More precisely, researchers have discovered that groups are more likely to reach a high-quality decision when their members engage in "vigilant decision making" (Janis and Mann 1977). Vigilant decision making occurs when group members carefully and painstakingly examine and reexamine the information upon which a consequential decision is based. According to Janis (1982), it is this kind of persevering effort that helps a group overcome negative groupthink forces that can lead it to a remarkably bad decision.

A third factor that appears to affect group performance is the *quality of thinking* that occurs among group members as they attempt to reach a collective decision. In particular, studies have discovered that the ability of a group to reach a high-quality decision is dependent on its members' ability to draw correct or warranted inferences from information bearing on the decision (Gouran, Hirokawa, and Martz 1986). In other words, a group is more likely to reach a high-quality decision when its members are able to draw appropriate conclusions from decision-relevant data available to them. NASA's regrettable decision to launch the ill-fated space shuttle *Challenger* in the face of information suggesting a postponement of that launch provides a good example of this point. During the pre-launch deliberation, engineers from Morton Thiokol, manufacturers of the solid-fuel rocket boosters that propelled the shuttle, provided NASA decision makers with data indicating that a crucial component of the rocket motor had malfunctioned on previous shuttle flights when

launch temperatures fell below 52° Fahrenheit. Because the temperature at the time of the *Challenger* launch was expected to be 32°F, the conclusion that NASA *should* have drawn from those data was that the component was likely to malfunction on this flight as well. Such a conclusion would obviously justify a decision to postpone the launch until the temperature reached or exceeded 52 degrees. Instead, the conclusion that NASA decision makers *actually* drew from the data was that, since malfunctions of the rocket component had not resulted in any serious problems with previous shuttle flights, there was no reason to believe that any problems would result in the present instance. This conclusion supported the decision to proceed with the launch of the *Challenger*—a decision that ultimately cost the lives of all seven crew members (Hirokawa, Gouran, and Martz 1988).

A fourth factor known to affect group decision-making performance is the reasoning system its members employ in reaching a decision. A group's "reasoning system" refers to the way group members go about making a choice from among a set of alternatives (Hirokawa and Keyton 1991). Peter Senge, in his influential book *The Fifth Discipline* (1990), observes that groups usually employ either "rational" or "political" reasoning in arriving at a decision. A *rational* system is one in which the group arrives at a final decision by carefully considering the positive and negative qualities of all available choices and then selecting the alternative that offers the most positive, and least negative, attributes. A *political* reasoning system, on the other hand, is one in which "factors other than the intrinsic merits of alternative courses of action weigh in making decisions—factors such as building one's own power base, or 'looking good,' or 'pleasing the boss' " (Senge 1990, 60). In short, a group using a political reasoning system is guided by self-interests and selects either the most expedient alternative or the alternative that offers the path of least resistance. According to Senge, groups are more likely to arrive at high-quality decisions when they employ rational, as opposed to political, reasoning systems in arriving at decisions (p. 60).

Importance of Group Communication

While it is clear that group decision-making performance is affected by a variety of factors, many researchers suggest that the quality of communication that occurs as a group attempts to reach a decision may well be the single most important determinant of group decision-making performance (see, e.g., Collins and Guetzkow 1964; Gouran and Hirokawa 1983; Hackman and Morris 1975; Janis and Mann 1977; Hirokawa 1982, 1986; Hirokawa and Salazar 1999; McGrath 1984; Taylor and Faust 1952). Such a conclusion, for instance, is implied in Ivan Steiner's (1972, 9) equation:

> *Actual (group) productivity* = [potential (group) productivity] – [losses due to faulty processes]

How does a group's communication affect the quality of its decision making? Early theorists speculated that group communication served as a medium or channel through which the true determinants of group decision performance were able to exert their influence. Specifically, it was suggested that group discussion affects the quality of group performance in three general ways.

First, *discussion allows group members to distribute and pool available informational resources necessary for effective decision making and problem solving.* Bamlund (1959), for example, maintained that open discussion is especially important for successful group decision making when the group is characterized by an unequal distribution of vital information. Here the opportunity for group discussion enables informed individuals to disseminate information that is needed by the group to reach a high-quality choice. A similar point is made by Leavitt (1951), who argued that group discussion facilitates effective group performance when it results in the effective centralization of information in the hands of people who need it to help the group arrive at

a high-quality decision. Here the true determinant of group performance is assumed to be the presence of relevant information, and group communication provides the medium through which this information is distributed among group members and subsequently brought to bear on the decision task.

A second view holds that *discussion allows group members to catch and remedy errors of individual judgment.* According to Taylor and Faust (1952), the principal reason why groups generally outperform individual decision makers is because the discussion of ideas, suggestions, and rationales for preferred choices tends to expose informational, judgmental, and reasoning deficiencies within individual members that might go undetected if those individuals were making decisions on their own. Moreover, group discussion provides the opportunity for members to point out and correct these problems before they can contribute to a regrettable final decision. In this case, the true determinant of group decision-making effectiveness is the occurrence of judgment errors by group members, and group interaction provides a medium for detecting and correcting these errors before they can adversely affect group performance.

A third perspective views *discussion as a means for intra-group persuasion.* Riecken (1958) suggested that group discussion affects group decision performance by serving as a medium for persuasion among group members. He notes that group discussion provides members with the opportunity to present and support their decisional preferences and, in so doing, to try to convince others to go along with those alternatives. According to Riecken, the overall quality of a group's decision will often depend on the decision preference of the group's most persuasive member(s). A similar notion is provided by Shaw and Penrod (1962). They suggest that group discussion provides members with the opportunity to convince others to accept and utilize available information in arriving at a collective choice. Their research indicated that the presence of knowledgeable group members does not necessarily lead to high levels of group performance unless those individuals are able to persuade others to accept and utilize the information they possess in arriving at a group decision. According to this view, then, the actual determinants of group performance are the amount and quality of information group members possess, the quality of the alternatives they favor, and their ability to persuade others to accept their information and/or decisional preferences. Group communication thus represents a convenient opportunity for those individuals to display their persuasive skills in convincing others to accept their informational or decisional preferences.

Communication as an Active Medium

In contrast to earlier theorists, who viewed the group discussion process as a more or less passive medium that allows the actual factors that affect group decision performance to exert their influence on the group, recent theorists have advocated the more *active* role that communication plays in effective group decision making. This perspective assumes that group communication is more than a convenient channel that group members use to distribute information or make their preferences known to others in the group. Rather, it is a social instrument (or tool) that group members use to create (or constitute) group decisions. As a social tool, however, communication in a group can exert its own distorting and biasing effects on group decisions (Poole and Hirokawa 1986).

A theory of group decision-making effectiveness that adopts an active view of the group communication process is the *Functional Communication Theory*. Briefly, this theory is based on two general assumptions: First, all decision-making tasks are characterized by certain requirements that have to be fulfilled in order for a group to reach a high-quality decision; and second, group communication represents the means by which group members attempt to fulfill the critical requirements of their task. In short,

Functional Communication Theory adopts an instrumental view of group communication and sees it as the primary "means by which group members attempt to meet the requisites for successful group decision making" (Gouran and Hirokawa 1983).

Functional Communication Theory

Briefly, Functional Communication Theory begins by viewing group "decisions" as the culmination of a series of smaller "sub-decisions" made by the group in regard to four general questions (Hirokawa and Scheerhorn 1986):

1. Does the present situation require us to make a choice of some kind?

2. What do we want to achieve or accomplish in making a choice?

3. What choices are available to us?

4. What are the desirable and undesirable aspects of each choice?

Functional Communication Theory asserts that group members collectively arrive at "answers" to these four questions by interacting (or communicating) with each other. These answers constitute the group's "decision logic system." It is from this "logic system" that a group's overall decision is assumed to emerge (Hirokawa and Keyton 1990). It is important to emphasize that although these four issues are presented in a seemingly logical order, Functional Communication Theory does *not* assert that the order in which members address them is crucial for group decision-making effectiveness. Actually, consistent with Marshall Scott Poole's developmental theory of group decision making (Poole 1983), Functional Communication Theory acknowledges that groups display a great deal of variability and idiosyncrasy in the way they address these four issues during their decision-making interaction.

By conceptualizing the group decision-making process as a series of sub-decisions contributing to the selection and justification of an overall choice, Functional Communication Theory identifies four ways in which group communication can affect group decision-making performance (Gouran and Hirokawa 1993).

First, group interaction can *influence the sub-decisions group members collectively make regarding the choice-making situation.* One common error occurring at this point in the group decision-making process is the failure to recognize the existence of a problem that could be remedied by an appropriate decision. An example of this can be drawn from a university committee I recently served on. This group was charged with the task of determining whether changes should be made to the University's human rights policies. Several of the committee were very vocal in their belief that no human rights problems currently exist at the University of Iowa, while others were equally adamant that such problems do exist on campus. The point here is a simple one: Since our recommendations, and the *quality* of those recommendations, would depend on the conclusions we reached regarding the existence of human rights problems on campus, if there were no problems but we wrongly concluded that they existed, we would be likely to make a bad decision by calling for unnecessary changes in recruitment and admissions policies. On the other hand, if there *were* human rights problems on campus but we concluded that none existed, we were equally likely to make a bad decision by recommending that no changes be made to the University's human rights policies.

A second way group communication can affect decision-making performance is by *influencing the criteria the group employs in reaching a final decision.* As suggested earlier, group members usually are cognizant of specific outcomes they hope or expect to realize as a result of their choice making. For instance, university committees usually make decisions to "improve" the state of affairs on campus, or "make better use" of existing resources. These objectives generally serve as the criteria (or standards) the group employs in evaluating alternative choices. Breakdowns in this facet of the decision-

making process can thus have detrimental effects on the final decisions made by a group.

The space shuttle *Challenger* accident provides a tragic example of how the use of inappropriate criteria can result in highly regrettable group decisions. On the morning of January 28, 1986, the *Challenger* lifted majestically off its launching pad at the Kennedy Space Center. A mere 73 seconds into its flight, in full view of millions of horrified observers, the spacecraft exploded, killing all seven of its crew, including an elementary school teacher named Christa McAuliffe. Almost immediately, President Reagan appointed a special commission, headed by former Secretary of State and Attorney General William P. Rogers, to determine the actual or probable cause or causes of the accident. After a grueling five-month investigation, highlighted by a number of public hearings, the commission uncovered disturbing evidence that the decision to launch the *Challenger* was made in the presence of information questioning the safety of the mission. It thus concluded that "flawed decision making" contributed to the tragic accident.

Many have debated whether the decision-making process involved in the *Challenger* disaster was actually as flawed as the Rogers Commission indicated. What is undisputed is the fact that NASA decision makers appeared to employ decisional criteria inconsistent with historical precedents involving manned space flights. Traditionally, decisions involving manned space flights were governed by the "safety first" criterion. That is, a launch should be canceled if there is any doubt regarding the success of the mission or the safety of the crew. In the case of the *Challenger*, however, it appears that different criteria were operating during the decision-making process. Several participants testified in public hearings that they felt "pressured" to maintain the ambitious schedule that NASA had established for the shuttle program (Gouran, Hirokawa, and Martz 1986). This pressure was further exacerbated by some participants' desire not to disappoint or inconvenience the national media, which had focused significant attention on this particular launch because it involved a civilian crew member whose job it was to symbolize the inseparability of space exploration and science education. In short, it appears that the decision makers responsible for the *Challenger* launch, while still concerned with safety, were also influenced by the objective of maintaining their launch schedule. This concern may have overridden the long-standing "safety first" criterion and contributed to the ill-advised decision to launch the *Challenger.*

A third way group communication can affect group decision-making performance is by *influencing the range of choices a group considers in reaching a final decision.* The quality of a group's final decision obviously depends on the quality of options available to it. Simply stated, a group cannot be expected to make a "good" choice if it does not possess "good" options to choose from. The choices a group generates through its brainstorming interaction thus play a crucial role in effective decision making.

To illustrate this point, suppose the president of a university leaves that institution to take a similar position at another university. Immediately, a search committee is created to find a suitable replacement for the departed president. For the sake of this example, suppose the committee was unable to entice any well-qualified individuals to apply for the job. At this point, the committee would either have to postpone making a choice until at least one well-qualified individual applied or select a candidate who lacked the expertise and experience necessary to continue the success that the university had achieved under the leadership of the departed president. Suppose further the Board of Regents of the university is unwilling to extend the search, and thus the committee is *forced* to choose from an inferior list of candidates. There is no reason to expect such a group to make a "good" decision. This example may seem absurd to you, but groups often feel compelled to make decisions even when they do not have a good set

of alternatives from which to choose (Gouran 1982).

A fourth way group communication can affect decision-making performance is by *influencing the group's assessment of the desirable and undesirable features of alternative choices.* Since a group usually relies on its evaluation of the positive and negative aspects of available choices to make a final decision, breakdowns at this stage of the decision-making process can directly affect a group's ability to make a high-quality choice. There are at least four types of evaluation errors that can adversely affect group decision-making performance: (1) failure to recognize the positive qualities of available choices, (2) failure to recognize the negative qualities of available choices, (3) overestimation of the positive qualities of available choices, and (4) overestimation of the negative qualities of alternative choices.

An example drawn from my conversations with college coaches will illustrate this problem. By and large, most of the coaches I talked to said they do not evaluate prospective high school athletes on the basis of their high school accomplishments but rather on their *projected performance* at the collegiate level. In other words, in observing and evaluating a high school athlete, they speculate what she or he will, and will not, be able to do at the collegiate level of competition.

One kind of mistake a coaching staff can make is to overlook an athlete's positive qualities. For instance, coaches may overlook her "intelligence" or "strong work ethic" in evaluating the athlete. This oversight can cause a college to bypass her in favor of an athlete who does not develop as fully as they would like.

In the same way, coaches can easily overlook negative qualities of the athlete. The National Football League (NFL) and the National Basketball League (NBA) are littered with examples of "first round draft picks" who never lived up to their "can't miss" star billing. The Green Bay Packers, for example, drafted an offensive lineman in the first round some years ago only to discover later that this player's athletic achievements in college were enhanced by the use of drugs (steroids) that were banned by the NFL. Needless to say, this individual had a short-lived and unsuccessful stint in the NFL. In short, by failing to recognize those negative aspects, the executives for the Green Bay Packers made a regrettable first-round draft choice.

Bad decisions can also result from a group's overestimation of the positive or negative aspects of alternative choices. Doug Flutie and Kurt Warner, outstanding quarterbacks in the NFL, are cases in point. Neither Flutie nor Warner were drafted by any NFL teams when they came out of college because many scouts believed they did not possess the size, speed, or arm strength to be good NFL quarterbacks. Both individuals proved their critics and detractors wrong by demonstrating on the field of play that they had other attributes which enabled them to overcome the "limitations" that caused them to be rejected by NFL teams. Simply put, groups sometimes make bad decisions by shying away from choices that they *should* have made but did not make because they put too much stock in the limitations of particular alternatives.

Summary and Conclusions

It should be clear at this point that effective group decision making usually does not happen by accident. In most cases, a group is able to make a high-quality choice because the way group members communicate and interact with each other in arriving at a final choice is characterized by (1) proper understanding of the problem or situation; (2) appropriate choice-making objectives; and (3) accurate evaluation of the positive and negative qualities of available choices. In the same way, errors occurring in one or more of those areas are likely to lead to a regrettable group decision.

I must point out that it is very easy for errors to occur in various phases of the group's interaction and reasoning processes. In fact, errors occurring in one phase can facilitate additional errors in subsequent phases. The important question that remains to be an-

swered is why these errors occur in the first place.

In his book *Crucial Decisions*, Irving Janis (1989) advances a constraints model that provides a structure and typology for understanding why errors occur in the decision-making interaction of groups. Janis suggests that three factors—what he calls *cognitive*, *affiliative*, and *egocentric constraints*—can lead to errors in various phases of the group's interaction and reasoning processes.

Cognitive constraints come into play when the members of a decision-making group confront a task for which little information is available, time is sharply limited, and/or the matter to be resolved is beyond the ordinary level of complexity. According to Janis, the presence of cognitive constraints can cause a group to resort to standard operating procedures in making choices rather than to vigilantly perform the essential requirements of the task. The health care teams I work with provide excellent examples of this. Sometimes, because of scheduling problems or unanticipated delays, the teams must attend to patients in less time than they would like. In these "crisis" situations, the teams often rely on what I call "habits of mind"—that is, conventional wisdom about what a problem is and what should be done about it—to make more efficient use of the limited time they have with these patients. In doing so, they attend to various functional requirements in a cursory manner, rather than in the detailed, vigilant manner expected of them.

Affiliative constraints usually occur when relationships among group members are a dominant concern and members fear either deterioration in such relationships or undue influence from one or more individuals whose thinking is not in line with majority sentiments. For example, I have noticed that the development of close friendships among health care team members sometimes hinders those individuals from engaging in "tough-minded" questioning of each other's assessments and recommendations. In post-rotation interviews, such individuals often admitted they deliberately refrained from "making an issue" of something because they wanted to preserve the camaraderie that had been fostered within the team. In short, the presence of "affiliative constraints" can hinder a group's efforts to effectively address functional requirements during group interaction.

Egocentric constraints are likely when at least one group member has a highly pronounced need for control or is otherwise driven by personal motivations. In my experiences with health care teams, "egocentric constraints" are most likely to emerge when a team member perceives himself/herself to be of higher status than other group members. In these instances, the individual will attempt to "take over" the team by dominating the discussion and telling others what to do and how they should do it. In short, the presence of a controlling group member often results in the ineffective performance of functional requirements because the group addresses only those functions that the controlling member feels it necessary for the team to address.

When any of these constraints becomes dominant, the interests of effective group decision making are likely to be undermined. Understanding how these constraints affect the role that communication plays in group decision-making performance represents an important priority for future small group communication researchers. Clearly, there is still much we need to understand about the role that group communication plays in effective or ineffective group decision making. Fortunately, the theoretical perspective discussed in this essay provides us with a useful framework for better understanding this role. As we discover more about how communicative forces, affected by cognitive, affiliative, and egocentric constraints, positively and negatively influence the decision-making process employed by a group in arriving at a decision, we will be in a much better position to offer warranted prescriptions for improving the quality of group interaction and performance. For the moment, however, it may be sufficient for groups to simply recognize the interaction and reasoning processes they are employing

to arrive at a decision, and to be aware of breakdowns that can occur in those processes, as well as the consequences of those breakdowns. Such self-conscious deliberation can pay big dividends in ensuring effective group decision making.

References

Bamlund, D. C. (1959). "A comparative study of individual, majority, and group judgment." *Journal of Abnormal and Social Psychology* 58: 55–60.

Brilhart, J. K., and Galanes, G. J. (1989). *Effective Group Discussion* (6th ed.). Dubuque, IA: Wm. C. Brown.

Gouran, D. S. (1982). *Making Decisions in Groups: Choices and Consequences.* Glenview, IL: Scott Foresman.

Gouran, D. S., and Hirokawa, R. Y. (1993). "The role of communication in decision-making groups: A functional perspective." In M.S. Mander (ed.), *Communications in Transition* (pp. 168–185). New York: Praeger.

Gouran, D. S., Hirokawa, R. Y, and Martz, A. E. (1986). "A critical analysis of factors related to decisional processes involved in the *Challenger* disaster." *Central States Speech Journal* 37: 119–135.

Hackman, J. R., and Morris, C. G. (1975). "Group tasks, group interaction process, and group performance effectiveness: A review and proposed integration." In L. Berkowitz (ed.), *Advances in Experimental Social Psychology* 8: 45–99. New York: Academic Press.

Hirokawa, R. Y, Gouran, D. S., and Martz, A. E. (1988). "Understanding the sources of faulty group decision making: A lesson from the *Challenger* disaster." *Small Group Behavior* 19: 411–433.

Hirokawa, R. Y, and Scheerhorn, D. R. (1986). "Communication in faulty group decision making." In R. Y. Hirokawa and M. S. Poole (eds.), *Communication and Group Decision Making* (pp. 63–80). Beverly Hills, CA: Sage.

Janis, I. L. (1982). *Victims of Groupthink* (2nd ed.). Boston: Houghton Mifflin.

Janis, I. L., and Mann, L. (1977). *Decision Making.* New York: Free Press.

Kelley, H. H., and Thibaut, J. W. (1969). "Group problem solving." In G. Lindzey and E. Aronson (eds.), *Handbook of Social Psychology* (pp. 1–101). Cambridge, MA: Addison-Wesley.

Lawler, E., and Mohrman, S. (1985, January-February). "Quality circles after the fad." *Harvard Business Review* (pp. 65–71).

Leavitt, H. J. (1951). "Some effects of certain communication patterns on group performance." *Journal of Abnormal and Social Psychology* 46: 38–50.

Poole, M. S., and Hirokawa, R. Y. (1986). "Communication and group decision making: A critical assessment." In R. Y. Hirokawa and M. S. Poole (eds.), *Communication and Group Decision Making* (pp. 15–31). Beverly Hills, CA: Sage.

Report of the Presidential Commission on the Space Shuttle *Challenger* Disaster. (1986). Washington DC: Alderson Reporting.

Riecken, H. W. (1958). "The effects of talkativeness on ability to influence group solutions to problems." *Sociometry* 21: 309–321.

Shaw, M. E., and Penrod, W. T. (1962). "Does more information available to a group always improve group performance? *Sociometry* 25: 377–390.

Taylor, D. W., and Faust, W. L. (1952). "Twenty questions: Efficiency in problem solving as a function of size of group. *Journal of Experimental Psychology* 44: 360–368.

Chapter 13
New Communication Technologies and Teams

Craig R. Scott

The growth of the Internet and groupware technologies, increased interest in online meetings, and movements toward virtual teaming all point to the importance of new communication technologies (NCTs) supporting teams. This chapter begins by clarifying what is meant by the term NCTs, and then offers four basic types: routine group communication technologies, meeting/project tools, document management/storage technologies, and coordination/collaboration tools. Scott also notes that the changing nature of NCTs demands that we focus on key dimensions differentiating these tools generally rather than examining each specific new technology as it emerges. The chapter then summarizes research on team-based NCTs in three contexts: education, organizations, and the research laboratory. Scott notes that team performance is generally improved by at least some NCTs; however, there may also be unanticipated (and sometimes undesirable) effects of such technologies, including changing team roles and greater surveillance of team members. Scott concludes his chapter by noting some directions for future work in this area and by suggesting that students of group communication can benefit greatly from a solid familiarity with and working knowledge of these new technologies.

Various communication technologies are used extensively by a variety of groups and teams in our society. For example, a cross-functional team in a business organization may be composed of a dozen members, all of whom use joint calendars on their computers and PDAs (personal data assistants) to schedule meetings and projects with one another. At those meetings, the teams may engage in a great deal of face-to-face interaction. But even when meetings take place with everyone in the same room, the teams might utilize technologies such as a group decision support systems as they make key decisions. Additionally, they might invite an expert about their work to join them via a video-conference. Afterward, the minutes from the meeting might be posted to the group's webpage on the company intranet. Between those meetings, they use a group mailing list and advanced voicemail systems to share information as they work towards team goals. Also, during some especially busy times, calls on their land line or mobile (cell) phones are quite the norm.

Consider another example: a team of three to four MBA students working together virtually, as they pursue their degrees through an online university. This team uses Internet chat tools to discuss assignments and projects, and it supplements this interaction with audio and desktop video connections linking the team members. Electronic bulletin boards facilitate discussion forums, where team members can explore issues pertaining to their coursework. As the team prepares its papers, it may use document management and group collaboration tools found in most word processing programs. And, of course, these documents are exchanged through various mail attachment and file-sharing programs that facilitate group communication.

These two teams vary—in terms of size, goals, and even the degree to which members are in one another's presence. However, both make use of various communication (as well as coordination and collaboration) technologies. Examples such as these are not extraordinary. Recent societal conditions and technological developments have created an environment conducive to the rapid development of group communication technologies (Coleman 1995). Computer-based technology to support group interaction already constitutes a multi-billion dollar world-wide industry, with the growth of the World Wide Web (WWW), the Internet, and widespread use of various groupware programs serving as additional indicators of our readiness for technologies that support teams/groups (Coleman 1995; Grudin and Poltrock 1997; Khoshafian and Buckiewicz 1995). Already, group support technologies have been used by millions of people and are a key resource in more than 1,500 organizations (Briggs, Nunamaker, and Sprague 1998; Nunamaker 1997). The web conferencing industry is also poised for tremendous growth in the coming years (Santalesa 2002). And, with a recent *Information Week* survey of business technology professionals suggesting that a majority of U.S. organizations are in the process of moving toward online meetings (Zaino 2002), there seems to be little debate about the importance of these new communication technologies for teams.

This chapter provides an overview of some of the key topics related to group communication technologies. The chapter is organized as follows. First, let us consider some important terminology and definitions. Then, I classify some existing group communication technologies. Next, let us examine the various contexts where teams use these technologies—focusing predominantly on applications and research findings with groups in educational contexts, organizations, and research laboratories. Finally, I briefly consider some contemporary issues surrounding new communication technologies (NCTs) and teams.

Terminology and Definitions

When someone starts talking about "new communication technology," you most likely conjure up images of computers and other electronic devices. Computers are certainly a key technology supporting group communication in various contexts. However, computers are just one kind of "new" technology that groups and teams use to support their communication.

Communication Technologies

Before explaining what makes a communication technology "new," let us explain what a "communication technology" is. A communication "technology" is any device/tool/machine/technique used to help accomplish the exchange of messages. These technologies mediate messages and include things like paper, drums, carrier pigeons, telephones, the Internet, and computers. Such a list of communication technologies illustrates three facts: (a) Communication technologies have a rather long history that predates the rise of the "new" media described below; (b) Some technologies are used directly by the communicator (end-user or interface technologies), while others provide the infrastructure over which the message travels (enabling technologies); (c) Technologies that serve to mediate communication may also serve other (noncommunication) purposes.

New Communication Technologies

"New" communication technologies are usually faster than older forms of mediated communication, can more easily overcome geographic barriers, and provide greater interactivity even though they do not always require people to be connected at the same time (Rice and Bair 1984; Lievrouw 1999). They are often hybrids of existing technologies (such as the mobile communication device that combines paging, email, fax, and phone functions), and are usually digital in nature. But what makes communication technology "new?" The term "new" is fairly subjective—what is "new" today may not be "new" tomorrow.

I will use the term *new communication technology* to refer to *those digital technologies that emerged after the mass media (e.g., television, newspapers) and that provide communicators with greater interactivity and control.* Sometimes the term computer-mediated communication (CMC) is used to describe such technologies. However, while some CMC technologies (those that support text-based communication over computers) are certainly a type of NCT, there are other NCTs that are not usually considered computer-based (e.g., mobile communication devices, videoconferencing, etc.).

In general, NCTs were created to support individual productivity, interpersonal communication, or organization-wide efforts (Grudin 1994; Grudin and Poltrock 1997). Only recently has attention focused on the ways NCTs can support groups and teams. Yet the terms describing this new focus on groups and teams, and the types of technologies that support them, are already numerous: "computer-supported collaborative work (CSCW), groupware, teamware, meetingware, electronic meeting systems (EMSs), group decision support systems (GDSSs), group support systems (GSSs), computer-mediated communication systems (CMCSs), collaborative computing, collaborative support systems, work-group computing, and multiuser applications" (Scott 1999, 438).

By focusing on new communication technologies that are either regularly used by groups/teams, or designed specifically for them, we arrive at an appropriate focal point for this chapter. To focus even more sharply, let me provide two final limitations here: First, the emphasis is on the transactional exchange of messages between team/group members—thus, technologies that focus mainly on information provision (announcements on a class web page) or that are used simply for information searching (e.g., databases) and do not involve direct human-human interaction are not addressed in this chapter. Second, fine distinctions can be made between technologies that support group communication versus those that facilitate coordination (e.g., group calendars) and collaboration (e.g., shared whiteboard). We will be mindful of those distinctions as we focus on new technologies that support group/team communication.

Team Technologies and Key Theoretical Dimensions

Having clarified what new communication technologies for teams/groups means, let us examine these specific technologies in more detail.

NCTs for Teams

There are many different types of NCTs that are used by groups/teams. Because they cannot all be addressed here, we will discuss four major categories of NCTs: routine group communication technologies, meeting/project systems, document management/storage capabilities, and coordination/collaboration tools.

Routine Group Communication Technologies. There are several NCTs that groups/teams use for their regular, ongoing interaction with other group members. In many cases, these are the same technologies that two people might use to interact—but with some slight variations they become very useful group communication technologies. *Group email* is an obvious example. Group email can include listservs, where team members are placed on a list ("subscribed") and all members on the list receive all messages sent to that list. Listservs, or mail lists, are regularly archived to provide a full record of team communication for later reference. These emails, like those sent to specific individuals, can carry attachments, which is especially important for groups that are working on projects requiring a great deal of information sharing. Another tool for routine group communication is *voicemail.* Voicemail, especially when it is used as more than an answering machine, can facilitate a great deal of project work for teams. Not only can detailed messages and updates be provided for individual team members, but messages can also be edited and forwarded to other team members or even sent to a voice mailbox for the whole group. Although the telephone itself is not considered a "new" technology, *advanced phone features* and *mobile phone devices* can do much to support teamwork. For example, three-way and multiparty calls, available on many phone systems, facilitate immediate and ongoing group communication. Even features such as caller-ID may help someone know when a fellow team member is trying to reach her or him. These features are available not only on most landline phones but on mobile communication devices as well, which also facilitates team members staying in touch. A final example in this area are *instant messaging* technologies, which can provide team members who are online together the ability to simultaneously discuss project work in a real-time chat-like environment.

Meeting/Project Tools. The set of technologies most specifically designed with groups/teams in mind falls into this category. Meetings require coordination and scheduling, are likely to have an agenda, and are often focused on very important issues. To support these needs, a number of *electronic meeting systems (EMSs)* have emerged to help provide mediated team sessions. Four main types of EMSs are audioconferencing, audio/videoconferencing, computer conferencing, and group (decision) support systems. *Audioconferencing* refers to meetings where team members are connected via telephone at two or more sites (it can also occur through computers via Internet telephony). Although this may take place with team members at their individual desk, workstation, or home, it more often involves some subgroup gathered in a conference room using a speakerphone to interact with one or more other subgroups who may have a similar setup at their sites. *Videoconferencing*, which usually means audio and video, is much like audioconferencing in that it involves some people at one location interacting with other team members at another location. A key difference, however, is that while most rooms can easily be equipped with a phone and speaker system, only a handful of rooms are equipped with the substantially more expensive videoconferencing equipment. Thus, *meeting room videoconferencing* happens only in designated spaces where the necessary cameras, monitors, and other equipment are available (though *desktop videoconferencing* may occur through networked computers

equipped with cameras). Some popular group tools, such as *NetMeeting*, support audio and video connections, as well as allow for real-time computer-mediated collaboration—all from one's desktop.

One of the more specialized group-relevant EMSs is the group decision support system (GDSS). GDSSs combine communication, decision support, and computer technologies to assist with team problem solving. A GDSS includes sophisticated software that operates on networked computers to allow team members to engage in typical meeting activities (brainstorming, prioritizing, discussion, setting criteria, selecting alternatives, evaluation, etc.). Although GDSSs can usually be used by team members anytime/anywhere, historically these systems have been used most frequently in a decision room where all the team members are co-present but interacting in large part through the computer system. This distinguishes GDSSs from other EMSs that support team members who are not all co-present.

Why use the GDSS when everyone is together in the same room anyway? These systems attempt to overcome some of the typical problems in most team meetings (i.e., domination of the discussion by a few members, status of people getting in the way of focusing on quality ideas, meetings taking too long, etc.). They do this in several ways, but the two most important here are (a) anonymous input, and (b) parallel participation. When people input their ideas and do priority/evaluation votes anonymously, they presumably do not have to worry about being ridiculed or sanctioned and can be more honest/open; thus, the anonymity helps to provide voice to certain members and forces the team to focus on the quality of ideas and not the status of the contributors. Parallel participation is made possible because everyone is typing/reading simultaneously without having to wait their turn to speak, as is typical in most meetings. Parallel participation not only allows the group to discuss more material in a shorter amount of time, but it at least partially prevents certain people from always dominating the meeting.

Document Management/Storage Technologies. For many teams, their work is largely information based, but even for others who work on more tangible products, progress still has to be regularly documented. Thus, a fair amount of team communication centers on the creation, modification, and storage of documents. Although the tools discussed here can be used individually, they have particular utility for teamwork. As teams work on these documents, there is a need for group writing, editing of others' comments, incorporation of suggested changes, making the document accessible to others for review, and storing the work in such a way as to preserve the full history of the document. Several technologies exist to support these activities. *Word processing features* can often be very useful, though most users do not actively utilize these tools. For example, in Microsoft Word, the most commonly used word processing software today, one or more team members can take a recently created file and use the *track changes* tools to line edit documents, to accept or reject changes, and even to compare two versions of a document for key differences. Other tools allow one to highlight key text for other team members and to insert comments for suggested revisions of work. All these tools provide the team with powerful group editing functions as they provide feedback to one another about the document. Additionally, the documents frequently associated with teamwork undergo numerous revisions, and it is often useful to have a history of the revisions and changes made for project management. Other features in programs such as Word allow team members to save each version of the document so as to keep a complete history of the work—which can be especially valuable when the team decides to reincorporate earlier material into a final draft even though it had been edited out at some point during the project.

In addition to the word processing features, the second set of technologies relevant to document management involves making work accessible to all team members. Some common office systems allow for shared folders where work is kept so that others can access the most current version of it. Other groups may find it useful to post information to team bulletin boards or web sites where group members can then access and download that information as authorized.

Coordination/Collaboration Tools. As noted earlier, it can be difficult to separate the important coordination and collaboration functions that technologies can provide from their communication functions. Thus, it is useful to briefly mention some of these systems here. *Groupware, teamware,* or *meetingware* are sophisticated computer-mediated tools that assist groups with vital coordination and collaboration functions (and provide some communication tools as well). Most common here are group calendars that coordinate schedules and meetings online (assuming everyone is keeping their own calendar current!) without contacting each individual member. Further, these tools can provide shared folders that also alert team members as to important due dates. In addition to office systems, such as LotusNotes and Outlook, which provide these sorts of features, a number of web-based groupware and conferencing systems are also available. Some examples are *www.intranets.com, www.smart groups.com, www.webex.com, www. eroom.com, www.centra.com,* and *www. groups.yahoo.com.* Although each of these services provide some basic communication tools for group members, their real support for team communication is their ability to help coordinate subsequent communication meetings/projects.

Finally, let me make a quick comment about collaboration. NetMeeting provides some tools that offer useful examples of computer-mediated team collaboration, where group members are jointly working on something (such as a document). The file/application sharing tool permits a number of team members to view a document jointly and collaborate on its creation. NetMeeting's whiteboard tool and other types of *electronic whiteboards* allow team members in different locations to jointly work on problem solving and have their contributions appear on everyone's screen (or on a remote whiteboard). In these cases, not only is the collaboration often assisted by other group communication tools, but that collaboration also may be vital to ongoing group communication.

Theory-Based Dimensions of NCTs for Teams

Since I have just described some of the NCTs currently available for groups and teams, you may find it odd that I would now suggest that focusing on specific technologies is actually not a good thing. What I mean is that focusing on each individual technology (or perhaps even the categories of technologies just described) and trying to determine whether it is appropriate for your group or team could lead to problems. These technologies tend to come and go, and (as is characteristic of the new media) they often morph (merge) into each other. Email systems that allow you to send voice and video mail are one example. Unified messaging systems that take your faxes and emails and read them to you over the phone also illustrate these changes. Even more obvious to most of us are the mobile communication devices that are no longer just a cordless phone but provide paging, email, fax, and web access. Thus, if you try to understand every NCT and all possible combinations of them in the future, you would have a difficult time making sense of NCTs for teams. As an alternative, it is preferable to focus on key dimensions, frameworks, and theories that begin to describe what various technologies have in common. If we can do this, then we are better equipped to understand each new technology as it emerges.

In a previous essay (Scott 1999), I identified several frameworks and theories for categorizing and making sense of the work relevant to team NCTs. Theories specifically focused on team technology use include adaptive structuration theory (DeSanctis and Poole 1994; Poole and DeSanctis 1990, 1992) and self-organizing systems theory (Contractor and Seibold 1993). Although the details of these complex theories are beyond the scope of this chapter, such perspectives provide useful insights into team technology use.

More valuable to this chapter are the general organizing frameworks. One common framework focuses on the number of senders and receivers involved in using the technology (Huseman and Miles 1988). In this model, there are technologies with one sender to one receiver (e.g., telephones), one sender to many receivers (e.g., web page), many senders to one receiver (e.g., executive information system), and many senders to many receivers (a public electronic bulletin board). Although generally useful, such a framework largely overlooks the few-to-few exchanges most relevant to group communication (Lipnack and Stamps 2000). Moreover, such models are still of limited value because (a) many technologies can support several if not all these options, and (b) the number of senders and receivers is likely not the most important theoretical dimension along which various communication technologies differ.

A preferred set of dimensions for understanding communication technologies—including NCTs—for group and teams is presented most clearly in work by Finn (Finn and Lane 1998; Lievrouw and Finn 1990). This work describes communication technologies along five dimensions. The first dimension is *time*, which concerns whether the technology requires people to be "connected" at the same time (synchronous) or at different times (asynchronous). An audioconference requires participants to meet synchronously, whereas voicemail works as an asynchronous technology. The second dimension is *space*, which focuses on whether the communicators using the technology are co-located or dispersed. A decision room GDSS involves participants who are located in the same physical room using the technology, whereas mobile communication devices are used when communicators are dispersed. Some technologies, such as videoconferencing meetings, generally support dispersed communicators even though there may be multiple people at each site who are co-located. The third dimension is labeled *capacity*, and focuses primarily on the content carried by the technology. The four main types of content in use currently are text, sound/audio, still image, and moving image. Most GDSSs involve text as the content, whereas wireless telephones carry sound/audio. Still images are found in traditional media such newspapers and magazines, as well as newer media including the World Wide Web. Finally, moving images are illustrated by desktop videoconferencing systems. Of course, several tools are capable of multiple types of content (i.e., multimedia).

The final two dimensions are actually secondary in nature because they are based largely on the combinations of the previous three dimensions. *Interactivity* refers to the technology's ability to support two-way exchanges. A telephone conversation, for example, is highly interactive and allows for feedback through the same channel. Most mass media are considered noninteractive in this sense because they are used primarily for broadcasting messages, with little, if any, focus on getting feedback from message recipients. Even some of the new media that are more asynchronous in nature (e.g., voicemail) are generally less interactive than synchronous new media (e.g., online chat tools). The final dimension is *control*, which refers to the ability and options that the communicator has to actively create, edit/manipulate, and store messages. For example, digital and text-based technologies, especially those that are asynchronous, are easily manipulated. Consider, for example, the email message that one can easily forward to others after making changes to the content of the message. Other types of content are more difficult to edit with most technologies (e.g., a paper fax), and synchronous technologies also pose additional problems for message alteration and storage. Meeting room videoconferencing, for example, does not provide most users with much control over content creation, editing, and storage—in large part because of the live (synchronous) exchange of moving images using cameras and monitors that provide only limited user options.

These five dimensions can be a very useful way to think about communication technologies that support groups and teams. When one is trying to determine what tool would work best for a certain situation, what matters most is not the specific technology. Rather, the key questions are whether it is synchronous or asynchronous (time), whether participants are going to be co-located or dispersed (space), what type of content will need to be conveyed (capacity), what level of two-way exchange is needed (interactivity), and how much users need to be able to actively create, change, and store content (control). Of course, there could be other questions to ask as well. Munter (1998), for instance, suggests that choosing technologies also depends on issues such as group expectations, group size, and resource availability. Clearly, though, understanding dimensions such as these can allow you to make informed decisions about which technologies your group or team needs so its members can effectively communicate with one another. Moreover, the dimensions also allow us to understand the ways in which tools like voicemail and email are alike (asynchronous, dispersed, moderate interactivity) and different (audio versus text, moderate control versus high control).

Key Contexts and Research Findings

Generally, NCTs can be used in any context where group interaction occurs. For example, every member of a family unit may have a wireless phone that allows them to stay in touch with each other. Or, consider certain social support groups that may exist online and take advantage of the anonymity provided by certain NCTs (e.g., chat tools, electronic bulletin boards). However, we tend to see the most widespread use of NCTs to assist groups and teams in three general contexts: education, organizations, and the research laboratory. Let us examine these three contexts and some of the general research conclusions applicable to them.

Education

As students, some of you have direct experience with the use of technologies to support learning teams. These might include live chat and discussion forums on bulletin boards as student groups analyze organizational cases; sophisticated online simulations that include group discussion, voting, and writing tools; or any of several other technologies used by instructors to provide learning opportunities for students. Brandon and Hollingshead (1999) note that "the emerging field of computer-supported collaborative learning (CSCL) seeks to combine classroom-based collaborative learning theory with theory and research on CMC in order to provide a foundation for understanding how CMC-based group projects can enhance learning" (p. 110). Indeed the focus of CSCL is with online groups, making it very relevant here. Brandon and Hollingshead's work in this area provides not only a review of research on mostly asynchronous text-based computer systems but develops a model of CSCL theory and research in the education context.

Brandon and Hollingshead (1999) note that summaries of work in this area have found that collaborative learning promotes higher achievement, higher-level reasoning, more ideas and solutions, and greater learning transfer than is typically found with individualistic learning strategies. However, most of that research was not based on technology-supported groups. In response to the lack of both theory and research in this area, Brandon and Hollingshead propose a model of CSCL theory and research. Several components of their model emphasize NCTs and teamwork. In this model, there are four general inputs to CSCL: social-behavioral inputs (including netiquette-based social context and electronic social context), social-cognitive inputs, course-CSCL fit (including the rationale for NCT use), and student variables (including experience and comfort in working with computers). The impact of these areas on group and individual learning is moderated by the communication technology and by various instructor variables. Finally, learning level may be related to several outcomes (e.g., knowledge, technology skills, satisfaction, etc.). Because their model emphasizes the role of NCTs (at least computer-based ones), it is useful to more thoroughly consider some of the research relevant to this framework.

With regard to the role of technology in establishing the social context, Hiltz and Wellman (1997) found that asynchronous links can help create a feeling of group learning—and may be aided by getting-acquainted events at the start of a project. Brandon and Hollingshead (1999) also suggest that appropriate and inappropriate technology use should be taught to groups (online groups such as those found on Usenet already have such guidelines). These might include the following types of undesirable actions: incorrect/novice use of technology, bandwidth waste (long or off-topic postings), violation of network-wide conventions, violation of specific newsgroup behaviors, inappropriate language, and factual errors (McLaughlin, Osborne, and Smith 1995). As for student variables, Witmer (1998) notes that research indicates student comfort with technology can impact performance. Comfort level is a major component of many views of experience (King and Xia 1999); thus, it is not surprising that experience with technology emerges as a main predictor of use and likelihood to use various group and nongroup NCTs (King and Xia 1999; Scott and Rockwell 1997). Most importantly, the effects of the various inputs on CSCL are moderated by communication technologies. Among the research studies here, Gay and Lentini (1995) found that online groups using multiple channels (chat, drawing tools, audio/video conferencing) had more extensive discussion. Additionally, Berge (1995) notes that asynchronous computer conferencing results in online groups taking longer to complete class projects.

Other valuable research in this area exists, such as Flanagin's (1999) case study of anonymous student teams and their use of a web-based groupware program. However, an overall conclusion about the state of CSCL literature based on Brandon and Hollingshead's (1999) review is that there really is very little in the way of solid research findings. There is a great deal of speculation and some anecdotal evidence, but we still know very little about online groups and their communication in the educational context. It seems likely, however, that this will be a growing area of research in the years ahead, thanks in part to models such as that proposed by Brandon and Hollingshead.

Organizations

In contrast to the education context, where research on team technology use and CSCL is still in relative infancy, work in this area from an organizational context is more established. A variety of organizational teams, both traditional and virtual, use the technologies described in this chapter for strategic planning, project coordination, product evaluation, self-assessment, and a host of other activities. The multidisciplinary field known as Computer-Supported Collaborative (sometimes Cooperative) Work (CSCW) has grown steadily since its beginnings in the mid-1980s (Khoshafian and Buckiewicz 1995), though research in this area is still much closer to its beginning than to its end (Briggs, Nunamaker, and Sprague 1998). Several recent reviews have attempted to summarize the growing body of research on team communication technologies in organizational contexts.

My review (Scott 1999) of the research in this area focuses on four key outcomes: performance (either quantity or quality of ideas/products), efficiency (usually time needed to accomplish goals), member satisfaction (with process and outcomes), and various communication-related variables (e.g., participation, influence, etc.). In general, my review suggests four conclusions about NCTs for organizational teams. First, team technologies improve both the quantity and quality of performance as compared to what was found in face-to-face teams—and this seems especially true of GDSS technologies. Second, the evidence points to greater efficiency with team NCTs as compared to groups without that support. Third, research on member satisfaction is somewhat mixed. In general, GDSS supported teams were as

satisfied or more satisfied than their face-to-face counterparts; however, teams using other, less sophisticated NCTs were often less satisfied. Finally, participation was generally greater for teams using GDSS than for traditional face-to-face interactions; however, participation was often less when other technologies (e.g., computer conferencing) were used to support the team.

Another recent review of findings in this area reveals similar results for organizational teams. Collins-Jarvis and Fulk's (1993; see also Fulk and Collins-Jarvis 2001) review of outcomes (decision quality, group efficiency, and member satisfaction) associated with electronic meeting systems (teleconferencing, GDSS, and computer conferencing) provides several conclusions. They found that computer conferencing and GDSS groups produced decisions of equal, if not better, quality than their face-to-face counterparts in the field studies they reviewed. Collins-Jarvis and Fulk also concluded that GDSS-supported organizational groups were more efficient than non-GDSS groups, which is consistent with my review. As for member satisfaction, GDSS group members were as satisfied as, if not more so than, face-to-face groups.

There are a number of studies on team NCTs in the organizational context. My earlier review (Scott 1999) of work from five years in the mid-1990s revealed 50 published studies. The research suggests some real benefits for groups and teams supported by NCTs—especially for performance, efficiency, and participation levels. Additionally, these benefits seem to be more associated with GDSS technologies than most other types examined. However, one should be aware of some limitations in this research also. First, some of it is clearly not as rigorous as might be found in more controlled settings. Second, and perhaps more important, not only is there evidence that different NCTs vary in terms of their effects on groups, but there is also evidence that they vary in terms of level of group member support, how they are used, and what kinds of tasks they are used for.

Research Laboratory

The majority of the NCT research on groups and teams has occurred in laboratory settings. Benbasat and Lim's (1993) review of 31 experimental studies, and McGrath and Hollingshead's (1994) review of 51 studies in this area, almost all involve laboratory-based teams. Additionally, Scott (1999) reviewed over 80 studies of laboratory teams in the mid-1990s alone. As with the organizational context, these recent reviews provide us with a useful picture of the research findings in this area.

In general, research from the laboratory teams has found that NCTs tend to result in improved performance. For instance, teams using GDSS technologies tended to outperform their face-to-face counterparts, at least on more quantitative measures of output; however, when teams did not perform as well, they were typically using audio-conferencing or computer conferencing technologies. However, there is no laboratory evidence that NCTs improve group efficiency. For example, teams using NCTs for a single, short meeting were not as efficient as their face-to-face counterparts—which may be due in part to the longer "startup time" and/or initial confusion for the technology-supported groups (Scott 1999). Findings are mixed with regard to member satisfaction. Usually when technology-supported team members were more satisfied than their face-to-face counterparts, they were using GDSS technologies rather than other types of NCTs. Finally, in terms of communication outcomes, GDSS groups participated more than face-to-face interactants, but computer conferencing team members participated less. Furthermore, there is evidence suggesting that the status of members persists in technology-supported meetings (despite the efforts to remove status through anonymity and other means).

Although the research in this context is generally the most scientifically rigorous, the laboratory studies also suffer from some questionable generalizability: do team members think and behave in a laboratory setting in ways that are comparable to what they might do in an organizational or even educational context? Although these studies do work to maintain some consistency with the factors that would be experienced by teams in other contexts, there are always limitations on the extent to which conclusions from this area of research can be applied to nonlaboratory groups. Additionally, most of these studies have also tended to focus on specific technologies. Usually ignored are specific aspects/features/dimensions of technologies. As a result, even with the sizable body of research in this context, it is difficult to make claims that cut across all variations of a technology—much less generalizations that apply to a wide range of even team-based NCTs.

Issues and Directions

It seems appropriate to close the chapter by examining four key issues associated with NCTs for teams, as well as suggesting several directions for future work in this area.

Key Issues

Although much of the research on NCTs for groups and teams tends to focus on specific variables and outcomes, much less is said about the unanticipated consequences of using NCTs, as well as what might be called the "dark side" of these tools. Unexpected, or ironic, use has been explored with team technologies, largely through adaptive structuration theory (DeSanctis and Poole 1994; Poole and DeSanctis 1990, 1992). As Scott, Quinn, Timmerman, and Garrett (1999) note, group communication technologies are especially subject to social influences and thus represent a set of innovations in which the actual use of the technology may well vary from a designer's initial intent (ironic use). Poole, DeSanctis, Kirsch, and Jackson (1995) concluded in their study of four teams using a GDSS that the teams integrated the technology into their group processes in quite different ways. Sometimes the technology was used in ways intended by the systems designers; in other cases, the technology was used "inappropriately" and contributed to poor performance. If team-based NCTs are especially subject to this ironic use, it is important that team members and other interested parties consider the positive and negative consequences that may result from such use. Although deviations from designer, manager, or teacher intent can be a problem and lead to uncertainty and confusion, such variations may also result in more functional use of the technology for the team, as members discover new and creative ways to utilize the features of the technologies for their own needs.

Another unanticipated effect of NCTs are changing group roles. For example, most of the EMS tools require technographers or chauffeurs to run the software and/or technical experts to facilitate the meeting connections. With other, more routine, team communication technologies, it may be the more experienced members who readily take on traditional leadership roles in the group because of their ability to use the tools effectively. With all these technologies, automatic records are kept—effectively eliminating the role of record keeper/secretary. In other ways, the asynchronous nature of some technologies, the anonymity provided or perceived, and the parallel processing in tools such as a GDSS may change who is able to dominate meetings, who participates, who chooses to "clown" around, and even who is able to fill influential leadership roles.

Additionally, there are clearly dark sides to these technologies. Like most NCTs, many team-based tools can also be surveillance technologies (see Botan 1996). The tools that allow us to communicate and collaborate can also serve to monitor our performance, keep logs of group members' activities, spy on team members, and invade our privacy in other ways. Team NCTs seem especially subject to this because of the openness one must generally use when interacting with teams. To the extent that such openness (e.g., file sharing, joint calendars) allows for less privacy, concerns about monitoring and surveillance become salient. Relatedly, these technologies invade our privacy in another way—by making members readily accessible to other team members and thus blurring boundaries between private/public and home/work. Although a variety of NCTs contribute to this blurring, team technologies may be even more of a problem, given group pressures to be accessible.

One final potential dark side centers on what is called technological determinism. This term refers to the belief or acceptance that technologies determine/shape/cause events. For example, a belief that a new videoconferencing will lead to improved productivity and financial savings is a technologically deterministic view. There is danger in assuming that technologies, simply by their presence, have such effects. A more useful way to think about all this is to consider how people use technologies. It is likely that the combination of the technologies available and their use in practice (in various team, organizational, and social contexts) is what actually shapes various outcomes.

Future Directions

Making any bold predictions about the future of NCTs for groups and teams would be of little value, largely because it is difficult to do so with any accuracy. However, there are some key trends that I have noted elsewhere relevant to group NCTs (Scott 1999). First, these technologies will continue to become increasingly available, thanks in large part to web-based systems, more portable technologies/systems, falling costs, and development of Internet2 technologies. Internet2 is essentially an effort to advance tomorrow's Internet so as to support new applications and technology; team collaboration is likely to be a major focus of such efforts. Second, team-based NCTs will continue to become integrated into other systems so as to become nearly transparent for most users; furthermore, the convergence of technologies that already support teams will provide users with new technologies and increased options for collaboration, coordination, and communication. Third, growth in virtual teaming seems certain to continue, given the reduced geographic constraints associated with these technologies (see Potter and Balthazard 2002; Shockley-Zalabak 2002).

Elsewhere (Scott 1999), I offer some specific directions for research on group/team NCTs, including a focus on specific variables (e.g., anonymity, feedback), processual and longitudinal studies, and continued research in various contexts where team-based NCTs are potentially of value. Additionally, there is a need for not only more research but continued theory development specific to team communication technologies. A focus on key dimensions of team NCTs and how they interact with users and context may provide for very useful theorizing in this area. Inevitably, research unguided by relevant theory and frameworks is of limited value once today's technologies change or when new technologies come along.

Conclusion

There is little doubt that the movement toward teams—in educational and organizational contexts especially—and the technologies to support them is more than a fad. Regardless of what your chosen career will be after graduation, there is a strong likelihood that you will find yourself working in teams or groups of some sort. This trend demands that students of group communication have at least a familiarity with, and preferably a solid working knowledge of, NCTs for groups and teams. Such familiarity and knowledge position us well in a world where teams and technologies to support them are playing an increasingly important role.

Author's Note

I would like to acknowledge Erik Timmerman and Karen Cornetto for their helpful comments on this chapter as it was under preparation.

References

Benbasat, I., and Lim, L. (1993). "The effects of group, task, context, and technology variables on the usefulness of group support systems: A meta-analysis of experimental studies." *Small Group Research* 24: 430–462.

Berge, Z. L. (1995). "Facilitating computer conferencing: Recommendations from the field." *Educational Technology* 35: 22–30.

Botan, C. (1996). "Communication work and electronic surveillance: A model for predicting panoptic effects." *Communication Monographs* 63: 293–313.

Brandon, D. P., and Hollingshead, A. P. (1999). "Collaborative learning and computer-supported groups." *Communication Education* 48: 109–126.

Briggs, R. O., Nunamaker, J. F., Jr., and Sprague, R. H., Jr. (1998). "1001 unanswered research questions in GSS." *Journal of Management Information Systems* 14: 3–21.

Coleman, D. (1995). "Groupware: Technology and applications." In D. Coleman and R. Khanna (eds.), *Groupware: Technology and Applications* (pp. 3–41). Upper Saddle River, NJ: Prentice-Hall.

Collins-Jarvis, L., and Fulk, J. (1993, November). Decision outcomes in face-to-face and electronically-mediated group meetings: A 1993 research review. Paper presented at the meeting of the Speech Communication Association, Miami, FL.

Contractor, N. S., and Seibold, D. R. (1993). "Theoretical frameworks for the study of structuring processes in group decision support systems: Adaptive structuration theory and self-organizing systems theory." *Human Communication Research* 19: 528–563.

DeSanctis, G., and Poole, M. S. (1994). "Capturing the complexity in advanced technology use: Adaptive structuration theory." *Organization Science* 5: 121–147.

Finn, T. A., and Lane, D. R. (1998, July). A conceptual framework for organizing communication and information systems. Paper presented at the International Communication Association Conference, Jerusalem, Israel.

Flanagin, A. J. (1999). "Theoretical and Pedagogical Issues in Computer-Mediated Interaction and Instruction: Lessons from the Use of a Collaborative Instructional Technology." *Electronic Journal of Communication* 9. Retrieved August 22, 2002 from *http://www.cios.org/getfile/Flanagin_v9n199*.

Fulk, J., and Collins-Jarvis, L. (2001). "Wired Meetings: Technological Mediation of Organizational Gatherings." In F. M. Jabin and L. L. Putnam (eds.), *The New Handbook of Organizational Communication:*

Advances in Theory, Research, and Methods (pp. 624–663). Thousand Oaks, CA: Sage.

Gay, G., and Lentini, M. (1995). "Use of collaborative resources in a networked collaborative design environment." *Journal of Computer-Mediated Communication* 1: 1–12.

Grudin, J. (1994). "Groupware and social dynamics: Eight challenges for developers." *Communications of the ACM* 37: 92–105.

Grudin, J., and Poltrock, S. E. (1997). "Computer-supported cooperative work and groupware." In M. V. Zelkowitz (ed.), *Advances in Computers* (pp. 269–320). San Diego, CA: Academic Press.

Hiltz, S. R., and Wellman, B. (1997). "Asynchronous learning networks as a virtual classroom." *Communications of the ACM* 40: 44–49.

Huseman, R. C., and Miles, E. W. (1988). "Organizational communications in the information age: Implications of computer based systems." *Journal of Management* 14: 181–204.

Khoshafian, S., and Buckiewicz, M. (1995). *Introduction to Groupware, Workflow, and Workgroup Computing.* New York: John Wiley & Sons.

King, R. C., and Xia, W. (1999). "Media appropriateness: Effects of experience on communication media choice." In K. E. Kendall (ed.), *Emerging Information Technologies: Improving Decisions, Cooperation, and Infrastructure* (pp. 143–175). Thousand Oaks, CA: Sage.

Lievrouw, L. A. (1999, May). "New media: Deciding what's new about new media" (pp. 10–11). *ICA News.*

Lievrouw, L. A., and Finn, T. A. (1990). "Identifying the common dimensions of communication: The communications systems model." In B. Ruben and L. Lievrouw (eds.), *Mediation, Information and Communication: Information and Behavior*, Vol. 3, (37–65). New Brunswick, NJ: Transaction.

Lipnack, J., and Stamps, J. (2000). *Virtual Teams: People Working Across Boundaries with Technology* (2nd Edition). New York: John Wiley & Sons.

McGrath, J. E., and Hollingshead, A. B. (1994). *Groups Interacting with Technology.* Thousand Oaks, CA: Sage.

McLaughlin, M. L., Osborne, K. K., and Smith, C. B. (1995). "Standards of conduct on Usenet." In S. E. Jones (ed.), *Cybersociety: Computer-Mediated Communication and Community* (pp. 90–111). Thousand Oaks, CA: Sage.

Munter, M. (1998). "Meeting technology: From low-tech to high-tech." *Business Communication Quarterly* 61: 80–87.

Nunamaker, J. F., Jr. (1997). "Future research in group support systems: Needs, some questions and possible directions." *International Journal of Human-Computer Studies* 47: 357–385.

Poole, M. S., and DeSanctis, G. (1990). "Understanding the use of group decision support systems: The theory of adaptive structuration." In J. Fulk and C. Steinfield (eds.), *Organizations and Communication Technology* (pp. 175–195). Newbury Park, CA: Sage.

———. (1992). "Microlevel structuration in computer-supported group decision making." *Human Communication Research* 19: 5–49.

Poole, M. S., DeSanctis, G., Kirsch, L., and Jackson, M. (1995). "Group decision support systems as facilitators of quality team efforts." In L. R. Frey (ed.), *Innovations in Group Facilitation: Applications in Natural Settings* (pp. 299–321). Cresskill, NJ: Hampton Press.

Potter, R. E., and Balthazard, P. A. (2002). "Virtual team interaction styles: Assessment and effects." *International Journal of Human-Computer Studies*, 56: 423–443.

Rice, R. E., and Bair, J. H. (1984). "New organizational media and productivity." In R. E. Rice and Associates (eds.), *The New Media: Communication, Research and Technology* (pp. 198–215). Beverly Hills, CA: Sage.

Santalesa, R. (2002, April). "Virtual Meeting Places." *Computer Shopper*, pp. 142–149.

Scott, C. R. (1999). "Communication technology and group communication." In L. R. Frey (ed.), D. S. Gouran, and M. S. Poole (assoc. eds.), *The Handbook of Group Communication Theory and Research* (pp. 432–472). Thousand Oaks, CA: Sage.

Scott, C. R., Quinn, L., Timmerman, C. E., and Garrett, D. (1999). "Ironic uses of group communication technology: Evidence from meeting transcripts and interviews with group decision support system users." *Communication Quarterly* 46: 353–374.

Scott, C. R., and Rockwell, S. C. (1997). "The effect of communication, writing, and technology apprehension on likelihood to use new communication technologies." *Communication Education* 46: 44–62.

Shockley-Zalabak, P. (2002). "Protean places: Teams across time and space." *Journal of*

Applied Communication Research 30: 231–250.

Witmer, D. F. (1998). "Introduction to computer-mediated communication: A master syllabus for teaching communication technology." *Communication Education* 47: 162–173.

Zaino, J. (2002). "Employee collaboration on the upswing." *InformationWeek.com.* Retrieved February 18, 2002 from *http://www.Informationweek.com/story/IWK200 20207S0008.*

Chapter 14
Characteristics of Effective Health Care Teams

Randy Y. Hirokawa
Daniel H. DeGooyer, Jr.
Kathleen S. Valde

This chapter reports an interesting study that uses narrative analysis to identify perceived influences on health care team performance. The authors report five general factors affecting health care team success or failure. The first factor is external support—that is, the assistance or hindrance the group members receive from sources outside the group. The second factor is member attributes—that is, the knowledge, skills, and motivation level of group members. The third factor is relationships—the quality of interpersonal relationships among team members. The fourth factor is organization, which includes the leadership, organization, roles, norms, goals, and procedures used by the team to complete its task. The fifth factor is process; this factor pertains to the exchange of information and ideas among group members, as well as the procedures used by group members to complete the group's task. The authors conclude their chapter by suggesting that the influences on health care team performance, while varied, are not as numerous as some might believe. Rather, the authors maintain that there appear to be some consistent themes associated with team success and failure, which, in turn, suggests there are some reliable predictors of health care team performance.

It is time for doctors and nurses to stop fighting and to start collaborating. . . . [The public] doesn't much care about our differences or our professional nuances.

It wants an organized system of care provided by a seamless web of high-quality professionals whose abilities span all the relevant health services. . . . (Bulger 1993, 3)

Roger Bulger's call for interdisciplinary team-based solutions to health care problems reflects a growing trend in America's health care delivery system: health care institutions are increasingly turning to interdisciplinary teams to provide a wide range of health care services, from behavior management to organ transplantation (Miccolo and Spanier 1993). Indeed, interdisciplinary teams are becoming a functional necessity as health care institutions strive to restructure the delivery of services to increase efficiency and improve patient outcomes (Robertson and McDaniel 1995).

In their recent assessment of critical care management in the 1990s, Miccolo and Spanier (1993) argue that several driving forces today virtually mandate a collaborative, team-based model of health care delivery. They include (a) the presence of an increasingly articulate consumer group, aided by the media, that continues to raise serious questions about the quality and cost of the health care they receive; (b) a growing concern among health care professionals about the fragmented, impersonal care often delivered to patients; (c) a shortage of nurses and other allied health professionals that continues to pose a significant threat to patient care in many parts of the United States; (d) the continued promotion of collaborative approaches to health care delivery by various health profession organizations; and (e) the emergence of new laws and health care structures calling for more efficient, less redundant, and more orderly health care delivery systems.

The expanding role of interdisciplinary teams in health care delivery is not necessarily a cause for optimism. While there is mounting evidence that the quality of patient care, as well as patient and provider satisfaction, are improved in a collaborative practice setting (e.g., Addleton, Tratnack, and Donat 1991; Helmreich and Schaefer 1994; Knaus, Draper, Wagner, and Zimmerman 1986; Lenkman and Gribbins 1994; Robertson and McDaniel 1995; Runciman 1989), decades of group performance research in the social and behavioral sciences also indicates that groups are not magic bullets. The literature clearly suggests that groups are capable of failing as easily as succeeding (e.g., Hackman 1990; Janis 1982; McGrath 1984, 1997). The point is that reliance on interdisciplinary teams to deliver health care must be accompanied by the realization that teams are capable of delivering both good and bad care. The key is to minimize risk by maximizing the likelihood that interdisciplinary health care teams will deliver high-quality care.

Efforts to ensure effective interdisciplinary health care team performance necessitates a thorough understanding of the factors that promote and impede the performance of such groups. It comes as no surprise that the question of health care team effectiveness has attracted the interest of many in the health professions (Pew Health Professions Commission 1993). What is surprising, however, is the fact that very little research has engaged in the comprehensive and systematic study of the factors that affect the performance of interdisciplinary health care teams (Bednash 1995).

Efforts to identify the influences on interdisciplinary health care team performance have been hampered by the absence of models of health care team effectiveness. To date, the vast majority of research on team performance has focused on task-performing teams embedded in public or private production or service organizations (Ilgen 1999). While these investigations have yielded a number of models of team performance (e.g., Cohen, Ledford, and Spreitzer 1996; Fleishman and Zaccaro 1992; Gladstein 1987; Guzzo 1986; Hackman 1990; Katzenbach and Smith 1993; Larson and LaFasto 1989; Morgan, Glickman, Woodward, Blaiwes, and Salas 1986), their applicability to the health care context is sus-

pect because the health care organization is purported to possess unique qualities not present in the traditional business organization (e.g., House 1981; Ray and Miller 1993; Kreps and Thornton 1992). In short, with a few exceptions (e.g., Gitlin, Lyons, and Kolodner 1994; Helmreich and Schaefer 1994; Kumpfer, Turner, Hopkins, and Librett 1993), the study of health care team performance has not been guided by models of team effectiveness derived from data specific to the health care setting.

This essay draws on data obtained in a recent study of health care teams.[1] Members of various types of multiprofessional and interdisciplinary health care teams were asked to provide stories of team successes and failures. These narratives were analyzed to identify perceived influences on health care team effectiveness and ineffectiveness. In this chapter, we give particular attention to influences related to group communication processes.

Factors Associated with Health Care Team Success and Failure

Health care team members perceive five general factors as influencing health care team success and failure. They include: (a) External support—assistance or hindrance from sources outside of, and generally beyond the control of, the group; (b) Member attributes—knowledge and skills of group members; (c) Relationship—interpersonal relationships among group members; (d) Organization—leadership, organization, roles, norms, goals, and procedures of the group; and (e) Process—exchange of information and ideas among group members, as well as the procedures employed in completing the group task.

External Support

The first factor associated with health care team success and failure is external support. Six percent of the stories of team success referred to benefits of feedback and support from individuals outside of the team:

I would have to say that we would never have been successful if we didn't have the backing of the Chief-of-Staff and the Hospital Administrator . . . they were totally committed to a team approach and did everything they could to help us succeed.

In contrast, 10 percent of team failure stories attributed ineffectiveness to such external factors as lack of support by administrators:

Management wasn't very supportive of the team . . . in fact, they deliberately did things to hinder our progress. . . . I would have to say that they were the greatest barrier to our success.

Stories of health care team success and failure underscore the potential value of administration/management support for team effectiveness. Health care teams typically exist and operate within an organizational infrastructure. The amount of support they receive from the management of the organization can have a powerful effect on team performance. One particular story illustrates the potential influence of administration support on team performance:

Management wasn't very supportive of our team or the team concept in general. They expected us to work as a team, but provided us with no training, no incentives or rewards, and expected us to meet after hours after we had performed our normal duties. They also undermined us on several occasions by refusing to support our recommendations. Needless to say, the team concept didn't last long in the hospital.

This example illustrates the importance of administrators communicating with and about teams in a consistent manner. While the administrators in the preceding example explicitly emphasized team work in how tasks and responsibilities were structured, implicitly they communicated a lack of support for teams in the ways they rewarded people for their participation on teams. Essentially, the lack of training and rewards, as well as the expectations for additional time and productivity, communicated to employees that teamwork was not valued or respected by the administrators of this organization.

Member Attributes

A second factor associated with team success and failure is member attributes. Thirty-two percent of the success stories credit member attributes for team effectiveness. In contrast, 92 percent of the failure stories contained a reference to member attributes as explanations for faulty team performance. This factor was characterized by two subthemes: (1) knowledge and skills, and (2) motivation.

Knowledge and skills was among the most commonly mentioned member attributes in both success and failure stories. Team members associated success with people having knowledge that they could share with the group—e.g., "Several members of our team had lots of prior clinical experience that they were able to pass on to the rest of us . . . we relied on their knowledge to help us make sound decisions." Failure stories frequently mentioned insufficient knowledge as a deficiency among group members—e.g., "None of us had enough knowledge or experience to recognize that the patient wasn't suffering from the flu but was actually a victim of carbon monoxide poisoning."

Both the success and failure stories reiterated the perception that health care team performance is necessarily dependent on the clinical competency of its members. That is, the stories of team success frequently mentioned the importance of knowledgeable and skillful members as a reason for their group's success; stories of team failure frequently mentioned insufficient knowledge and skills of team members as a reason for group ineffectiveness. In fact, member incompetence was the most frequently mentioned reason for team failure. While the precise nature and amount of knowledge and skills required of team members is likely to depend on the type of health care team involved and the nature of its task, the narratives examined in this study suggest that the expertise of team members should at least match the most complex and challenging tasks the team is likely to encounter. One particular story illustrates the importance of having knowledgeable team members:

> I was a member of a National Guard Medical Field Team. We were on weekend maneuvers in July and it was very hot and humid. One of the soldiers was brought in with what we initially thought was heat exhaustion. We began treating him for that condition, but he didn't respond to the treatment and seemed to be getting worse. Then one of the team members recognized that his symptoms were more indicative of a heat stroke (much more serious and life-threatening than heat exhaustion), so we immediately changed our treatment and the patient responded well to it. I'm convinced that had we not had this knowledgeable team member with us, we would have misdiagnosed the problem and possibly lost the patient.

Having skilled and competent members is essential to health care teams; there is no replacement for knowledge and ability in providing medical care. However, it is not sufficient to have skilled and competent members. Skill and competence has an effect only to the extent of members' ability to communicate their knowledge to others. If the team member in the preceding scenario had been unable to convey his or her suspicions or to convince others of their legitimacy, the skills and competence of that member may not have been enough to save this particular patient. Health care providers need to be able to communicate their knowledge to others in ways that enable other team members to trust and respect the information and insights they bring to the team.

In addition to skills and knowledge, the narratives indicated that *motivation* was a key member attribute. Success stories suggested that team members need to be highly motivated (e.g., "We did well because we had highly motivated members who quite simply worked their butts off") and to have high levels of dedication and commitment (e.g., "Each member of the team was a consummate professional with total dedication and commitment to the success of each transplant procedure"). In contrast, failure stories associated a lack of motivation with team

failures (e.g., "Team members were just tired, burned out, I guess, so no one had the desire or energy to put forth the effort necessary to get the job done").

The findings of this study also underscore the importance of hard work. Both the success and failure stories contained numerous references to the beneficial effects of hard-working team members, or conversely, the detrimental effects of unmotivated team members. Of course, a high level of effort, by itself, may not be sufficient for health care team success. Rather, what appears to be important is the fact that team members function interdependently. In other words, effective health care teams may do well because group members cover each other, so crucial tasks are never ignored or neglected. As one respondent put it:

> When someone is 'crashing' [when a patient is dying] nobody says, 'Sorry— that's not in my job description.' It also happens in less critical situations, though. Success of a team depends on a low level of hierarchical thinking, and a great deal of respect for all duties that contribute to the successful functioning of the unit. Everyone has to be good at what they do, but they also have to be willing and able to back each other up so that no matter how hairy it gets, we can provide the best care possible for the patient.

The ability to "back each other up" is related to communication. Group members can only back each other up if they know each other's tasks and responsibilities. Knowing other people's tasks can result from observation, but it most often comes from group members talking with each other, and learning from each other, not just what needs to be done but how best to do it.

Relationship

The narratives highlight relationships as a third factor associated with health care team successes and failures. Thirty-five percent of the team success stories underscored the importance of relational factors in accounting for group effectiveness. Within this general theme, the most frequent subthemes were *mutual respect:*

> I think we were successful because we all respected and affirmed each other's value and contribution to the team . . . everyone's opinions and views were listened to and taken into account seriously,

and *group cohesiveness:*

> I would attribute our success to the fact that we were a tight-knit team . . . we covered for each other, and picked each other up, so that even if someone was having a bad day, we were still able to get the job done as a team."

Interestingly, fewer team failure stories (9 percent) contained references to relationships among group members. When relationship themes did appear, they pertained mainly to *interpersonal conflicts:*

> Our team was characterized by considerable tension between the Surgeon and the SIC nurse . . . the rest of us either got dragged into it, or found ourselves walking on eggshells around them, so in the end their conflict affected our ability to work well together as a team,

or *power plays:*

> At our very first team meeting, the doctor immediately took charge and said, 'Look, if anything goes wrong and the patient sues, I'm the one who's gonna get sued. . . . I pay the million-dollar malpractice insurance, so we're gonna do things my way.'. . . At that point the rest of us figured why put in any effort since he's gonna do things his way anyway."

The examples provided here demonstrate the intersection of relationship themes and communication in team effectiveness. In the story of team success, the participant notes the importance of affirming people and of listening to each other—both important elements of communication. Further, the failure stories provide examples of relationships having hostile communicative environments, where people fear communicating their ideas to other people. While relationships are not necessarily communication, we cannot overlook the degree to which the "quality" of the relationship influences peo-

ple's communication with each other— their willingness to talk with other members of the team, as well as the tone of the conversations.

Organization

The fourth factor associated with team success and failure is organization (structure). Forty-seven percent of the success stories were characterized by references to the importance of team organization, while 58 percent of the team failure stories contained references to organizational aspects of the group. The narratives emphasized two subthemes pertaining to organization: (1) clarity of roles and responsibilities, and (2) leadership.

Health care team success was associated with common goals and clear roles and responsibilities. For example, one participant reported: "The secret to our success was simple—we all had the same common goal—to do everything we could for the patient's health and well-being." Another respondent wrote: "We were successful because each of us knew what his/ her specific role in the group was, and we accepted those roles and worked hard to become more efficient and effective at whatever our job was." In contrast, health care team failure was associated with unclear roles and responsibilities (e.g., "We didn't do well because none of us seemed to have a firm handle on what our roles were, either individually or as a team").

Our analysis of the success and failure stories underscores the likely importance of clear roles and responsibilities. The success stories contained frequent references to the importance of the team members knowing precisely what they are supposed to do, while the failure stories contained equally frequent references to ambiguous roles and duties as an explanation for team ineffectiveness. The importance of clear roles and responsibilities is rather obvious: When team members have specific assigned duties, they know exactly what is expected of them and can more easily apply their knowledge and skills. However, when team members are not sure what they are supposed to do, they find it more difficult to make valuable contributions to the team. As one respondent explains:

> Our success was based on the fact that each one of us had a very specific job with clearly specified responsibilities and assignments and was efficient and competent at it. We could move in, set up, and be performing surgery within a day. The only way this is possible is if each of us performs our jobs precisely and collectively nothing is neglected or overlooked.

Of course, group members' understanding of roles and responsibilities is based on those roles and responsibilities being clearly communicated to them. Team members must talk to each other so each knows what he or she is responsible for, as well as what others in the team expect of him or her.

In addition to highlighting the necessity of clear roles and responsibilities, the narratives pointed to leadership as an important organizational subtheme. Success stories identified good leadership as a contributing factor to effective health care team performance (e.g., "Our success was due to the efforts of our team leader—she motivated us and was cool under pressure . . . even when things weren't going well, she could figure out what was going wrong and tell us what to do to correct it"). Conversely, narratives of health care team failures often emphasized poor leadership (e.g., "We did poorly because the doctor in charge played mind games with people and pitted people against each other so that no one cooperated with each other, and on top of that refused to take an active role in providing any guidance for the group").

Interestingly, while only five stories attributed team success to good leadership, twenty-one stories attributed team failure to poor leadership. This suggests that poor leadership may have a greater impact on team performance than good leadership. As one respondent put it: " . . . while a good leader can add tremendously to the group effort, a bad leader will definitely sink the group like a dead weight." The detrimental influence of poor team leadership is evident in the following story:

> I was a member of a psychiatric assessment team at a psychiatric hospital. We met each day to discuss the progress of the patients currently at the hospital. The leader of our team (an MD) was the worst leader you could imagine—he was close-minded, condescending, domineering, thought he knew it all, micro-managed everything, and worse of all, played people off against each other. He singlehandedly created a climate of distrust and low morale, not to mention high stress, such that everyone wanted off the team as quickly as possible. Needless to say, our team messed up on several patient assessments, the worse of which was a patient who was diagnosed as having organic brain deterioration when, in fact, he was suffering from post-traumatic stress disorder.

Our findings also indicate that how leaders communicate with team members is an important facet of leadership effectiveness or ineffectiveness. Communication is vital to good leadership: leaders need to be able to clearly articulate their ideas and expectations, to persuade team members, and to delegate tasks and responsibilities fairly, without micro-managing others. Poor communication skills can be a major obstacle for people who aspire to lead.

Process

The fifth and final factor associated with team success and failure in the narratives we studied is group process. Thirty-two percent of the success stories contained references to the importance of group process for effective team performance. Included in this thematic category were references to *hard work* (e.g., "Bottomline, we were successful because we put in long hours, worked hard, and did exhaustive research to make sure that our recommendations would produce the desired outcomes for the patient"); *overlapping effort* (e.g., "We helped each other out . . . no one restricted themselves to only their roles . . . there aren't a lot of gaps when everyone works like this"); and *effective communication* (e.g., "Our success was due to good communication—we discussed each case thoroughly, really listened to each other, and made sure we understood what others were saying and opened [ourselves] up to understanding the viewpoints of other people").

In comparison, 54 percent of the failure stories contained references to faulty group process as an explanation for team ineffectiveness. Specific references included *poor communication* (e.g., "The basic problem was that the information people needed to get their jobs done didn't get to them in a timely manner if it got there at all"); *insufficient effort* (e.g., "Although none of us would admit it at the time, our failure was due to the fact that people were neglecting their duties and responsibilities and expecting others to cover for them . . . [and as a result] important tasks got overlooked"); and *ineffective procedures* (e.g., "[the whole team concept] was new to us and so we really didn't know what we were doing and we didn't have the benefit of established procedures and guidelines to follow, so we just flew by the seat of our pants and not very well unfortunately").

Of particular salience to this chapter is the finding that the stories of team success and failure highlight the importance of effective group communication. Success stories contained numerous references to the importance of effective listening, open exchange of ideas, and timely and effective dissemination of information to team members who needed it. Failure stories, on the other hand, contained nearly twice as many references to the detrimental influence of poor listening, close-minded interaction among team members, and the absence of proper information flow among team members. This suggests that poor group communication may be especially problematic for team success. One particular story underscores the problems of poor group communication:

> I was a member of a purchase team for a MRI scanner. Basically, the hospital administrator, behind closed doors with a vendor, made the purchase without consulting with any of us. After we found out, we tried to talk to the administrator, but he wouldn't listen to us. As a result, the hospital ended up purchasing a MRI scanner that was soon obsolete because it used the wrong kind of magnets (resistive magnets). To make matters worse, it was discovered that we didn't have adequate space to install the MRI scanner because the administrator never consulted with the building engineers and just assumed that the MRI scanner would fit in the existing CT suite. All of these problems could have been easily avoided if the administrator had taken the time to talk with various members of the team before making the purchase.

Tables 14.1 and 14.2 summarize the findings of the health care team study.

Table 14.1

Summary of Differences Between Success and Failure Narratives

Theme	Story Type		
	Success (N = 78)	Failure (N = 59)	Z-score
External Force	5 (6%)	6 (10%)	−0.68
Member Attribute	25 (32%)	54 (92%)	−12.14*
Relationship	27 (35%)	5 (9%)	2.17*
Organization	37 (47%)	34 (58%)	−0.47
Process	25 (32%)	32 (54%)	−4.06*

* $p < .05$

Table 14.2

Summary of Themes and Respective Major Subthemes
of Success and Failure Narratives

Theme	Success Stories, Subthemes	Failure Stories, Subthemes
External	$N = 5$, External feedback Administration support	$N = 6$, Administrative nonsupport Chance
Member Attribute	$N = 25$, Knowledge and skills High motivation Dedication and commitment	$N = 54$, Insufficient knowledge and skills Lack of motivation
Relationship	$N = 27$, Mutual respect Group cohesiveness	$N = 5$, Interpersonal conflicts Power plays
Organization	$N = 37$, Common goals Clear roles and responsibilities Good leadership	$N = 34$, Poor leadership Poorly defined roles
Process	$N = 25$, Hard work Overlapping effort Effective communication	$N = 32$, Insufficient effort Ineffective procedures Poor coomunication

Conclusion

In his book *Groups That Work (and Those That Don't)*, Hackman (1990) cautions us that task group performance is the result of many different factors that "do not come in separate, easily distinguishable packages" (8). Our discussion of factors associated with health care team effectiveness supports Hackman's proposition. At the same time, this discussion also suggests that the influence on health care team performance is not as infinite as some might believe. Rather, there appear to be some consistent themes associated with stories of team success and failure that suggest some reliable predictors of health care team effectiveness.[2] What are needed at this point are empirical studies that test the validity of recounted influences on health care team performance.

Finally, the findings of this study point to the need to focus specific attention on health care team ineffectiveness. Much of the extant literature emphasizes the importance of success in teams and groups but gives less attention to understanding team failures. The assumption in the literature seems to be that what does not contribute to a team's success will necessarily contribute to a team's failure. However, the findings of this study suggest that the influences on group success and failure do not necessarily exist on opposite ends of a continuum. Indeed, this study suggests that the absence of facilitative influences on group success does not necessarily lead to group failure, and vice versa. A second and related area to focus on in pinpointing ineffectiveness is the importance of communication within ineffective teams. This finding indicates that communication becomes noteworthy to team members only when it does not work. Again, such a finding directs further research toward the communicative aspects of ineffective teams. As the narratives for this study demonstrate, health care team failure does happen. Future research should thus investigate specifically the determinants of such failure, in order to minimize their occurrence.

Author's Note

The second and third authors are listed alphabetically to reflect their equal contribution to this study. The authors thank Thomas Socha for his review of a previous draft of this chapter.

Notes

1. The information presented in this essay is based on the findings of a previous study, Narrative Accounts of Health Care Team

Performance by Hirokawa, DeGooyer, and Valde (2000). The goal of the previous study was to provide empirical groundwork for the development of a model of health care team performance that would serve as a useful guide for the systematic study of interdisciplinary health care team effectiveness. That study drew on the method of narrative accounting (Polkinghorne 1988) to identify potential influences on health care team performance. The procedures for the study consisted of having participants complete a three-part survey. The first section asked for sex, age, and occupation/profession of the storyteller. The second section asked the respondent to: "Recall your most memorable experience of health care team success. In narrative (or story) form, please provide a detailed account of that success—that is, describe what happened, explain why you think it was a success, and indicate what contributed to your team's success. Please tell your story in as much detail as possible." The third section asked group members to: "Recall your most memorable experience of health care team failure. In narrative (or story) form, please provide a detailed account of that failure—that is, describe what happened, explain why you think it was a failure, and indicate what contributed to your team's failure. Please tell your story in as much detail as possible." A total of 137 usable stories (78 success stories and 59 failure stories) were obtained from the participants. A variety of teams were represented, including medical assessment (27 percent), behavior modification (22 percent), critical/intensive care (21 percent), geriatric care (15 percent), organ transplantation (11 percent), and miscellaneous others (4 percent). These stories and themes were then coded using inductive analysis (Glaser and Strauss 1967).

2. An overall comparison of the frequency of those themes between success and failure stories revealed a significant association between themes and story type (X^2 (4, N = 250) = 27.42, $p < .01$). A comparison of the standardized frequencies (expressed as proportions) revealed significant differences between the group success and failure stories in regard to three themes: relationships (Success = 35%; Failure = 9%; $z = 2.17$, $p < .05$); process (Success = 32%; Failure = 54%; $z = -4.06$, $p < .05$); and member attribute (Success = 32%; Failure = 92%; $z = -12.14$, $p < .05$). No significant difference was observed between the success and failure stories in regard to organization

factors (Success = 47%; Failure = 58%, $z = -0.47$, $p > .05$) and external factors (Success = 6%; Failure = 10%, $z = -0.68$, $p > .05$). The power to detect significant differences in proportion was .96.

References

Addleton, R. L., Tratnack, S. A., and Donat, D. C. (1991). "Hospital-based multidisciplinary training in the care of seriously mentally ill patients." *Hospital and Community Psychiatry* 42: 60–61.

Bednash, P. (1995). Interdisciplinary education and practice. Unpublished position statement. American Association of Colleges of Nursing. Washington, DC.

Bulger, R. J. (1993). A vision for the future of health professions education. Keynote address delivered to the First Congress of Health Professions Education. Washington, DC.

Cohen, S. G., Ledford, G. E., and Spreitzer, G. M. (1996). "A predictive model of self-managing work team effectiveness." *Human Relations* 49: 643–676.

Fleishman, E. A., and Zaccaro, S. J. (1992). "Toward a taxonomy of team performance functions." In R. W. Sweezey and E. Salas (eds.), *Teams: Their Training and Performance* (pp. 31–56). Norwood, NJ: Ablex.

Gitlin, L. N., Lyons, K. J., and Kolodner, E. (1994). "A model to build collaborative research for educational teams of health professionals in gerontology." *Educational Gerontology* 20: 15–34.

Gladstein, D. L. (1987). "Groups in context: A model of task effectiveness." *Administrative Science Quarterly* 29: 499–517.

Glaser, B. G., and Strauss, A. L. (1967). *The Discovery of Grounded Theory: Strategies for Qualitative Research*. Chicago: Aldine Publishing Company.

Guzzo, R. A. (1986). "Group decision making and group effectiveness in organizations." In P. S. Goodman and Associates (eds.), *Designing Effective Work Groups*. San Francisco: Jossey-Bass.

Hackman, J. R. (1990). *Groups That Work (and Those That Don't): Creating Conditions for Effective Teamwork*. San Francisco, CA: Jossey-Bass.

Helmreich, R. L., and Schaefer, H. (1994). "Team performance in the operating room." In M. S. Bogner (ed.), *Human Error in Medicine* (pp. 225–253). Hillsdale, NJ: Lawrence Erlbaum.

Hirokawa, R. Y., DeGooyer, D., and Valde, K. (2000). Narrative accounts of health care team performance. Paper presented at the National Communication Association Annual Conference, Seattle.

House, J. S. (1981). *Work Stress and Social Support*. Reading, MA: Addison-Wesley.

Ilgen, D. R. (1999). "Teams embedded in organizations: Some implications." *American Psychologist* 54: 129–139.

Janis, I. L. (1982). *Victims of Groupthink*. Boston: Houghton Mifflin.

Katzenbach, J. R., and Smith, D. K. (1993). *The Wisdom of Teams: Creating the High-Performance Organization*. New York: Harper Collins Publishers.

Knaus, W. A., Draper, E. A., Wagner, D. P., and Zimmerman, J. E. (1986). "An evaluation of outcome from intensive care in major medical centers." *Annals of Internal Medicine* 104: 410–418.

Kreps, G. L., and Thornton, B. C. (1992). *Health Communication: Theory and Practice*. Prospects Heights, IL: Waveland Press.

Kumpfer, K. L., Turner, C., Hopkins, R., and Librett, J. (1993). "Leadership and team effectiveness in community coalitions for the prevention of alcohol and other drug abuse." *Health Education Research* 8: 359–374.

Larson, C. E., and LaFasto, F. M. (1989). *Teamwork*. Newbury Park, CA: Sage.

Lenkman, S., and Gribbins, R. (1994). "Multidisciplinary teams in the acute care setting." *Holistic Nursing Practice* 8: 81–87.

McGrath, J. E. (1984). *Groups: Interaction and Performance*. Englewood Cliffs, NJ: Prentice-Hall.

McGrath, J. E. (1997). "Small group research, that once and future field: An interpretation of the past with an eye to the future." *Group Dynamics* 1: 7–27.

Miccolo, M. A., and Spanier, A. H. (1993). "Critical care management in the 1990s: Making collaborative practice work." *Critical Care Unit Management* 9: 443–453.

Morgan, B. B., Jr., Glickman, A. S., Woodward, E. A., Blaiwes, A., and Salas, E. (1986). *Measurement of Team Behaviors in a Navy Environment* (NTSC Report No. 86–014). Orlando, FL: Naval Training System Center.

Pew Health Professions Commission. (February 1993). *Health Professions Education for the Future: Schools in Service to the Nation*. San Francisco: Pew Commission.

Polkinghorne, D. E. (1988). *Narrative Knowing and the Human Science*. Albany, NY: State University of New York Press.

Pritchard, R. D. (1995). *Productivity Measurement and Improvement: Organizational Case Studies*. Westport, CT: Praeger.

Ray, E. B., and Miller, K. I. (1993). "Communication in health-care organizations." In B. C. Thornton and G. L. Kreps (eds.), *Perspectives on Health Communication* (pp. 102–116). Prospects Heights, IL: Waveland Press.

Robertson, K. E., and McDaniel, A. M. (1995). "Interdisciplinary professional education: A collaborative clinical teaching project." *American Journal of Pharmaceutical Education* 59: 131–136.

Runciman, P. (1989). "Health assessment of the elderly in health professions education: The case of shared learning." *Journal of Advanced Nursing* 14: 111–119.

Chapter 15
Teaming with Emotion

The Impact of Emotionality on Work-Team Collaboration

Carolyn C. Clark
Richard W. Sline

In the final chapter in this section, Clark and Sline discuss a descriptive study of the role of emotions in group and team performance. The authors found important differences between the role of emotions in what they call "positive" and "negative" triggering events. A "triggering" event is one that produces emotional experiences in group members. Clark and Sline found that emotions like anger are always associated with negative episodes in the group, while emotions like joy are associated with positive episodes. They also found that certain emotions (like anger) are more likely to be suppressed in a group than other ones (like joy). Perhaps the most important finding of this study, however, is that negative emotional expression in a group does not necessarily have a negative influence on team collaboration.

Scholars of group communication have paid little attention to the impact of emotional expression on team interaction, although recent developments demonstrate that this is a timely and vital issue. These developments include the rapid spread of permanent work teams in American businesses and the recognition of emotional expression as a central aspect of team interaction. This chapter describes these trends, traces recent scholarship addressing emotional expression in the workplace, and summarizes a study that focuses on the role of emotionality in the communication processes of tightly coupled work teams.

Team Structures

The popularity of work teams in modern corporations stems in part from today's intense global competition and the increasing complexity of the business environment. This complexity has forced American industry to explore alternative production strategies based on flexibility and quick response time rather than on standard mass production. Organizations facing high uncertainty in their environments tend to mimic innovations that have already been implemented by successful companies. Leading U.S. firms such as Xerox, Procter and Gamble, and General Motors, for example, have drawn on Japan's use of participative structures by instituting self-directed teams, and a multitude of U.S. firms have followed suit. In support of these changes, former Harvard economist and U.S. Secretary of Labor Robert Reich (1983, 1987) has proclaimed that teamwork structures are the most effective means for corporations to respond to the complexities of global competition and high-speed information processing in today's global market.

Emotional Expression and Teamwork

Such structural revisions, of course, are never easy to execute. In fact, significant organizational changes almost always develop in roller-coaster fashion, involving setbacks as well as advances. For example, even though the adoption of team structures may confer on workers a greater sense of responsibility, teamwork has been no panacea. In fact, there are several aspects of team communication that tend to foster anxiety and emotional tension among team members. The interdependency involved in successful teamwork demands a great deal of emotional energy and can highlight dissension. You can imagine the irritations that might develop among team members who are working closely with the same group of people day after day, as they attempt to collaborate in performing tasks under time pressures. Besides this, the responsibility of joint decision making intensifies every member's information load. Since fewer decisions are delegated to individuals, the amount of material to be kept track of can snowball as each member sifts through data in order to contribute intelligently to group decisions. Finally, the de-emphasis of traditional upward-downward channels of communication and the incorporation of lateral communication among teammates can generate additional anxiety because employees must learn to adjust to new patterns of communication.[1] Thus interdependency, increased information load, and changed communication patterns heighten the strain experienced by team members and increase the potential for emotional outbreaks. If emotions are managed appropriately, however, these same strong feelings can actually forge solid interpersonal relationships among teammates. In this way, emotional expression can function as either a bonding mechanism or a deterrent to collaboration.

Prior Research on Emotionality in the Workplace

Emotion has been identified as a crucial communication construct, a driving force that plays a significant role in sculpting the beliefs, attitudes, and values through which meaning and relationships are created and maintained in organizations. Pace and Faules (1983, 193) have defined relationships as "emotional connection[s]" between interacting individuals. Weick (1979) contends that shared feelings contribute more to group cohesiveness than shared opinions do, and Collins (1981) has asserted that "emotional energy" plays a primary role in successful interaction. It has also been recognized that, given the shift from traditional hierarchies of command to participative structures, it is no longer feasible for employees to suppress and ignore emotions in work contexts.

In Western tradition, however, reason, cognition, and thinking (i.e., "rationality") have been theoretically set in opposition to passion, affect, and feeling (i.e., "emotionality"). Organizational life has historically acclaimed and encouraged rationality, while it has considered emotionality to be either irrational or illegitimate. Managers typically treat emotionality either as inappropriate demeanor or as a commodity that can be used to increase organizational productivity. Zaleznik (1989) refers to the first conception (i.e., emotional expression as inappropriate demeanor) as the prevailing corporate code. He explains that according to this code, emotions detract from effective decision making and should be suppressed on the job. Managers who subscribe to this code assume that people are capable of ignoring their emotions and can make decisions and perform tasks based purely on rational goals, such as the maximization of profits. Managers fear that in situations where emotions are expressed openly, employees might not take their tasks seriously, or tension among team members might escalate. In support of this view, scholars of small group communication have also observed that strongly expressed emotion can act as a disruptive breakpoint in group communication, particularly if the expression violates procedural norms.

The second conception (i.e., emotions as commodities) has been referred to by Hochschild (1983) as "emotional labor." Emotional labor is illustrated in the jobs of flight attendants, whose performance is judged by their ability to paste on smiles and retain them, no matter how they are feeling inside. Van Maanen's (1991) description of the "feeling business" at Disneyland provides another example of emotional labor. At Disneyland, employees (or "performers") are constantly monitored by supervisors to ensure that they never express any signs of insincerity, sleepiness, or boredom in view of the guests. These accounts serve as poignant reminders of the potential for abusing emotionality as a business commodity.

Organizational scholars point out that emotions have been devalued by rational models of organizing and urge the development of alternative conceptualizations that honor emotional expression at work. Recent inquiries in the field of communication have exposed this "myth of rationality" as a social construction and claim that the suppression of emotions can generate feelings of alienation and fragmentation. Mumby and Putnam (1992) argue that a healthier working environment would be one in which feelings are not viewed instrumentally. They advocate the endorsement of a "bounded emotionality"[2] in which emotional expression at work, as long as it is kept within certain bounds, should be clearly permissible. Constraints on emotional expression should not be imposed by organizational mandate but by each person's consideration for his or her coworkers. According to this perspective, emotionality is not viewed as a commodity but as an important constituent of communication that can enhance creativity, interrelatedness, mutual respect, a sense of community, and an appreciation of diversity among team members.

Empirical studies grounded in this perspective of bounded emotionality confirm the profound benefits of emotional expression at work and recognize the potential for detrimental effects when emotional expression exceeds certain bounds. Trujillo (1983), for example, suggests that expressive communication increases the togetherness of workers because the sharing of playful episodes functions as a powerful social force. Such episodes help define workers' social reality and create an expectation of smoothness in organizational life. In situations where the expression of playful emotions has become the norm, disruptive sentiments such as hostility are less likely to occur. The constructive expression of emotion among group members has also been associated with increased participant involvement and satisfaction. In addition, Zaleznik (1989, 122) argues that emotions should be viewed as a source of valuable information. The expression of emotions, he contends, encourages communication and thinking and leads to improved problem definition and potential resolution, whereas restricting the expression of emotions reduces cooperation and "constricts individuals in their ability to grow." On the other hand, Wellins, Byham, and Wilson (1991) maintain that a pivotal emotional event in a team's life can prompt the team to "catapult into a more advanced or regressed state" in its development as a group. Kanter (1989) concedes that if emotional bonds among particular team members become too strong (i.e., cliques, romances, etc.), openness, collaboration, and trust among the team as a whole will usually diminish. Bocialetti (1988) suggests that although the withholding of emotions may result in worker stress, suppression of critical feedback, and lowered motivation, when emotional expression becomes too intense there may be unwanted repercussions such as disruption of task activities, intimidation, or an unbusinesslike atmosphere.

Research Questions

Because we agree with the view that emotional expression is not inappropriate in the workplace and that emotionality is an issue of critical importance to communication scholars as well as practitioners, we designed a study to explore the impact of emotional expression on collaboration in work teams. We drew our sample from an organization that arranges staffing to fill in on a temporary basis for physicians around the country who are taking leaves of absence. The organization is structured into permanent work teams. All of the teams conform to Weick's (1979) characterization of "tightly coupled teams." That is, members have overlapping tasks, shared goals, a high frequency of interaction, and mutual fate control.

We investigated the following issues:

1. The types of events team members reported as being "triggers" of emotional reactions.

2. Members' perceptions of how those triggering events influence subsequent team collaboration.

3. The types of emotions that team members perceive they are expressing.

4. Characteristics related to the expression of specific types of emotions.

Method

Since this paper represents one portion of a larger investigation of emotional expression within highly interdependent work teams, we will only outline the procedures relevant to this study.

Subjects and Procedures

One hundred and ninety questionnaires were distributed to members of 18 interdependent work teams in a health care staffing organization. Often work teams are characterized as merely subsets of individuals working together on a regular basis (Farace, Monge, and Russell 1977). Our study, however, focuses on teams that are tightly coupled, with members having overlapping tasks, shared goals, and a high frequency of interaction and fate control (Ancona and Nadler 1989; Weick 1979). Members also share "outcome interdependence" (Shea and Guzzo 1987), that is, their compensation is based on team and organization success, as well as individual performance.

Open-ended descriptions of two emotional events (one negative and one positive) which occurred in the presence of other team members were elicited from each respondent. A six-category list of basic emotion clusters (love, joy surprise, anger, sadness, and fear) proposed by Ekman (1973) and verified by Shaver, Schwartz, Kirson, and O'Conner (1987) allowed respondents to rank up to three emotions they felt during the episode in order of strength. Based on the work of Shaver et al., the meaning of each emotion cluster was clarified by a list of related terms (i.e., LOVE—liking, compassion, longing, desire; FEAR—panic, worry, nervousness, uneasiness). Team members were given the opportunity to report multiple emotion types for each triggering event since they might have experienced a sequence of emotions as events unfolded (Aylwin 1985).

Suppression of emotions was measured by asking respondents if there was anything else they wanted to say during the emotional event but chose not to. Those indicating that they suppressed information were asked to explain what they wanted to say and why they did not say it. In addition, five-point Likert scale questions were used to measure the perceived intensity of the emotion.

Respondents also evaluated the impact of the emotional incidents on eight team collaboration variables using five-point Likert scales (1 and 2 represent decreased values; 3 signifies no change; 4 and 5 indicate increased values). Four of these variables (trust among team members, willingness to collaborate, willingness to accept differences among members, and willingness to place team goals above individual goals) were averaged to provide a team relationship score. The remaining variables (openness in sharing information, frequency of team talk, quality of team discussions, and inclusion of all team members in discussions) were averaged to provide an overall score for team communication behavior. The variables selected were based on Larson and LaFasto's (1989) "Team Excellence" system that had been adopted by the organization as its model and language for teamwork. At the time this study was administered, each respondent had previously received a copy of *Teamwork: What Must Go Right, What Can Go Wrong* (Larson and LaFasto 1989) and participated in a series of cross-team "concept learning groups" in which the "Team Excellence" concepts had been discussed and analyzed within the context of employee experiences. Therefore, the outcome variables selected to measure team collaboration—relationships and communication effectiveness—had high potential for significant shared meaning among respondents.

Data Analysis

Eighty-six useable questionnaires were returned, representing a 45% return rate. A total of 83 positive emotional incidents and 85 negative emotional events were reported (n = 168).

First, the researchers independently generated preliminary categories to describe triggering events, using Miles and Huberman's (1984) "clustering" technique. These preliminary categories were integrated into two master sets, one for negative and one for positive events. Next, the researchers jointly unitized the open-ended descriptions, selecting the portion of each anecdote that reflected the primary impetus for the respondent's emotional reaction. Sixty-three percent of the responses were then independently categorized by the researchers to test for reliability. Absolute agreement was .86 and reliability was .85 (Scott's pi) for both negative and positive events (Scott 1955). The remaining events were classified independently.

Chi square tests were used to examine the relationship between kind of triggering context and type of subsequently felt emotion, the significance of differences among the frequency of emotion types experienced by team members, and the extent to which emotions were suppressed by team members. T-tests were run to compare emotional intensity of various suppressed emotions. Paired t-tests were used to analyze the differences in the relationships of positive and negative emotional triggering events with subsequent perception of team collaboration.

Triggering Events

The purpose of our first research question was to construct a typology of events that team members reported as being triggers of emotional reactions. Typologies are valuable because they allow comparisons among the various categories of triggering events and other variables.

Our typology divides both negative and positive triggering events into two main categories (individual-directed and team-directed), depending on whose action it was that impelled the emotional episode and therefore became the recipient of the emotional outburst. Each of these main categories is further divided into subcategories corresponding to Bales's (1950) distinction between task and socioemotional activities. Figures 15.1 and 15.2 provide lists of these categories, along with definitions and representative accounts from our respondents.

Figure 15.1

Negative Triggering Events

1. Individual-directed

   a. Task criticism: Team member receives task-related criticism in the presence of teammates.

   > "I received feedback that I was allowing details to slip through the cracks."
   > "I was questioned as to what I was actually doing all day."

   b. Socioemotional criticism: Team member is personally criticized in the presence of teammates for attitudes, personality traits, or interpersonal behavior.

   > "I felt like I was free-falling forever from a large jet when I was chewed out for not being supportive enough of my team."
   > "My feelings were hurt when I received written feedback from my teammates that they were reluctant to be open and direct with me because I would always overreact and cry."

2. Team-directed

   a. Imperious behavior: Individuals or subgroups of the team behave in ways that communicate superiority, arrogance, favoritism, or cliquishness to other team members.

Figure 15.1 (continued)

Negative Triggering Events

> "One teammate treated us as if we were beneath her, acting as if she was the master and I was the servant."
> "A small group of our teammates excluded the rest of us from a social activity that was intended for the entire team."

b. Noncollaborative behavior: A team member's actions communicate attitudes (such as lack of cooperation, support, and trust) that detract from the team's ability to cooperate.

> "One team member referred to the team's upcoming retreat as 'bullshit.'"
> "One team member was unwilling to relocate her own work station, even though it would improve the team's functioning."

Figure 15.2

Positive Triggering Events

1. **Individual-directed:**
   a. Task recognition: Team member receives recognition in front of teammates for a job well done.

   > "My teammates gave me a real shot in the arm when they congratulated me for pulling in some big contracts for the company."
   > "I was selected to represent the company at an important industry meeting."

   b. Socioemotional recognition: Team member receives praise for personal traits and supportive behaviors.

   > "I was thanked by my superior for having had the courage to give her constructive, negative feedback."
   > "My teammates decorated my work station and gave me roses in celebration of my tenth anniversary with the company."

2. **Team-directed:**
   a. Team pride: Team member feels good about the task accomplishments of teammates.

   > "The whole team was jumping around and patting each other on their backs when we finished a difficult assignment on very short notice."
   > "The company CEO called our team together to tell us how impressed and amazed he was with our accomplishments."

   b. Team spirit: Team member feels positive about being part of the team.

   > "My teammates worked overtime to cover her responsibilities so she could take time off to care for a critically ill family member."

When we compared frequencies, we found that the negative emotional events reported by our respondents were typically associated with criticism for *socioemotional* behavior and that the majority of these were situations in which the team was threatened (see Table 15.1). Conversely, positive emo-tional episodes were usually associated with praise that was directed at individuals and was based on *task-related* performance (see Table 15.2).

There are several possible explanations for these findings. Poor team collaboration may have been cited more frequently

Table 15.1

Percentages of Negative Triggering Events

Target of Triggering Event	Percentage	Kind of Behavior	Percentage
Individual-directed	38	Task-related	19
Team-directed	60	Socioemotional-related	79
Other	2	Other	2

Table 15.2

Percentages of Positive Triggering Events

Target of Triggering Event	Percentage	Kind of Behavior	Percentage
Individual-directed	65	Task-related	57
Team-directed	30	Socioemotional-related	39
Other	5	Other	4

as a source of negative emotions than criticism directed at individuals simply because personal criticism occurs less frequently. Common observation, however, does not support this hypothesis. A second potential explanation stems from the tendency of members of well-functioning teams to construct a strong sense of group identity, pride, and unified commitment. This climate may engender feelings of protectiveness toward the team as an entity, so events involving teammates seem more striking than those that only concern oneself.

On the other hand, the fact that praise directed at individuals was most frequently associated with positive emotions might be attributable to people's natural tendency to "feel good" when they can clearly take individual credit for the accomplishment. If others have been involved, the feelings of responsibility for the success may be attenuated. Another explanation may be that when an achievement comes from a shared effort in which no individual is clearly identifiable as the source of the success, leaders may perceive less reason for recognizing the accomplishment.

Fisher and Ury's (1981) popular work, *Getting to Yes*, may provide some clues in interpreting the finding that negative emotions were primarily reported as springing from relational triggering events, whereas positive emotions were most frequently initiated by recognition for task-related achievements. These authors contend that during emotional situations, individuals frequently fail to "separate the people from the problem" (Fisher and Ury 1981, 11). That is, when an individual behaves in a way that is not pleasing to us, we may judge this to be a personal attack, draw hasty inferences regarding that person's intentions, conclude that the other places little value on our relationship, and react by trying to defend our own egos. If we are focused on the task, however, we are less prone to react in a negatively emotional manner and can evaluate the conflict more objectively.

An alternate but related intuitive explanation may be that when we are reproached by teammates for committing task errors, the mistakes may be viewed as one-time slips that can be corrected in the future. The perception of personal traits as displeasing, however, is seen as more threatening, more difficult to change, and perhaps even taboo to discuss.

A third possible explanation for this tendency is that organizational reward systems typically assign credit for task achievements rather than for relational competence; thus, we become conditioned to associate success at work with task accomplishment. Knowledge- or skills-based pay programs, for example, are growing in popularity with organizations structured with teamwork designs. Performance-based incentive systems, which reward individual and/or team accomplishments, are equally popular. In fact, the organization in this study has an incentive program that rewards a combination of individual, team, and company performance. Individual recognition for task accomplishment provides these workers with salient, positive emotional experiences, particularly when such recognition is made in the presence of the entire organization.

Influence on Team Collaboration

Our second question centers on how negative and positive triggering events influenced perceptions of subsequent team collaboration. Collaboration is a vital construct to explore in studies of team interaction because it is considered to be a foundation for success. We measured two aspects of collaboration—*relationships* and *communication*. We chose these two measures because the characteristics of successful team relationships and communication had been extensively discussed and analyzed in this company's ongoing training program for upgrading employees' team collaboration skills, so all team members were likely to share similar meanings for these terms.

When we analyzed the data, we found that most members perceived that team relationships had improved after positive emotional events and had remained essentially unchanged after negative emotional events. Even more notably, most respondents reported that team communication had improved following emotional events, regardless of whether the events were positive or negative in nature.

This sequence implies—in contrast to Zaleznik's (1989) explanation of the corporate code, which advocates the suppression of emotions in the workplace—that the expression of emotions, both positive and negative, may not have the debilitating effect on subsequent team collaboration that managers typically expect. In fact, our respondents' open-ended descriptions of these events suggest that emotional expression frequently has a cathartic effect of relieving pent-up tension and functions to bring team members closer together.

Types of Emotions

Our third research question elicited the types of emotions experienced by participants. Several authors have used bipolar schemes (i.e., they have lumped all negative emotions into one category, and all positive emotions into another). However, bipolar classifications may be obscuring important distinctions, such as possible dissimilarities between the implications of anger and those of fear. To explore such possible disparities, we supplied respondents with Ekman's (1973) well-known typology of emotions and asked them to indicate the cluster that most closely represented their feelings during each emotional episode (see Table 15.3).

Sixty-seven percent of our team members selected anger as the emotional cluster that best described the way they felt during the negative episode, and 77 percent chose joy as the primary emotion they felt during the positive episode.

Table 15.3

Emotional Clusters

Cluster	Examples of Constituent Emotions
Anger	Annoyance, grouchiness, frustration, bitterness, scorn, disgust, envy, torment
Sadness	Hurt, unhappiness, disappointment, regret, embarrassment, rejection, sympathy
Surprise	Amazement, astonishment
Fear	Panic, worry, nervousness, uneasiness
Joy	Happiness, satisfaction, enthusiasm, relief, contentment, pride
Love	Liking, compassion, longing, desire

Table 15.4

Percentages of Emotional Clusters Reported by Waldron and Krone Compared to Those Reported by Clark and Sline

Emotion Cluster	Waldron and Krone		Clark and Sline	
	Negative	Positive	Negative	Positive
Anger	48%	0%	67%	0%
Sadness	39	0	18	0
Surprise	11	3	11	18
Fear	37	0	5	0
Joy	0	83	0	77
Love	0	7	0	5

Note: Waldron and Krone's respondents reported multiple emotions; therefore, the percentages do not sum to 100.

These choices coincide with those identified by Waldron and Krone (1991) in their study of employees functioning in a nonteamwork design (see Table 15.4). At first glance, we interpreted the prevalence of anger and joy in both studies as an indication that emotions experienced in the workplace might follow similar patterns, regardless of work design.

Characteristics of Anger

Because anger appeared to be such a commonly felt emotion, we then compared the characteristics of anger to those of other negative emotions. Upon analyzing the data in more depth, however, we noted that 78 percent of the team-directed negative events were associated with anger, while more than half (53 percent) of the individual-directed events were associated with other emotions (see Table 15.5). This led us to revise *our* previous notion that emotions might function similarly in all work settings; instead, we surmised that there might indeed be some deeper connection between anger and team-directed situations.

Table 15.5

Comparison of Anger to Other Emotional Clusters

Target of Triggering Event	Anger	Other
Individual-directed	47%	53%
Team-directed	78%	22%

We also discovered that anger was suppressed more than other emotions (see Table 15.6). Goffman (1969) has proposed that employees' choices of when and how to express their emotions may function as "control moves." On the other hand, Sutton and Rafaeli (1988) have suggested that displays of emotion may be related to perceived relational consequences. Many people, for example, consider anger, like conflict, to be detrimental to relationships and therefore attempt to subdue angry feelings. A related explanation may be that members of highly interdependent work teams have been socialized to place the team's needs above individual needs. Team members who suppress their anger may do so because they believe that the need to maintain a collaborative climate on the team is more important than a personal need for expression.

Table 15.6

Suppression of Anger During Negative Episodes

Target of Triggering Event	Suppressed	Expressed
Anger	84%	16%
Other emotions	54%	46%

We reasoned that suppression could also be a function of the intensity of the emotion. When we tested this hunch, we found that expressed anger was usually reported as being more intense than suppressed anger (see Figure 15.3). It seems that individuals are no longer capable of exercising choice and containing their anger when it surpasses a certain threshold of intensity.

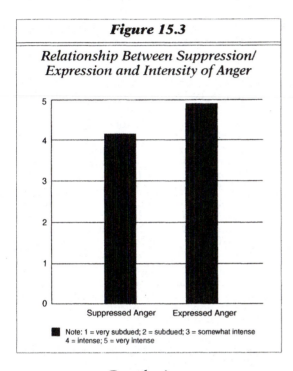

Figure 15.3

Relationship Between Suppression/ Expression and Intensity of Anger

Note: 1 = very subdued; 2 = subdued; 3 = somewhat intense 4 = intense; 5 = very intense

Conclusions

Because of the exploratory nature of this study, the specific results must be viewed as tentative. The findings do, however, suggest some general trends and reveal areas for future research.

This preliminary typology of triggering events suggests that important differences exist among individual-directed and team-directed emotional encounters, as well as between task and relational dimensions. Moreover, negative triggering events seem to exhibit characteristics that are qualitatively different from positive events. In addition, the role of anger in team interaction appears to be unique. Perhaps the most significant finding, however, is that negative emotional expression among our respondents did not generally have a negative influence on team collaboration. This discovery lends support to Mumby and Putnam's (1992) contention

that organizations do not need to stifle emotional expression for fear of its consequences but should acknowledge emotionality as a natural component of human interaction and allow team members to create their own norms for managing emotionality. Furthermore, this study suggests that additional examination of the role of anger in team interaction could be fruitful. Finally, these findings prompt us to advocate detailed research aimed at discerning the conditions under which emotional displays exceed the threshold of being beneficial and begin to push the envelope of bounded emotionality too far.

Notes

1. Barker, Melville, and Pacanowsky (1993) have argued that a breakdown of the communication hierarchy does not necessarily imply that the traditional roots of control in the organization have been altered; in the majority of cases it is merely the surface patterns of communication that have changed.

2. The phrase "bounded emotionality" parallels "bounded rationality," a term coined by Simon (1976) to portray the fact that human decision making cannot be truly rational. We are all bounded by our own perceptual biases and cognitive limitations, so that the choices we make are at best sufficient rather than optimal.

References

Ancona, D., and Nadler, D. (1989, Fall). "Top hats and executive tales: Designing the senior team." *Sloan Management Review*, 19–22.

Aylwin, J. (1985). *Structure in Thought and Feeling.* New York: Methuen.

Bales. R. F. (1950). "A set of categories for the analysis of small group interaction." *American Sociological Review* 15: 257–263.

Barker, J. R., Melville, C. W., and Pacanowsky, M. E. (1993). "Self-directed teams at XEL: Changes in communication practices during a program of cultural transformation." *Journal of Applied Communication Research* 21(4): 297–312.

Bocialetti, G. (1988). "Teams and the management of emotion." In W. B. Reddy (ed.), *Team Building: Blueprints for Productivity and Satisfaction*. Alexandria, VA: NTL Institute.

Clark, C. L., and Sline, R. W. (1992). Teaming with emotion: The impact of emotionality on team collaboration. Paper presented at the annual meeting of the Speech Communication Association, Chicago, IL.

Collins, R. (1981). "On the microfoundations of macrosociology." *American Journal of Sociology* 86: 984–1014.

Ekman, P. (1973). "Cross culture studies of facial expression." In P. Ekman (ed.), *Darwin and Facial Expression—A Century of Research in Review* (pp. 169–222). NY: Academic Press.

Farace, R., Monge, P., and Russell, H. (1977). *Communicating and Organizing*. Reading, MA: Addison-Wesley.

Fisher, R., and Ury, W. (1981). *Getting to Yes: Negotiating Agreement Without Giving In*. Boston: Houghton Mifflin.

Goffman, E. (1969). *Strategic Interaction*. Philadelphia: University of Pennsylvania Press.

Hochschild, A. R. (1983). *The Managed Heart*. Berkeley: University of California Press.

Kanter, R. (1989). *When Giants Learn to Dance*. New York: Simon and Schuster, Inc.

Larson, C., and LaFasto, F. (1989). *Teamwork: What Must Go Right, What Can Go Wrong*. Newbury Park, CA: Sage.

Miles, M. B., and Huberman, A. M. (1984). *Qualitative Data Analysis: A Sourcebook of New Methods*. Beverly Hills, CA: Sage.

Mumby, D., and Putnam, L. (1992). "The politics of emotion: A feminist reading of bounded rationality." *The Academy of Management Review* 17: 465–486.

Pace, R. W., and Faules, D. F. (1983). *Organizational Communication* (2nd ed.). Englewood Cliffs, NJ: Prentice Hall.

Reich, R. (1983). "The next American frontier." *The Atlantic Monthly* 251(3): 43–58.

Reich, R. (1987). "Entrepreneurship reconsidered: The team as hero." *Harvard Business Review* 65(3): 77–83.

Scott, W. S. (1955). "Reliability of content analysis: The case of nominal scale coding." *Living Research*, 19, 321–325.

Shea, G. P., and Guzzo, R. A. (1987). "Group effectiveness: What really matters?" *Sloan Management Review, 28 (3)*, 25–31.

Shaver, P., Schwartz, J., Kirson, D., and O'Conner, C. (1987). "Emotion knowledge: Further exploration of a prototype approach." *Journal of Personality and Social Psychology, 52*, 1061–1086.

Simon, H. A. (1976). *Administrative Behavior* (3rd ed.). New York: Free Press.

Sutton, R. I., and Rafaeli, A. (1988). "Untangling the relationship between displayed emotions and organizational sales: The case of convenience stores." *Academy of Management Journal* 31: 461–487.

Trujillo. N. (1983). "Performing Mintzberg's roles: The nature of managerial communication." In L. L. Putnam and M. E. Pacanowsky (eds.), *Communication and Organizations: An Interpretive Approach*. Newbury Park, CA: Sage.

Van Maanen, J. (1991). "The smile factory: Work at Disneyland." In P. J. Frost, L. F. Moore, M. R. Louis, C. C. Lundberg, and J. Martin (eds.), *Reframing Organizational Culture*. Newbury Park, CA: Sage.

Waldron, V. R., and Krone. K. J. (1991). "The experience and expression of emotion in the workplace: A study of a corrections organization." *Management Communication Quarterly* 4: 287–309.

Weick, K. E. (1979). *The Social Psychology of Organizing* (2nd ed.). New York: Random House.

Wellins, R., Byham, W., and Wilson, J. (1991). *Empowered Teams: Creating Self-Directed Work Groups that Improve Quality, Productivity and Participation*. San Francisco: Jossey-Bass.

Zaleznik, A. (1989). *The Managerial Mystique: Restoring Leadership in Business*. New York: Harper and Row.

Part VI

Leadership in Groups

Leadership is crucial for effective group action. Seldom does a group or team do well unless someone in the group directs and coordinates the various activities of group members.

Since the beginning of civilization, people have sought answers to the questions of who becomes a leader and why. Interest in leaders and leadership is as strong today as in the past, and scholars from a variety of academic disciplines have produced extensive literature on the topic, yet answers to questions of leaders and leadership have proven elusive. There is no consensus why, and under what circumstances, some become leaders and others remain followers, no universal theory of leadership, and no precise formula for producing leaders.

The study of leaders and leadership has been complicated by conceptual slippage between these two terms. *Leader* refers to a position within the group structure, or to a person who occupies such a position. *Leadership* refers to the process of influencing group activities toward goal achievement (Shaw 1981, 317). Since the person who most influences group activities is often seen as its leader, the two terms are often used interchangeably. However, insofar as the person who occupies the position of group leader is not the only one who can exert influence in the group, "leader" and

"leadership" must be seen as distinctly different aspects of small groups.

Four Approaches to Studying Leadership

The study of leaders and leadership in the context of small group communication has historically been guided by four conceptual approaches:

Trait approach. Early research on group leaders and leadership was based on the general assumption that leaders are people who possess certain inherent personal characteristics that allow them to exercise leadership in a group. Research in this tradition thus focused on the search for individual traits and characteristics that distinguish leaders from nonleaders. John Geier (1967) conducted a well-known group communication study in this tradition. The author studied leader emergence in 16 five-member task-oriented groups using three research methods: (1) direct observation, (2) interviews of group members, and (3) analysis of diaries kept by group members. He found that group leaders emerge through a two-stage process in which would-be contenders for the leader position are *eliminated* on the basis of their negative traits. Through a series of such rejections, a leader finally emerges. In particular, Geier found that leader candidates were eliminated if they were uninformed about the task, nonparticipative, extremely rigid, or too authoritarian, or if they uttered offensive verbalizations. While the trait approach to group leadership has a certain amount of common-sense appeal, researchers have, for the most part, been unsuccessful in identifying a set of traits that universally distinguish leaders from nonleaders (Bass and Stogdill 1990).

Style approach. The style approach to the study of group leaders and leadership is premised on the belief that leaders display different behavioral patterns in exercising leadership, which, in turn, have a direct impact on group performance. White and Lippitt (1968) conducted a landmark study in this tradition. The researchers studied the effects of three different styles of group leadership on group satisfaction, cohesiveness, and productivity—*authoritarian* (where the leader determined all policies for the group members and told them what to do), *democratic* (where the leader encouraged the group to make its own policies and asked group members what they wanted to do), and *laissez-faire* (where leaders refused to help the group choose its policy and neither asked nor told group members what to do). The study found that the democratic style was associated with greater group satisfaction and cohesiveness than either the authoritarian or *laissez-faire* styles. However, with regard to group productivity, there was no significant difference between the authoritarian and democratic leadership styles, though groups with both styles of leadership outpaced the groups with *laissez-faire* leaders. The problem with the style approach to the study of group leadership is that the concept of "style" is difficult to translate into distinct and unique behavioral patterns. Clearly, there are many different "styles" of group leadership, and distinctions among them often involve very subtle behavioral differences (Barge and Hirokawa 1989).

Situational approach. The situational approach to the study of group leadership assumes that leadership is a function of the interaction between the leader's and followers' personalities, and the social situation in which the group finds itself. The work of Fred Fiedler (1978) best exemplifies this approach. Fiedler identified two general types of group leaders—those who are "people oriented" and those who are "task oriented"—and provided evidence to show that each style of leadership is best suited for different group situations. Task-oriented leaders tend to be most effective in situations that either highly favor the leader, or do not favor him or her at all. In contrast, people-oriented leaders are best in situations where members are moderately favorable toward the leader. Although the situational approach reveals the complexity of the leadership phenomenon, it fails to provide more than a superficial insight into this complexity. Thus, the approach suggests an indeterminable number of possible situational influences on group leaders and leadership. In short, the number of variables that group leadership is potentially contingent on is virtually impossible to comprehend (Fisher 1986, 203–204).

Functional approach. The functional approach to studying group leaders focuses on the duties or responsibilities (i.e., functions) performed by those who emerge as leaders in groups. Research by Beatrice Schultz and her associates on the role of the "reminder" in group decision making (Schultz, Ketrow, and Urban 1995) is an illustration of this research approach. The researchers found that the person occupying the "reminder role"— that is, the person who imposes a rational structure on the group's deliberations without interrupting the ongoing interaction—often emerges as the leader of the group. The major problem with the functional approach is its inability to specify a limited set of functions that are uniquely related to group leadership. Fisher (1986) cautions that the "incredible complexity associated with leadership functions (e.g., the number of different communicative functions potentially linked to leadership, the changes in leadership functions effected by task situations and combinations of group members)" makes it highly unlikely that a set of task and social functions unique to leadership will ever be found.

The chapters in this section take us beyond the four traditional approaches discussed above and bring us up-to-date on what is known about the communicative aspects of group leaders and leadership.

References

Barge, J. K., and Hirokawa, R. Y. (1989). "Toward a communication competency model of group leadership." *Small Group Behavior*, 20: 167–189.

Bass, B. M., and Stogdill, R. M. (1990). *Bass and Stogdill's Handbook of Leadership: Theory, Research, and Managerial Applications*, 3rd Edition. New York: The Free Press.

Fiedler, F. E. (1978). "The contingency model and the dynamics of the leadership process." In L. Berkowitz (ed.), *Advances in Experimental Social Psychology* Volume II (pp. 59–112). New York: Academic Press.

Fisher, B. A. (1986). "Leadership: When does the difference make a difference?" In R. Y. Hirokawa and M. S. Poole (eds.), *Communication and Group Decision-Making* (pp. 197–218). Beverly Hills, CA: Sage.

Geier, J. G. (1967). "A trait approach to the study of leadership in small groups." *Journal of Communication*, 17: 316–323.

Schultz, B., Ketrow, S. M., and Urban, D. M. (1995). "Improving decision quality in the small group: The role of the reminder." *Small Group Research*, 26: 521–541.

Shaw, M. E. (1981). *Group Dynamics: The Psychology of Small Group Behavior*. New York: McGraw-Hill.

White, R., and Lippitt, R. (1968). "Leader behavior and member reaction in three 'social climates.'" In D. Cartwright and A. Zander (eds.), *Group Dynamics: Research and Theory*, 3rd Edition (pp. 318–335). New York: Harper. ✦

Chapter 16
Leadership as the Art of Counteractive Influence in Decision-Making and Problem-Solving Groups

Dennis S. Gouran

Gouran portrays group leadership as the art of getting a group back onto its "goal path" when the interaction of its members has taken it astray. The author argues that groups can avoid serious breakdowns and frustrations if the members and, in particular, the group's leader, are aware of ever-present obstacles that stand in the way of effective group performance. Gouran offers advice concerning how group leaders can confront and counteract the negative influences of authority relations, pressures for uniformity, status struggles, disruptive behavior, and incompatibility between individual and group goals.

When people hear the term *leader* in the context of decision-making and problem-solving groups, they typically think of it as referring to a person who occupies a formal position that carries specified responsibilities and gives the occupant certain rights that others do not enjoy. Among other things, a leader, we think, is the person who: (a) calls a meeting to order; (b) announces the agenda; (c) guides discussion; (d) asks members for input; (e) summarizes interaction; (f) articulates the conclusion the members have reached; and, if need be, (g) serves as the spokesperson for the group in other venues. The performance of such activities, we understandably believe, constitutes *leadership*.

There is nothing wrong with thinking about leaders and leadership in this frame of reference; however, to do so exclusively is to view leadership and those who enact it from a very narrow perspective—a view that probably obscures the most critical aspects of what a person does when he or she functions as a leader in a decision-making or problem-solving group. The purpose of this essay is to provide a more expansive view of leadership, one that invests it with considerably more importance than the execution of prescribed and expected responsibilities. It portrays leadership as the *art of counteractive influence*—a view that is implicit in a more general perspective on communication in decision-making and problem-solving groups called the Functional Theory of Communication in Decision-Making and Problem-Solving Groups (Gouran and Hirokawa 1996); this theory is discussed elsewhere in this volume (see Chapter 4). This view is also more directly evident in Irving Janis's (1989) Constraints Model of Policymaking Processes. The view is also implicit, even if somewhat subtly, in Kevin Barge's (1994) Communication Skill Model of Leadership.

Coming to understand and appreciate the notion of leadership as the art of counteractive influence is easier if one has some familiarity with the ways in which theorists historically have portrayed leadership and how conceptions of it have evolved over the approximately one century that the subject has been of scholarly interest. With such familiarity, moreover, one can begin to see the roots of the perspective on which the present essay focuses. The section that follows provides an overview of several of the more dominant and influential historical perspectives.

General Perspectives on Leadership

From the beginning of the formal study of leadership, the phenomena to which it refers have been inseparably fused with the concept of social influence. Noting the large number of definitions apparent in scholarly literature, Peter Northouse (2001a) offers one he seems to feel is either compatible with, or subsumes, most of the others. "Leadership," according to Northouse, is "a process whereby an individual influences a group of individuals to achieve a common goal" (3). What that process entails, however, varies in relation to the theoretical lens through which one views leadership. For convenience, you can think in terms of three general perspectives: trait, stylistic, and situational. I discuss each below.

The Trait Perspective on Leadership

Those who subscribe to the trait perspective on leadership are of the belief that some individuals possess particular characteristics that others lack and that it is these characteristics that enable them both to secure positions of leadership and to exercise influence successfully once they occupy them (Bass 1990). Early thinking from this perspective reflected the presumption that leaders inherit these traits. The genetic view, however, garnered little support in research evidence and eventually gave way to the view that the qualities that enable one to accede to a position of leadership and to succeed there are most likely acquired.

The five qualities that seem to have the most consistent relationship to leadership emergence, Northouse (2001b) notes, are: (a) intelligence; (b) self-confidence; (c) determination; (d) integrity; and (e) sociability. That these are the same ones that best equip a person in a position of leadership to exercise influence is less clear because those who view leadership from the trait perspective have largely refrained from investigating the relationship of these traits to the outcomes that groups achieve. The presumption is one that Ernest Bormann (1969), moreover, has clearly challenged in his observation from research on leaderless groups at the University of Minnesota that what enables a person to move into a position of leadership is not what enables him or her to maintain it (see especially Chapters 10 and 12, pp. 201–225, 244–260).

Despite the absence of confirmation that particular traits are common both to the emergence of leaders and their success in the role, the trait perspective nevertheless is compatible with the understanding of leadership as the exercise of influence. To date, however, it has not provided much insight into how the traits give rise to the behavior necessary for a person either to emerge as a leader in a group or to have impact on how well the members perform. In these respects—the latter, in particular—the trait perspective is perhaps the most primitive and nonspecific of the three general ones that have provided the foundation for our understanding of what leadership is and how it functions in decision-making and problem-solving groups.

A view of leadership characterized as "transformational" (see Burns 1978) is one that shows promise of improving our understanding of how certain leadership traits, or personal qualities, enable one to exercise influence. Transformational leaders reportedly are: (a) charismatic; (b) visionary; (c) intellectually stimulating; and (d) highly considerate of the well-being of others (Avolio 1999). Those possessing these qualities, theoretically speaking, have better prospects than others for being viewed as leaders and also have greater impact on others' performance than those lacking such attributes. In principle, because transformational leaders are charismatic, others are attentive to what they have to say. In addition, their ability to articulate visions gives others a sense of purpose. Finally, such leaders ostensibly impel others to action by stimulating a sense of confidence that the leader's visions are realizable and by instilling in them the feeling that someone genuinely cares about their well-being. The adequacy of this explanation, however, remains to be established unequivocally.

The Stylistic Perspective on Leadership

In response to the general failure of scholars to identify a set of traits that uniformly distinguish leaders from nonleaders or that account for how people in positions of leadership exercise influence, as Barge (1994) notes, attention in some quarters began shifting from personal qualities to the characteristic ways in which leaders behave. Spurring this change in focus was work in the late 1930s and 1940s by Kurt Lewin and his associates in the area of child development (see Lewin, Lippitt, and White 1939). In the research, adult leaders systematically varied their behavior in dealing with children performing group tasks, so as to be autocratic at times, democratic at others, and *laissez-faire* at still others. The investigators were interested in the effects on performance and affective responses that such variations would have and which manner of behavior was consistently most effective, regardless of the personal characteristics of the leader. Hence, the stylistic perspective was born.

Those following in the line of research that Lewin launched discovered over time that the three categories mentioned above were insufficient to capture the variations in the styles that leaders actually exhibit. What subsequently occurred, then, was a concerted effort to identify the full range of styles. Style, scholars began to discern, was a reflection of how a leader balanced concern about subordinates with concern about tasks; consequently, style was manifest in a variety of specific forms.

The most comprehensive typology to emerge in scholarship relating style to these two types of concerns was that developed originally by Robert Blake and Jane Mouton (1964) in connection with their now familiar "Managerial Grid" and later refined by Robert Blake and Anne McCanse (1991). The current listing of styles related to the Managerial Grid has the following categories: (1) Impoverished; (2) Country Club; (3) Authority-Compliance; (4) Middle of the Road; (5) Team; (6) Paternalistic/Maternalistic; and (7) Opportunistic. The last two of these are hybrids. The first style reflects low concern for task and others, the fifth, high concern for both, and the remaining three, different combinations of concern. An unfortunate by-product of the effort to identify styles and what contributes to leaders' preferences for them was a reduction of interest in the extent to which a leader's characteristic way of behaving affects the outcomes that decision-making and problem-solving groups, in particular, achieve.

When those interested in the stylistic perspective on leadership first began amassing empirical evidence, it appeared that leaders exhibiting a democratic, other-centered style had more positive consequences for more aspects of the performance and the affective responses of the members of the group than did their *laissez-faire* and more autocratic, task-centered counterparts. With the emergence of more exhaustive and refined inventories of leadership styles, such as the Managerial Grid, the team-management style seemed to rise to the top in regard to presumed effectiveness, even though scholars had become less concerned with outcomes. That particular style has much in common with the older, less precisely defined concept of democratic style.

Even though research emanating from the stylistic perspective historically appears to have established grounds for believing that particular styles (namely, democratic and team-management) generally promote more positive consequences than others, there is certainly no basis for feeling that the relationships are anywhere close to being universal (Shaw 1981). In fact, by the mid-1900s, some scholars began to recognize that the search for a one-best-style was apt to be as futile as that involving universal traits and, hence, began to think in different terms. With this change in thinking came a new perspective, one to which those who were writing about leadership began to apply the label "situational."

The Situational Perspective on Leadership

The situational perspective on leadership is not quite as easy to characterize as the trait and stylistic perspectives, but, in general, it entails the notion that the style of leadership that maximizes the performance of groups and leads to other desired outcomes depends on how well the behavior the style embodies is suited to the characteristics of the situation in which a person attempting to exercise leadership finds himself or herself. With this realization came a host of specific theories too numerous to review in this article. Four are worth noting, however, as they have had considerable exposure within the last forty years and continue to enjoy popularity as structures for understanding leadership and its effects. The four are: (a) Life-Cycle Theory; (b) Path-Goal Theory; (c) Contingency Theory; and (d) Leader-Member Exchange Theory.

Life-Cycle Theory. In 1969, Paul Hersey and Kenneth Blanchard introduced the so-called "Life-Cycle Theory of Leadership," which Blanchard and other associates later revised (see Blanchard, Zigarmi, and Zigarmi 1985). In its simplest form, the theory posits that the style of leadership that is appropriate for one to adopt depends on the developmental (originally, maturity) level of the members of a group. Developmental level is a reflection of the willingness and ability of the members of a group to perform a given task.

At the lowest level of development, a directing style is theoretically best. As development increases, the appropriate style shifts from coaching to supporting to delegating, in that order. The key situational concern for a leader in choosing a style, according to this theory, is how well equipped, with respect to motivation and skill, the members of a group are to perform the task they have before them at the time they are to undertake it. This assessment, if erroneous, can have unfortunate consequences in the form of poor decisions and ineffective solutions to problems.

Path-Goal Theory. From the perspective of Path-Goal Theory, which is a formulation developed by Robert House and Gary Dessler (see House 1996; House and Dessler 1974), the critical concerns in choosing a leadership style are the apparent motivation of group members and removing obstacles that may adversely affect that motivation. Motivation, the theory holds, is determined by: (a) group members' perception that they have the ability to complete a task; (b) their belief that they have the opportunity to do so; and (c) the expectation of a positive payoff.

Different aspects of the environment in which a group functions can exert a negative influence on any of these factors. A leader, in turn, must choose the style (directive, supportive, participative, or achievement-oriented) that will enable him or her to mitigate, if not eliminate, whatever is acting as a negative constraint on motivation. For instance, if a task is ambiguous and, thus, is creating doubt among group members that they can successfully complete it, a leader probably should adopt a directive style. If a task is unsatisfying, a leader may need to adopt a supportive style. A participative style seems to work best when group members have needs for control and no apparent means for satisfying them. Finally, an achievement-oriented style would be most likely to motivate group members who like challenges but see no particular value accruing to them for performing a particular task. When this is the case, the style in question may enable groups members to see a psychological payoff.

Contingency Theory. "Contingency Theory" is virtually synonymous with the name of Fred Fiedler (1967), who added complexity to the situational perspective well beyond that of either Life-Cycle Theory or Path-Goal Theory. Fiedler's (1964) Contingency Model of Leadership Effectiveness portrays the style of leadership appropriate in any given situation as a complex function of: (a) the favorability of a leader's relationship with subordinates (positive or negative); (b) the power in the position (strong or weak); and (c) the structure of the task to be performed (structured or unstructured). The most favorable conditions for a leader would be to have positive relationships with subordinates, position power, and a structured task. Their opposites would pose the least favorable conditions.

According to Fiedler, individuals who see their least preferred coworkers in unfavorable terms (Low LPCs) tend to be task-oriented and function best at either extreme in the conditions identified above, whereas their High LPC counterparts (those who see least preferred coworkers in relatively favorable terms) appear to function best in intermediate conditions. Fiedler (1967) cites a good deal of research to support his claims.

Unlike others who subscribe to a situational view of leadership, Fiedler does not see the implication of his theory to be the need for leaders to adjust their styles to particular sets of circumstances. Rather, he contends that leaders should be placed in positions for which their personalities (as reflected by their standing on an LPC measure) and related characteristic styles provide a good match. This is a controversial theoretical posture, and the theory that follows points to a quite different conclusion concerning the practical aspects of the style/situation relationship.

Leader-Member Exchange Theory. The last of the four theories in this section, originally called "Vertical Dyad Linkage Theory," currently carries the label "Leader-Member Exchange Theory," or LMX Theory, for short. The individual most strongly associated with this theory is George Graen, but he has been joined over the years by others who have become attracted to it and contributed to its overall evolution (see Graen 1976; Graen and Cashman 1975; Graen and Uhl-Bien 1991). LMX Theory, in its present form, assumes that leaders are inherently unable to maintain the same relationship with everyone for whom they may have leadership responsibility. That inability can easily lead to the formation of in-groups and out-groups, which, in turn, may result in less than optimum performance by those who see themselves as comprising the out-group. Treating everyone similarly, moreover, may only further contribute to the problem, according to the theory, because everyone in a group has different needs, and uniform

leader behavior ironically leads to differential satisfaction of such needs.

To be effective, a leader, the theory posits, should relate differently to his or her subordinates and attempt, in the process, to engage in high-quality interaction with each. In the original version, the accent was not on high-quality interaction. The presumption was that the formation of in-groups and out-groups resulting from differential treatment would motivate those finding themselves in out-groups to become members of in-groups. Research did not provide warrant for this expectation. As a result, the later formulation portrayed out-group formation as undesirable, and the theory subsequently addressed means by which such development could be prevented, primarily by means of engaging in high-quality interaction with all subordinates.

LMX theory, it should be clear, takes the situational perspective to as great an extreme as Contingency Theory, but in the opposite direction. Whereas Contingency Theory accents stability in leader behavior, LMX Theory emphasizes maximum flexibility. On the other hand, like Contingency Theory, LMX Theory qualifies as normative, owing to its prescriptions for how leaders should behave.

Implications of Prior Perspectives for the Emergence of a New Perspective—The View of Leadership as Counteractive Influence

The general perspectives that have guided much of our thinking over the years about leadership in groups, as well as in other types of social entities, all reinforce—albeit rather differently—the view of leadership as the exercise of influence. From the trait perspective, one is able to have positive impact on the performance of a group by virtue of one's possession of particular qualities that contribute to others' positive responses to attempted influence. From the stylistic perspective, it is the manner in which one behaves that seems to have the greatest bearing on responses to attempted influence. Finally, from the situational perspective, leadership effectiveness is largely a matter of one's behaving in a manner that is appropriate for the given set of circumstances in which he or she is serving as leader.

With the exception of Path-Goal Theory as a specific manifestation of the situational perspective, little of the work that has emanated from these three perspectives has made clear precisely what occurs when a person acting as a leader succeeds in exercising influence in ways that yield positive outcomes. Path-Goal Theory provides an important clue, namely, that a leader who exercises influence in some way is functioning to remove what otherwise would be impediments (in this case, lack of motivation) to the achievement of desired objectives (for instance, successful performance of a task, the development and maintenance of good relationships among members, and the cultivation of skills that may be necessary on future occasions). In short, from the vantage point of Path-Goal Theory, leadership appears to be counteractive in nature.

Unfortunately, and as the other theories under the rubric of the "situational perspective" suggest, lack of motivation is not the only obstacle that individuals in positions of leadership encounter and with which they must contend. Others include: (a) members' skill level; (b) their readiness to perform a particular task; (c) the group's maturity relative to the task; (d) members' needs; (e) the quality of their relationships with the leader; (f) the personality attributes of both the leader and the members; and (g) a variety of task characteristics, such as difficulty, clarity, familiarity, and solution multiplicity (see Shaw 1981, 365–377 for a more complete listing of task characteristics). If lack of motivation were the only obstacle to successful group performance, then Path-Goal Theory might be all that we need to have a useful way of thinking about leadership and to develop effective means for enacting it. As noted, however, it is not; hence, a more encompassing view of leadership as counteractive influence within one or more

accommodating theoretical structures appears to be necessary.

Leadership as Counteractive Influence—A More Encompassing View and Its Theoretical Moorings

In 1982, Gouran introduced the notion of leadership as the "art of counteractive influence" (p. 147) in respect to decision-making and problem-solving discussions. Using a travel metaphor, not unlike that of House and Dessler (1974) in their development of the Path-Goal Theory of Leadership, Gouran (1982) likened group process to a journey in which communicative behavior is the vehicle by which the members of a group move from a starting point to a destination. In the course of the journey, if the participants encounter no obstacles, there is no need for leadership to steer them in the right direction or to help them navigate the "road" on which they have embarked. In this view, leadership only becomes necessary and important when there are obstacles to avert or, in some instances, to remove. The categories of obstacles to which a leader may need to direct counteractive influence, according to Gouran, are: (a) substantive, (b) interpersonal, (c) procedural, and (d) ethical.

Gouran (1984) subsequently identified five categories for which leadership in the form of counteractive influence is apt to be necessary if decision-making or problem-solving groups are to achieve the goal of making sound, warranted choices. A leader, or any person functioning as such, Gouran contended, has to be equipped to overcome obstacles posed by: (a) authority relations; (b) pressure for uniformity; (c) status differentiation; (d) disruptive behavior; and (e) incompatibility between individual and collective goals. Specific strategies for counteracting these obstacles consist of such actions as: (a) establishing resistance to authority in ways that are nonthreatening; (b) trying to restore a focus on substantive concerns; (c) making group norms salient and reminding higher-status members of the need to observe them; (d) attempting to convert antagonistic comments into constructive input; and (e) looking for overarching goals that accommodate both those of individuals and of the group as a whole.

Up to the point that Gouran published the article summarized in the preceding paragraph, the theoretical underpinnings for leadership as the exercise of counteractive influence were neither particularly clear nor very precise. In fact, the foundation was rather eclectic and constituted an amalgam of various strands of scholarly thought. Concurrent and subsequent academic work leading to the development and evolution of three different theoretical perspectives, however, did much to provide better bases for thinking about leadership in these terms. The most pertinent developments were Dennis Gouran and Randy Hirokawa's (1996) Functional Theory of Communication in Decision-Making and Problem-Solving Groups, Irving Janis's (1989) Constraints Model of Policymaking Processes, and Kevin Barge's (1994) Communication Skill Model of Leadership.

Gouran and Hirokawa's Functional Theory of Communication in Decision-Making and Problem-Solving Groups

At the time that Gouran (1982) was introducing the notion of leadership as counteractive influence, he and his colleague Randy Hirokawa were also developing the initial version of their Functional Theory of Communication in Decision-Making and Problem-Solving Groups (see Gouran and Hirokawa 1983). This theory reduces to the fundamental notion that the likelihood of a decision-making or problem-solving group's making an appropriate choice is in direct proportion to the extent to which communication serves to ensure that the critical requirements of the task are satisfied. Hence, it provides the larger theoretical structure in which to embed the concept of leadership as counteractive influence. It also makes clearer the focus of leadership. From the functional perspective, whenever the requirements of a decision-making or problem-solving task are not being adequately addressed in the ongoing interaction of group members, the need for leadership, intervention, or counteractive influence, if you will, comes into play.

In its most recent form, functional theory, as articulated by Gouran and Hirokawa (1996), identifies the following five requirements that need to be satisfied for decision-making or problem-solving groups to maximize their chances for making the best possible choices: "(a) showing correct understanding of the issue to be resolved; (b) determining the minimal characteristics any alternative, to be acceptable, must possess; (c) identifying a relevant and realistic set of alternatives; (d) examining carefully the alternatives in relationship to each previously agreed-upon characteristic of an acceptable choice; and (e) selecting the alternative that analysis reveals to be most likely to have the desired characteristics" (76–77). The implicit role of leadership from the functional perspective on decision-making and problem-solving discussion is for those attempting to lead it to communicate in ways that counteract whatever may be limiting a group's ability to satisfy these specific requirements.

Gouran and Hirokawa (1986) identified a domain of counteractive influence for the context of decision-making and problem-solving discussions that refined, as well as added to, the five types of specific obstacles Gouran (1984) had previously articulated. Among the most common obstacles to effective performance (viz., satisfying the five requirements listed above), according to Gouran and Hirokawa, are: (a) the utilization of faulty information by group members; (b) erroneous inferences drawn from information; (c) a reliance on faulty or otherwise questionable assumptions; (d) the misperception of the issues to be resolved; (e) the misevaluation of alternatives; (f) violations of procedural norms; and (g) undue influence of high-status members (see Gouran and Hirokawa [1986, 82–83] for elaboration of each category and representative illustrations).

Although Gouran and Hirokawa (1986) made mention of some very general forms that counteractive influence might take in efforts to address these seven kinds of situations, offering prescriptions was not their purpose. Their more basic concern was alerting readers to the classes of obstacles that do, in fact, inhibit progress along a decision-making or problem-solving group's goal path, and for which researchers need to develop an agenda that would yield specific information concerning the relative utility of different types of counteractive responses.

The view of leadership as serving particular functions has been in existence for some time. In fact, Kenneth Benne and Paul Sheats (1948) developed an inventory consisting of: (a) task functions (e.g., initiating ideas, seeking and giving opinions, elaborating ideas, and providing orientation) and (b) relational functions (e.g., being supportive of others, attempting to manage conflicts, relieving tension, and building cohesion). What makes more recent thinking different is the focus on how such functions serve the members of groups in averting or overcoming problems that complicate efforts to fulfill essential task requirements.

Janis's Constraints Model of Policymaking Processes

The view of leadership as counteractive influence gained increased currency when Irving Janis (1989), who had earlier introduced strategies for counteracting extreme concurrence seeking in planning groups and others experiencing groupthink (see Janis 1982), extended the notion to ineffective decision making in general. He did so in a discussion of some 19 general measures he identified for dealing with a wide variety of obstacles to informed judgment posed by cognitive, affiliative, and egocentric constraints. Such constraints pose problems because, as in the case of the set of obstacles that Gouran and Hirokawa (1986) identified, the consequence of their presence is a sharply reduced likelihood of a decision-making or problem-solving group's being able to satisfy the requirements of its task in a way that contributes to optimal choice.

Cognitive Constraints. Cognitive constraints arise when group members feel pressured by limited time and information

or are uncomfortable because the complexity of the task appears to exceed the upper boundaries of their ability. On such occasions, those involved may resort to mental shortcuts called *heuristics* (see Bazerman 2002; Nisbett and Ross 1980) to make decisions and solve related problems. These heuristics may lead the parties involved to rely on analogies, check for the existence of standard operating procedures, or seize on the first option that seems to have merit for resolving the matter under consideration. They may also engage in what Janis and Mann (1977) refer to as "defensive avoidance" (p. 86), or putting off choices in the hope that the need for making them will dissipate.

Affiliative Constraints. When the desire of at least some members of a group to maintain a congenial climate supersedes their interest in performing effectively, it is likely that they are under the influence of some form of affiliative constraint. These types of individuals also resort to heuristics (rules, if you will), such as "Don't rock the boat" or "Don't upset the applecart," that have as their principal aim the preservation of group harmony. Participants, in some instances, may even try to rig meetings in advance, so as to prevent later conflict and unpleasantness. Failing in that, they may pressure those not "following the party line" to conform. When the goal of preserving harmony is dominant, failure to meet the requirements of decision-making and problem-solving tasks becomes all the more probable.

Egocentric Constraints. Strong desires for personal gain and for preventing others from realizing such gains among the members of a group, when evident, suggest the presence of egocentric constraints. Under the influence of egocentric constraints, a climate of "every person for him- or herself" is apt to develop, and participants relate to one another in a competitive and often affectively dysfunctional manner. In so doing, they resort to heuristics that encourage domination, retaliation, and opportunism. As with the other two categories of constraints, the heuristics associated with egocentric constraints provide little basis for suspecting that a group will perform a decision-making or problem-solving task competently.

Janis (1989) identified numerous practices that leaders might attempt under different circumstances to address problems resulting from cognitive, affiliative, and egocentric constraints and the heuristics to which they give rise. For instance, when the members of a group are inclined to endorse the first alternative that appears to make sense as an action, a leader might wish to emphasize that it is better to be too cautious than too risk-prone, encouraging more thought and deliberation. As a further illustration, to reduce pressure for uniformity, a leader could emphasize the need for members of groups to be aware of their tendency to try to gain compliance on the basis of majority sentiment rather than argument and evidence. As yet another example, a person in a position of leadership might express strong moral disapproval of apparently self-serving efforts by group members to steer choices in particular directions—and certainly should do so if such efforts are conspicuously self-serving.

From the examples above, Janis, in the sorts of suggestions he makes for responding to group members' interaction when cognitive, affiliative, and egocentric constraints are driving the group, clearly sees leadership as the exercise of counteractive influence. It is also evident that he believes such counteractive responses as he has exemplified and recommends for those in positions of leadership improve the chances that the members of decision-making and problem-solving groups will effectively perform their tasks. In these respects, Janis's constraints model and its implications for the practice of leadership are highly compatible with the views stemming from Gouran and Hirokawa's (1996) functional perspective.

Barge's Communication Skill Model of Leadership

Also compatible with Gouran and Hirokawa's theory and how it relates to leadership (although perhaps not in so obvious a way as Janis's constraints model) is Kevin Barge's (1994) Communication Skill Model of Leadership. Drawing heavily on the work of Karl Weick (1978) and Aubrey Fisher (1985), Barge (1994) sees leadership as being constituted in two broad forms of mediation: (a) object and (b) action. Both varieties of mediation assist one in the management of complexity. Barge casts the skills related to object and action mediation into conventional communication terms. He sees object mediation as requiring encoding skills primarily. Action mediation entails the application of decoding skills.

In his model, Barge divides object mediation into the categories of: (a) networking (acquiring information) and (b) sense making (the interpretation of information by means of evaluation and data-splitting). He identifies two categories of action mediation: (a) decision making and (b) relational management. Relational management further includes: (a) defining roles; (b) motivating subordinates; and (c) facilitating the resolution of conflicts.

Barge goes into considerable detail concerning what one can do to engage in each of the four forms of mediation mentioned. For instance, he discusses both how to become networked and how to acquire useful information once one has a network. He also presents and assesses a number of useful aids for making sense of information for those who have need to use it. Barge further discusses what leaders need to know about making decisions in order to assist others to perform effectively in enacting the process. Finally, he draws from numerous sources to develop guidelines one can follow in attempting to define roles, motivate, and manage conflicts. Less important for purposes of this essay than specific leadership practices that Barge introduces are the respects in which his approach to conceiving leadership comports with the views of Gouran and Hirokawa (1996) and Janis (1989).

Although Barge never employs the term *counteractive influence*, his views of leadership and what it entails are undeniably in sync with the concept. Mediation is a form of intervention. The need for intervention, moreover, arises under circumstances in which some type of problem exists, and for which normal aspects of performance are proving to be inadequate. If everything were going well in the process of group decision making or problem solving, presumably intervention and, hence, mediation would be unnecessary, which, incidentally, is implicit in the increased presence of self-managed teams in contemporary organizations (see Hill 2001) and in practices suggested in Stephen Kerr's (1977) Leadership Substitutes Theory.

When one looks beneath the surface of Barge's (1994) Communication Skill Model of Leadership, it soon becomes evident that he is implicitly suggesting that the sorts of interventions for engaging in object and action mediation that he identifies serve the function of counteracting conditions that represent sources of interference in a decision-making or problem-solving group's ability to satisfy the requirements of its task. If the group lacks information, the leader functions to help the members acquire what they need. If the members are having difficulty interpreting information, the leader's role is to help them make sense of it. If the group members do not know how best to engage in decision making or problem solving, it becomes the responsibility of the leader to assist them to learn. Finally, if the group is beset with relational problems that are adversely affecting the members' ability to perform a decision-making or problem-solving task, a leader (or someone performing in that capacity) likely needs to engage in an appropriate form of relational management. When the members of decision-making and problem-solving groups are not experiencing any of these sorts of difficulties, mediation, and hence leadership, would appear to have little, if any, function or necessity.

Why the Art of Counteractive Influence?

At this point, you could reasonably ask why it is necessary to define leadership as the "art of counteractive influence." It prob-

ably is not necessary. However, I have chosen to characterize leadership as an art for two reasons. I address them below.

First, research, to a very real extent, has not caught up to theory. Those whose theoretical perspectives are most accommodating to the notion of leadership as counteractive influence have, as yet, been largely restricted to offering advice in terms of of actions one *might* take—not necessarily *should* take—in response to particular categories of obstacles. Janis (1989) even goes so far as to present the measures he invites practitioners to consider within the framework of a set of hypotheses, which suggests that he is not completely confident that they would have the sort of impact one might reasonably presume. Gouran and Hirokawa (1996) and Barge (1994) are, in their own ways, equally tentative. Thus, the exercise of leadership continues to involve a substantial element of subjective judgment. The sorts of considerations introduced throughout this essay, however, may contribute to making such judgments better-informed ones.

Second, I have chosen to use the term *art* to emphasize that, despite what we have learned about the phenomenon of leadership in decision-making and problem-solving groups, some inexplicable aspects of it remain when one is attempting to account for its effectiveness. On any given occasion, two individuals engaged in the same behavior might succeed at quite different levels in counteracting, or otherwise overcoming, a set of conditions that are impairing a decision-making or problem-solving group's potential for successfully meeting the requirements its task imposes. One might do very well, and the other could fail abysmally. Although the likelihood of such an extreme difference in the exercise of counteractive influence is not great, there does appear to be a kind of intuitive feel that some individuals have and others do not for the enactment of certain types of communicative behavior; it is very difficult to detect but it nonetheless can produce differences in leadership success. While I do not endorse the cliché sometimes applied to leadership ability ("Some people have it, and others do not"), people can vary in subtle ways that seem to defy description and that do, in fact, make a difference in how others respond to what, on the surface, appear to be nearly identical acts of attempted influence. Capitalizing on those subtleties that give one greater advantage definitely appears to be something of an art.

Conclusion

Leadership is an elusive phenomenon, especially in the context of decision-making and problem-solving discussions. When one carefully considers the various ways of studying and theorizing about leadership, however, one can see the seemingly diverse threads of thought begin to interweave and converge on a common point. Prior scholarship (see especially Barge 1994; Gouran and Hirokawa 1996; Janis 1989) suggests that, at its most fundamental level, leadership consists of the behavior required (whether of someone in a designated position of authority or not) when the members of a decision-making or problem-solving group are experiencing difficulty in satisfying the requirements for making the best realistically possible choices. In this regard, it is not only appropriate, but it makes sense, to conceive of it as the art of counteractive influence.

References

Avolio, B. J. (1999). *Full Leadership Development: Building the Vital Forces in Organizations*. Thousand Oaks, CA: Sage.

Barge, J. K. (1994). *Leadership: Communication Skills for Organizations and Groups*. New York: St. Martin's Press.

Bass, B. M. (1990). *Bass and Stogdill's Handbook of Leadership* (3rd ed.). New York: Free Press.

Bazerman, M. (2002). *Judgment in Managerial Decision Making* (5th ed.). New York: John Wiley and Sons.

Benne, K. D., and Sheats, P. (1948). "Functional roles of group members." *Journal of Social Issues* 4: 41–49.

Blake, R. R., and Mouton, J. S. (1964). *The Managerial Grid*. Houston, TX: Gulf.

Blake, R. R., and McCanse, A. A. (1991). *Leadership Dilemmas—Grid Solutions*. Houston, TX: Gulf.

Blanchard, K. H., Zigarmi, P., and , Zigarmi, D. (1985). *Leadership and the One Minute Manager: Increasing Effectiveness Through Situational Leadership*. New York: William Morrow.

Bormann, E. G. (1969). *Discussion and Group Methods: Theory and Practice*. New York: Harper and Row.

Burns, J. M. (1978). *Leadership*. New York: Harper and Row.

Fiedler, F. E. (1964). "A contingency model of leadership effectiveness." In L. Berkowitz (ed.), *Advances in Experimental Social Psychology* (Vol. 1): 149–190. New York: Academic Press.

——. (1967). *A Theory of Leadership Effectiveness*. New York: McGraw-Hill.

Fisher, B. A. (1985). "Leadership as medium. Treating complexity in group communication research." *Small Group Behavior* 16: 167–196.

Gouran, D. S. (1982). *Making Decisions in Groups: Choices and Consequences*. Glenview, IL: Scott, Foresman.

——. (1984). "Principles of counteractive influence in decision-making and problem-solving groups." In R. S. Cathcart and L. A. Samovar (eds.), *Small Group Communication: A Reader* (4th edition, pp. 166–181). Dubuque, IA: William C. Brown.

Gouran, D. S., and Hirokawa, R. Y. (1983). "The role of communication in decision-making groups: A functional perspective." In M. S. Mander (ed.), *Communications in Transition* (pp. 168–185). New York: Praeger.

——. (1986). "Counteractive functions of communication in effective group decision-making." In R. Y. Hirokawa and M. S. Poole (eds.), *Communication and Group Decision Making* (pp. 81–90). Beverly Hills, CA: Sage.

——. (1996). "Functional theory and communication in decision-making and problem-solving groups: An expanded view." In R. Y. Hirokawa and M. S. Poole (eds.), *Communication and Group Decision Making* (pp. 55–80). Thousand Oaks, CA: Sage.

Graen, G. B. (1976). "Role-making process within complex organizations." In M. D. Dunnette (ed.), *Handbook of Industrial and Organizational Psychology* (pp. 1202–1245). Chicago: Rand McNally.

Graen, G. B, and Cashman, J. (1975). "A role-making model of leadership in formal organizations: A developmental approach." In J. G. Hunt and L. L. Larson (eds.), *Leadership Frontiers* (pp. 143–166). Kent, OH: Kent State University Press.

Graen, G. B., and Uhl-Bien, M. (1991). "Relationship-based approach to leadership. Development of Leader-Member Exchange (LMX) Theory over 25 years: Applying a multi-level multi-domain perspective." *Leadership Quarterly* 6: 219–247.

Hersey, P., and Blanchard, K. H. (1969). "Life-cycle theory of leadership." *Training and Development Journal* 23: 26–34.

Hill, S. K. E.(2001). "Team leadership." In P. G. Northouse (ed.), *Leadership: Theory and Practice* (2nd ed., pp. 161–187). Thousand Oaks, CA: Sage.

House, R. J. (1996). "Path-Goal Theory of leadership: Lessons, legacy, and a reformulated theory." *Leadership Quarterly* 7: 323–352.

House, R. J., and Dessler, G. (1974). "The Path-Goal Theory of leadership: Some post hoc and a priori tests." In J. G. Hunt and L. L. Larson (eds.), *Contingency Approaches to Leadership* (pp. 29–55). Carbondale: Southern Illinois University Press.

Janis, I. L. (1982). *Groupthink: Psychological Studies of Policy Decisions and Fiascoes* (2nd ed.). Boston: Houghton Mifflin.

——. (1989). *Crucial Decisions: Leadership in Policymaking and Crisis Management.* New York: Free Press.

Janis, I. L., and Mann, L. (1977). *Decision Making: A Psychological Analysis of Conflict,* *Choice, and Commitment.* New York: Free Press.

Kerr, S. (1977). "Substitutes for leadership: Some implications for organizational design." *Organization and Administrative Sciences* 8: 135–146.

Lewin, K., Lippitt, R, and White, R. K. (1939). "Patterns of aggressive behavior in experimentally created "social climates." *Journal of Psychology* 10: 271–299.

Nisbett, R., and Ross, L. (1980). *Human Inference: Strategies and Shortcomings of Social Judgment.* Englewood Cliffs, NJ: Prentice-Hall.

Northhouse, P. G. (2001a). "Introduction." In P. G. Northouse (ed.). *Leadership: Theory and Practice* (2nd ed., pp. 1–13). Thousand Oaks, CA: Sage.

——. (2001b). "Trait approach." In P. G. Northouse (ed.). *Leadership: Theory and Practice* (2nd ed., pp. 15–33). Thousand Oaks, CA: Sage.

Shaw, M. E. (1981). *Group Dynamics: The Psychology of Small Group Behavior* (3rd ed.). New York: McGraw-Hill.

Weick, K. E. (1978). "The spines of leaders." In M. McCall and M. Lombardo (eds.), *Leadership: Where Else Can We Go?* (pp. 37–61). Durham, NC: Duke University Press.

Chapter 17
Leadership and Gender

Challenging Assumptions and Recognizing Resources

Susan B. Shimanoff
Mercilee M. Jenkins

This chapter illustrates the relationship between gender and group leadership. It presents a comprehensive review of research devoted to differences between and similarities of women and men in group leadership roles. The authors expose (and refute) many myths about women as leaders (e.g., women are more emotional and less task-oriented than men) and point out how gender alone can limit women's leadership opportunities and effectiveness. Shimanoff and Jenkins conclude the chapter with practical suggestions for identifying and overcoming barriers to women becoming group leaders.

Among the many roles group members can perform, the role of leader has received more attention from researchers than any other. What is a leader? In the studies we reviewed for this article we identified four major approaches to defining "leader": (1) the person named by the group as the leader, (2) the person who group members *perceive* to be performing leader-like behaviors, (3) the person who has the greatest influence on the group's final decision, and (4) the *actual performance* of leadership behaviors. It is our position that the fourth approach is the best one.

Who a group names as leader or who members perceive as being the leader may be influenced by stereotypes or selective perception. This is particularly important when comparing females and males. Research has shown that even when they perform the same behaviors, males are often given more leadership credit than females (Brown and Geis 1984; Geis, Boston, and Hoffman 1985; Butler 1984). Further, when women with inclinations to lead were not named the leader, they still performed leader-like behaviors (Nyquist and Spence 1986).

Leadership behaviors may lead to a greater say in a group's decision, but a group member can get what he or she wants in other ways as well. For example, a group may acquiesce to a member's desires because it feels manipulated, apathetic, generous, exhausted, or frustrated. Stake (1981) argued that getting one's way should be perceived as dominance instead of necessarily leadership, and we agree.

Leadership, it seems to us, is best understood as the behaviors that help a group to achieve its goals. Previous researchers have associated the following behaviors with leadership: appropriate procedural suggestions, sound opinions, relevant information, frequent participation, active listening, supporting group members, and asking for the opinions of other group members. When one focuses on *who* is called the leader, leadership is seen as belonging to one person, but when one concentrates on *behaviors*, leadership can be performed by multiple members and can be the responsibility of the group as a whole rather than a single person.

However, most of the previous research has taken a single-person approach to leadership, and when we reviewed this literature we were struck by the prejudice against women. Research has demonstrated that there are far more similarities than differences in the leadership behaviors of women and men, and that they are equally effective. Still, women are less likely to be pre-selected as leaders, and the same leadership behavior is often evaluated more positively when attributed to a male than a female. In exploring gender and leadership, we would like to address five topics: (1) the behaviors of male and female leaders, (2) the effectiveness of female and male leaders, (3) the effects of sex-role stereotypes, (4) the role of group dynamics, and (5) practical suggestions for challenging false assumptions and for recognizing the resources that both women and men bring to group interactions.

Leadership Behaviors of Females and Males

The most common claim in regard to stylistic differences has been that women are more concerned with the social-emotional dimensions of group process and men are more concerned with getting the job done (Anderson and Blanchard 1982; Denmark 1977; Hollander and Yoder 1980). However, researchers have found either no differences or minimal ones (about 4 percent) regarding these two types of behaviors by female and male leaders (Anderson and Blanchard 1982; Dobbins and Platz 1986).

Task Behaviors

In problem-solving groups, the talk of both men and women is predominately task related and this intensifies when one is the leader: "approximately 91 percent of a male leader's behavior is devoted to active task behavior (giving answers) and approximately 88 percent of a female leader's behavior is active task behavior" (Anderson and Blanchard 1982, 135). Women emphasize production, whether they are classified as task or relational leader types, and they continue their strong contributions to task endeavors even when the group is doing well; men tend to reduce their task contributions under similar circumstances (Millard and Smith 1985).

Further, one study of actual leadership behavior in student problem-solving, groups found that female leaders devoted a greater proportion of their total communication to task issues than male leaders (Wood 1981), and in other studies males have been shown to make more off-task comments than females (Gigliotti 1988; Winther and Green 1987). Fortunately, group members have indicated that they were equally satisfied with male and female leaders who exhibited equal

frequencies of task-oriented behaviors (Alderton and Jurma 1980).

Leaders are more likely than other members to make procedural suggestions for how a group should conduct its business; this is true for both males and females (Bunyi and Andrews 1985; Andrews 1984). In addition, Hirokawa (1980) found that constructive procedural discussions were more typical of effective groups than ineffective ones. Making procedural suggestions seems to be one of women's strengths. In resolving conflicts, Carrocci (1985) found that women generated twice as many procedural suggestions as men did.

Two other task-related behaviors that may be particularly important for women are (1) demonstrated expertise and (2) the use of evidence. When expertise is low or members do not use evidence, males in the group are evaluated more positively than females. When women and men are equal in expertise and their use of evidence, however, they tend to be evaluated similarly (Bradley 1980, 1981; Wentworth, Keyse, and Anderson 1984).

Owen (1986) maintained that when women emerge as leaders in mixed-sex groups it is largely because they have worked substantially harder than any member. In addition, the women he observed were most likely to be the ones who provided organizational skills, suggested procedures, set the agenda, and took the notes. We find it interesting that a traditionally female task—taking the minutes—was one of the behaviors that contributed to a woman becoming a leader. This task provided her useful information that she could then use to guide the group's interaction.

One factor that has been shown to influence task behaviors is performance self-esteem. Persons with high performance self-esteem see themselves as productive, assertive, responsible, competent, articulate, powerful, persuasive, willing to take a stand, and forceful (Stake 1979), and they are more likely to be selected as leaders than those with low performance self-esteem (Andrews 1984).

Group members with high performance self-esteem are more likely to provide relevant information, sound opinions, appropriate procedural suggestions, and counterarguments, and to get the group to embrace their perspective (Andrews 1984; Stake and Stake 1979). The performance of these behaviors leads group members to view them as leaders.

Females, however, typically have lower performance self-esteem than males (Stake 1979), and performance self-esteem is more related to their leadership behaviors than it is for men (Stake and Stake 1979). On the other hand, efforts to increase a woman's performance self-esteem increase her leadership behaviors and her influence on group decisions (Stake 1983), especially if group members are given time to assimilate positive information about her abilities (Stake 1981). Further, when females are thought to be superior on a task, they have as much influence as males, and this boost in self-confidence and influence carry over to subsequent dyads (Pugh and Wahrman 1983).

Social-Emotional Behaviors

When the behaviors of male and female leaders differ, women are likely to meet the social-emotional needs of group members slightly more (Anderson and Blanchard 1982). Women leaders were rated as more interpersonally warm during initial interactions than male leaders (Goktepe and Schneier 1989; Spillman, Spillman, and Reinking 1981). Interestingly, positive social-emotional behaviors frequently contribute more to group satisfaction than task-related behaviors (Schriesheim 1982). Further, group members think that they are just as likely as leaders to perform task behaviors and negative social-emotional behaviors, but that leaders are much more likely to perform positive social-emotional behaviors than nonleaders (Schneier and Bartol, 1980).

If the degree to which women meet the social-emotional needs of group members was more often acknowledged, we might come to associate women with leadership more frequently. Instead, group members tend to expect even more from women, and when they are not *more* responsive than males to the needs of others, group members tend to evaluate women more harshly (Faranda, 1981; Helgesen, 1990; Russell, Rush, and Herd, 1988; Wright, 1976). Similarly, three separate studies have shown that females using an authoritarian style of leadership were perceived less favorably than males using the same style (Faranda, 1981; Haccoun, Haccoun, and Sallay, 1978; Jago and Vroom, 1982). It is not surprising, then, that sometimes women use a more democratic or participative style than men (Baird and Bradley 1979; Helgesen 1990; Jago and, Vroom 1982; Begins and Sundstrom 1989; Rosenfeld and Fowler 1976).

Men were particularly satisfied with the leadership of women when they led by providing orientation, information, and clarification; by asking for the men's opinions; by not giving more suggestions or disagreements than their male partners; and by having equal influence on the groups' decisions (Stake 1981). Likewise, Alderton and Jurma (1980) reported that female leaders agreed more with followers than male leaders did, but in spite of this, group members were more likely to disagree with female leaders than male leaders. These studies suggest that women support group members more, but receive less support in return.

To provide effective socio-emotional messages, one must be a good listener. Listening has also been strongly linked to effective leadership. When listening skills, speaking ability, and traditional management behaviors like organizing work, setting goals, and influencing others were compared, listening was the most related to group satisfaction and effectiveness (Willer and Henderson, 1988). Several scholars have noted that listening skills are especially important to women (Belenky, Clichy, Goldberger and Tarule 1986; Gilligan 1982; Helgesen 1990). In her analysis of women executives, Heigesen (1990) observed that the women valued "listening as a way of making others feel comfortable and important, and as a means of encouraging others to find their own voices and grow" (244–245).

Combined Task and Social-Emotional Leadership

In combination, the studies on the task and social-emotional behaviors of leaders show that while women may show more concern with interpersonal relationships, they also devote considerable energy to the group's task. Further, group members expect women leaders to perform well in both task and social-emotional dimensions (Cirincione-Coles 1975; Jenkins 1980). Similar research has also been reported dealing with African-American versus Caucasian business students. Thomas and Littig (1985) found that African-American students have a tendency to self-report a more highly structured management style, coupled most often with high consideration.

While this approach may have advantages for group members, Dumas's (1980) study of African-American women managers indicated the possible negative consequences for leaders trying to do it all. African-American women managers report that they are often expected to fulfill the "Black Mammy" role (to take care of everyone's needs at the expense of her own) or risk being seen as the "Terrible Mother" (selfish, punitive, and frightening). These overwhelming expectations often force the women to choose between burning out in an effort to fulfill them or incurring the anger of their subordinates. What might prove more constructive is a shared understanding that fulfilling the social-emotional and task needs of a group is the collective responsibility of all members.

Women's Ways of Interacting[1]

Many studies indicate that girls and women interact differently than men in same-sex groups (Maltz and Borker 1982). Research on all-female groups suggest that girls and women have an equalitarian ideology among themselves (Goodwin 1980; Helgesen 1990; Maltz and Borker 1982) and that they sanction members who directly confront each other (Jenkins 1984; Wilensky 1988). Similarly, females report greater dis-

satisfaction than males in autocratically led groups (Kushell and Newton 1986).

Some writers of popular self-help books have asserted that women do not do as well as men in business because their relative inexperience with competitive team sports makes it more difficult for them to be good team players (Harragan 1977; Hennig and Jardim 1976). In contrast to these assumptions, though, women have been found to be more cooperative and supportive (Jenkins 1984), while men are described as more self-assertive and competitive (Maltz and Borker 1982). Given their greater efforts at cooperation, it would seem that women may be the "real team players" (Nelson 1988). For example, both women and men on predominately female research teams noted the differences in the way group members worked together when compared to mixed or male-dominated groups. They described the group as an open, cooperative but challenging, and supportive context where learning and growth were promoted (Nelson 1988).

If women interact differently in groups, it seems likely that they would also lead differently. Although men and women agree on many ideal traits for leaders, women are more likely to desire leaders who are "cooperative, empathetic, supportive, democratic, and calm," while men are more likely to desire leaders who are "demanding, active, aggressive, rational, and decision-oriented" (Graves and Powell 1982, 690). Men are more prone to hierarchical leadership, and women are more likely to rotate leadership (Aries 1976; Helgesen 1990; Wyatt 1988). In keeping with this approach women may see leadership more in terms of facilitation and organization rather than power and dominance (Owen 1986; Wyatt 1988).

In Owen's groups of college students, and in Wyatt's group of women weavers, members were reluctant to call themselves leaders and instead described their roles in the group in terms of organizing and facilitating the group to reach its goal. Nelson (1988) further suggests that this facilitative style of leadership allows leaders to model the behavior they want to see in group members. Thus, when women lead differently than men, we should not assume they need to change their behavior.

These studies indicate that female leadership styles may have some advantages not previously recognized in studies of mixed-sex groups. Helgesen (1990) details four case studies of successful female leaders in organizations and outlines why she believes these women are effective: (1) they create a web of associations through which they communicate with all levels of the organization; (2) they are able to be spontaneous as leaders and respond to situations with flexibility; (3) they tend to break down barriers between employees; and (4) they are effective transmitters of information and ideas throughout the organization.

The women see themselves as "being in the middle of things. Not at the top, but in the center; not reaching down, but reaching out" (Helgesen 1990, 45–46). Using the metaphor of a web, Helgesen (1990) describes this type of leadership as more connected and inclusive: "You can't break a web into single lines or individual components without tearing the fabric, injuring the whole" (49).

Women's metaphors for leadership reflect less traditional ways of thinking about this process. A woman in a class on small group communication said a leader is like a sponge. A leader should absorb all that the group produces and then be prepared to give it back whenever the group requests it. Helgesen (1990) furnishes similarly enlightening metaphors from women executives. A leader is a teacher, a magician (making changes while serving others and maintaining one's personal identity), a gardener ("watering flowers, helping them to flourish and grow" [xiv]), and a transmitter ("picking up signals from everywhere, then beeping them out to where they need to go" [27]). These metaphors reflect a much more participative view of leadership than the more traditional concepts of power and dominance.

Summary

Across the studies on leadership behavior, it can be said that in problem-solving groups both female and male leaders concentrate on task-related behaviors, but that females are slightly more responsive to the social-emotional needs of group members and tend to be more attentive listeners. Males are inclined to talk more, which may increase their power, but women can be equally effective in using evidence and making procedural suggestions, two key behaviors for leaders. Further, features more typically associated with women, such as inclusion, spontaneity, equalitarianism, and dissemination of information, have been shown to be important leadership skills.

The evidence on leadership style indicates that members generally seem to prefer both male and female leaders to be task oriented, but prefer females to be more responsive to social-emotional needs than males; women leaders seem to comply with these demands. Still, as Baird and Bradley (1979) noted, it is possible that because of sex-role biases, a female leader may need to be superior to a male leader to be rated equally.

Effectiveness and Group Satisfaction

Anderson and Blanchard (1982) reviewed 71 reported findings regarding group members' satisfaction with and the effectiveness of leaders. They found that in 77 percent of the cases, male and female leaders were rated equally; 14 percent favored male leaders and 8 percent favored female leaders. Clearly there is not a consistent preference for male or female leaders. This same pattern was observed in naturally occurring groups, experimental/laboratory groups, case studies, and simulated groups. They also found no consistent preference for a stereotypical feminine (social-emotional) or masculine (task) style of leadership for either males or females. Additional evidence for the lack of difference in effectiveness of male and female leaders is provided by two sets of extensive field research projects dealing with military groups and sensitive or encounter groups.

Rice and his colleagues have conducted research focusing on women at West Point since the first coeducational class. In a group that met only for a short time, males with conservative views toward women rated female leaders lower than male leaders on initiating structure, but males with liberal views toward women rated female leaders higher than male leaders (Rice, Bender, and Vitters 1980).

In later studies, male cadets were rated slightly higher (about 8 percent) on overall leadership ability than female cadets by their peers and superiors (Rice, Yoder, Adams, Priest, and Prince 1984), but male and female leaders were rated equally successful and skillful by their followers (Rice, Instone, and Adams 1984). Similarly, another study found that male and female squad leaders were rated equally positively by their followers (Adams, Rice, and Instone 1984). Collectively these studies suggest that if people are asked to rate females and males when they have had only limited contact, they will sometimes resort to their preconceived attitudes, but after extended interactions, group members rate male and female leaders as equally effective.

Another type of group that has been studied extensively in the field is self-reflective groups from the Tavistock Institute in England. The groups are composed of psychology undergraduate and graduate students who are themselves studying group processes. These groups are typically assigned one of two types of leaders: those who are supposed to be emotionally responsive and those who are supposed to remain emotionally detached and merely comment on the group process.

The research on the effects of gender on leadership in these groups is not consistent. In some cases emotionally responsive women were rated as the most effective (Wright 1976), and at other times they were considered the least effective (Morrison and Stein 1985). In one study, emotionally detached males and females were rated equally as leaders (Morrison and Stein 1985), but in another study this detachment resulted in female leaders being perceived as more potent and active and male leaders receiving more

positive messages (Wright 1976). In still another study, male co-leaders were perceived as more potent, active, instrumental, and insightful than female co-leaders, but female and male co-leaders were rated equally on skills and emotional responsiveness. Further, group members behaved similarly regardless of whether the female or male was the first or second in command (Greene, Morrison, and Tischler 1981; Tischler, Morrison, Greene, and Stewart 1986). Across these studies, there is no consistent evidence that Tavistock groups are more effective or satisfied if a female or male assumes the position of leader.

Summary

Collectively the studies on effectiveness and satisfaction demonstrate that groups are equally satisfied with effective leaders of either gender and that generally women and men lead equally well. If males and females exhibit the same behaviors as leaders and they are equally effective one would expect them to emerge as leaders equally. Yet, more men than women are in positions of power. What will account for this discrepancy? One possibility is the biasing effects of sex-role stereotypes.

Sex-Role Stereotypes

Porter and Geis (1981) remind us that in our culture becoming a leader is tied to the perceptions of others:

Leadership is a social phenomenon. Becoming a leader depends on acting like a leader, but even more crucially, it depends on being seen by others as a leader. In our society people do not become leaders by their own individual fate. They become leaders by being appointed to the position, being elected to it, or by emerging over time as the group member to whom others look for guidance. In every case leadership depends on recognition by others, by fellow group members or by those doing the voting or appointing (39).

Evaluations of Identical Messages

Given that leadership depends on the *recognition* of others, it is important that we ascertain how observers evaluate the same behaviors when they are performed by a female or a male. Across several studies there tends to be a pro-male bias; that is, males are more often rated more positively than females for the same behavior (Butler and Geis 1990; Nieva and Gutek 1980). Still, this is not always the case. Four factors would appear to help to reduce sex-role biases: (1) additional, unambiguous, and relevant information, (2) sex-role-neutral tasks, (3) positive evaluations by others, and (4) actual interaction with the person (Brown and Geis 1984; Butler 1984; Butterfield and Powell 1981; Heilman and Martell 1986; Nieva and Gutek 1980; Seifert and Miller 1988).

When group members were neither praised nor blamed by others, Brown and Geis (1984) found that observers rated males as: (a) showing significantly more leadership, (b) having higher-quality contributions, (c) being more desirable for hiring, (d) meriting a higher salary, and (e) meriting a more responsible job than females. The actual behavior of males and females in this case did not differ. The same behavior was evaluated differently merely on the basis of whether a male or a female performed that behavior.

Recent research has also noted that sex-role biases may have become more subtle. In three studies where males and females were rated equally as leaders for performing the same behaviors, males were nonetheless rated more positively than females in other ways. For example, two different studies found that for the same behaviors, female leaders were rated as bossier, more dominating, more emotional, less warm, less sensitive, and less attractive than male leaders (Brown and Geis 1984; Butler 1984). In addition, group members expressed greater disapproval of identical ideas when those ideas were presented by a woman, but more approval when the suggestions were made by a man (Butler and Geis 1990). In Seifert and Miller's (1988) study, the very same message was rated as clearer when attributed to a male leader rather than a female leader. Further, in several studies, even people who firmly believed they held equalitarian or feminist attitudes nonetheless discriminated against female leaders in more subtle, unconscious ways (Butler 1984; Butler and Geis 1990; Porter and Geis 1981; Porter, Geis, Cooper, and Newman 1985).

Effects of Sex-Role Attitudes on Behavior

Reinforcing or challenging sex-role attitudes also has an effect on group dynamics. Group size and shared attitudes affect the leadership emergence of females and males, and the behaviors of group members (Porter et al. 1985). Males with traditional sex-role attitudes were more likely to dominate the group interaction if the group was comprised of four members sharing their attitudes than if there were only two such members. On the other hand, groups comprised of four androgynous members acted in a more equalitarian manner than groups of two such members. That is, the more other group members share one's attitudes about sex-roles, the more likely one is to behave in accordance with those attitudes; the shared attitudes serve to reinforce each other.

Further, *reminding* people of their own attitudes toward sex-role stereotype affected group interactions and leadership emergence. Groups who held equalitarian attitudes behaved in a more equalitarian manner when they were reminded of those attitudes than when they were not, while groups who held more traditional sex-role attitudes had more male dominance when they were reminded of their attitudes than when they were not. Porter et al. (1985) argued that sex-role "scripts" for males and females may be so ingrained in our habitual, subconscious behavior that the scripts will override equalitarian attitudes unless such attitudes are reinforced by reminders and interaction with others who value equality.

Designating a Leader

Another type of sex-role bias has been demonstrated in studies in which groups are given little or no time to interact before selecting their leaders. A series of studies has examined the role of viewing oneself as possessing "dominant" qualities (e.g., self-confident, articulate, forceful, persistent, logical, and responsible) and being designated the leader (Carbonell 1984; Fleischer and Chertkoff 1986; Megargee 1969; Nyquist and Spence 1986). In same-sex groups in which gender differences are not an issue, the dominant person is named the leader 70 percent of the time. However, for mixed-sex dyads the pattern is quite different. When the more dominant person is male, he is named the leader 84 percent of the time, but when the more dominant person is female, she is named the leader only 41 percent of the time on the average and sometimes only 20 percent. Further, when both partners are high in dispositional dominance, the male rather than the female was named the leader 71 percent of the time (Davis and Gilbert 1989).[2]

A similar kind of bias occurred in Porter and Geis's (1981) study of the effects of seating arrangements on perceived leadership. When observers looked at photographs of same-sex groups, they thought the person at the head of the table was the most likely to lead, contribute, talk, and dominate. When the same males and females were shown in mixed-sex groups, the males at the heads of the tables were again designated the leaders, but females at the heads of the tables were not perceived as leaders.

Summary

It is disturbing that a person's gender *alone* could change how the very same message or person is evaluated. These sex-role biases may have serious consequences for hiring and promoting women into leadership positions, especially when group members have had little opportunity to interact. Still, it can be useful to acknowledge this bias. Women, who have become discouraged because their words and ideas seem to carry less weight than the same ones expressed by their male colleagues, can stop wondering if the situation would be better if they had only behaved differently.

These studies, as well as those on leadership style, cast doubt on the appropriateness of special training programs for women per se to enhance their leadership skills, but the findings indicate the need to make groups aware of their biases and means for reducing them. Research has demonstrated that concrete and specific information is "more effective and less ambiguous than global discussions in reducing sex-role-biased attitudes (Auerbach, Kilmann, Gackenbach, and Julian 1980; Heilman and Martell 1986). Reinforcing equalitarian attitudes has also been shown to be effective in reducing male dominance.

Group Dynamics

Several studies have indicated that if groups are allowed to interact before choosing a leader they are more likely to make their decision on the basis of performance rather than gender. For example, Schneier and Bartol (1980) found that after fifteen weeks of working on various projects 50 different groups were equally likely to name a female or a male as their leader, as were the 28 groups who met for six to 15 weeks in Goktepe and Schneier's (1989) study. Similarly, a high-dominant woman was named as the leader over a low-dominant male only 36 percent of the time when they did not interact, but when they worked on a project before selecting the leader, her ascendancy rose to 71 percent (Davis and Gilbert 1989). Even in a male-defined domain, such as the military, males and females were evaluated equally on actual performance over time (Rice, Instone, and Adams 1984). Thus, simply allowing group members to witness the strengths of individual men and women helps to reduce sex-role biases.

In addition, how people behave toward each other and how others interact with leaders have been shown to have a profound effect on leaders' behavior. For example, leaders produced more task, and less negative social-emotional, behaviors when followers asked them for direction than when group members tried to control the leader's behavior (Beckhouse, Tanur, Weiler, and Weinstein 1975). If group members treat each other on the basis of mutual respect rather than sex-role biases, potential leaders are more likely to act like leaders. In the sections that follow we will discuss various aspects of group dynamics that affect leadership.

Patterns of Interaction

Numerous studies have indicated that the amount of participation is positively correlated with leadership. People who talk more frequently are named as leaders more often than less talkative members of a group (Fisher 1985). Wentworth, Keyser, and Anderson (1984) report that this relationship is almost two times stronger for women than men. Being one of the first group members to speak may also influence who is perceived as a leader. In Fleischer and Chertkoff's (1986) study of dyads, the person who spoke first was selected as the leader 60 percent of the time. Lamb (1981) found that the earlier a woman spoke in a group, the more she participated. Kimble, Yoshikawa, and Zehr (1981) reported that the first woman to speak in a group was viewed as the most assertive, while the assertiveness scores of males were unrelated to the order in which they spoke. These studies suggest a stronger relationship for women than for men regarding initiation, amount of speech, and influence in groups.

The overall greater verbosity of men may be due to various aspects of small group interaction. For example, when presenting the same information and arguments, women received more negative feedback than males (Butler and Geis 1990). This kind of reaction could easily discourage the participation of women. In addition, there is some evidence that men and women may have different rules for taking turns speaking. Some studies have indicated that females are more likely to call on other members or invite them to speak while males are more likely to allow whoever speaks first to have the floor (Aries 1976; Jenkins 1984). An invitation to speak rather than having to fight for the floor might increase the participation of women.

Shimanoff (1984) also discusses how group members could manipulate the turn-taking rules to influence who emerges as the leader. Consistently returning the floor to a particular person, or to coalition members, can shape who is the most active participant, as well as who is perceived as the most competent, and thus who leads the group. Groups seeking equalitarian participation may wish to guard against such manipulation. On the other hand, it may be a useful tool if others are unfairly discriminating against particular members.

Groups may also influence the participation of women by the degree to which women are interrupted. Zimmerman and West (1975) demonstrated that interruptions lead to the original speaker falling silent, and many studies have found that women are more likely to get interrupted than men (e.g., Brooks 1982; Kennedy and Camden 1983; Octigan and Niederman 1979; West and Zimmerman 1983; Willis and Williams 1976; Zimmerman and West 1975). It is also worth noting that although Dindia (1987) found no gender differences for many types of interruptions, she discovered that males were more likely to interrupt women to change the subject than the reverse. Davis and Gilbert (1989) also reported equal levels of interruptions by males and females, but that high-dominant persons were more likely to interrupt than low dominant persons.

Acknowledging that interruptive patterns may be gender related could be useful. When males and females were told that "research has shown that male speakers are more likely than female speakers to interrupt partners in conversation," the interruptive behavior of both males and females dramatically decreased (for males from 88 interruptions to 29 [decrease of 67 percent] for females from 34 interruptions to 7 [decrease of 79 percent]) (Octigan and Niedennan 1979).

Members may also wish to monitor their own verbosity in an effort to equalize participation. This awareness may be particularly relevant for men who tend to talk more than women in groups (Thome, Kramarae, and Henley 1983). If women participate equally in discussions, groups may then need to watch their attitudes.

Edelsky's (1981) research on group partici-pation demonstrated that when women merely speak as much as men they are often thought of as being overly talkative. At the end of her study when she recognized this perceptual bias even in herself, Edelsky wrote: "Perhaps our subjective impression of a talkative woman is simply one who talks as much as the average man" (1981, 415).

Group Composition

Group composition can also influence leadership emergence. In one study of triads, when males were in the majority they emerged as the leader 100 percent of the time. When females were in the majority they were more likely to serve as leaders, but this increase was not statistically significant (Bunyi and Andrews 1985). Similarly, Schneier and Bartol (1980) reported that as the number of women in a group increased the likelihood that a female would emerge as the leader increased. Other studies have in-dicated that women have more trouble get-ting group members to treat them equally if they are the solo representative of their sex or in a small minority than when a man is the only male or a token (Craig and Sherif 1986; Fairhurst and Snavely 1983; Ott 1989; Wolman and Frank 1975).

Expertise and Validation

Assumed or attributed expertise increases the likelihood that one will emerge as the leader or be evaluated more positively (Bunyi and Andrews 1985; Dobbins, Stuart, Pence, and Sgro 1985; Fleischer and Chertkoff 1986; Offermann 1986). Some-times group members assume expertise on the basis of sex-role stereotypes. For exam-ple, males were most likely to be named as the leader if the task required stereotypically masculine or neutral expertise (e.g., invest-ment or entertainment), while females and males were equally likely to emerge as lead-ers if stereotypically feminine expertise was required (e.g., a wedding) (Wentworth and Anderson 1984).

External validation of women leaders is also important. It increases the possibility that her work will be valued by herself and others (Brown and Geis 1984; Butler 1984;

Dobbins, Stuart, Pence, and Sgro 1985; Fleischer and Chertkoff 1986; Pheterson, Kiesler and Goldberg, 1971; Peck 1978; Stake 1983). This validation is especially important because the credibility of women is often challenged. Further, vali-dation can yield more leadership. Fe-males who were told they were selected as leaders because of their skills performed more leadership behaviors than women who thought the position had come to them by chance, even though their actual abilities were identical (Eskilson and Wiley 1976).

The mere presence of a female author-ity figure has been shown to increase the credibility of other women (Butler 1984; Etaugh, Houtler, and Ptasnik 1988; Geis, Boston, and Hoffman 1985). Similarly, a woman's abilities will be rated more fa-vorably if one is exposed to success stories about other women in similar circum-stances (Heilman and Martell 1986). Posi-tive validation can lead to increases in performance self-esteem and conse-quently more leadership behaviors (Stake 1983). More should be done to increase women's levels of performance self-es-teem because as Stake and Stake (1979) write: "When females have confidence in their abilities, they do assert themselves" (82). The achievements of women should be acclaimed by authority figures, group members, and women themselves.

Summary

The studies on group dynamics lead us to conclude that an individual group member cannot by himself or herself or-chestrate who will become a leader. Groups are systems; that is, the behavior of one group member influences the be-havior of others. Interacting before desig-nating a leader, striving for more equalitarian interactions and balanced groups, and validating the accomplish-ments of women are all ways of increasing the probability that the most effective per-sons will lead.

Practical Suggestions

This essay has identified several barriers to women becoming leaders. Since groups are typically more productive and satisfied when the most qualified persons lead and since those persons are as likely to be women as men, we would now like to highlight ways for reducing these barriers.

Before we do, we need to note still another kind of bias. Most of the research on leadership has been limited to groups comprised of persons who are white and middle-class. This limitation in the research has affected what we have been able to write about in this chapter, and we want to acknowledge that shortcoming. Just as new studies that include women where they were previously neglected have altered conceptions of effective leadership (Helgesen, 1990), we suspect that the investigations of more diverse groups, cultures, and leadership styles will bring further modifications in how leadership ought to be viewed.

Based on the studies we have reviewed in this chapter, we make the following recommendations for groups who wish to maximize effective leadership. Group members should:

1. Acknowledge and challenge sex-role biases.

2. Affirm equalitarian attitudes and remind group members of their value.

3. Celebrate the "traditional" strengths of women.

4. Increase the visibility and support of female role models.

5. Validate the performance and self-confidence of women.

6. Designate leaders only after interacting, if at all.

7. Listen attentively.

8. Support group members and treat them with respect.

9. Ask others for their opinions; invite others to participate.

10. Draw upon the strengths of all group members; recognize the contributions of each as a valuable resource.

11. Make procedural suggestions.

12. Offer relevant information.

13. Provide evidence for claims.

14. Be an active participant, but monitor your own verbosity.

15. Discourage unequal interruptions; especially those that change the subject.

16. Learn from diverse groups and individuals.

Conclusion

At the beginning of this chapter we recommended that groups view *leadership* as the responsibility of all members rather than concentrate on one person fulfilling the role of lone *leader*. Leadership is the performance of behaviors that help a group reach its goals. It includes behaviors like making procedural suggestions, offering sound opinions, providing relevant information, and presenting counterarguments. Both men and women do these behaviors well and often with equal frequency. Leadership also involves listening attentively, supporting group members, and asking for the opinions of others; women are expected to perform these behaviors—and they do so with slightly more frequency than men.

Groups have many needs. A group-centered approach to leadership taps into the talents and energies of all its members. Consequently, it is likely to be healthier and more effective than if it had tried to rely on a single individual. So far, women seem more willing to embrace the ideal of shared leadership than men. Ideally, each group member would match her or his strengths to the group's needs. If different members serve as facilitator, organizer, note taker, attentive listener, sponge, teacher, gardener, transmitter, magician, or whatever else the group needs, then a lone leader would not have to be the "Black Mammy" or "Iron Maiden," and the entire group could be empowered to fulfill its goal.

Notes

1. Scholars who have identified "women's ways" of leading or interacting in groups have noted that not all women behave in this manner and that many men utilize the same skills and values (Heigesen 1990; Nelson 1988). Still, they have been called women's ways because they were more typical of women than men. In a similar vein we want to acknowledge that the research shows considerable variability; that is, one cannot claim that all males or all females lead in a particular way. Both women and men lead effectively and poorly; some members of both sexes are autocratic, democratic, sensitive, demanding, responsive, detached, and so forth.

2. We found comparing the results for the dispositional dominance literature with those for performance self-esteem interesting. The scales used in both studies (i.e., dispositional dominance and performance self-esteem) seemed very similar and yet for the most part the results were very different. Again we think whether the groups chose their leaders before or after interacting is the best explanation for this difference. When groups interacted, males and females were equally likely to emerge as the leader in both types of studies. It was only when they did not interact that males emerged more often. It just happens that most of the studies using dispositional dominance did not involve interaction, while group members did interact in the performance self-esteem study.

References

Adams, J., Rice, R. W., and Instone, D. (1984). "Follower attitudes toward women and judgments concerning performance by female and male leaders." *Academy of Management Journal* 27: 639–643.

Alderton, S. M., and Jurma, W. E. (1980). "Genderless/gender related task leader communication and group satisfaction: A test of two hypotheses." *Southern Speech Communication Journal* 46: 48–60.

Anderson, L. R., and Blanchard, P. N. (1982). "Sex differences in task and social-emotional behavior." *Basic and Applied Social Psychology* 3: 109–139.

Andrews, P. H. (1984). "Performance-self-esteem and perception of leadership emergence: A comparative study of men and women." *Western Journal of Speech Communication* 48: 1–13.

Aries, E. (1976). "Interaction patterns and themes of male, female, and mixed groups." *Small Group Behavior* 7: 7–18.

Auerbach, S. M., Kilmann, P. R., Gackenbach, J. I., and Julian, A., III. (1980). "Profeminist group experience: Effects of group composition on males' attitudinal and affect response." *Small Group Behavior* 11: 50–65.

Baird, J. E., and Bradley, P. H. (1979). "Styles of management and communication: A comparative study of men and women." *Communication Monographs* 46: 101–111.

Beckhouse, L., Tanur, I., Weiler, J., and Weinstein, E. (1975). "And some men have leadership thrung upon them." *Journal of Personality and Social Psychology* 31: 557–566.

Beleaky, M. R, Clinchy, B. M.; Goldberger, N. R., and Tarule, J. M. (1986). *Women's Ways of Knowing: The Development of Self, Voice, and Mind.* New York: Basic Books.

Bradley, P. H. (1980). "Sex, competence and opinion deviation: An expectation states approach. " *Communication Monographs* 47: 105–110.

——. (1981). "The folklinguistics of women's speech: An empirical examination." *Communication Monographs* 48: 73–90.

Brooks, V. R. (1982). "Sex differences in student dominance behavior in female and male professors' classrooms." *Sex Roles* 8: 683–690.

Brown, V., and Geis, F. L. (1984). "Turning lead into gold: Evaluations of men and women leaders and the alchemy of social consensus." *Journal of Personality and Social Psychology* 46: 811–824.

Bunyi, J. A., and Andrews, P. H. (1985). "Gender and leadership emergence: An experimental study." *Southern Speech Communication Journal* 50: 246–260.

Butler, D. (1984). "Can social consensus bias evaluations of emergent leaders?" Unpublished master's thesis, University of Delaware.

Butler, D., and Geis, F. L. (1990). "Nonverbal affect responses to male and female leaders: Implications for leadership evaluations." *Journal of Personality and Social Psychology* 58: 48–59.

Butterfield, D. A., and Powell, G. N. (1981). "Effect of group performance, leader sex, and rater sex on ratings of leader behavior." *Organizational Behavior and Human Performance* 28: 129–141.

Carbonell, J. L. (1984). "Sex roles and leadership revisited." *Journal of Applied Psychology* 65: 44–49.

Carrocci, N. M. (1985). "Perceiving and responding to interpersonal conflict." *Central States Speech Journal* 36: 215–228.

Cirincione-Colei, K. (1975). "The administrator: Male and female?" *Journal of Teacher Education* 26: 326–328.

Craig, J. M., and Sherif, C. W. (1986). "The effectiveness of men and women in problem-solving groups as a function of group gender composition." *Sex Roles* 14: 435–466.

Davis, B. M., and Gilbert, L. A. (1989). "Effect of dispositional and situational influences on women's dominance expression in mixed-sex dyads." *Journal of Personality and Social Psychology* 57: 294–300.

Denmark, F. L. (1977). "Styles of leadership." *Psychology of Women Quarterly* 2: 99–113.

Dindia, K. (1987). "The effects of sex of subject and sex of partner on interruptions." *Human Communication Research* 13: 345–371.

Dobbins, G. H., and Platz, S. (1986). "Sex differences in leadership: How real are they?" *Academy of Management Review* 11: 118–127.

Dobbins, G. H., Stuart, C., Pence, E. C., and Sgro, J. A. (1985). "Cognitive mechanisms mediating the biasing effects of leader sex on ratings of leader behavior." *Sex Roles* 12: 549–560.

Dumas, R. G. (1980). "Dilemmas of black females in leadership." In Rose LaFrances-Rodgers (ed.), *The Black Women*. Beverly Hills, CA: Sage, 203–215.

Edelsky, C. (1981). "Who's got the floor?" *Language in Society* 10: 383–421.

Eskilson, A., and Wiley, M. G. (1976). "Sex composition and leadership in small groups." *Sociometry* 39: 194–200.

Etaugh, C., Houtler, B. D., and Ptasnik, P. (1988). "Evaluating competence of women and men: Effects of experimenter gender and group gender composition." *Psychology of Women Quarterly* 12: 191–200.

Fairhurst, G. T, and Snavely, B. K. (1983). "A test of social isolation of male token." *Academy of Management Journal* 26: 353–361.

Faranda, J. A. (1981). "The influence of sex-role stereotypes on the evaluations of male and female leaders." *Dissertation Abstracts* 42(5B): 21–28.

Fisher, B. A. (1985). "Leadership as medium: Treating complexity in group communication research." *Small Group Behavior* 16: 167–196.

Fleischer, R. A., and Chertkoff, J. M. (1986). "Effects of dominance and sex on leader selection in dyadic work groups." *Journal of Personality and Social Psychology* 50: 94–99.

Geis, F. L., Boston, M. B., and Hoffman, N. (1985). "Sex of authority role models and achievement by men and women: Leadership performance and recognition." *Journal of Personality and Social Psychology* 49: 636–653.

Gigliotti, R. J. (1988). "Sex differences in children's task-group performance: Status/norm or ability?" *Small Group Behavior* 19: 273–293.

Gilligan, C. (1982). *In a Differen[t] Voice: Psychological Theory and Women's Development*. Cambridge, MA: Harvard University Press.

Goktepe, J. R., and Schneier, C. E. (1989). "Role of sex and gender roles, and attraction in predicting emergent leaders." *Journal of Applied Psychology* 74: 165–167.

Goodwin, M. H. (1980). "Directive-response speech sequences in girls' and boys' task activities." In S. McConnell-Ginet, R. Borker, and N. Furinan (eds.), *Women and Language in Literature and Society* (pp. 157–173). New York: Praeger.

Graves, L. M., and Powell, G. N. (1982). "Sex differences in implicit theories of leadership: An initial investigation." *Psychological Reports* 50: 689–690.

Greene, L. R., Morrison, T. L., and Tischier, N. G. (1981). "Gender and authority: Effects on perceptions of small group co-leaders." *Small Group Behavior* 12: 401–413.

Haccoun, D. M., Haccoun, R. R., and Sallay, G. (1979). "Sex differences in the appropriateness of supervisory styles: A non-management view." *Journal of Applied Psychology* 63: 124–127.

Harragan, B. L. (1977). *Games Mother Never Taught You*. New York: Warner.

Heilman, M. E., and Martell, R. E. (1986). "Exposure to successful women: Antidote to sex discrimination in applicant screening decisions?" *Organizational Behavior and Human Decision Processes* 37: 376–390.

Helgesen, S. (1990). *The Female Advantage: Women's Ways of Leadership*. New York: Doubleday.

Hennig, M., and Jardim, A. (1976). *The Managerial Women*. New York: Pocket Books.

Hirokawa, R. Y. (1980). "A comparative analysis of communication patterns within effective and ineffective decision-making groups." *Communication Monographs* 47: 312–321.

Hollander, E. P., and Yoder, J. (1980). "Some issues in comparing women and men leaders." *Basic and Applied Social Psychology* 1: 267–280.

Jago, A. G., and Vroom, V. H. (1982). "Sex differences in the incidence and evaluation of participative leader behavior." *Journal of Applied Psychology* 67: 776–783.

Jenkins, M. M. (1994). "The story is in the telling: A cooperative style of conversation among women." In S. Tromel-Plotz (ed.), *Gewalt durch Sprache: die Vergewaltigung van Frauen in Gesprachen.* Frankfurt an Main: Fischer Taschenbuch Verlag.

Jenkins, M. (1980). "Toward a model of human leadership." In C. Berryman and V. A. Eman (eds.), *Communication, Language, and Sex* (pp. 149–158). Rowley, MA: Newbury House.

Kennedy, C. W., and Camden, C. T. (1983). "A new look at interruptions." *Western Journal of Speech Communication* 47: 45–58.

Kimble, C. E., Yoshikawa, J. C., and Zehr, H. D. (1981). "Vocal and verbal assertiveness in same-sex and mixed-sex groups." *Journal of Personality and Social Psychology* 40: 1047–1054.

Kushell, E., and Newton, R. (1986). "Gender, leadership style, and subordinate satisfaction: An experiment." *Sex Roles* 14: 203–210.

Lamb, T. A. (1981). "Nonverbal and paraverbal control in dyads and triads: Sex or power differences." *Social Psychology Quarterly* 44: 49–53.

Maltz, D. N., and Borker, R. A. (1982). "A cultural approach to male-female communication." In J. J. Gumperz (ed.), *Language and Social Identity* (pp. 196–216). New York: Cambridge.

Megargee, E. I. (1969). "Influence of sex roles on the manifestation of leadership." *Journal of Applied Psychology* 53: 377–382.

Millard, R. J., and Smith, K. H. (1985). "Moderating effects of leader sex on the relation between leader style and perceived behavior patterns." *Genetic, Social, and General Psychology Monographs* 111: 305–316.

Morrison, T. L., and Stein, D. D. (1985). "Member reaction to male and female leaders in two types of group experiences." *Journal of Social Psychology* 125: 7–16.

Nelson, N. W. (1988). "Women's ways: Interactive patterns in predominantly female research teams." In B. Bate and A. Taylor (eds.), *Women Communicating: Studies of Women's Talk* (pp. 199–232). Ablex Publishing.

Nieva, V. F., and Gutek, B. A. (1980). "Sex effects on evaluation." *Academy of Management Review* 5: 267–276.

Nyquist, L. V., and Spence, J. T. (1996). "Effects of dispositional dominance and sex role expectations on leadership behaviors." *Journal of Personality and Social Psychology* 50: 87–93.

Octigan, M., and Niederman, S. (1979). "Male dominance in conversations." *Frontiers* 4: 50–54.

Offermann, L. R. (1986). "Visibility and evaluation of female and male leaders." *Sex Roles* 14: 533–544.

Ott, E. M. (1989). "Effects of the male-female ratio at work." *Psychology of Women Quarterly* 13: 41–57.

Owen, W. F. (1986). "Rhetorical themes of emergent female leaders." *Small Group Behavior* 17: 475–486.

Peck, T. (1978). "When women evaluate women, Nothing succeeds like success: The differential effects of status upon evaluations of male and female professional ability." *Sex Roles* 4: 205–213.

Pheterson, G., Kiesler, S., and Goldberg, P. (1971). "Evaluation of the performance of women as a function of their sex, achievement, and personal history." *Journal of Personality and Social Psychology* 19: 114–118.

Porter, N., and Geis, F. (1981). "Women and nonverbal leadership cues: When seeing is not believing." In C. Mayo and N. M. Henley (eds.), *Gender and Nonverbal Behavior* (pp. 39–61). New York: Springer-Verlag.

Porter, N., Geis, F., Cooper, E., and Newman, E. (1985). "Androgyny and leadership in mixed-sex groups." *Journal of Personality and Social Psychology* 49: 808–823.

Pugh, M. D., and Wahrman, R. (1983). "Neutralizing sexism in mixed-sex groups: Do women have to be better than men?" *American Journal of Sociology* 88: 746–762.

Ragins, B. R., and Sundstrom, E. (1989). "Gender and power in organizations: A longitudinal perspective." *Psychological Bulletin* 105: 51–88.

Rice, R. W., Bender, L. R., and Vitters, A. G. (1980). "Leader sex, follower attitudes toward women and leadership effectiveness: A laboratory experiment." *Organizational Behavior and Human Performance* 25: 46–78.

Rice, R. W., Instone, D., and Adams, J. (1984). "Leader sex, leader success, and leadership process: Two field studies." *Journal of Applied Psychology* 69: 12–31.

Rice, R. W., Yoder, J. D., Adams, J., Priest, R. F., and Prince H. T., II. (1984). "Leadership rating for male and female military cadets." *Sex Roles* 10: 885–902.

Rosenfeld, L. R., and Fowler, G. D. (1976). "Personality, sex, and leadership style." *Communication Monographs* 43: 320–324.

Russell, J. E. A., Rush, M. C., and Herd, A. M. (1988). "An exploration of women's expectations of effective male and female leadership." *Sex Roles* 18: 279–287.

Schneier, C., and Bartol, K. M. (1980). "Sex effects in emergent leadership." *Journal of Applied Psychology* 65: 341–345.

Schriesheim, C. A. (1982). "The great high consideration-high initiating structure leadership myth: Evidence on its generalizability." *Journal of Social Psychology* 116: 221–228.

Seifert, C., and Miller, C. E. (1988). "'Subordinates' perceptions of leaders in task-performing dyads: Effects on sex of leader and subordinate, method of leader selection, and performance feedback." *Sex Roles* 19: 13–28.

Shimanoff, S. B. (1984). "Coordinating group interaction via communication rules." In R. S. Cathcart and L. A. Samovar (eds.). *Small Group Communication: A Reader* (pp. 31–44). Dubuque, IA: Wm. C. Brown.

Spillman, B., Spillman, R., and Reinking, K. (1981). "Leadership emergence: Dynamic analysis of the effects of sex and androgyny." *Small Group Behavior* 12: 139–157.

Stake, J. E. (1979). "The ability/performance dimension of self-esteem: Implications for women's achievement behavior." *Psychology of Women Quarterly* 3: 365–377.

——. (1981). "Promoting leadership behaviors in low performance-self-esteem women in task-oriented mixed-sex dyads." *Journal of Personality* 49: 401–414.

——. (1983). "Situation and person-centered approaches to promoting leadership in low performance-self-esteem women." *Journal of Personality* 51: 62–77.

Stake, J. E., and Stake, M. N. (1979). "Performance-self-esteem and dominance behavior in mixed-sex dyads." *Journal of Personality* 47: 71–84.

Thomas, V. G., and Littig, L. A. (1985). "Typology of leadership style: Examining gender and race effects." *Bulletin of the Psychonomic Society* 23: 132–134.

Thorne, B., Kramarae, C., and Henley, N. (1983). *Language, Gender and Society*. Rowley, Mass: Newbury House.

Tischer, N., Morrison. T., Greene, L. R., and Stewart, M. S. (1986). "Work and defensive processes in small groups: Effects of leader gender and authority position." *Psychiatry* 49: 241–252.

Wentworth, D. K., and Anderson, L. R. (1984). "Emergent leadership as a function of sex and task type." *Sex Roles* 11: 513–524.

West, C., and Zimmerman, D. H. (1983). "Small insults: A study of interruptions in cross-sex conversations between unacquainted persons." In B. Thorne, C. Kramarae, and N. Henley (eds.), *Language, Gender, and Society* (pp. 103–118). Rowley, MA: Newbury House.

Wilensky, J. (1988). Women and Conflict. Paper presented at the Fifteenth Annual Student Conference in Communication.

Willer, L. R., and Henderson, L. S. (1988). Employees' perceptions of managers' communication competence versus traditional management behaviors. Paper presented at the Academy of Management Conference, Anaheim, CA.

Willis, F. N., and Williams, S. J. (1976). "Simultaneous talking in conversation and sex of speakers." *Perceptual and Motor Skills* 43: 1067–1070.

Winther, D. A., and Green, S. B. (1987). "Another look at gender-related differences in leadership." *Sex Roles* 16: 41–58.

Wolman, C., and Frank, H. (1975). "The solo woman in a professional peer group." *American Journal of Orthopsychiatry* 45: 164–171.

Wood, J. T. (1981). "Sex differences in group communication: Directions for research in speech communication." *Journal of Group Psychotherapy, Psychodrama, and Sociometry* 34: 24–31.

Wright, F. (1976). "The effects of style and sex of consultants and sex of members in self-study groups." *Small Group Behavior* 7: 433–456.

Wyatt, N. (1988). "Shared leadership in the weavers guild." In B. Bate and A. Taylor (eds.), *Women Communicating: Studies of Women's Talk* (pp. 147–176). Norwood, NJ: Ablex Publishing.

Zimmerman, D. H., and West, C. (1975). "Sex roles: Interruptions and silences in conversations." In B. Thorne and N. Henley (eds.), *Language and Sex: Difference and Dominance* (pp. 105–129). Rowley, MA: Newbury House.

Chapter 18
Leadership as Organizing

J. Kevin Barge

This chapter presents an alternative conception of group leadership—viewing it as a form of organizing. Barge examines the research on group leadership and concludes, "leadership is a form of mediation that mediates between information environments, group actions, and group outcomes." He provides a model of leadership that (1) accounts for the complexity and uniqueness of situated leadership behavior, and (2) provides an explanation of how certain individuals may be effective across situations. The chapter concludes with an explanation of how individuals become more complex and skillful organizers.

For many decades organizational and group researchers have focused on identifying the characteristics of effective leadership. Some theorists suggest that effective leadership is best characterized by a set of personality traits such as intelligence or physical traits such as height and weight (Stogdill 1948). Others contend that leadership is best defined by a set of overt behaviors that comprise a leadership style. Leadership styles have been typically characterized in terms of the amount of task and relational behavior a leader exhibits (Blake and Mouton 1978; Schriesheim and Kerr 1974) or the degree to which a leader allows followers to participate in decision making (White and Lippitt 1960). Researchers differ on whether or not a single set of traits or behaviors characterizes effective leadership. "One best style" theorists argue that possessing certain traits or mastering a single set of behaviors allows an individual to be an effective leader across all situations (Blake and Mouton 1978). Situational or contingency theorists maintain that the needed traits or behaviors must be matched to the situation in order to be an effective leader (Fiedler 1967; Vroom and Yetton 1973; Hersey and Blanchard 1982; House and Mitchell 1974).

The emerging picture of leadership research from the last few decades is a complex and contradictory one. Yet, most current theories do not adequately account for this complexity. For example, a common method for reducing leadership's complexity is to focus on either the traits or the behaviors characterizing leadership, but not both. This all or nothing method oversimplifies the leadership process because theorists are forced into an unenviable position of either emphasizing that leadership is ultimately manifested through complex communication behaviors or stressing the complex cognitive processes people use when selecting behaviors to perform; one is at the exclusion of the other. Another common method for reducing leadership's complexity is to single out the one set of traits or behaviors that leaders must possess or perform to be effective. Those who argue "one best style" of leadership exists across situations are unable to refute the mounting evidence in support of the position that leadership effectiveness is influenced or determined by situational factors. While situational leadership theorists address this problem by identifying key contingencies that influence the effectiveness of a given set of traits or styles, the approach introduces a new set of problems because situationalism limits researchers in developing generalizable theories of leadership (Bass 1981) that can aid in the identification and development of leaders (Mumford 1986).

A central question confronting leadership studies is how to manage its complexity. Can the complexity of leadership be captured by using either traditional trait or behavioral theories? Is the complexity of leadership adequately modeled by either "one best style" or situational leadership theories? Some theorists maintain that viewing leadership as a form of organizing addresses some of these concerns (Fisher 1985, 1986; Weick 1978). Based on Ashby's (1968) law of requisite variety, leadership from an organizing perspective recognizes that complexity can alone regulate complexity. The objective of viewing leadership as a form of organizing is to identify the processes that allow leaders to process information in more complex manners and behave in more complex fashions.

The purpose of this essay is to examine how researchers have traditionally treated complexity in leadership research and to sketch out an alternative approach to the study of leadership. By viewing leadership as a form of organizing, a generalizable model of leadership can be developed that: (1) accounts for the complexity and uniqueness of situated leadership behavior, and (2) provides an explanation of how certain individuals may be effective across situations. A set of theoretical propositions is presented in the conclusion of the essay.

Complexity and Leadership

Effective leaders exhibit considerable complexity in how they analyze and make sense of situations and in the range and depth of behaviors they perform during a discussion. Effective leaders are complex information-processors who are sensitive to the subtle qualities of individuals and the group environment. For example, transformational and charismatic leaders are closely attuned to the unique qualities and characteristics of their subordinates. They consider a follower's needs, skills, and abilities, and they recognize the constraints the organizational and group environment places upon the individual followers (Bass et al. 1987; Conger and Kanungo 1987).

Effective leaders also draw upon complex behavioral repertoires when managing individuals and the small group environment. Fisher (1986) suggests leadership may be the degree of complexity in the leader's behaviors instead of the frequency of certain types

of acts. For example, functionalist views of leadership suggest as leaders perform more of a particular leadership function, they are more likely to emerge as effective leaders (Knutson and Kowitz 1975). Repeating the same behavior over and over to fulfill a leadership function ensures a leader of being perceived as effective. However, leadership behavior is much more complex as leaders adapt their actions to the environment versus relying on standardized response patterns (Ellis 1979). Effective leaders need to adjust their behavior according to the group's level of development (Dies 1977), the psychological maturity of the follower (Hersey and Blanchard 1982), or the set of goals pursued by the leader (Vroom and Yetton 1973). A genuine mark of leaders according to Fisher (1985) is their ability to draw upon a complex repertoire of behaviors when adapting to changing situation versus relying on a single set of stylized behaviors.

Despite acknowledging that leadership is inherently complex, most theorists continue to reduce leadership's complexity into more manageable forms. Organizational and group researchers have typically reduced the complexity of leadership using one of three strategies (Fisher 1985). First, theorists have tried *to simplify the complexity of leadership through statistical and conceptual means*. The former is exemplified by the Ohio State Leadership Studies which employed factor analysis to group a number of micro behaviors into larger macro behavioral styles. The individual behaviors of scheduling, maintaining performance standards, enforcing work deadlines, offering encouragement, and "needling" subordinates were all collapsed into a macro behavioral style known as initiating structure (Schriesheim and Kerr 1974). The latter is exemplified by leadership style theorists who contend that there exists one best style of leadership which is effective across all situations (Blake and Mouton 1978; White and Lippitt 1960). By arguing that one best style exists, the complexity inherent to the leadership process is diminished by ignoring situational factors such as the nature of the task which may alter the needed styles.

Similarly, theorists have also reduced the complexity of leadership by equating a person with the leadership process. Leadership is reduced to a role in the group with typically one or two individuals within the group occupying the leadership role (Bales and Slater 1955). This is known as the entitative view of leadership where "the 'entity' is the leader; leadership being treated as a leader characteristic whether identifiable in what leaders do, or in their underlying characteristics" (Hosking 1988, 152). This is particularly problematic because some evidence indicates that the leadership contributions of the entire group versus the one or two members occupying the "leadership" role make a difference upon group productivity (Barge 1989).

A second strategy for treating complexity in leadership research is to *treat leadership's complexity as a problem to be solved.* Several popular situational leadership theories incorporate complexity into their conceptualizations by specifying contextual or moderating variables that influence leader behavior. By identifying the important contingencies of leadership, researchers are better able to specify the influence of specific types of behaviors in given situations. Howell, Dorfman, and Kerr (1986, p. 99) elaborate:

> Since some moderators have a positive effect on subordinate criteria measures, while others have a negative effect or no effect at all, a leader must know which *types* of moderators are present in order to develop a successful strategy for influencing subordinates.

While such an approach recognizes the complexity of the leadership situation, it also introduces the problem of determining which situational variables are most important. What criteria shall be used to decide which situational factors are important and which are not important? The number of individual, task, and social variables that could conceivably influence leadership are bewildering. As Fisher (1985) points out, situational theories open a Pandora's box of available situational factors to consider.

Third, researchers have tried to reduce the complexity of leadership *by manipulating the design of their research studies.* Surveys using self-report methods are commonly used as research techniques to relate leadership to power (Mowday 1979), motivation (Tyagi 1985; Kohli 1985), and organizational commitment (Stevens, Beyer, and Trice 1978; Morris and Sherman 1981). This type of methodology employs a selected measure of leadership, has the leaders provide a self-rating of their leadership behaviors or has the leader's followers provide the rating, and then subsequently correlates it to whatever the outcome is of interest to the researcher. In addition, more sophisticated questionnaire designs include measures of moderating variables serving to influence the direction and strength of the relationship between leadership and the designated outcome. However, such a methodology minimizes examination of the process of leadership and the sequential patterning of messages within conversation (Watson 1982). Using survey methods, the frequency of a leader's behavior can be examined in relation to selected outcomes; but the complexity of leadership behavior, as marked by the selection, timing, and sequencing of messages, or the developmental change across time cannot be measured.

Leadership as Organizing

Small groups must effectively manage the environmental obstacles they encounter and their internal group processes in order to accomplish their work. In order to do this, groups create a social order that allows them to successfully process inputs and transform them into outputs. The social order is a set of rules and norms that aid the group in solving problems and accomplishing its task. Hosking (1988, p. 163) has recognized:

> Perhaps the most fundamental dilemma is that which underlies the achievement of 'flexible social order'.

The dilemma is how to achieve a degree of order which is sufficient for core problems to continue to be solved, whilst at the same time, not too much, perpetuating a rigid way of doing things as they have always been done.

Given this fundamental problem, researchers have shifted from viewing leadership as a form of social influence to a form of organizing (Weick 1978; Hosking 1988; Greico and Hosking 1987; Brown and Hosking 1986; Fisher 1985, 1986). From this perspective, leadership is viewed as a process that either implicitly or explicitly aids the group in negotiating the social order.

Weick (1978) initially proposed viewing leadership as a form of organizing. According to Weick (1979), task groups are usually faced with a variety of task and interpersonal problems which must be overcome effectively in order for groups to be productive. Among these problems is the need to reduce ambiguous and equivocal information to a manageable level of understanding and action. That is, effective group performance necessitates that group members devise a set of rules and procedures, or an organizing system, suitable for limiting the number of plausible meanings and appropriate courses of action that can be derived from available information. As Weick sees it, then, the basic function of leadership is to assist the group in creating this organizing system, as well as overcoming other existing barriers to successful goal achievement.

The organizing system consists of assembly rules and interacts. Organizational members manage equivocality by imposing meaning on organizational events. Upon encountering equivocal events, organizational members utilize their past experiences and interpretations as criteria for interpreting these events. These criteria or *assembly rules* act as causal maps for making sense of the available information and planning subsequent action. For example, a work group may be charged with planning a series of activities to promote better personal health by organizational members. Few of the committee members, however, are genuinely interested in or excited about performing this task. As a result, they may adopt the assembly rule of effort whereby they select behaviors and cycles of behaviors whose completion requires little effort. All information coming into the group and behaviors performed during discussion will be done with a minimal amount of effort expended by group members. All actions will be performed with an eye towards conserving energy and effort.

Assembly rules, in turn, guide the performance of *communication cycles.* Putnam and Sorenson (1982) explain that a communication cycle consists of messages (acts) which are performed, responses to those messages (interacts), and changes prompted by the responses (double interacts). Using the preceding example, when evaluating a proposed health activity, a group using the effort assembly rule may perform the following communication cycle: Person A proposes solution::Person B agrees and praises the solution::Person A agrees and praises the solution. Such a communication cycle reflects a minimal amount of effort exhibited by the group members who easily accepted the initial solution proposed by the individual without engaging in an active, thoughtful critique of the ideas. Behaviors such as disagreeing with the idea, challenging the assumptions underlying the proposal, or extending the initial proposal are infrequent because they would require a higher level of effort than suggested by the assembly rule. Weick (1979) contends that increases in the number of assembly rules applied to manage equivocality decrease the number and variety of communication cycles. This is because only a few communication cycles will meet the requirements posed by the assembly rules.

Leadership becomes the process of helping groups apply appropriate assembly rules and initiating needed communication cycles to successfully adapt to their environment and accomplish goals. In short, leadership is a form of mediation that mediates among information environments, group actions, and group outcomes. According to Weick (1978), leaders must be skilled at object and action mediation. *Object mediation* refers to the ability of leaders to collect and gather accurate imprints of the group's environment. Good object mediators possess complex receptor systems that allow them to register a situation in greater detail. On the other hand, *action mediation* refers to the ability to perform a variety of actions that aid groups in overcoming obstacles. Leadership from an organizing perspective attempts to specify how leaders may become more complex information processors (object mediators) and behavioral performers (action mediators) who are able to create organizing systems that effectively deal with the group's environment.

Communication, Skill, and Organizing

Researchers viewing leadership as a form of organizing attempt to explain how individuals may become more complex and skillful organizers. Metcalfe (1982) suggests leaders may become skillful organizers by: (1) expanding their choice of perceptions regarding situations, and (2) increasing their behavioral repertoires. As a result, leadership as organizing focuses on the basic decoding and encoding skills that allow individuals to act in more complex and skillful fashions. Skills are the specific abilities required to competently perform a given task. In this case, the task is helping the group organize itself to overcome group and environmental obstacles. The general assumption underlying this perspective is that competent leaders are skillful performers who decode and encode messages that facilitate the group accomplishing its goal.

A truly comprehensive accounting of skillful performance must include both psychological and behavioral aspects of encoding and decoding (Spitzberg and Cupach 1984). Most leadership approaches, however, tend to emphasize one element over the other when attempting to define *skill*. For example, Fiedler and Garcia (1987) equate skill with an individual's personal resources, cognitive and psychological in nature, as represented by knowledge, expertise, and competence. On the other hand, Metcalfe (1982)

defines skill as an overt behavioral performance that facilitates goal achievement. While the former approach can specify the required abilities to interpret and act within situations, it is yet possible that individuals are unskilled behaviorally to act appropriately within a given situation. This is analogous to "knowing" what to do but being unable to "do it." A different problem arises when viewing skills solely as a form of behavioral performance. If an individual performs poorly, the researcher is unable to distinguish whether the poor performance is due to a behavioral deficit, a lack of knowledge, or a combination of both. For this reason, skills are defined generally as the abilities to perform a task which may involve both cognitive and behavioral abilities.

Consistent with Weick's (1979) model of organizing, a comprehensive leadership model must address three broad processes aimed at completing the task of organizing the group: (1) Sense making—how individuals decode ambiguous information and diagnose situation, (2) Decision making—how individuals select messages to aid the group in overcoming environmental obstacles, and (3) Performance—how individuals actually encode the selected message and with what effect. Each of these processes is associated with specific skills that facilitate successful performance.

Sense Making and Organizing

Effective leaders are good object mediators who are sensitive to the information environment and who fully process information. If leaders are to be successful information processors: (1) they must expose themselves to the organization's values, beliefs, and norms, (2) they must be sensitive to the nuances of organizational events, and (3) they must be able to examine organizational events from a variety of perspectives.

Networking. Leaders must initially collect imprints of the environment in order to assess what obstacles confront the group when accomplishing its overall task. Networking is a skill that is central to initially gathering this information and subsequently processing it. By successfully networking within the group and its surrounding environment, group leaders collect valuable information regarding the nature of the problems confronting the group and the appropriate lines of action. Networking allows individuals to enlarge their knowledge of both the group's environment and its members and understand the processes that are considered appropriate within the organization (Hosking 1988). This enlarged knowledge base, in turn, allows individuals to efficiently and effectively identify problems, develop solutions, and select and implement policy.

Effective networking is strategic in the sense that leaders gain knowledge of central problems confronting the group that require resolution. This knowledge enables them to "make sense" of group activity and distinguish among genuine and pseudo problems. This is critical to group effectiveness because treating a pseudo problem as genuine can trigger negative consequences. For example, an organization may traditionally experience a decrease in profits during the summer quarter. The leader of a work team in the organization who is less experienced and not well socialized into the organization may view this as a pressing problem to be solved and attempt to "shake things up" to remedy the problem. This may cause resentment and ill will by the team members because the more experienced members recognize that the business profits are cyclical and tend to be lower in summer. For them, this temporary drop in profits is a pseudo versus a real problem.

Data Splitting. Weick (1979) argues that individuals use cause maps or scripts to interpret organizational events. Throughout their membership in the organization, individuals develop scripts for interpreting events and sequencing their own subsequent actions. As a result, cognitive scripts serve a useful function in helping individuals make sense of the environment. For example, organizations sometimes have "hazing rituals" whereby older organizational members tease newer organizational members. Such rituals may be a normal process of initiation

and socialization into the organization. Organizational members who are aware of this ritual may use the script governing the hazing ritual to interpret the teasing as just another hurdle imposed by the organization to get ahead and not view it as a personal affront.

Gioia and Poole (1984) observe that scripts are useful because they help reduce the cognitive complexity of decision making. However, they may be problematic when they are overused because leaders may fail to be aware of the subtle differences that distinguish one particular problem or situation from another. In fact, leaders who rely heavily on organizational scripts may overlook the uniqueness of events confronting them and inadequately interpret and classify these events. For example, in their study of the effects of implicit leadership theories or prototypes, Lord and his associates (Cronshaw and Lord 1987; Phillips and Lord 1981, 1986; Phillips 1984) discovered that people tend to attribute certain types of behaviors to leaders even if they are not exhibited, provided the leader has performed some behaviors that are characteristic of leadership. Phillips and Lord (1986) argue that subordinates are poor at accurately accounting for the specific behaviors exhibited by the leader when they use leadership prototypes. Similarly, leaders may tend to encode strong interrelated images into their memory when strong organizational scripts exist. This leads to several assumptions regarding what elements are important in a situation, the causal relationships among elements, decision premises, appropriate actions, and the ordering of the elements. As a result, leaders may attend to attribute certain qualities to a situation or problem that are not really there. They may classify a problem according to a few details and gloss over or ignore other unique characteristics of the problem.

Data splitting is a skill that helps leaders to be attentive to the individual and fine-grained details of a situation. Data splitting helps leaders account step-by-step for the unique details relevant to the situation. Data splitting involves doubting that the incoming picture presented by the information automatically matches their existing cognitive template or script. Rather, leaders must split the incoming data apart into smaller and separate units in order to account for the uniqueness of the situation. This notion is similar to Phillips and Lord's (1986) suggestion that followers need to be trained to separate out independent leader behaviors in order to provide more accurate ratings of a leader's behavior. Specifically, they suggest that subordinates need to be trained to encode behaviors on an independent basis rather than to integrate them when encoded. While such techniques may require considerable effort by subordinates, this can improve the behavioral-level accuracy of their descriptions of their superiors. Therefore, to enhance behavioral accuracy, leaders must learn to separate differing aspects of incoming information.

Dialectical Thinking. The ability to view situations from multiple perspectives is positively associated with accurately diagnosing problems and generating quality solutions (Schweiger et al. 1986). The skill of dialectical thinking represents one method for examining problems from varying perspectives. Dialectical thinking involves shifting from viewing problems and solutions as either/or to both/and (Mitroff 1978). To think dialectically, a leader must be prepared to admit that the underlying cause of a problem and its extreme opposite make sense simultaneously or are equally valid. For example, a group member may perform poorly during a group meeting. Rather than immediately attribute the poor performance to a lack of effort, the leader using dialectical thinking may accept that lack of effort is simultaneously the right cause and is not the right cause for the poor performance. The leader may then reason through alternative explanations such as a lack of knowledge for the cause of poor performance. Such thinking leads to a more precise and thorough understanding of a problem by producing as many alternative conceptualizations of the problem and solutions as possible.

Dialectical thinking has been correlated with improved problem solving in the strategic decision-making literature. Several decision theorists have shown that dialectical thinking facilitates a thorough analysis of problems and their appropriate resolution (Mitroff 1982; Mitroff and Mason 1981; Mitroff and Emshoff 1979; Schwenk 1982) and produces higher quality decisions than more passive inquiry modes such as consensus-building (Schweiger, Sandberg, and Ragan 1986). One reason that dialectical thinking may improve problem analysis is that it prevents managers from relying too heavily on a set of standardized patterns. Mitroff (1978) suggests that most leaders react to situations out of habit employing a single frame of reference to view the situation. By actively debating the assumptions underlying the problem and solutions, leaders will be more likely to analyze the situation correctly. Dialectical thinking allows more effective leaders to employ at least two independent frames of reference to avoid solving the wrong problem.

Dialectical thinking can also improve the entire group's ability to dissect, analyze, and solve problems. According to Bass et al. (1987, p. 75), more effective leaders view situations from multiple perspectives and encourage their followers to do so as well:

> Transforming leaders help subordinates to think about old problems in new ways. Followers are supported for questioning their own beliefs and values and, when appropriate, those of their leaders, which may be outdated or inappropriate for solving the current problems confronting their organizations. As a consequence of being intellectually stimulated by their leader, followers develop their own capabilities to solve future problems that the leader may not have anticipated.

By viewing a situation from multiple perspectives, leaders avoid working on the wrong problem and gain additional insight into the nuances and subtleties of the problem. Furthermore, by encouraging followers to view problems in new ways and challenging traditional ways of doing things, the group expands its ability to view problems in new ways. This, in turn, expands the group's ability to analyze problems more accurately and generate more creative and novel solutions.

Decision Making and Organizing

Weick (1978) argues that effective leaders initially must focus on object mediation in order to capture rich and diverse impressions of the environment. The skills of networking, data splitting, and dialectical thinking assist leaders in the sense-making process by helping them form complex and differentiated impressions. Once leaders have analyzed and made sense of the situation, they must then focus on action mediation. Simply, they must select actions that facilitate the group accomplishing its task. Two skills involved in deciding which behaviors leaders will perform are: (1) choice making, and (2) articulation.

Choice Making. The leader must ultimately decide what actions will facilitate the group accomplishing its task or overcoming its environmental obstacles. In essence, leadership involves choosing among alternative courses of action and selecting those actions that will maximize the group accomplishing its overall task. Mumford (1986) points out that leadership involves making decisions in regards to attaining specific goals that will lead to attaining the overall task. Upon making sense of the situation, leaders will have a sense of the priority of particular problems and the root causes underlying the existence of particular problems. They must then decide what goals they wish to achieve which subsequently limits range of actions they may select to perform.

Within the leadership literature, two general types of leadership goals have been articulated: (a) task, and (b) socioemotional (Bales and Strodtbeck 1951; Benne and Sheets 1948; Blake and Mouton 1978). Goals are collective objectives or endpoints that the group wishes to achieve. Table 18.1 contains a typology of leadership goals. *Task goals* are objectives that relate to accomplishing the group's overall task or mission. Such objectives include recognizing the need for decision, problem diagnosis, solution generation, solution evaluation and ad-

aptation, and implementation planning. Mumford (1986) implicitly recognizes that these goals comprise important steps in the problem-solving process. The task goals presented in Figure 18.1 are consistent with Dewey's (1910) steps of critical thinking. These categories have also been

---

Table 18.1

A Typology of Leadership Goals

Task Goals	Relational Goals
1. Establishment of Operating Procedures	1. Conflict Management
2. Problem Definition	2. Motivation
3. Solution Generation	3. Affect
4. Solution Evaluation	4. Loyalty
5. Implementation Planning	5. Contribution to the Group

Figure 18.1

The Process of Skillful Leadership

Information Inputs

↓

Sense-Making Skills
Networking
Data Splitting
Dialectical Thinking

Decision-Making Skills
Choice Making
Articulation

↓

Performance Skills

↓

Actual Performance of Behavior

↓

Assessed Skill of Leader
Appropriateness
Effectiveness

used by a variety of functional researchers investigating small groups (Hirokawa 1983, 1985, 1988; Poole 1983). In order to address the obstacles confronting the group, leadership involves selecting behaviors that accomplish some or all of these goals.

Socio-emotional goals are non-task related goals which attempt to establish and maintain interpersonal relationships (i.e. conflict management, friendship, cohesiveness, or good will). The typology of socio-emotional goals stems from several tributaries. Dienesch and Liden (1986) argue that leaders and followers try to establish their relationships within three parameters: (1) affect, (2) loyalty, and (3) contribution to exchange. These three parameters may also represent three goals that leaders and followers try to achieve during group discussion. Furthermore, as leadership is the process of negotiation of social order, conflicts inevitably arise which must be managed in the negotiation process (Hosking 1988). Therefore, one socioemotional goal entails the smoothing over, avoiding, or managing of conflict. Finally, most leadership theories concur that leaders must motivate their subordinates (Likert 1967; Fiedler 1967; Blake and Mouton 1978). Therefore, motivation is included as a critical goal.

Articulation. Leaders must not only possess skill in selecting messages which facilitate goal achievement, they must also be skilled at articulating their messages at a sufficient level of abstraction so that followers can understand and comprehend them (Eisenberg 1984). Appropriate articulation is partially determined by the norms and behavioral patterns existing within the social group. Particularly strong scripts not only contain prescriptions for what constitutes appropriate behavior but also their progressive sequence. By being aware of the organizational scripts that operate within an organization or group, leaders have a working knowledge of how they are to speak to others in appropriate ways.

Scripts can set expectations for both social and task behavior. Scripts structure expectations regarding the *social environment*. The social environment consists of the unfolding collective interpretation of the rules,

metaphors, and expectations that guide and regulate role relationships and interaction. Scripts also structure expectations regarding the *task environment*. Poole (1983) suggests that the task environment consists, in part, of the group's intersubjective task representation or "design logic" that depicts the strategy for how a decision is to be made. Groups develop patterns of solving problems or a problem-solving style that sets forth the way a group approaches a problem.

Leaders facilitate the organizing process when they articulate their directions, suggestions, or questions in a manner that followers can understand and view as appropriate. Using Harris's (1979) model of competence, leaders may vary in their skill level of articulation. First, leaders may be *minimally articulate*. Such individuals do not understand the demands of the group and the rules for appropriate and well-sequenced talk. They are "outside" the system looking in. For example, a Protestant at a bar mitzvah may not understand the rules guiding the ceremony and may, therefore, be unable to sequence his or her messages. Second, leaders may be *satisfactorily articulate*. At this skill level, leaders are able to articulate appropriately as they understand the demands and rules of the group. They are able to work appropriately within the existing system. For example, stereotypical bureaucrats understand how the organization operates and are able to phrase their requests in manners that are appropriate and effective given the organization. Third, leaders may be *optimally articulate*. Leaders at this skill level not only can operate within the existing system, but they are able to transcend the system and articulate a new organizing system which supplants the initial one. In terms of organizing, leaders need to be at least satisfactorily articulate in order to convey to other group members the actions that need to be taken.

Performance and Organizing

Leadership is ultimately executed through communication. While the skills involved in sense making and decision making improve the likelihood leaders will select behaviors that facilitate groups accomplishing their goal, they may not be able to actually perform the behavior. That is, they are unable to translate their selected behavior into action. This may stem from a lack of practice, or experience, or simply fatigue (McFall 1982). A practical example of this occurrence is the classic weekend golfer. Many weekend golfers know what they theoretically need to do to hit the ball correctly. Yet, these same golfers continually slice the ball into out-of-bounds or hit the ball into water hazards and sand traps. This poor execution (and golf swing!) may stem from a lack of practice and experience or a long week of exhaustive work. Similarly, group leaders may know what they need to criticize a proposed solution, but are unprepared for giving solid and effective criticism. As a result, they are unable to criticize effectively the proposed solution.

Performance skills refer to the ability of the individual to successfully execute a particular behavior. Successful performance or skilled behavior is marked by two qualities. First, skillful behavior is characterized by *appropriateness*. For example, theorists have defined inappropriate behavior as unnecessarily abrasive, intense, or bizarre (Getter and Nowinski 1981), hostile (Numbers and Chapman 1982), and non-sanctioned social behavior (Spitzberg and Cupach 1984). In terms of group appropriateness, appropriateness may therefore be defined as behaviors that conform to the existing group norms, myths, and metaphors (Gioia and Poole 1984). Second, skillful performance is characterized by *effectiveness*. Organizing serves an instrumental function by facilitating individuals or groups in achieving goals. Therefore, performance is skillful to the extent that it allows the individuals to accomplish goals. This is consistent with interpersonal definitions of effectiveness which characterize it as the achievement of interpersonal goals (Argyris 1968; Spivack, Platt, and Shure 1976; Breen et al. 1977; Foote and Cottrell 1955; Fitts 1970). If a leader's actions are to be perceived as skilled, they must therefore be both perceived as appropriate and effective.

Discussion and Conclusions

This essay has articulated a general model of leadership based upon the idea that leadership is a form of organizing which helps groups organize themselves to achieve their task. This model is presented in Figure 18.1. Specifically, the model suggests that leadership can be broken down into three broad processes: (1) sense making, (2) decision making, and (3) performance. Furthermore, within each of these processes there are particular encoding and decoding skills that facilitate leaders performing behaviors that aid the group in overcoming their obstacles. For example, sense making can be broken down to include the skills of networking, data splitting, and dialectical thinking. While these activities are presented in a linear manner, they may be nonlinear as subsequent activities can influence initial ones. For example, skillful performance may influence the individual's ability to subsequently network which directly influences the individual's ability to make sense of the organizational environment (Hosking 1988). This model yields several theoretical propositions for viewing *leadership as organizing*.

The underlying premise of viewing leadership as organizing is that only complexity can regulate complexity. Skillful organizers' thoughts and behaviors must be at least as complex as the information environment they confront. Simply, difficult problems with many possible solutions to select from require that the processing of the problem be more complex and extensive if the group is to effectively understand and solve the problem. If leaders are ineffective at networking, data splitting, or dialectical thinking, they will be unable to collect accurate imprints and form more complex or fine-grained impressions of the environment. This, in turn, reduces the quality of information they have available to determine what behaviors will facilitate organizing the group towards accomplishing its goal. Poor sense-making and decision-making skills decrease the perceptual and behavioral complexity of leaders. This ultimately diminishes their ability to adapt to the organizational environment. A leader's failure to exhibit complexity in behavior may also be linked to lowered perceptions of competence by other group members because the leader does not have a broad repertoire of behaviors to draw upon. Less complex organizers may rely on standardized responses to particular problems and have a limited number of actions they can perform if their initial response fails. The underlying assumption is that these processes and skills will remain constant in their applicability across situations but their level of depth and complexity will change according to the situation. This line of reasoning leads to the following propositions.

Proposition 1: The complexity of the sense-making, decision-making, and performance skills must equal or exceed the complexity of the information environment if leadership is to help the group overcome its obstacles.

Proposition 2: Individuals who are highly skilled in sense making and decision making and who possess broad behavioral repertoires will be perceived as acting appropriately and will exhibit more variety in their behavior.

An example may be useful at this point. Following is a list of questions that leaders may ask when they encounter and manage obstacles in the group environment. The questions are grouped according to the type of skill they reflect. However, such questions may also be used in other activities.

Networking

1. Have I talked to all the concerned parties with regard to the decision?

2. Who possesses unique insight into the problem? Have I talked to that person?

3. Who has a sense of history about the problem?

4. Is this problem a recurring one? Who would have access to that information?

Data Splitting

1. Is this problem really the same as problems I have faced before?

2. What elements are causing the problem?

3. What is different about this problem from similar problems that I have dealt with in the past?

4. When does this problem seem to occur?

5. Who seems to be involved with this problem?

6. Why does this problem seem to be occurring?

7. What are the consequences of the problem if I do not manage it? What happens if I solve the problem? What happens if I don't solve the problem?

Dialectical Thinking

1. What do I think is the primary reason for the problem? What are the arguments for this position?

2. If I rule out what I think is the primary cause of the problem, what are some other possible causes of the problem? What are the arguments supporting this position?

3. When I pit these competing positions against one another in a debate, which set of arguments from #1 and #2 are superior? What are the underlying assumptions of each position? Which assumptions are most valid?

4. Which assumptions and arguments have survived the debate and analysis?

5. How can I synthesize the two competing positions together? What is my final analysis?

Decision Making

1. What are the goals that I want to achieve?

2. Is there a conflict between achieving my task and relational goals? If so, which one is more important? Is there a way to balance them off?

3. What are some possible behaviors I could perform in order to achieve those goals?

4. Which of these behaviors is most likely to help me accomplish these goals?

Articulation

1. How do I phrase my messages so that they can be understood by my subordinates?

2. Are there any social, organizational, or legal constraints on what I can say?

3. Do I think I can say what I want to say well? Can I articulate what I want to be understood by my followers? If I can't, is there another kind of behavior that I can perform that would allow me to achieve my goal?

Regarding Proposition 1, a leader may need to address these questions in greater depth or ask new ones in order to solve highly complex problems. On the other hand, when a task is relatively simple, the leader may not need to ask as many questions or go into as much depth. Regarding Proposition 2, the assumption is that as leaders go through these basic processes in more depth, they will have made sense of the situation and planned and executed appropriate actions. Furthermore, as the available options they can select from increase, they will be able to exhibit more and varied kinds of behaviors and different sequences of behavior when needed.

While sense-making and selection skills may independently affect the organizing process, they also influence one another. Sense-making and selection skills need to be tightly coupled or linked prior to a leader performing particular behaviors. That is, choice making and articulation should directly flow from the sense-making process. Initially, sense-making activities should be loosely coupled or connected to selection activities so the leader can concentrate on forming accurate and detailed impressions of the organizational environment (Weick 1978). However, once those impressions have been collected, sense-making must be tightly coupled with the decision-making

process. By tightly coupling sense making and decision making, the chances that leaders will perform irrelevant, ineffective, or inappropriate behaviors are diminished. This is because once leaders have established a valid interpretation of the situation, it is more likely they will address this problem versus focusing on other irrelevant problems. This line of reasoning leads to the following proposition.

Proposition 3: Sense-making and selection skills must be tightly coupled initially for skillful behavioral performance.

While tightly coupled sense-making and decision-making processes enhance the organizing process, they do not guarantee the behavioral complexity of leaders. For example, leaders may be highly accomplished sense makers as they are able to dissect situations accurately and select appropriate behaviors. However, if leaders are constrained by their ability to articulate their ideas and plans, they will not be able to translate the complexity of their ideas into actual performance. Simply, we may know what we want to say and do, but cannot put it into words or actions. Therefore, the articulation ability of an individual moderates the influence of the leader's sense-making abilities.

Proposition 4: The behavioral complexity of leadership is diminished when the articulation skills rigidly conform to organizational norms, regulations, and myths (i.e. satisfactorily articulate) even when the leader is a highly skilled sense maker.

Finally, the various sense-making skills interact and moderate one another. It is possible for an individual to be active in the network and still be perceived as an unskilled communicator and organizer. High activity within social networks within organizations can expose individuals to a variety of information. However, if individuals rely heavily on the strong scripts they possess, they may gloss over important details contained within the situation. Furthermore, if they are poor dialectical thinkers they may not be able to sufficiently analyze the situation in order to avoid solving irrelevant problems. Therefore, the knowledge that individuals gain from networking may not be positively related to behavioral complexity if the information is used poorly.

Proposition 5: Networking is negatively associated with the complexity of leadership behavior when data splitting and dialectical thinking skills are poor.

This essay has proceeded from the assumption that leaders need to develop particular skills that allow them to view situations in more complex ways and display variety in their behavior when needed. Since group situations vary greatly, evolve over time, and are unique, identifying specific personality traits and behaviors that guarantee effectiveness in a given group at a given point in time is difficult. Therefore, leadership from an organizing perspective is not geared toward identifying what specific behaviors leaders must perform in a given situation to be effective or what the match between specific leadership traits and the situation must be. The thrust of this essay is to suggest that leaders need to be adaptable to the evolving group situation and that leaders need to possess and perform skills that enhance their adaptability in situations. The skills identified in Figure 18.1 do not specify what precise behaviors need to be performed in specific situations. Rather, it specifies some of the basic processes and skills that allow individuals to successfully analyze situations and select and execute appropriate behaviors across a variety of situations. These skills should enhance the adaptability of leaders and ultimately translate into more effective and well-organized groups.

References

Argyris, C. (1968). "The nature of competence-acquisition activities and their relationship to therapy." In W. G. Bennis, E. H. Schein, F. Steele, and D. E. Berlew (eds.), *Interpersonal Dynamics: Essays and Reading on Human Interaction.* Homewood, IL: Irwin.

Ashby, W. R. (1968). "Variety, constraint, and the law of requisite variety." In W. Buckley (ed.), *Modern Systems Research for the Behavioral Scientist.* Durham, NC: Duke University Press.

Bales, R. F., and Slater, P. E. (1955). "Role differentiation in small decision-making groups." In T. Parsons (ed.), *The Family, Socialization, and Interaction Process.* Glencoe, IL: Free Press.

Bales, R. F., and Strodtbeck, F. L. (1951). "Phases in group problem solving." *Journal of Abnormal and Social Psychology* 46: 485–495.

Barge, J. K. (1989). "Leadership as medium: A leaderless group discussion model." *Communication Quarterly* 37(4): 237–247.

Bass, B. M. (1981). *Slogdill's Handbook of Leadership.* New York: The Free Press.

Bass, B. M., Waldman, D. A., Avolio, B. J., and Bebb, M. (1987). "Transformational leadership and the falling dominos effect." *Group and Organizational Studies* 12(1): 73–87.

Benne, K., and Sheets, S. (1948). "Functional roles of group members." *Journal of Social Issues* 4: 41–49.

Blake, R. R., and Mouton, J. S. (1978). *The Managerial Grid.* Houston: Gulf.

Breen, P., Donlon, T. F., and Whitaker, U. (1977). *Teaching and Assessing Interpersonal Competence: A CAEL Handbook.* Columbia, NJ: CAEL.

Brown, M. H., and Hosking, D. M. (1986). "Distributed leadership and skilled performance as successful organization in social movements." *Human Relations* 39(1): 65–79.

Conger, J. A., and Kanungo, R. N. (1987). "Toward a behavioral theory of charismatic leadership in organizational settings." *Academy of Management Review* 12(4): 637–647.

Cronshaw, S. F., and Lord, R. G. (1987). "Effects of categorization, attribution, and encoding processes on leadership perceptions." *Journal of Applied Psychology* 72(1): 97–106.

Dewey, J. (1910). *How We Think.* Boston: D. C. Heath.

Dienesch, R. M., and Liden, R. C. (1986). "Leader-member exchange model of leadership: A critique and further development." *Academy of Management Review* 11(3): 618–634.

Dies, R. R. (1977). "Pragmatics of leadership in psychotherapy and encounter group research." *Small Group Behavior* 8: 229–248.

Eisenberg, E. M. (1984). "Ambiguity as strategy in organizational communication." *Communication Monographs* 51: 227–242.

Ellis, D. G. (1979). "Relational control in two group systems." *Communication Monographs* 46: 153–166.

Fiedler, F. E. (1967). *A Theory of Leadership Effectiveness.* New York: McGraw-Hill.

Fiedler, F. E., and Garcia, J. E. (1987). *New Approaches to Effective Leadership: Cognitive Resources and Organizational Performance.* New York: John Wiley.

Fisher, B. A. (1985). "Leadership as medium: Treating complexity in group communication research." *Small Group Behavior* 16(2): 167–196.

———. (1986). "Leadership: When does the difference make a difference?" In R. Y. Hirokawa and M. S. Poole (eds.), *Communication and Group Decision-Making* (pp. 197–218). Beverly Hills: Sage.

Fitts, W. H. (1970). *Interpersonal Competence: The Wheel Model.* Studies on the self-concept and rehabilitation: Research monograph No. 2. Dede Wallace Center, Nashville, TN: W. H. Fitts.

Foote, N. N., and Cottrell, L. S., Jr. (1955). *Identity and Interpersonal Competence.* Chicago: University of Chicago Press.

Getter, H., and Nowinski, J. K. (1981). "A free response test of interpersonal effectiveness." *Journal of Personality Assessment* 45: 301–308.

Gioia, D. A., and Poole, P. P. (1984). "Scripts in organizational behavior." *Academy of Management Review* 9(3): 449–459,

Grieco, M. S., and Hosking, D. M. (1987). "Networking, exchange, and skill." *International Studies of Management and Organization* 17(1): 75–87.

Harris, L. M. (1979). Communication competence: Empirical tests of a systemic model. Unpublished doctoral dissertation, University of Massachusetts, Amherst.

Hersey, P., and Blanchard, K. (1982). *Management of Organizational Behavior.* Englewood Cliffs, NJ: Prentice-Hall.

Hirokawa, R. Y. (1983). "Group communication and problem-solving effectiveness: An investigation of group phases." *Human Communication Research* 9(4): 291–305.

———. (1985). "Discussion procedures and decision-making: A test of functional perspective." *Human Communication Research* 12: 203–224.

———. (1988). "Group communication and decision-making performance: A continued test of the functional perspective." *Human Communication Research* 14(4): 487–515.

Hosking, D. M. (1988). "Organizing, leadership and skillful process." *Journal of Management Studies* 25(2): 147–166.

House, R. J., and Mitchell, T. R. (I 974). "Path goal theory of leadership." *Journal of Contemporary Business* 5: 81–97.

Howell, J. P., Dorfman, P. W., and Kerr, S. (1986). "Moderator variables in leadership research." *Academy of Management Review* 11(1): 88–102.

Knutson, T. J., and Kowitz, A. C. (1975). "Orientation behavior, leadership, and consensus: A possible functional relationship." *Communication Monographs* 42: 107–114.

Kohli, A. K. (1985). "Some unexplored supervisory behaviors and their influence on salespeople's role clarity, specific self-esteem, job satisfaction, and motivation." *Journal of Marketing Research* 22: 424–433.

Likert, R. (1967). *The Human Organization.* New York: McGraw-Hill.

McFall, R. M. (1982). "A review and reformulation of the concept of social skills." *Behavioral Assessment* 4: 1–31.

Metcalfe, B. M. A. (1982). "Leadership: Extrapolating from theory and research to practical skills training." *Journal of Management Studies* 19(3): 295–305.

Mitroff, I. I. (1978). "Systematic problem solving. In M. M. Lombardo and M. W. McCall (eds.), *Leadership: Where Else Can We Go?* (pp. 129–143). Durham, NC: Duke University Press.

———. (1982). "Dialectic squared: A fundamental difference in perception of the meanings of some key concepts in social science." *Decision Sciences* 13: 222–224.

Mitroff, I. I., and Emshoff, J. R. (1979). "On strategic assumption-making: A dialectical approach to policy and planning." *Academy of Management Review* 4: 1–12.

Mitroff, I. I., and Mason, R. O. (1981). "The metaphysics of policy and planning: A reply to Cosier." *Academy of Management Review* 6: 649–651.

Morris, J. H., and Sherman, J. D. (1981). "Generalizability of an organizational commitment model." *Academy of Management Journal* 24: 512–526.

Mowday, R. T. (1979). "Leader characteristics, self-confidence, and methods of upward influence in organizational decision situations." *Academy of Management Journal* 22(4): 709–725.

Mumford, M. D. (1986). "Leadership in the organizational context: A conceptual approach and its applications." *Journal of Applied Social Psychology* 16(6): 508–531.

Numbers, J. S., and Chapman, L. J. (1982). "Social deficits in hypothetically psychosis-prone college women." *Journal of Abnormal Psychology* 91: 255–260.

Phillips, J. S. (1984). "The accuracy of leadership ratings: A cognitive categorization perspective." *Organizational Behavior and Human Performance* 33: 125–138.

Phillips, J. S., and Lord, R. G. (1981). "Causal attributions and perceptions of leadership." *Organizational Behavior and Human Performance* 28: 143–163.

———. (1986). "Notes on the practical and theoretical consequences of implicit leadership theories for the future of leadership measurement." *Journal of Management* 12(1): 31–41.

Poole, M. S. (1983). "Decision development in small groups III: A multiple sequence model of group decision-making." *Communication Monographs* 50: 321–341.

Putnam, L. L., and Sorenson, R. L. (1982). "Equivocal messages in organizations." *Human Communication Research* 8(2): 114–132.

Schriesheim, C., and Kerr, S. (1974). "Psychometric properties of the Ohio State Leadership Scales." *Psychological Bulletin* 81(11): 756–765.

Schweiger, D. M., Sandberg, W. R., and Ragan, J. W. (1986). "Group approaches for improving strategic decision making: A comparative analysis of dialectical inquiry, devil's advocacy, and consensus." *Academy of Management Journal* 29(1): 51–71.

Schwenk, C. R. (1982). "Dialectical inquiry into strategic decision making: A comment on the continuing debate." *Strategic Management Journal* 3: 371–373.

Spitzberg, B. H., and Cupach, W. R. (1984). *Interpersonal Communication Competence.* Beverly Hills: Sage.

Spivack, G., Platt, J. J., and Shure, M. B. (1976). *The Problem-Solving Approach to Adjustment.* San Francisco: Jossey-Bass.

Stevens, J. M., Beyer, J. M., and Trice, H. M. (1978). "Assessing personal, role, and organizational predictors of managerial commitment." *Academy of Management Journal* 21: 380–396.

Stogdill, R. M. (1948). "Personal factors associated with leaderships: A survey of the literature." *Journal of Psychology* 25: 35–71.

Tyagi, P. K. (1985). "Relative importance of key job dimensions and leadership behaviors in motivating salesperson work performance." *Journal of Marketing* 49: 76–86.

Watson, K. M. (1982). "An analysis of communication patterns: A method for discriminating leader and subordinate roles." *Academy of Management Journal* 25(1): 107–120.

Weick, K. E. (1978). "The spines of leaders." In M. McCall and M. Lombardo (eds.), *Leadership: Where Else Can We Go?* (pp. 37–61). Durham, NC: Duke University Press.

———. (1979). *The Social Psychology of Organizing.* Reading, MA: Addison-Wesley.

White, R., and Lippitt, R. (1960). *Autocracy and Democracy.* New York: Harper.

Vroom, V. H., and Yetton, P. W. (1973). *Leadership and Decision-Making.* Pittsburgh: University of Pittsburgh Press.

Part VII

Diversity in Groups

When Confucius said, "Human beings draw close to one another by their common nature, but habits and customs keep them apart," he might well have been addressing a problem that small groups face today. Diversity (or difference)—the very thing that can cause groups to be a wealth of talent, knowledge, insight, and wisdom—can also be the reason that the individuals fail to work well together.

Problems with accepting people's differences are not new to contemporary society. Wandering nomads, religious missionaries, and conquering soldiers have been encountering people different from themselves since the beginning of time. Those early meetings, like some meetings today, were often confusing and hostile. In the twenty-first century, intercultural contacts are more common and, in many ways, more significant than those early meetings. But being aware of some of the hurdles that groups face when dealing with differences can make members better able to see obstacles, to overcome them, and to use the group's diversity to its advantage.

What Is Culture?

Culture is ubiquitous, multidimensional, complex, and all-pervasive. Defining it, therefore, has been a complicated and involved process. As early as 1952, Kroeber and Kluckholm listed 164 definitions of cul-

ture that they found in the anthropology literature. Some definitions emphasized culture as a set of knowledge and beliefs; others emphasized culture as a set of behaviors. Some definitions focused on the material aspects of culture (e.g., books, films), while others focused on the nonmaterial aspects of everyday life (e.g., attitudes, values). Of course, many new definitions have appeared since (Martin and Nakayama 2000).

For our purposes, we define culture as the *sum total of beliefs, values, attitudes, meanings, perceptions, customs, practices, language, and other artifacts of social life that are learned, shared, and passed on by a group of people.* Culture, then, is the "instruction manual" we carry around in our heads to help us make sense of, and behave appropriately in, everyday life.

While there is considerable disagreement about what culture is, and what the boundaries of culture are, there is a great deal of agreement concerning the major characteristics of culture: culture is *learned*, culture is *shared*, and culture is *passed on from generation to generation*.

Culture is learned. An important characteristic of culture is that it is learned. Human beings are not born with a built-in "instructional manual" on how to get along in everyday life. We learn what to believe (and disbelieve), we learn what to perceive (and ignore), we learn what to value (and devalue), we learn what to like (and dislike), and so forth. The lessons we learn about culture usually come from our daily interactions with others who share that culture—first with family and people in the neighborhood, at school, at youth groups, at college, at work, and so on (Hofstede 1991).

Culture is shared. Culture is a collective experience because the aspects that constitute culture (e.g., attitudes, values, beliefs, practices) are shared with people who live in and experience the same social environment. To say that aspects of culture are shared means to say that multiple members of the group understand or do something in the same way. For example, members of a group are said to share an attitude when they respond in the same way (positively or negatively) to the same stimulus.

Culture is passed on. To say that culture is "learned" also implies that culture can be passed on from one group member to another, and that this passing on of culture can occur over an extended period of time. Hence, the culture of a group can remain long after group membership has changed. For example, the Communication Studies Department at the University of Iowa is characterized by what people call the "Iowa Tradition." The "Iowa Tradition" is a set of attitudes, values, beliefs, and ways of doing things that make the department unique, unlike communication departments elsewhere. No one knows when the "Iowa Tradition" was created, but current members of the department learned about it from past members of the department, and these current members, in turn, pass it on to new members who enter the department.

International Concerns

Marshall McLuhan's (1964; McLuhan and Fiore 1967, 1968) *global village* prophecy is now a reality. The world is indeed "shrinking" and we appear to live in a common "village." Jet airlines allow tourists, business people, athletes, diplomats, and even terrorists to be anywhere in the world within hours. Even when physical mobility is difficult, communication satellites, high-speed digital communication, and the Internet link people from different nations and cultures in ways unimaginable even a few decades ago. New communication technologies (like those described by Robyn Parker in Chapter 3 and Craig Scott in Chapter 13) now allow us to form work groups with people who live on the other side of the world.

Not everything is positive about this new freedom to associate with people from different cultures. When one leaves the boundaries of one's own culture, one finds that cultural differences often go far beyond differences in language, foods, currency, living conditions, and modes of transportation. One encounters drastic differences of attitudes, values, beliefs, practices, customs, and perceptions. One discovers cultural idiosyncrasies in the use of space and time, the treatment of women and the elderly, and even in the meaning of truth. As the events of September 11, 2001 tragically revealed, the inability to respect and accept cultural differences makes the global village a very dangerous place to live in today. It also makes it very difficult (if not impossible) for people from different parts of the world to work together to tackle global issues, or even less complicated business problems.

Domestic Concerns

Similar concerns with diversity and cultural differences exist within our own boundaries. The United States has long been a "melting pot" for different ethnic groups (and the cultures they bring with them), and the blending continues as people from Asia, Central and South America, Cuba, Haiti, and Mexico have entered the United States and become part of the new society. Additionally, people in the United States who previously remained in the shadow of the dominant, mainstream "American" culture are now becoming more visible and vocal. Native Americans, African Americans, homosexuals, the disabled, the elderly, women, the homeless, and others are crying out for—indeed demanding—recognition and a place in the new global village. All this means that contact and association with people from different cultural backgrounds is becoming a normal part of our daily lives.

Membership in groups characterized by diversity troubles many people. The behavior and thinking of people from cultures different from one's own sometimes appear strange, even bizarre, and such people frequently fail to meet our expectations. Language barriers make interaction and communication with people from different cultures even more challenging and difficult. Not surprisingly, we encounter people who say: "I do not want to be a part of a diverse group. I want to associate and work only with people who resemble me."

No doubt, diversity in a group presents challenges for the members of that group. It is not easy working with people who think differently from us; who do things different from us; who perceive things differently from us; and who value things differently from us. But as the chapters in this section reveal, the challenges presented by group diversity pale in comparison to the potential benefits and gain that it offers.

References

Kroeber, A. L., and Kluckholm, C. (1952). "Culture: A critical review of the concepts and definitions." Papers of the Peabody Mueseum of American Archaeology and Ethnology, 47, 1–223.

Martin, J. N., and Nakayama, T. K. (2000). *Intercultural Communication in Context*, 2nd Edition. Mountain View, CA: Mayfield Publishing Co.

Hofstede, G. (1991). *Cultures and Organizations: Software of the Mind.* London: McGraw-Hill.

McLuhan, M. (1964). *Understanding Media.* New York: Mentor.

McLuhan, M., and Fiore, Q. (1967). *The Medium Is the Massage.* New York: Bantam.

———. (1968). *War and Peace in the Global Village.* New York: Bantam. ✦

Chapter 19
Sex, Gender, and Communication in Small Groups

Nina M. Reich
Julia T. Wood

The authors of this chapter are careful to differentiate between sex and gender, not only conceptually, but also in terms of their influence on how people interact in groups and teams. By engaging in an extensive review of the research literature, Reich and Wood convincingly argue that actual differences in the way women and men communicate in groups are less important than perceptions of those differences. They conclude that "deeply ensconced cultural views of how women and men should communicate in groups affect perceptions of how they actually communicate and how appropriate and effective they are."

Think about groups in which you have participated. Have you ever felt that some members dominated others—talked over others, interrupted, spoke with excessive volume? Have you felt that some members focused mainly on asserting themselves and their ideas whereas other members focused primarily on connecting ideas among group members and strengthening group climate? It is likely that you have noticed communication patterns such as these. It is also likely that some of the patterns you have noticed are linked to the sex or gender of group members.

In this chapter, we will consider how sex and gender influence group communication. If you watch shows such as *Oprah* or read popular books such as John Gray's *Men Are From Mars, Women Are From Venus*, you may think that men and women communicate in radically different ways. If so, read on. This chapter will help you evaluate stereotypes such as those in John Gray's work. Actually, men and women are from the same planet, and their communication isn't as different or difficult as interplanetary communication. There are both similarities and differences between women's and men's communication.

In this chapter, we want to understand how sex and gender influence communication in groups. The first section of the chapter distinguishes between sex and gender, two concepts that are often confused. Next we will discuss general differences in how men and women communicate in groups. The third section of the chapter focuses on sex and gender influences on decision making and conflict in groups. The final section of the chapter considers how gender may affect both enactment and perception of leadership in groups. Throughout this chapter, we invite you to step outside of the communication patterns you have learned until now and think about making informed choices about how you want to communicate at different moments in the life of groups. You may find that you want to develop both masculine and feminine communication styles to enhance your effectiveness in various aspects of group interaction.

After reading this chapter, you should be aware of gendered communication tendencies. Insight into gendered communication styles will allow you to understand and interact effectively with group members who employ both masculine and feminine communication patterns. In addition, you will be empowered to choose the style of communication you want to use in various situations. This will increase your effectiveness when communicating in group contexts.

Sex and Gender

You have heard the terms *feminine* and *masculine* as well as the terms *women* and *men*. The former terms refer to gender and the latter to sex, which are distinct phenomena. *Women, men, male,* and *female* are words that specify sex, which biology determines. In contrast, feminine and masculine are words that designate genders, which are meanings for each sex that society constructs and sustains. Before we can understand gendered communication patterns, we need to clarify what gender is and how it differs from sex.

Sex

Sex is determined by genetic codes that program biological features. Of the 23 pairs of human chromosomes, one pair controls sex. Usually this unit has two chromosomes, one of which is always an X chromosome. If the second chromosome is a Y, the fetus is male; if it is an X, the fetus is female. (Other combinations have occurred: XYY, XXY, XO, and XXX.) During gestation, genetic codes direct the production of hormones so that fetuses develop genitalia and secondary sex characteristics consistent with their genetic makeup. (Again there are exceptions, usually caused by medical interventions. See Wood 2003 for a more thorough discussion.)

We rely on biological features to classify people as male and female: external genitalia (the clitoris and vagina for a female, the penis and testes for a male) and internal sex organs (the uterus and ovaries in females, the prostate in males). Hormones also control secondary sex characteristics such as percentage of body fat (females have more fat to protect the womb when a fetus is present), how much muscle exists, and amount of body hair. There are also differences in male and female brains. Females generally have greater specialization in the right hemisphere, which controls integrative and creative thinking, while males typically have more developed left lobes, which govern analytic and abstract thought. Usually females also have a better-developed corpus callosum, which is the bundles of nerves connecting the two brain lobes. This anatomical difference suggests that women may be better able to cross to the left hemisphere than men are to cross to the right (Hines 1992). All of these are sex differences controlled by biology.

Gender

Gender is considerably more complex than sex. You might think of gender as the cultural meaning of sex. A culture constructs gender by arbitrarily assigning certain qualities, activities, and roles to each sex and by then weaving these assignments into the fabric of social life. Children spend much time in sex-segregated groups. In addition, others teach children to embody social prescriptions for gender by treating boys and girls differently and by expecting different behaviors from them. Thus, we are not born with a gender, but we become gendered as we internalize and then embody society's views of femininity and masculinity. Thus, gender is a social creation—not an innate, individual characteristic.

Gender refers to social beliefs and values that specify what sex *means* and what it allows and precludes in a particular society at a specific time. Because there is diversity among societies and each one changes over time, the meaning of gender is neither universal nor stable. Instead, femininity and masculinity reflect the beliefs and values of particular cultures in certain eras.

It should now be clear to you that gender and sex are not synonymous. Sex is biological, whereas gender is socially constructed. Sex is an individual property, whereas gender is a social construction. Sex is innate whereas gender is learned and therefore changeable. Sex is established by genetics and biology, whereas gender is produced and reproduced by particular societies at particular times. Barring surgery, sex is permanent, whereas gender varies over time and across cultures.

Whereas our sex stays the same across situations, we may choose to embody different genders in different situations. For instance, both women and men may adopt more typically masculine task-oriented behaviors when a group is facing a deadline to complete its work. Conversely, both men and women may adopt more conventionally feminine inclinations to be interpersonally sensitive when a group is experiencing tension or demoralization. These examples remind us that we do not have to limit ourselves to only masculine or feminine styles of communication when we interact in groups. We can make choices so that our communication is effective in varying situations that call for equally varying communication behaviors. As a member of groups, you can make choices about your gender—or genders, as you might choose to adopt behaviors that our society associates with both femininity and masculinity. Awareness of your capacity to choose how to communicate leads us to the concept of androgyny.

Androgyny

The idea that we are not locked into only masculine or feminine identities inspired a line of research launched by Sandra Bem. In the seventies, Sandra Bem (1974) coined the term *androgyny*, based on the Greek words *andro* for male and *gyne* for female. Androgyny refers to a person's psychological sex role, or gender—how feminine and how masculine a person is. Bem pointed out that most of us think about gender as a single continuum in which masculinity is one pole and femininity is the other, opposite pole. This view of gender implies that we are either masculine or feminine, but not both.

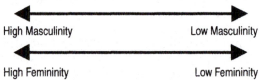

Bem proposed an alternative way of thinking about gender. She believed it was more accurate and more productive to think about gender as two separate continua on which each of us can place ourself: one masculine, one feminine.

Bem thought that each of us has both qualities that our society regards as feminine and qualities that our society perceives as masculine. Some of us have many feminine qualities and few masculine ones; some of us have many masculine qualities and few feminine ones; and some of us have a number of both feminine and masculine qualities. According to Bem, the two sets of qualities are not oppositional but highly complementary. For example, someone who has the conventionally masculine quality of aggressiveness would benefit from also having the conventionally feminine quality of sensitivity to others. In combination the two qualities correct each other and render the person balanced and adaptable.

Bem thought the ideal was for each person to be comfortable and skilled in feminine and masculine behaviors. She observed that different situations and goals call for different kinds of behaviors. Thus, she reasoned, a person who is competent in a broad repertoire of behaviors is likely to be effective in a wide range of contexts, whereas someone who has a narrower set of behaviors will be competent in a correspondingly narrower set of situations.

Research has provided some support for Bem's ideas. Compared to sex-typed individuals, androgynous people are more flexible, have higher self-esteem, and are more effective in interacting with a range of people (Heath 1991; Heilburn 1986). A long-term study of adults found that androgynous people are also more likely to be successful in their professional and personal lives than their sex-typed counterparts (Heath 1991). Further, research has shown that the most effective leadership includes both conventionally feminine qualities such as relationship building and conventionally masculine qualities such as focusing on achievement (Cann and Siegfried 1990).

Since Bem's groundbreaking work, there have been criticisms of the concept of androgyny. Perhaps the most important criticism is that the concept reproduces and hardens the dichotomy between masculine and feminine. In so doing, it undermines its own effort to get beyond rigid divisions between men and women, masculinity and femininity (Bem 1993). Even with this weakness, the idea of androgyny is useful because it highlights the fact that we are not confined to one set of behaviors. Thus, it opens options for you as a communicator

Sex, Gender, and Communication Patterns in Groups

In opening this chapter, we noted that differences between men's and women's ways of communicating are not as great as John Gray and other popular writers claim. There are many similarities in how the sexes communicate in groups and other contexts (Aries 1996; Burleson in press):

- Both women and men act to achieve goals.
- Both women and men are ambitious.
- Both women and men value supportive relationships with others.
- Both women and men seek and exercise leadership.
- Both women and men can be assertive and deferential.

In addition to many similarities in how women and men typically communicate, there are also some differences. The differences are generally matters of degree or extent rather than absolute contrasts. We'll discuss four broad sex-related tendencies that often surface in group communication.

Instrumental and Expressive Communication

One of the most noted sex differences in communication concerns tendencies to use communication for expressive or instrumental purposes. *Expressive* communication emphasizes feelings, connections between people, and personal disclosures. Communication is perceived as an end, or goal, in its own right. The goal of communicating is to share oneself with others and to build relationships. *Instrumental* communication emphasizes accomplishing something—solving a problem, making a decision, or presenting information. Communication is per-

ceived as a means to an end—the end of doing something or achieving some goal. Although members of both sexes communicate expressively and instrumentally, women generally engage in more expressive communication than men, and men generally engage in more instrumental communication than women (Fletcher 1999; Fletcher, Jordan, and Miller 2000; Harris 1998; Johnson 1996; Mulac 1998).

Tendencies toward instrumental or expressive communication styles show up in a variety of ways in group situations. Members who prioritize expressive communication are likely to engage in "small talk" before meetings start and during meetings. They work to build personal relationships between members and see these relationships as central to effective group work. Members who place primary emphasis on instrumental communication may perceive personal talk as a distraction from the task at hand.

Task and Relationship Foci in Communication

Closely related to expressive and instrumental tendencies are sex-linked inclinations to emphasize group tasks or relationships among members. Obviously, these two are not mutually exclusive since effective groups achieve tasks and maintain good relationships among members. Yet the extent to which members emphasize task or relationship varies in sex-related ways. Generally women place more emphasis on relationships than men, and generally men place more emphasis on tasks than women. Researchers report that women are more likely than men to communicate caring and to want to help others (Fletcher et al. 2000; Lunneborg 1990; Otten 1995).

Recently we participated in a week-long leadership development program. On the first day participants were assigned to groups and told to develop a recommendation for solving a fictitious company's problem. In our group, several members immediately focused on the goal—what kind of solution we should generate. Two members of the group resisted an initial focus on the outcome and wanted to discuss why they were attending this program and what they hoped to gain from it. Later in the activity the members who were focused on the outcome were pushing for a final group report, writing down key points and supporting arguments. The two members who were more focused on process asked questions such as "Have we all agreed to that?" "Pat, do you have anything to add?" "Is everyone comfortable that we understand the problem well enough to proceed with considering solutions?" "Chris, have we considered your reservations sufficiently?" For the members focused on outcome, the only important goal was to generate a recommendation. On the other hand, the members who were focused on process placed high value on participation and interpersonal relationships. To them, attending to all members and building good relationships between members were essential to developing a good recommendation and keeping the team cohesive.

Individual and Group Orientation

A third sex-related difference is the tendency to emphasize individual effort and contributions or to emphasize the group as a whole. Perhaps you have been in groups where one person seemed to seek the spotlight—wanted his or her ideas to be noticed and credited to him or her. This behavior is an example of an individualistic orientation, in which a person asserts himself or herself in order to gain personal status and control. In contrast, some members of groups focus more on the team or group. Their communication works to build connections between ideas, to respond to others, and to draw everyone into discussion (Fletcher et al. 2000; Tannen 1990, 1995). This behavior exemplifies a team orientation, in which a person places greater emphasis on building the team than on winning personal status and credit.

Ella Baker's work in the civil rights movement exemplifies group-centered leadership (Payne 1989). Baker was concerned that blacks were relying too heavily on high-profile individual leaders such as Martin Luther King, Jr. and Malcolm X. In Baker's opinion,

achieving civil rights required widespread active participation of blacks. Her leadership consisted of encouraging ordinary black citizens to get involved with the civil rights movement and to exercise "grassroots leadership" in defining goals and empowering themselves (Wyatt 2002).

Forcefulness

A fourth sex-related difference in group communication is forcefulness. Research shows that men typically communicate more forcefully than women. Forcefulness includes several communication behaviors. First, it involves how much a person talks. Although folklore tells us that women "talk all the time," research shows that in many contexts men actually talk more than women. This tendency is particularly evident in task situations, where men generally talk more and for longer periods of time than women (Aries 1987; Austin, Salehi, and Leffler 1987).

Forcefulness is also demonstrated when a person controls conversation by engaging in strategies to keep himself or herself prominent in the discussion. One way to do this is engage in self-promotion—calling others' attention to your ideas, your contributions, or your achievements. Communication scholars Zorn and Murphy (1996) report that men are more likely than women to feel comfortable promoting themselves and taking credit for their ideas and accomplishments. Men are also more likely than women to interrupt others and move a group's communication back to them and their issues (Anderson and Leaper 1998). Another strategy for controlling conversation is to reroute comments. For instance, in a group Charles might say, "I disagree with Jan's suggestion because of an experience I had with that plan." If Wilson wants to reroute the conversation, he might state, "You're right, Charles—we need to consider our experiences when evaluating Jan's suggestion. One experience I had is. . . ." Notice how Wilson uses Charles' comment as a jump-off point for introducing his own ideas, thus rerouting the conversation and the group's attention. Conversational control is also maintained by silence, or refusal to respond to others' comments. When there is no response, a line of conversation dies (DeFrancisco 1991).

Forcefulness is also demonstrated by *how* people communicate in groups. Compared to women, men generally communicate more assertively and directly, using both verbal and nonverbal behaviors to add emphasis to their ideas (Tannen 1990, 1995). Men are more likely than women to say, "This is the proposal we should go with." Women are more likely than men to say, "I think this is a strong proposal. What do the rest of you think?" Men are more likely than women to use strong volume and powerful hand and body movements to add emphasis to their ideas.

Think again about groups in which you have participated. Did you notice the four broad areas of sex-related differences in communication that we have discussed? Did you notice that some members communicate more expressively, whereas other members communicate more instrumentally? Did some members focus more on task and others more on relationships? Did some members seem more interested in asserting themselves individually while other members seemed more oriented toward the overall group or team? Did some members communicate more forcefully than others? Now ask yourself whether members in the groups you have been part of can be divided neatly by their sex on these four aspects of communication. The chances are good that some, but not all, women in groups that you have observed were expressive, oriented toward relationships and the team, and not especially forceful. It is also likely that some, but not all, men in your groups were instrumental, oriented toward task and individual status, and forceful.

Not all men communicate in the same ways. Not all women communicate in the same ways. And not all women and men conform to the communication patterns that research has identified as typical of each sex. Before leaving this discussion, we should highlight two qualifications to research findings about men's and women's communication.

Generalized Tendencies, Not Universal Dichotomies

The first qualification is that differences between women's and men's communication are general, not universal. Not all women communicate as a majority of women do, and not all men communicate as a majority of men do. Research that we will discuss in this chapter tells us only about general patterns. We need to keep in mind that there are exceptions to the general patterns that researchers have found. You may well discover that you are a living exception to some of the communication that is typical for your sex.

Differences as Matters of Degree, Not Absolute Opposites

The second qualification is that the sex-linked patterns researchers have identified are tendencies, or matters of degree. They are not rigid, absolute, or dichotomous differences (Burleson, in press). For example, in general, men tend to communicate more forcefully than women. This does not mean that women never communicate forcefully; it means only that, in general, women tend to express themselves less forcefully than men. Although women typically are more attentive than men to interpersonal dynamics in groups, some women are not interpersonally sensitive and some men recognize interpersonal issues and work to address them. Keeping these qualifications in mind will help you avoid faulty sex stereotypes, which do not hold up in everyday interactions with unique individuals.

Conflict Styles and Decision Making in Groups

Decision making and managing conflict are two of the most important aspects of communication in groups. In this section, we will look first at research on men's and women's styles of making decisions and dealing with conflict. Then we will explore how those general sex and gender differences unfold in group interaction.

Conflict Styles

As groups work together, conflicts inevitably arise. *Conflict* is defined as "an expressed struggle between at least two independent parties who perceive incompatible goals, scarce resources, and interference from the other party in achieving their goals" (Hocker and Wilmot 1991, 12).

Hocker and Wilmot (1991) identify five conflict styles that people use when attempting to make decisions or solve problems. The first is the *avoidance style*. The avoidance style is a passive approach in which a group member may disagree with other group members but will not speak up in order to avoid a conflict. The second style is *accommodation*. Accommodation is a highly cooperative approach in dealing with conflict and is often employed when the relationship of the group is more important to you than the problem at hand. A third conflict style is *competition*. This is a highly aggressive and uncooperative conflict style. For example, one group member may do "whatever it takes" to get his or her way even if it hurts the group relationship. Next is *collaboration*, also referred to as negotiation. This is a cooperative style that attempts to integrate all group members' opinions in order to make a decision that meets all of the group members' needs. The final conflict strategy is that of *compromise*. Compromising stresses a shared outcome. With this approach it is not uncommon for group members to give up personal needs for the betterment of the group.

While conflict may have both beneficial and harmful outcomes when attempting to make group decisions, conflict tends to affect groups positively when "it produces a better decision, increases cohesiveness and teamwork, enhances member understanding, and leads to satisfaction with both the process and the product" (Brilhart and Galanes 1998, 263). Because conflict can have both positive and negative effects on group decision making, it is important to ask how men and women manage conflict within groups.

You may have found from your own experiences that men and women tend to deal with conflict differently. It is also commonly believed that because, in general, men are more assertive and competitive in their communication styles that men are more likely to engage in competitive or avoidant conflict management behaviors. Similarly, many people think that, because women are viewed as more submissive and deferential than men, women may rely on cooperative behaviors. Along similar lines Canary and Spitzberg (1987) found that the topic of the conflict affected perceptions of women's and men's appropriateness and effectiveness in dealing with conflict. But note that this finding is about others' perceptions of men's and women's conflict styles; it does not tell us about the actual styles people use in group situations. So what does the research say about how men and women deal with conflict within groups?

Some research suggests that men and women view and approach conflicts differently. For instance, Berryman-Fink and Brunner (1987) found that males are more likely to report that they compete in conflict situations, while women report that they are more inclined to compromise. Other studies report that men and women are largely similar in their conflict styles (Bell, Chafetz, and Horn 1982; Canary, Cunningham, and Cody 1988; Sternberg and Soriano 1984; Gayle, Preiss, and Allen 1998). So how can we explain the discrepancy in research findings? The most informed answer is that sex is a factor, but not the only factor, that influences conflict style. Although men and women may have somewhat different general preferences for dealing with conflict, the style that any person actually uses is influenced by factors such as the expertise of group members and the task at hand. Agreeing with this, Cupach and Canary (1995) argue that views we hold about men and women's conflict styles are simplistic, and more often than not they are based on sex stereotypes, not on how women and men actually communicate.

When thinking about the conflict style that you adopt in groups, keep in mind that the conflict situation itself is a major factor that influences the style you are most likely to engage in when dealing with a group conflict. So, while sex may play a role in your overall preferred style of handling conflicts, conflict styles are also influenced by the task at hand, the expertise of the group members, and the nature of the group (Aries 1998). Although the sex of the individual clearly plays a role in decision-making processes within groups, it is important to be able to use any of the five conflict styles when attempting to solve problems. An integrative approach— that is, being able to engage in all five types of conflict styles—will allow you and other group members the flexibility that is necessary to productive group processes and outcomes.

Decision Making

Do women or men exert more influence on group decision making? Although research suggests that men generally are perceived as more competent than women, in actual group decision making, members will often defer to the individual who is perceived as having more expertise at the task at hand (Wood and Karten 1986). For example, if a man is perceived as the expert on a particular task, he will most likely control the decision-making process. Conversely, if a woman is perceived as the expert on another task, then the group members will most likely defer to the women as the expert decision maker (Canary and Emmers-Sommer 1997). Thus, perceived competence, or expertise, influences the amount of power an individual has and can exert. To the extent that group members adopt social views of women's and men's areas of expertise, gender may influence perceptions of competence.

Sex differences and perceptions of them also seem to vary over time in a group's life. For example, sex differences in influence tend to be greater early in a group's life than later (Aries 1996; Wheelan and Verdi 1992). As group members get to know each other over time, sex-stereotyped perceptions typically diminish. If you think about your own interactions, you may realize that sex stereotypes shape your first impressions, but those stereotypes fade as you get to know people. Similarly, it makes sense then that sex differences are more salient in the beginning of group interactions, before less obvious facets of group members emerge.

We should also note that sex-related differences in decision-making strategy and influence tend to be greater in groups that are very unbalanced—for instance, six men and one woman or eight blacks and one white (Aries 1996; Kanter 1977). On the basis of gender expectations, if a woman engages in a competitive conflict style in a group with a majority of male members, she may be viewed as highly "aggressive." Similarly, if a man in a group with a preponderance of female members engages in an accommodating conflict style, he may be viewed as "wimpy."

An important implication of the research we have discussed is that an individual's sex is not the most important influence on conflict style or decision-making processes.

Leadership in Groups

As you might suspect, some of the sex-related patterns in group communication discussed in the foregoing section also show up in leadership. The first parallel between members' communication and leaders' communication is that the sexes are more similar than dissimilar. After analyzing 25 studies of sex differences in leadership, Wilkins and Andersen (1991) concluded that there are no major differences in how women and men leaders communicate. Similarly, Powell (1993) reported that there are few significant sex differences in leadership effectiveness. Both women and men value being leaders and exerting influence. In leadership roles, both women and men are competent at directing and coordinating others, keeping a group on task, and producing high-quality results (Aries 1998; Fletcher et al. 2000).

Sex-Related Differences in Group Leadership

There are differences of degree in how women and men enact leadership. In general, women are more likely than men to use a collaborative, democratic style of leadership that shares power and enables others (Aries 1987; Eagly and Johnson 1990; Fletcher et al. 2000; Helgesen 1990; Lunneborg 1990; Rosener 1990). Men are more likely than women to use a directive, or even autocratic, leadership style that maintains their status (Eagly and Karau 1991; Eagly and Johnson 1990). Men in leadership roles also tend to be more reluctant than women to share information, preferring instead to keep information to themselves as a means of enhancing their personal power (Helgeson 1990; Natalle 1996).

Perceptions Versus Actual Communication

Before leaving our discussion of sex differences in leadership, we should note that whether women and men actually lead differently is only part of the issue. At least as relevant is the question of how others perceive women's and men's leadership. Staley (1988) found that beliefs that women and men are different prompt some people to perceive women leaders are ineffective. In other words, people who think men are stronger, more decisive, and more professionally competent are likely to evaluate women leaders as ineffective even if the women are doing everything an effective male leader would do.

Several studies have shown that women and men may be perceived and judged differently even when they communicate in the *very same ways*. Women and men who were research confederates were trained to employ identical leadership behaviors. The women were judged negatively when they used a directive communication style; the men were not. When men communicated directively, they were judged as strong leaders, whereas women who communicated directively were judged as aggressive or bitchy (Baird 1981; Butler and Geis 1990). It seems that women who are assertive and not particularly sensitive to others' feelings may be judged negatively because they are violating cultural prescriptions for femininity. Men who are assertive and not especially sensitive to others' feelings are less likely to suffer negative judgments because those behaviors do not violate cultural expectations for masculinity. This makes sense in light of Beebe and Barge's Chapter 24 in this book, where they point out that one criterion of communication competence is appropriateness—acting in ways that are perceived as permissible within a given culture. Women leaders who violate social expectations of femininity may be judged as inappropriate communicators and therefore as ineffective leaders.

Clear evidence that many people presume men are more likely to be leaders than women comes from an interesting study conducted by Valian (1998), a professor of psychology and linguistics who is interested in how sex and gender stereotypes shape perceptions. She conducted an experiment to find out whether college students are equally likely to perceive women and men as leaders. Students were asked to identify the leader in photos of people seated around a conference table. When the people in the photo were all men or all women, students overwhelmingly chose the person at the head of the table as the leader. Students also selected the person at the head of the table as the leader when the photo showed both women and men and a man was seated at the head of the table. However, when both women and men were in the photo and a woman was at the head of the table, students selected the woman at the head as the leader only half the time. Valian's study and others we have discussed remind us that perceptions of leaders have as much to do with the person perceiving as with the leader and what she or he does.

Have you heard of "bully broads?" This is an especially dramatic illustration of the extent to which gendered expectations shape our views of what is appropriate and inappropriate leadership behavior. Jean Hollands is a Silicon Valley executive coach whose special focus is training women leaders to communicate in ways that are nurturing, soft, unaggressive—in a word, feminine. According to Hollands (2001), the rules for effective leadership are different for women and men. She says that nobody likes a bullying leader, but men can get away with it and women cannot. Men who bully subordinates may not be liked, but they get results because being aggressive, even overbearing, is consistent with cultural views of men. Women who bully subordinates, however, are likely to get resentment and to find their careers derailed because aggressive communication is inconsistent with cultural views of women. Hollands' solution is to coach women leaders to be more feminine—to speak softly, wear conventionally feminine clothes, smile, defer to others, and even cry. Although it is tempting to dismiss Hollands' workshops for bully broads as trivial, keep in mind that her clients include women managers from premier companies such as Cisco, Hewlett-Packard, Sun Microsystems, and Lockheed-Martin.

Summary

In this chapter, we have seen that sex and gender are one influence on patterns of communication in groups. Just as important, we have seen that sex and gender are not the only—and perhaps not the most important—influence on how people interact in groups and teams. We have also seen that how actual women and men communicate may be less important than how others perceive their communication. Deeply ensconced cultural views of how women and men *should* communicate affect perceptions of how they *actually* communicate and how appropriate and effective they are.

As you think about how this chapter applies to your own communication in groups, remember that your sex and gender influence, but do not determine, how you communicate in groups and other contexts. You can choose how to communicate, basing your choices on your goals, the situation in which you find yourself, and the expectations and tendencies of those with whom you interact. And you can choose to alter your ways of communicating as interaction evolves over time in groups.

References

Anderson, K., and Leaper, C. (1998). "Meta-analyses of gender effects on conversational interruption: Who, what, when, where, and how." *Sex Roles* 39: 225–252.

Aries, E. (1987). "Gender and communication." In P. Shaver and C. Hendrick (eds.), *Sex and Gender* (pp. 292–299). St. Paul, MN: West.

———. (1996). *Men and Women in Interaction: Reconsidering the Differences.* New York: Oxford University Press.

———. (1998). "Gender differences in interaction." In D. Canary and K. Dindia (eds.), *Sex Differences and Similarities in Communication: Critical Essays and Empirical Investigations of Sex and Gender in Interaction* (pp. 65–81). Mahwah, NJ: Erlbaum.

Austin, A., Salehi, M., and Leffler, A. (1987). "Gender and developmental differences in children's conversation." *Sex Roles* 16: 497–510.

Baird, J., and Bradley, P. (1979). "Styles of management and communication: A comparative study of men and women." *Communication Monographs* 46: 101–111.

Bell, D., Chafetz, J. S., and Horn, L. (1982). "Marital conflict resolution: A study of strategies and outcomes." *Journal of Family Issues* 3: 111–131.

Bem, S. (1974). "The measurement of psychological androgyny." *Journal of Clinical and Consulting Psychology* 42: 155–162.

Berryman-Fink, C., and Brunner, C. (1987). "The effects of sex of source and target on interpersonal conflict management styles." *Southern Speech Communication Journal* 53: 33–48.

Bradley, P. (1981). "The folk-linguistics of women's speech: An empirical investigation." *Communication Monographs* 48: 73–90.

Brilhart, J., and Galanes, G. (1998). *Group Discussion* (9th ed.). Boston: McGraw-Hill.

Burleson, B. (in press). "The experience and effects of emotional support: What the study of cultural and gender differences can tell us about close relationships, emotion, and interpersonal communication." *Personal Relationships.*

Butler, D., and Geis, F. (1990). "Nonverbal affect responses to male and female leaders: Implications for leadership." *Journal of Personality and Social Psychology* 58: 48–59.

Canary, D. J., Cunningham, E. M., and Cody, M. J. (1988). "Goal types, gender, and locus of control in managing interpersonal conflict." *Communication Research* 15: 426–446.

Canary, D., and Emmers-Sommer, T. (1997). *Sex and Gender Differences in Personal Relationships*. New York: Guilford Press.

Canary, D., and Spitzberg, B. (1987). "Appropriateness and effectiveness perceptions of conflict strategies." *Human Communication Research* 14: 93–118.

Cann, A., and Siegfried, W. (1990). "Gender stereotypes and dimensions of effective leader behavior." *Sex Roles* 56: 565–576.

Cupach, W., and Canary, D. (1995). "Managing conflict and anger: Investigating the sex stereotype hypothesis." In P. Kalbfleisch and M. Cody (eds.), *Gender, Power, and Communication in Human Relationships* (pp. 233–252). Hillsdale, NJ: Lawrence Erlbaum.

DeFrancisco, V. (1991). "The sounds of silence: How men silence women in marital relations." *Discourse and Society* 2: 413–423.

Eagly, A., and Johnson, B. (1990). "Gender and leadership style: A meta-analysis." *Psychological Bulletin* 108: 233–256.

Eagly, A., and Karau, S. (1991). "Gender and the emergence of leaders: A meta-analysis." *Journal of Personality and Social Psychology* 60: 687–710.

Fletcher, J. (1999). *Disappearing Acts: Gender, Power and Relational Practice at Work*. Cambridge, MA: MIT Press.

Fletcher, J., Jordan, J., and Miller, J. (2000). "Women and the workplace: Applications of a psychodynamic theory." *American Journal of Psychoanalysis* 60: 243–261.

Gayle, B., Preiss, R., and Allen, M. (1998). "Embedded gender expectations: A covariate analysis of conflict situations and issues." *Communication Research Reports* 15: 379–387.

Gray, J. (1992). *Men Are from Mars, Women Are from Venus*. New York: HarperCollins.

Harris, J. (1998). *The Nurture Assumption*. New York: Simon and Schuster/Free Press.

Heath, D. (1991). *Fulfilling Lives: Paths to Maturing and Success*. San Francisco: Jossey-Bass.

Heilbrun, A. (1986). "Androgyny as a type and androgyny as a behavior: Implications for gender schema in males and females." *Sex Roles* 14: 123–139.

Helgesen, S. (1990). *The Female Advantage: Women's Ways of Leadership*. New York: Doubleday.

Hines, M. (1992, April 19). [Untitled report]. *Health Information Communication Network* 5: 2.

Hocker, J., and Wilmot, W. (1991). *Interpersonal Conflict* (3rd ed.). Dubuque, IA: Brown Publishers.

Hollands, J. (2001). *Same Game, Different Rules: How to Get Ahead Without Being a Bully Broad, Ice Queen, or Other Ms. Understood*. New York: McGraw-Hill.

Johnson, F. (1996). "Friendships among women: Closeness in dialogue." In J. Wood (ed.), *Gendered Relationships* (pp. 79–94). Mountain View, CA: Mayfield.

Kanter, R. (1977). *Men and Women of the Corporation*. New York: Basic.

Leaper, C. (1996). "The relationship of play activity and gender to parent and child sex-typed communication." *International Journal of Behavioral Development* 19: 689–703.

Lunneborg, P. (1990). *Women Changing Work*. Westport, CT: Greenwood.

Maltz, D., and Borker, R. (1982). "A cultural approach to male-female miscommunication." In J. J. Gumpertz (ed.), *Language and Social Identity* (pp. 196–216). Cambridge, UK: Cambridge University Press.

Mulac, A. (1998). "The gender-linked language effect: Do language differences really make a difference?" In D. Canary and K. Dindia (eds.), *Sex Differences and Similarities in Communication: Critical Essays and Empirical Investigations of Sex and Gender in Interaction* (pp. 127–153). Mahwah, NJ: Erlbaum.

Natalle, E. (1996). "Gendered issues in the workplace." In J. T. Wood (ed.), *Gendered Relationships* (pp. 253–274). Mountain View, CA: Mayfield.

Otten, A. (1995, January 27). "Women and men still see things differently." *Wall Street Journal*, p. B1.

Payne, C. (1989). "Ella Baker and models of social change." *Signs: Journal of Women in Culture and in Society* 14: 885–899.

Powell, G. (1993). *Women and Men in Management*. Newbury Park, CA: Sage.

Rosener, J. (1990). "Ways women lead." *Harvard Business Review* 68: 119–125.

Salazar, A., Hirokawa, R., Propp, K., Julian, K., and Leatham, G. (1994). "In search of true causes: Examination of the effect of group potential and group interaction on decision performance." *Human Communication Research* 20: 529–559.

Staley, C. (1988). "The communicative power of women managers: Doubts, dilemmas, and management development programs." In C. Valentine and N. Hoar (eds.), *Women and Communicative Power: Theory, Research, and Practice* (pp. 36–48). Anandale, VA: Speech Communication Association.

Sternberg, R., and Soriano, L. (1984). "Styles of conflict resolution." *Journal of Personality and Social Psychology* 47: 115–126.

Tannen, D. (1990). *You Just Don't Understand: Women and Men in Conversation.* New York: Morrow.

——. (1995). *Talking 9 to 5: Women and Men in the Workplace.* New York: Avon.

Valian, V. (1998). *Why So Slow? The Advancement of Women.* Boston: MIT Press.

Wheelan, S., and Verdi, A. (1992). "Differences in male and female patterns of communication in groups: A methodological artifact?" *Sex Roles* 27: 1–15.

Wilkins, B., and Andersen, P. (1991). "Gender differences and similarities in management communication." *Management Communication Quarterly* 5: 6–35.

Wood, J. (2002). "A critical response to John Gray's Mars and Venus portrayals of men, women and relationships." *Southern Communication Journal* 67: 201–210.

——. (2003). *Gendered Lives: Communication, Gender and Culture,* (5th ed.). Belmont, CA: Wadsworth.

Wood, W., and Karten, S. (1986). "Sex differences in interaction styles as a product of perceived sex differences in competence." *Journal of Personality and Social Psychology* 50: 341–347.

Wyatt, N. (2002). "Foregrounding feminist theory in group communication research." In L. Frey (ed.), *New Directions in Group Communication* (pp. 43–56). Thousand Oaks, CA: Sage.

Zorn, T., and Murphy, B. (1996). "Gendered interaction in professional relationships." In J. Wood (ed.), *Gendered Relationships* (pp. 213–232). Mountain View, CA: Mayfield.

Chapter 20
Communication in the Multicultural Group

Richard E. Porter
Larry A. Samovar

This chapter begins by explaining what culture is and how it impacts both perception and social interaction in groups. The authors then use specific examples to demonstrate how culture modifies and influences messages, displays of emotion, use of time, negotiation styles, and pace of communication in small group settings. Porter and Samovar conclude by discussing problems associated with racial, ethnic, and gender prejudice by looking at differences in cultural perceptions and values.

Today in the United States we find numerous cultures and co-cultures. Indeed, the United States is emerging rapidly as a diverse multicultural society. Some cultures are based on race: Black, Hispanic, Oriental, and Native American. Others are based on ethnic differences: Jew, Italian, German, Cambodian, and Mexican are but a few of the many ethnic cultures we find in the United States. There are also cultures based on socioeconomic differences. The culture of a Rockefeller or a Kennedy is vastly different from that of a third-generation welfare family living in Detroit. The magnitude of cultural diversity in the United States can be seen in New York City where 185 different countries are represented with substantial populations. It is also seen in the California public schools where there is no longer a majority segment of the population. Whites account for 49 percent of the student population while people of color account for 51 percent. Of that 51 percent, 31 percent are Hispanic, 9 percent are Black, and 11 percent Asian.[1] These statistics strongly suggest that intercultural contact is inevitable.

Furthermore, court decisions and legislative actions have forced increased intercultural contact. Equal opportunity and affirmative action employment practices, desegregation and integration of public schools, and the establishment of minority quotas for admission to unions, colleges, universities, and graduate and professional schools have increased intercultural contact.

Changes in immigration patterns have shifted segments of the world population. People from Vietnam, Cambodia, Laos, Cuba, Haiti, Colombia, Nicaragua, El Salvador, and Ecuador, among others, have entered the United States and become our neighbors. As these people try to adjust their lives to this culture, there are many opportunities for intercultural contacts in our daily lives.

Almost every facet of our lives finds us increasingly in the presence of and having greater awareness of others who are culturally different. Contacts with cultures that often appear unfamiliar, alien, and at times mysterious may now be a part of our day-to-day routine. We are no longer isolated from one another in time and space. Instead, we face each other on a daily basis.

With this momentum toward multiculturalism comes a cultural diversity that in the past has not received adequate recognition. If our society is to be one of peace where all people are accorded respect and dignity, we must learn to interact successfully with culturally diverse people.

Successful interaction within culturally diverse settings requires that we develop a facility for intercultural communication and learn to use it in a wide variety of communication situations. One of these situations, and the one we will examine, is the small group. Before considering this, however, brief attention will be given to the relationships between culture and communication.

Culture and Communication

The link between culture and communication is crucial to understanding intercultural communication because it is through the influence of culture that people learn to communicate. A Japanese, an Austrian, or an American learns to communicate like other Japanese, Austrians, or Americans. Their behavior conveys meaning because it is learned and shared; it is cultural. People perceive their world through categories, concepts, and labels that are products of their culture.

Culture

Culture is an all-encompassing form or pattern for living that is acquired through the process of being born into and raised in a particular society. Culture is complex, abstract, and pervasive. It impacts on many aspects of human social and communicative activity. Cultures develop around ways of life and value systems. Religious, philosophical, political, economic, and social role views may differ greatly from our own, as may communities, modes of life, forms of work, degrees of industrialization, and social organization. In these cases, we find people are noticeably different from ourselves in their ways of life, customs, and traditions. Even within dominant cultures we find diversity among co-cultures. Members of the drug culture, for instance, share values and perceptions of the world that are quite different than those shared by members of the white supremacy movement, gay community, or feminist movement.

Perception

One of culture's most significant effects is on the perceptual process. In its simplest sense, *perception is the internal process by which we select, evaluate, and organize the external environment*. In other words, perception is the conversion of the physical energies of our environment into meaningful experience. A number of corollary issues arise out of this definition that help explain the relationship between perception and culture. It is believed generally that people behave as they do because of the ways in which they perceive the world, and that these behaviors are learned as part of their cultural experiences. Whether in judging beauty or describing snow, we respond to stimuli as we do primarily because our culture has taught us to do so. We tend to notice, reflect on, and respond to those elements in our environment that are important to us. In the United States we might respond principally to a thing's size and cost while to the Japanese, color might be the important criterion. Culture tends to determine which are the important criteria of perception.

Cultural similarity in perception makes the sharing of meaning possible. The ways in which we communicate, the circumstances of our communication, the language and language style we use, and our nonverbal behaviors are primarily all responses to and functions of our culture. As cultures differ from one another, the communication practices and behaviors of individuals reared in those cultures will also be different.

Social Perception

Social perception is the process by which we construct our unique social realities by attributing meaning to the social objects and events we encounter in our environments. It is an extremely important aspect of communication. Culture conditions and structures our perceptual processes so that we develop culturally inspired perceptual sets. These sets not only help determine which external stimuli reach our awareness, but more importantly, they significantly influence the social aspect of perception—the social construction of reality by the attribution of meaning to these stimuli. The difficulties in communication caused by this perceptual variability can best be lowered by knowing about and understanding the cultural factors that are subject to variation and honestly and sincerely desiring to communicate successfully across cultural boundaries.

Intercultural Communication

The difficulties that cultural diversity poses for effective communication have given rise to the marriage of culture and communication and to the recognition of intercultural communication. Inherent in this fusion is the idea that intercultural communication entails the investigation of culture and the difficulties of communicating across cultural boundaries.

To help us understand what is involved in intercultural communication, we begin with a fundamental definition. *Intercultural communication is defined as a communication situation in which a message produced in one culture must be processed in another culture.* In other words, whenever a person who is a member of one culture sends a message—whether verbal or nonverbal, spoken or written—to someone who is a member of another culture, both are engaged in intercultural communication.

Intercultural communication can best be understood as cultural diversity in the perception of social objects and events. A central tenet of this position is that minor communication problems are often exaggerated by perceptual diversity. To understand the worlds and actions of others, we must try to understand their perceptual frames of reference. We must learn to understand how they perceive the world. In the ideal intercultural encounter we would hope for many overlapping experiences and a commonality of perceptions. Cultural diversity, however, tends to introduce us to dissimilar experiences, and hence, to varied and frequently strange and unfamiliar perceptions of the external world.

Communication Context

Any communicative interaction takes place within some social and physical context. When people are communicating within their culture they are usually aware of the context and it does little to hinder the communication. When people are engaged in intercultural communication, however, the context in which that communication takes place can have a strong impact. Unless both parties to intercultural communication are aware of how their culture affects the contextual element of communication, they can be in for some surprising communication difficulty.

We begin with the assumption that communicative behavior is governed by rules. By a rule, we mean a principle or regulation that governs conduct and procedure. In communication, rules act as a system of expected behavior patterns that organize interaction between individuals. Communication rules are both culturally and contextually bound. Although the social setting and situation may determine the type of rules that are appropriate, the culture determines the rules. In Iraq, for instance, a contextual rule prohibits females from having unfamiliar males visit them at home. In the United States, however, it is not considered socially inappropriate for unknown males to visit females at home. Rules dictate behavior by establishing appropriate responses to stimuli for a particular communication context.

Communication rules include both verbal and nonverbal components. The rules determine not only what should be said but how it should be said. Nonverbal rules apply to proper gestures, facial expressions, eye contact, proxemics, vocal tone, and body movements.

Unless one is prepared to function in the contextual environment of another culture, he or she may be in for an unpleasant experience. The intercultural situation can be one of high stress both physically and mentally. The effects of this stress may result in culture shock. In order to avoid culture shock, it is necessary to have a full understanding of communication context and how it varies culturally. We must remember that cultural contexts are neither right nor wrong, nor better nor worse; they are just different.

Intercultural Communication Within Multicultural Groups

Small group communication settings involve intercultural communication when a group is composed of people from diverse cultural backgrounds. This quite naturally occurs in international settings when people from various countries and cultures meet to discuss international politics, economics, and business. We may also find it in domestic areas when civic bodies attempt to solve problems within the community or when students representing various ethnic and racial backgrounds meet to recommend school policies and actions.

Small group communication is a complex process involving highly complicated interrelationships between many dynamic elements. The sharing of common goals or purposes, a social organization, the establishment of communication channels and the sharing of relevant beliefs and values are all recognized necessary ingredients for the emergence of a group and the development of an atmosphere suitable for small group communication. In general, a certain similarity between people is necessary for the creation of this atmosphere and the development of what Fisher calls *groupness*.[2] Successful small group formation and communication are difficult enough when group members are culturally similar, but when members are culturally diverse, the task may become formidable.

Intercultural small group communication occurs in both international and domestic settings. In either setting, however, successful intercultural communication is dependent on both a desire to communicate successfully and a recognition of cultural influences on communication processes.

A further aspect of culture that can have a significant effect on multicultural small group communication is what anthropologist Edward T. Hall has identified as the context dimension of culture.[3] According to this view, cultures vary along a context dimension that ranges from low to high. What this refers to as far as communication is concerned is the amount of shared cultural knowledge and background the communicators possess. Hall states:

> Any transaction can be characterized as high-, low-, or middle-context. HC transactions feature preprogrammed information that is in the receiver and in the setting, with only minimal information

in the transmitted message. LC transactions are the reverse. Most of the information must be in the transmitted message in order to make up for what is missing in the context.[4]

An example of where various cultures lie along the context dimension can be seen in Table 20.1.

Table 20.1
High- and Low-Context Cultures in Order
High-Context Cultures[5]

	Japanese
	Arab
	Greek
	Spanish
	Italian
	English
	French
	American
	Scandinavian
	German
	German-Swiss

Low-Context Cultures

In high-context cultures most of the information is either in the physical context or is internalized in the people who are a part of the interaction. In low-context cultures, however, most of the information is contained in the verbal message and very little is embedded in the context or within the participants. High-context cultures such as Japan, Korea, and Taiwan tend to be more aware of their surroundings and their environment and do not rely on verbal communication as their main information source. The Korean language contains a word *nunchi* that literally means being able to communicate through your eyes. In high-context cultures, so much information is available in the environment that it is unnecessary to state verbally that which is obvious. Oral statements of affection, for instance, are very rare because it is not necessary to restate what is communicated nonverbally. When the context says "You are welcome here," it is not necessary to state it orally.

This notion of context poses problems when members of a small group are from cultures that differ in context level. When we meet with members of high-context cultures, unless we have the requisite contextual programming, we are liable to have difficulty in communicating because the high-context messages do not contain sufficient information for us to gain true or complete meaning. What is worse, we may interpret a high-context message according to our low-context disposition and reach entirely the wrong meaning.

There are four aspects of cultural context that can affect multicultural small group discussion. First, verbal messages are extremely important in low-context cultures. It is in the verbal message that the information to be shared is coded. It is not readily available from the environment because people in low-context cultures do not tend to learn how to perceive the environment for information. Second, low-context people who rely primarily on verbal messages for information are perceived as less attractive and less credible by people from high-context cultures. Third, people in high-context cultures are more adept at reading nonverbal behavior and the environment. Fourth, people in high-context cultures have an expectation that others are also able to understand the unarticulated communication; hence, they do not speak as much as people from low-context cultures.

A consequence of cultural context can be seen by comparing Asian and American communication patterns. Asians usually assess the feelings and state of mind of those present. The harmony of the group is paramount, and they do not want to do anything that would lessen that harmony. Thus, they tend to give their opinions in an indirect manner.[6] Asiatic modes of communication can be labeled as defensive and situational. Their conversation often stops abruptly, or the subject is changed without obvious reason, as soon as a speaker feels that the listener does not agree totally with the expressed point of view or that feelings may have been hurt.[7]

On the other hand, Americans tend to be task oriented, direct, and businesslike. They want to get immediately to the heart of the matter. They depreciate what are considered to be irrelevant concerns such as individual feelings and urge immediate action to get the job done.

Cultural diversity in the concept of time can also affect multicultural small group communication. In American, Australian, German, English, Israeli, Swiss, and Scandinavian cultures, for example, time is treated as a valuable, tangible, and limited resource. Like money, time is saved, wasted, given, taken, made, spent, run out of, and budgeted. Because time is so valuable, it is used productively, and is compartmentalized into efficient intervals of activity.[8] In Oriental countries, such as Japan, China, and Korea, as well as Middle Eastern countries such as Saudi Arabia and Latin American countries such as Mexico, Brazil, and Chile, the cultural rules specify that people take their time before becoming engaged in activity. In many of these countries, meetings begin with extended social acquaintance and the establishment of social rapport over many cups of coffee or tea. The development of an extended social acquaintance does not mean five or ten minutes. It may take hours or perhaps even several meetings during which the group task may not even be mentioned in order to establish an appropriate social climate.

This diversity in the use of time can be frustrating to the American who is culturally biased toward rapid activity and being engaged. Americans work by deadlines, and once given a deadline, they race to meet or beat it. Giving a task a deadline heightens its importance and creates a sense of urgency. Deadlines elsewhere, however, may produce opposite results. An Arab may take a deadline as an insult. Arabs consider the drinking of coffee and chatting as doing something whereas the American sees it as doing nothing. Ethiopians attach prestige to things that take a long time.[9]

Culture also governs the process by which negotiation takes place. Perceptions of both the concept and the process differ culturally. For instance, in the Persian language the word for compromise does not mean a midway solution that both sides can accept as it does in English; instead, it means surrendering one's principles. Also, a mediator is seen as a meddler, someone who is bargaining uninvited. In India and the Middle East the process of negotiation is enjoyed. Negotiation is seen as an act of bargaining in which there is give and take. Each person sets out to obtain the best deal he or she can, and most enjoy the process of striking a bargain. The influence of Islam gives the Saudi businessman a strong sense of honor and of personal dignity. Although Saudis are often tough and skilled negotiators, an agreement will be honored to the letter. The same, of course, is expected in return.

The pace of conversation is another culturally influenced communication variable that can affect multicultural group communication. Asians prefer a reflective or slow pace. They often let other group members begin so that they can respond to arguments and set the pace once the other side has had its say. The Chinese are prone to seem passive and ask a lot of questions. They probe for information and conceal any eagerness they may feel. They listen carefully and give subtle hints about their requirements for reaching group consensus. The French and Koreans prefer to give their arguments first and then their conclusions. Americans begin with their position and then develop the evidence to support it. Chinese and Japanese tend to be very detail oriented, while Americans like to develop the big picture. Americans often are not trusted by members of other cultures because they omit perceived essential details.

Cultural diversity in rhetorical practices also influences the multicultural group. In Mexico and many Middle Eastern countries, people are selected to participate in multicultural groups because of their rhetorical skills. Among Arabs, "strong manhood is coextensive with strong rhetoric."[10] Educated and illiterate alike have extraordinary mastery of their language expressed through a rich vocabulary and well-rounded, complex phrases. In Western countries, gender is no longer much of a factor, but in Middle Eastern and Asian countries where women have little status, participants are nearly always men.

Another problem we may face in intercultural small group communication is the actual communication process itself. This is readily seen if we examine the differences in approach between Americans and Japanese. We Americans want to talk to the one in authority who can make tough decisions. We want to get down to business and drive a hard bargain, and we want answers now. We are busy; time is money, and we cannot fool around. The Japanese, however, are quite different in their approach. "If we were to place Japanese concepts of self and group at one end of a continuum it would be possible to produce an almost perfect paradigm by placing American concepts at the other."[11] In other words, Japanese concepts of self and group are essentially the opposite of our own. Some distinctions between American and Japanese concepts will be discussed in order to see how different approaches to group interaction influence communication.

Americans tend to view groups as being composed of individuals, in which the role of the individual is paramount. This concern with the individual is reflected in the American culture through admiration of "rugged individualism" and the desire to interact with the responsible party. The Japanese, on the other hand, have a selfless view of groups. The group is the social entity; individual identity is submerged for group identity.

This distinction between the concept of self in relation to groups is important in terms of decision making and the outcomes of intercultural negotiation. The American concept of individual importance leads to a notion of individual responsibility. A single, unique person is ultimately responsible for decisions and their consequences. This individual is also expected to accept blame for decisions that lead to bad consequences. In a sense, Americans want to know who to "hang" when things go wrong. The Japanese, however, operate in a group sense rather than an individual sense. Decisions result from group interaction and group consensus; the group, not the individual, is responsible for the consequences of its action, and when something goes wrong the group, not the individual, is held responsible. The extremes of this position are aptly described by Cathcart and Cathcart:

> This embodiment of group can be carried to the point where, in the extreme circumstances, those persons at the top of the group hierarchy feel constrained to answer for the misdeed of individual group members by committing *harikiri* (suicide) in order to erase the blot on the group's honor. The act of *harikiri* reflects a total denial of self and a complete loyalty to the group.[12]

Contrast this in your imagination, if you will. Can you imagine the president of a top U.S. corporation committing suicide because a machine shop supervisor made a poor decision that adversely affected profits and angered stockholders and customers?

In discussing the international dimension of intercultural communication, we have reviewed several cultural differences that might be found among participants in multicultural group interaction. The point here is to emphasize how culture affects our participation in small group communication and how it may influence our behaviors and the meanings—both social and literal—that we attribute to other people and to their messages.

Much of what we have viewed may seem trivial; to others, however, these matters are very important. If we are to be successful intercultural communicators, we must realize how seemingly insignificant matters can affect the dynamics of our intercultural groups.

When we shift our interest to the domestic dimension of intercultural communication, we are still faced with the problems of cultural diversity but in a way that frequently manifests itself in terms of trust, values, and expectations.

Inherent in a culturally diverse community are problems of racial, ethnic, and gender prejudice. There are many members of

the community who have grown up with negative beliefs about other races and ethnic backgrounds as well as the role and place of women. This is not a perception peculiar only to white Anglos; it is common across races and ethnic groups. This diversity in experience can lead to differences in ideas about who can be trusted. In an ideal group situation, everyone trusts each other; they do not feel that someone will try to do them harm. In many multicultural settings, though, the situation is different. Some people, because of their previous experiences and current expectations, may sense that others cannot be trusted, that they will ultimately harm or cheat them.

Frequently, culturally diversified groups are found when civic bodies or panels are formed. In this case the first effort is often to empanel as members a priest, a minister, a rabbi, a Black, an Oriental, and a Hispanic as well as women and representatives of other diverse groups within the community such as gays, civil libertarians, youth, welfare recipients, and senior citizens. However admirable this effort may be in terms of democratic institutions, it can result in artificially created groups whose compositions defy the formation of an atmosphere conducive to the cohesiveness and member satisfaction that are necessary for the feeling of "groupness" mentioned earlier. This is especially the case when there are culturally diverse values, beliefs, and attitudes. Whereas a natural group—one formed through the ongoing process of group dynamics—is composed of members who share similar relevant values, beliefs, and attitudes. Artificial groups—those we form by administrative action—may be composed of persons who have diverse value systems and who distrust or even dislike the cultural systems of each other. Toleration may be practiced, but it may not overcome differences in basic beliefs and values that influence the outcome of group interaction.

The value systems of people engaged in small group communication get in the way of their achieving consensus or agreement on an issue at times. When group members are from different cultures, this variance often amplifies the problem because of the influence culture has on the development of values. As cultural diversity increases, the chance of value conflict also increases. This aspect is especially a problem in final phases of discussions when decisions are being made. An example from a group-discussion class illustrates this point. A group had been formed at the beginning of the semester to discuss the common interest problem of divorce in the United States. For several weeks everything went well. During the initial phases of the discussion, agreement was easily reached on the nature of the problem, its extent, its effects, and even its causes. When the solution phase of the discussion began, however, difficulty soon developed. One member of the group of South American origin was a deeply devout Catholic. To him, the only possible solution was to make divorce illegal because it was an immoral act that should not be permitted. This alternative was his only answer; he was adamantly opposed to any other possible solution. The result was an initial attempt by other members of the group to communicate with him and attempt to have him modify his position or at least listen to alternatives that could be available to non-Catholics. This effort met with no success, and when it became evident that he would neither alter his position nor listen to other views, he was in effect banished from the group. He became a mere observer where he had once been an active participant; after a short time, he began to miss the discussions altogether. Here was a case where the prevailing belief-value system of the group was too different from his, and it soon became more rewarding for him not to be a member of the group than to continue his group membership. Consequently, he dropped out of the group.

Granted, this is an extreme example, but it does illustrate vividly the situation in which the value system of an individual derived from his cultural heritage was of sufficient strength to prevent him from interacting with his fellow students and to even consider their positions. We also must realize that although Catholicism transcends culture, it is mediated by various cultures. This was one case where the cultural tradition of this man's origin maximized Catholic dogma and made it a very strong part of his value system.

Similar situations can easily arise when we form groups that represent all views and interests within a community. Perhaps it will not always be so severe as to disrupt the group or lead to its disintegration, but it can lead to problems that must be understood and resolved before a group can form its identity and reach consensus. We must remember that some views are not compatible with others, just as some interests are not compatible with others. When diverse views and interests are forced to interact, the outcome may not be what is expected or desired, and may ultimately frustrate attempts to obtain representative views in the formulation of community policies.

In a multicultural community there are also problems of language differences. Because many people are new to the United States, they may have difficulty with the English language; they may not speak English or may not speak it sufficiently. Their command of the language may be inadequate, which can result in misunderstandings. Suspicion and feelings of uneasiness can develop when some members of the community speak a language that cannot be understood by others. The presence of diverse languages can create feelings of resentment among those who do not understand the languages being spoken.

Cultural differences in nonverbal behavior can also lead to difficulty in the multicultural group. It might be in the form of dress and appearance: A Black wearing a cornrow hairstyle or a Hindu wearing a turban can cause people to feel strange because they do not understand the self-significance of a person's appearance. Diverse nonverbal behavior may also be expressed in forms of greeting that employ special handshakes or embraces. Again, that which is different is viewed suspiciously.

Summary

Here we have emphasized the view that the chief problem in intercultural communication lies in social perception. We have suggested that culture strongly influences social perception, which leads to errors in the interpretation of messages. If there is to be successful intercultural communication within small groups in both domestic and international arenas, we must be aware of the cultural factors that affect communication in both our own cultures and the cultures of others. We must understand both cultural differences and cultural similarities. Understanding differences can help us recognize problems, and understanding similarities can help us become closer.

Notes

1. N. S. Mehta, S. Monroe, and D. Winbush, "Beyond the Melting Pot." *Time.* April 9, 1990, 28–31.

2. B. A. Fisher, *Small Group Decision Making Communication and the Group Process* (New York: McGraw-Hill, 1976).

3. Edward T. Hall, *Beyond Culture* (Garden City, NY: Doubleday, 1976).

4. Hall, 101.

5. L. Copeland and L. Griggs, *Going International: How to Make Friends and Deal Effectively in the Global Marketplace* (New York: Random House, 1985).

6. Jan Servaes, "Cultural Identity in East and West." *Howard Journal of Communications* 1 (1988), 68.

7. Servaes, 68.

8. Copeland and Griggs, 8.

9. Copeland and Griggs, 9.

10. R. Patai, *The Arab Mind*, rev. ed. (New York: Scribner's, 1983), 49.

11. D. Cathcart and R. Cathcart, "Japanese Social Experience and Concepts of Group." In L. Samovar and R. Porter (eds.), *Intercultural Communication: A Reader* 2d ed. (Belmont, CA: Wadsworth, 1976), 58.

12. Cathcart and Cathcart, 59–60.

Reprinted from: Richard E. Porter and Larry A. Samovar, "Communication in the Multicultural Group." In R. S. Cathcart, L. A. Samovar, and L. D. Henman (eds.), *Small Group Communication: Theory & Practice*, Seventh Edition. Published by Brown & Benchmark. Copyright © 1996 by Times Mirror Higher Education Group, Inc. Reprinted by permission of the authors. ✦

Chapter 21

Cross-Cultural and Intercultural Work Group Communication

John G. Oetzel
Mary Meares
Akiko Fukumoto

In this chapter the authors compare how Americans and Japanese engage in group work. They provide ample research evidence and realistic scenarios to support their claim that Americans tend to focus on task communication rather than relational communication, distribute turns unequally, use low-context communication, resolve conflicts with either cooperative or competitive approaches, and use majority-rule decision making. In contrast, Japanese tend to focus on relational communication more than task communication, distribute turns equally, use high-context communication, try to avoid conflicts, and engage in consensus decision making. The authors conclude that an awareness of cultural and communication differences between Japanese and Americans increases everyone's chances of creating and maintaining a constructive work group climate when participating in groups composed of Japanese and American members.

Japanese and Americans[1] have frequent workplace and academic interactions. Japan is the second leading import partner and the third leading export partner of the United States (Central Intelligence Agency 2000). In addition, 2,126 manufacturers have both Japanese and American affiliations (Japan External Trade Association 2001). There is extensive contact in schools as well, as Japanese students constitute the second-largest group of foreign students studying in the United States (NAFSA 2001). As a result of these factors, Japanese and Americans often find themselves working together in groups on a regular basis. It is therefore important to understand how these two cultures[2] influence communication in work groups.[3]

The purpose of this chapter is to describe how Japanese and American cultural backgrounds influence work group communication in homogeneous and culturally diverse groups. Homogeneous groups are composed of people with similar cultural backgrounds (i.e., all Japanese or all Americans), whereas culturally diverse groups are composed of people with different cultural backgrounds (i.e., both Japanese and Americans). The chapter is organized into three sections. First, we describe some cultural differences and similarities between Japan and the United States. Second, we compare work group communication in these two countries that results from their cultural backgrounds. Finally, we note how cultural differences affect work group communication in culturally diverse groups composed of both Japanese and Americans.

Comparing the Cultures of Japan and the United States

Cultures differ in numerous ways. One of the most popular approaches to understanding cultural differences is to identify dimensions of cultural variability that can be measured relative to various cultures. These dimensions are *etic* meanings. Etic meanings refer to culture-general ideas or behaviors that can be compared and contrasted between cultures. In contrast, *emic* meanings are culture-specific ideas or behaviors. These meanings are best represented by specific terms that are unique to a particular culture and do not have a direct comparison with other cultures. In this section, we describe four etic differences and include several emic examples to illustrate subtle variations of these general dimensions. The four etic differences are *individualism-collectivism, power distance, uncertainty avoidance,* and *face concerns.* These dimensions are the distinctions most useful for explaining work group communication differences between Japan and the United States.

We want to put forth one caveat before continuing. It is important to understand that while this chapter focuses on general cultural and communication differences between Japanese and American work groups, individuals from a given culture may have a unique, subjective interpretation of their culture and thus may have a unique communication style that varies considerably from the general patterns of that culture. For example, a U.S. national may not strongly identify with his or her culture and thus may not communicate in a manner consistent with U.S. cultural values.

Individualism-Collectivism

Individualism is a social pattern that consists of loosely linked individuals who view themselves as independent of collectives and who give priority to their personal goals over the goals of others (Triandis 1995). *Collectivism* is a social pattern consisting of closely linked individuals who see themselves as part of one or more collectives (family, co-workers, tribe, nation) and are willing to give priority to the goals of these collectives over their own personal goals (Triandis). In essence, members of collectivistic cultures draw on a "we" identity, while members of individualistic cultures draw on an "I" identity (Ting-Toomey 1988). Members of collectivistic cultures are concerned with maintaining relational harmony with members of their ingroups, whereas members of individualistic cultures emphasize self-realization and individuality.

Hofstede (1991) found that the United States was the most individualistic culture—out of 53 studied—and that Japan was much more collectivistic than the United States.

Overall, Japan is considered a moderately collectivistic culture. An important value for Japanese is *wa*, which can be roughly translated into English as harmony or purity, although there is no exact translation (Gudykunst and Nishida 1994). Communication in Japanese groups tends to avoid direct confrontation that would destroy the harmony and positive feelings in the group. The group and the feelings of collective cohesion and harmony are more important than the need for self-expression and individuality. In contrast, Americans are encouraged to express their individual ideas even when they are in conflict with others in a group. This strong individualistic expression can be difficult to reconcile with group harmony.

Differences in individualism and collectivism can also be seen in the differing cultural attitudes toward dependence. Americans often see themselves as independent and separate from others. Dependence and "co-dependence" are seen as limiting individual development and potential. Americans, although usually part of interdependent work and family groups, often express a fear of being part of a collective and losing individuality. Japanese, in contrast, value *amae*, or dependence on others (Gudykunst and Nishida 1994). Trusting, dependent relationships are valued and seen as a positive, cohesive bond in Japan.

Power Distance

Power distance is "the extent to which the less powerful members of institutions and organizations within a country expect and accept that power is distributed unequally" (Hofstede 1991, 28). Power distance includes attitudes about authority and relationships with authority figures. While all nations have a level of hierarchy in their society and organizations, some nations choose to de-emphasize hierarchy, and others find hierarchy necessary and even comforting. Individuals in large-power distance cultures emphasize status distinctions between members in a hierarchy. Managers, parents, and elected officials are highly respected and their position affords them a high status. As a result, subordinates do not question the authority of superiors, and superiors are benevolent leaders who make decisions for the well-being of the subordinates. In contrast, individuals in small–power distance cultures tend to minimize status differences among members in a hierarchy. As a result, decision making is shared with subordinates, and subordinates may disagree and challenge superiors in appropriate situations (e.g., when the superior makes a bad decision).

Hofstede (1991) found that there is a slight difference in the power distance scores of Japanese and Americans. Japan is classified as a large–power distance country and the United States is classified as a small–power distance country. However, the difference between the two countries is slight and thus there are some similarities in status and power. For example, in both countries, achieved status (e.g., monetary success or advancement in a company) is an important characteristic. However, there are differences in how power distance is enacted in the two countries.

In Japan, recognizing status and power difference is very important. In school or in the workplace, individuals with more years of experience are called *senpai* while junior members are *kohai*. Even if the two individuals are at the same rank in an organization, the *kohai* is expected to follow the directions of the *senpai*. Another example of the importance of recognizing status in Japan is the emphasis placed on using titles for superiors. In Japan, individuals address managers with a title such as *kakaricho* (a manager of a branch section), attach titles after a family name (e.g., Tanaka *kakaricho*), or add *san* after the title (e.g., *kakaricho-san*).

Japanese communication practices relevant to individual status contrast with predominant ways of interacting in the United States. For example, U.S. workers typically call superiors by their first names and work under an "open door" policy, where they can share concerns and suggestions with managers. These practices minimize the differences in status between two people rather than emphasize the differences between them.

Uncertainty Avoidance

Uncertainty avoidance is the degree to which people feel threatened by unknown situations and the extent to which they try to avoid those situations (Hofstede 1991). In high–uncertainty avoidance cultures, individuals strive for predictability in their lives. These individuals dislike ambiguity and thus prefer to have formal and written rules guiding behavior during interactions. Further, these individuals view conflict and change as negative and want career stability. In contrast, individuals in low–uncertainty avoidance cultures are less bothered by ambiguity and uncertainty. In fact, uncertainty creates the possibility of change, allowing for individual growth. These individuals like innovation and career change, and view conflict as having potential positive outcomes.

Hofstede (1991) found that Japan is a high uncertainty avoidance culture and the United States is a low uncertainty avoidance culture. The emphasis placed on *meishi*, business cards, can be used to help understand differences between Americans and Japanese with respect to both uncertainty avoidance and power distance. When two people meet for the first time in Japan, business cards are exchanged, not just for contact information but also for the important information about where the other stands in relation to one's own status. The information on status will help an individual reduce uncertainty about the relationship with the new person and determine interaction norms, such as the level of politeness in language and the length and depth of bowing.

Ironically, in some cases, Americans tend to avoid uncertainty more than Japanese, as observed in contracts and job descriptions. Contracts and job descriptions are written in detail, binding the parties involved to specific behaviors. In Japan, contracts and job descriptions are vague and ambiguous (based on U.S. standards) and can be revised and amended as necessary without regarding changes as a "breach of contract" (Yoshikawa 1982). While Japanese tend to seek perfection and precision for status differences and interaction norms, they embrace uncertainty for contracts and job descriptions. While Americans embrace uncertainty for many life situations and interactions, they value precision, clarity, and explicitness with regard to work obligations.

Face

Face is the claimed sense of favorable social self-worth and/or projected other-worth in a public situation (Ting-Toomey and Kurogi 1998). Face is a cluster of identity- and relation-based issues that simmer and surface before, during, and after communication interactions. Essentially, face is about the images we and others present, maintain, threaten, and bargain over. Face is associated with respect, honor, status, reputation, credibility, competence, family/network connection, loyalty, trust, relational indebtedness, and obligation issues.

The etic meaning of face comes from the locus or origin of face: self, other, or mutual. *Self-face* is the concern for one's own image, whereas *other-face* is the concern for another's image. *Mutual-face* is concern for both parties' images or the "image" of the relationship (Ting-Toomey and Kurogi 1998). A recent study illustrated that Americans are more self-face oriented and less other-face oriented than Japanese and that there is no difference in mutual-face concerns (Oetzel et al. 2000). Essentially, Americans are concerned with building up their own self-image, while Japanese are concerned with not causing others to lose face, as well as not having shame placed upon them for behaving inappropriately.

Tatemae and *honne* are concepts that help to illustrate how face influences communication in Japan. *Honne* refers to an individual's true ideas, dreams, and wishes, whereas *tatemae* is the outward presentation of one's self to society, which is bound by cultural standards. Japanese society places restrictions on what is acceptable to present, encouraging people to conform more to the group identity. These restrictions serve to reduce conflict and maintain harmony. Thus individuals are encouraged to use *tatemae* in public, especially during difficult situations

(e.g., conflict), to protect others' face. *Honne* is used in private situations with close friends in order to express true feelings. There is also a distinction between public and private face for Americans, exemplified through such concepts as tact and diplomacy. However, Americans are still encouraged to express their opinions even if they differ from those of others so long as they are presented in a tactful manner. Additionally, an individual who does not display honest feelings in public (e.g., says bad things about someone and then is nice to that person's face) is considered to be "two faced." Essentially, Americans believe that what is said and what is felt should be the same, whereas Japanese believe that it is appropriate in some situations to say something different than what is felt (Condon 1984).

Comparing Work Group Communication in Japanese and American Groups

The differences presented in the previous section lay the foundation for understanding Japanese and U.S. cultures in comparison to one another. These distinctions are important because culture influences the communication that occurs in work groups. In this section, we focus on five types of work group communication that have frequently been examined by earlier researchers: task and relational communication, turn taking, high- and low-context communication, conflict management, and decision-making styles. We define these concepts and identify similarities and differences in the communication patterns of Japanese and American work groups, using the four etic cultural patterns described earlier.

Task and Relational Communication

Group scholars have long recognized that there are two important interrelated dimensions to work groups: task and relational (Bales 1950). The *task* dimension concerns communication that focuses on understanding the goal of the group and accomplishing its work. Communication along the *relational* dimension emphasizes social support and relational maintenance that enhances the cohesiveness of the group. All groups have components of both task and relational communication. However, cultural values influence the way that the group prioritizes task and relational communication (Hofstede 1991; Oetzel and Bolton-Oetzel 1997). Specifically, Japanese tend to emphasize relational communication because of collectivistic values and uncertainty avoidance, whereas Americans tend to emphasize task communication because of individualistic values and uncertainty avoidance about work requirements. Americans like to "get down to business" and focus on task issues as soon as possible. Successful work helps the group members build trust in one another and continue a fruitful working relationship. It also helps to establish clarity about the work to be accomplished. In contrast, Japanese want to establish strong interpersonal relationships before working on tasks or conducting business. For the Japanese, relationship-building is essential at the outset of a group's deliberation for two reasons: First, it facilitates trust-building, and trust is seen as crucial for facilitating open group communication about the work. Second, sound interpersonal relationships among group members provide a framework for understanding each person's role and position in the group.

Turn Taking

Individuals accomplish work during group meetings through the process of turn taking. *Turn taking* refers to the exchange of the roles of speaker and listener in conversation (Duncan and Fiske 1977). A *turn* is an utterance by a single group member that conveys an idea, thought, or opinion. In Japan, group members try to distribute turns equally among all group members to ensure that all participate (Yamada 1990). Additionally, the distinction between turns is very clear, with a noticeable pause between turns. It is important for members to show respect to the other person's ideas by not interrupting and by giving thought to others' ideas and questions. These behaviors are the result of concern for the others' images and helping

all to feel valued during the conversation. In contrast, turns tend to be distributed unequally in the United States. At many meetings, a group has an agenda and the individual (e.g., a leader) who created the agenda will often dominate the discussion. Other group members "grab the floor" when they have something to say. Assertive individuals will talk more during group meetings than unassertive people. Additionally, interruptions in turn taking are common. Individuals who want to add something to the discussion often do so when they are ready, not necessarily when others finish their turn. These behaviors are consistent with individualism, but also with projecting a self-face of intelligence and credibility. That is, individuals will only talk if they have something of value to contribute.

During an actual turn, individuals use a particular style or pattern of communication to convey ideas. *Low-context communication* is meaning or intention conveyed through explicit verbal messages (Hall 1976). Low-context communication is direct, and the speaker is responsible for constructing a clear message that a listener can decode easily. *High-context communication* is meaning or intention conveyed through the context (e.g., social roles or situations) and nonverbal channels (Hall 1976). High-context communication is an indirect verbal mode, and the receiver assumes the responsibility of inferring the correct meaning (i.e., "reading between the lines"). Japanese group members tend to use high-context communication in discussions for several reasons. First, group members are collectivistic, are likely familiar with each other, and thus are skilled at interpreting each other's messages. Second, members want to protect the harmony of the group and thus do not want to directly offer opinions in case the opinions cause dissension. In contrast, Americans tend to use low-context communication because of individualistic and self-face concerns. Group members are unique individuals and no one could possibly know exactly what the others are thinking. They want to make sure that they are clearly understood and thus state opinions and ideas directly.

During group meetings, conflicts are possible as people discuss various ideas. *Conflict* is "the interaction of interdependent people who perceive opposition of goals, aims, and values, and who see the other party as potentially interfering with the realization of these goals" (Putnam and Poole 1987, 552). In high–uncertainty avoidance cultures like Japan, conflict is to be avoided because the outcomes are likely to be negative or at least unknown. In low–uncertainty avoidance cultures like the United States, conflict has the potential to stimulate growth and change. When conflict occurs, the manner in which conflict is managed determines its effect for the group. *Conflict management style* refers to general tendencies or modes of patterned responses to conflict in a variety of antagonistic interactive situations (Ting-Toomey 1997). Avoidance, cooperation, and competion are three predominant conflict management styles in work groups. *Avoidance* involves withdrawing from the issue and not directly addressing a disagreement. *Cooperation* involves considering both parties' interests and trying to find a mutually acceptable resolution to the issue. *Competition* involves putting one's own interests ahead of others in order to "win" the issue.

In the United States, group members tend to use both cooperation and competition during discussions (Oetzel 1998a, 1998b). Cooperation is the ideal, as the group prospers from working together. A well-performing group reflects highly on the individual group members. However, group members will compete if necessary to protect their interests. Avoidance is not a positive option because it does not allow for a thorough evaluation of ideas. These conflict management styles are the result of individualism and self-face concern since the styles focus on protecting individual interests and achieving success. In Japan, group members tend to avoid or cooperate (Oetzel 1998a, 1998b; Ting-Toomey et al. 1991). Avoidance helps to maintain the relational harmony of the group while cooperation facilitates the achievement of group goals. If direct confrontation of points of conflict is required, it

will often take place outside of formal group meetings. Competition is avoided because it threatens others' face and thus the collective.

Decisions are reached throughout a group's existence and can be the primary outcome of many work groups. *Decision-making style* is the manner in which decisions are reached in a group. Examples of decision-making styles include a single person making a decision (e.g., a leader), majority rule, and consensus. In Japan, group decision making is a process of gaining consensus through *nemawashi* (Ju 1994; Stewart 1993). *Nemawashi* literally means trimming a tree's roots prior to transplanting it. A person who initiates a proposal informally discusses the proposal and its implications with others in the group. In these informal, social interactions, the proposal is debated, critiqued, and revised. The purpose of these discussions is to gain support from other members in an effort to achieve consensus. In this manner, the individual initiating the proposal is able to save face because it is better to find out in private that there are problems with the proposal than to lose face in public. Once it is clear that a proposal is acceptable to everyone, a "formal" signing ceremony occurs and group members congratulate each other for doing good work.

In contrast, decisions in American work groups are often reached through direct confrontation about ideas. Proposals are initiated (by anyone in the group, but often by a leader) in the group meetings. There may be a notice (e.g., memo or e-mail) about the proposal, but the meeting is the primary place to discuss the proposal. Members may discuss the idea before the meeting, but primarily to find out what others think about the proposal and not to shape it. At the meeting, the proposal is presented and other group members debate, critique, and make suggestions. Members vote on the proposal, or an amended version of it. If the proposal receives a majority of votes, it is passed. Consensus is strived for, but it is not seen as a realistic goal because of the different opinions that may exist. This process reflects individualistic values and a relatively low-power distance. Specifically, members have the right to say what they feel, and if the proposal is good enough it will pass. Personal relationships, group harmony, and status are secondary concerns in many work group situations.

Intercultural Work Group Communication

The cross-cultural differences in work group communication that we have illustrated have important implications for what occurs in intercultural work groups composed of Japanese and Americans. Research on intercultural or culturally diverse work groups reveals two predominant findings: (a) cultural diversity can benefit work group performance because of the influx of unique ideas and opinions (McLeod, Lobel, and Cox 1996), and (b) cultural diversity can also lead to less effective communication processes because of the different communication styles that result from cultural differences (Cox 1994). The latter phenomenon is called *process difficulty* and is defined as communication processes that potentially interfere with the productivity of a group and that include high levels of conflict and tension, power struggles, lack of cooperation, lack of respect for group members, and inequality in turn taking (Watson and Michaelson 1988). It is important to understand how culture influences work group communication to facilitate group members in being successful. In this section, we explain why process difficulty occurs in culturally diverse groups, describe types of process difficulty in Japanese/U.S. groups, and provide several scenarios to illustrate these difficulties.

Problems, misunderstandings, and conflicts are likely to occur in intercultural groups because individuals tend to rely on norms and practices of interaction from their own cultural perspective (Nadler, Keeshan-Nadler, and Broome 1985). Members from one culture may use communication styles that do not correspond to the styles of members of a different culture. In essence, differences in the cultural backgrounds of the members of intercultural groups are likely to lead to more difficult communication processes than occur in homogeneous groups. These differences potentially create misunderstandings in communication, at least during the initial meetings of a work group. Oetzel (1998a) studied homogeneous and intercultural groups composed of Japanese and Americans working on a hypothetical decision-making task about a student allegedly caught cheating on a test. Oetzel found that the intercultural groups used fewer consensus decisions and had more inequality in the distribution of turns than did the homogeneous groups. These types of process difficulties in diverse groups composed of Japanese and Americans can be explained by examining the differences in cultural values between these two nations. We present three scenarios to illustrate intercultural communication and potential process difficulty in these types of work groups.

Scenario 1: Discussing Suggestions

Four group members, one Japanese and three Americans, worked at a large multinational organization located in the United States. They were developing a proposal for improving the computer networking of the company. One day Yoshi approached Bob with an idea about how to improve the proposal. Yoshi had arrived recently from Japan and decided to share his ideas with Bob, the member of the group with the longest tenure at the organization. Yoshi asked Bob what he thought about the idea. Bob said it sounded good and that he should share it with the rest of the group. At their weekly meeting, the following exchange took place.

Yoshi: . . . so, that is my proposal. What do you think?

Bob: I have some concerns about training costs. What you are proposing will require us to do a lot of new training that I'm not sure we are ready for.

Nicole: I agree with Bob and I'm also concerned whether our server can handle it.

Jose: Yes, I agree as well. However, I have some ideas for altering the proposal so that it can work.

The meeting continued for an hour as the members talked about the proposal and made addendums to it. At the end of the meeting, they were satisfied with the changes and felt the proposal was a great idea. The members appreciated Yoshi's ideas and were happy with his work, as he had "got the ball rolling." However, Yoshi felt hurt by the meeting and was especially angry with Bob because he had encouraged him to bring a "weak" proposal to the meeting and did not even have the courtesy to share his objections outside of the meeting. Rather than confront the other group members, Yoshi asked his supervisor to be assigned to a different work group.

This scenario helps to illustrate differences between Japanese and American cultures with regard to decision making, conflict, and high- and low-context communication. Yoshi practiced *nemawashi* by bringing the proposal to Bob outside of the formal meeting. He was trying to achieve consensus outside of the meeting to avoid direct confrontation and disagreement in the meeting. Additionally, he went to the senior member of the group (the *senpai*) to show respect for the authority that Bob presumably had (i.e., power distance). He expected Bob (as the senior member of the team) to offer advice and revision if they were needed. However, since Bob said to bring it to the meeting, Yoshi felt that the proposal was in good order. In the spirit of individualistic group meetings and the need to refine ideas through discussion and debate, Bob's suggestion to bring the proposal to the meeting meant, "We should discuss the idea and the meeting is an appropriate place." Bob, Mary, and Jose directly disagreed with the proposal because they found flaws in it. Their approach was low-context or direct to make sure their concerns with the proposal were clear and understood by everyone. The counterproposals were not attacks on Yoshi personally but rather on the ideas. Thus they felt they were not attacking Yoshi's face but rather were helping the group to perform well, which would help all involved. Yoshi did not feel this way since his idea was criticized in public rather than privately, violating his expectation of the meeting as a ritual of agreement in the spirit of *wa*, or harmony. Yoshi's response was to avoid the confrontation because of his collectivistic values and desire to protect his and others' face. The other three members directly confronted the conflict and engaged in what they felt was cooperative dialogue to "fix" the proposal. Overall, differences in individualism-collectivism, power distance, and face concerns help to explain the difficulties in communication that occurred in this scenario.

Scenario 2: Deciding on a Group Topic

Four university students were working on a group project. Yoko and Aya are Japanese students studying in the United States, while Anna and Kim are Americans. The group had to come up with a communication intervention to alleviate a social or health concern in the local community. The group was trying to figure out their topic. They had a meeting, where the following conversation took place.

Anna: I think we should focus on health care for the uninsured. (To Aya) What do you think?

Aya: (pauses a few seconds)

Kim: I think that is a good topic, but I wonder if there are some other issues we should be considering.

Yoko: (after a pause of 10 seconds in the conversation) I was reading in the paper yesterday about the dropout problem in local high schools. They reported that

Kim: (interrupting) Yes, that 12 percent of freshman never finish high school.

Anna: (overlapping Kim's statement). That's a great topic. We all have experiences in high school. We can use those. What do you think Aya?

Aya: (pauses a few moments) Hmm.

Kim: Come on Aya. This will be a great topic. I think we can bring a lot of different opinions and um. . . .

Anna: (overlapping Kim's statement) . . . experiences to the topic.

Aya: I guess so.

Anna and Kim: Great. We have a topic.

The meeting ended and Anna and Kim were very excited about the topic. They talked about how Yoko had a great idea and the topic would work out great. They were a little worried about Aya because she did not say much during the meeting. Yoko and Aya were a little concerned as well. Kim and Anna constantly interrupted them and each other for that matter. They also did not allow for careful thought about proposals. Yoko and Aya thought the topic would work fine, but they would have preferred to think and discuss the ideas a little more.

The differences in turn taking are largely the result of individualism-collectivism. Anna and Kim are likely more individualistic and less collectivistic than Aya and Yoko. Anna and Kim are assertive in expressing their views. Anna and Kim took most of the turns and even interrupted to share opinions. In contrast, Aya and Yoko did not take many turns and Aya tended to pause before speaking. Aya's pause likely reflects the fact that she found Anna's questions important and worthy of thought. She was probably surprised when Kim answered the questions directed to her. The differences have caused some confusion in both the Japanese and American students. At this point, both sets of students are not interpreting the others' behavior accurately because of the differences in cultural values.

Scenario 3: The Business Negotiation

In the third scenario, two companies were in a sales negotiation. The U.S. company wanted to sell a new technology to the Japanese company. The U.S. organization sent their two best sales representatives (in terms of sales productivity) to close the deal that had been initiated over e-mail. Malik and Mark met with two senior representatives (Taka Masumoto and Hiroshi Yokochi) of the Japanese company in Japan. Upon arriving at the company, the representatives exchanged business cards and greetings. The two U.S. sales representatives quickly glanced at the cards, put them in their pockets, and bowed to their hosts. The following conversation took place:

Mark: Thanks for meeting with us, Taka and Hiroshi. I am excited about the possibility of working together.

Malik: Yes, it's great to meet you! I think it will be great for both of our companies.

Masumoto: Yokochi-san and I are pleased to meet you. How was your trip?

Malik: Oh, it was great. I slept the whole way. Hey, can we talk about the proposal? I've drawn up a rough plan. The price is excellent.

Yokochi: We are glad you have made it here safely. We've planned a dinner for you this evening and then tomorrow a sightseeing excursion.

Mark: Well, dinner sounds nice, but we really need to get this business plan hammered out. Maybe we can just catch a bite at the hotel and make it a working dinner. We need to get working on this contract.

Masumoto: The Director would like to meet you at dinner and then we can go drinking.

Malik: Drinking? I think we have too much work for that! How about we take care of the contract first and then we can have some fun? My boss has authorized me to make a special deal for you. If we sign the contract, we'll take off 10 percent. Now, what do you think about this?

Yokochi: Perhaps we can talk about it later this week.

Mark: Oh, I think we need to do it as soon as possible. We can relax after the work is done.

The meeting ended shortly thereafter, and after a few days of sightseeing and dinners, Mark and Malik returned home without a sale.

In this situation, Malik and Mark insisted on getting down to business, whereas Masumoto and Yokochi wanted to take some time to get to know the Americans. Getting to know others involves learning about the credibility of the individuals and establishing a relationship of trust. This difference created a conflict that both parties attempted to deal with in their own way. Malik and Mark were very insistent on dealing with the proposal. This pursuit was competitive in order to accomplish their objectives. Further, they wanted to reduce their uncertainty about the contract and whether they were going to make a sale. Masumoto and Yokochi attempted to resolve the conflict by avoiding direct discussion of the conflict and attempting to establish a relationship. The Japanese perspective is one where personal relationships are more important than written contracts.

Additionally, the U.S. company and Mark and Malik did not follow Japanese status norms. First, the company sent individuals of comparatively low status. In Japan, the buyer has more status than the seller (Graham, Kim, Lin, and Robinson 1988), and thus the company should have sent representatives with status at least equal to that of the Japanese representatives. Second, Mark and Malik did not use the business cards appropriately to determine the status of their counterparts and reduce uncertainty about the position of the individuals involved in the negotiation. They used first names when last names and titles would have been more appropriate. Since the negotiation was in Japan and the Japanese were the buyers, the U.S. representatives needed to adjust their behaviors to the Japanese norms and expectations in order to increase their chances of making a sale.

Suggestions for Working in Japanese/ American Intercultural Work Groups

Throughout this chapter, we have illustrated Japanese and American cultures and their influence on work group communication. In the previous section, we illustrated how these cultural differences can cause difficulties in intercultural work groups. We now offer suggestions for improving the quality of communication in Japanese/ American intercultural work groups. The suggestions we offer have specific relevance for Japanese/American groups but also have the potential to benefit members of any intercultural group.

1. Practice mindful observation and interpret communication from people of different cultures from their perspective, not your own. One way to learn to see things from other perspectives is to follow the ODIS formula: *O*bserve, *D*escribe, *I*nterpret, and *S*uspend Evaluation (Ting-Toomey 1999; Ting-Toomey and Oetzel 2001).

   - *Observe* the behavior—Pay attention to the verbal and nonverbal communication of other group members.

   - *Describe* the behavior—Describe what is actually happening, not your explanation for that behavior. For example, in the second scenario, Anna and Kim might have described Aya's behavior as being quiet, not saying anything, and, perhaps might have noted that she avoided looking at them.

   - *Interpret* the behavior—Make a list of possible interpretations. Brainstorm as many reasons as you can for the behavior. For example, (a) Aya could be shy, (b) she might not feel well, (c) she could be uncomfortable speaking English, (d) she could be offended by something Kim or Anna said, (e) she could be uncomfortable with the topics, (f) she could be uncomfortable with the process, (g) she could be used to a slower conversation style with longer pauses, or (h) she could be distracted by something else. Keep going until you run out of possibilities.

   - *Suspend Evaluation.* Based on what you know about the culture, evaluate your list of possible interpretations and choose the one that you think is most likely. You may want to enlist the help of a "cultural informant," someone from that culture (or who is very familiar with the culture) who can help you to understand the behavior and choose the correct interpretation. In this case, Aya may be quiet for a combination of reasons, but probably a different conversation style is a good explanation. Overall, try to avoid evaluating the person's behavior on the basis of your standards.

2. Give the group time to develop and figure out differences and ways to work together. Intercultural groups, no matter which nationalities and cultures are represented, take more time to develop their norms and learn to work together. This time can be frustrating for group members who want to get the group task accomplished, but time is necessary. Communication styles and expectations are different for members of each group, but with patience and awareness, a group culture and norms can be developed through communication with all group members.

3. Seek ways to encourage group participation and cooperation. Americans are often dominant in groups because they come from a more individualistic culture and their norms for communication are to use direct, low-context language. Japanese members, in contrast, may not feel as comfortable participating with direct language and without having had time to consult with other members about the topic. The group members need to learn to monitor their own level of participation and not get carried away with the discussion, thereby excluding the other members. A thoughtful moderator or facilitator (in a formal or informal capacity) can help groups learn to include all voices in discussion and help individuals develop skills in participation and cooperation.

4. Talk about cultural differences. It is important to discuss differences without implying that the others should adapt to your way of doing things. Ask about the expectations of the other group members. For example, in the first scenario, Bob could have said, "I think you should take it to the group and let us debate it. Usually that's the way we develop proposals together." Yoshi could have said, "I'd like to have your opinions before going to the meeting. I'm concerned that the proposal will be shot down. In Japan, we try to talk to individuals before the meeting so we won't have a problem in the meeting." This discussion opens the door to talking about cultural differences and can help prevent conflicts and diffuse tension.

5. Try to expand your repertoire of what you feel comfortable with in group situations. If you are Japanese, you may want to practice talking about tasks before building relationships and being direct. You might want to develop skills and comfort in constructively confronting other team members' ideas in meetings. Try not to be offended when group members are critical of your ideas, but rather see it as a chance to hone the idea. In addition, try to realize that Americans may not be aware of status differences in the same way that you are. Do not be offended if they treat you as an equal in spite of the fact that you have different levels of status.

If you are an American, you might want to try talking to other members in private about proposed work ideas rather than bringing up conflicts in meetings or public spaces. If a Japanese member approaches you outside of a meeting, consider his or her need for resolving potential problems in private. Develop relationships with your Japanese co-workers and work on these relationships before focusing on tasks. Be aware of the importance of status and role in Japanese culture and show respect to high-status individuals. Also, work on being less direct and think about how your criticism may threaten the face concerns of other members of the group.

6. Be aware of individual differences within a culture. All individuals within a culture will not communicate in the same ways. A useful concept that can help illustrate variation within culture is self-construal. *Self-construal* is one's self-image and is composed of an independent and an interdependent self (Markus and Kitayama 1991). The independent construal of self involves the view that an individual is a unique entity with an individuated repertoire of feelings, cognitions, and motivations. In contrast, the *interdependent construal of self* involves an emphasis on the importance of relational connectedness (Markus and Kitayama 1991). Self-construals are similar to the cultural pattern of individualism-collectivism. Gudykunst et al. (1996) argue that the interdependent self-construal predominates in collectivistic cultures and the independent self-construal predominates in individualistic cultures. However, self-construals are based on individual and not cultural assessments. Thus there are independent individuals in Japan and interdependent individuals in the United States. These differences add a layer of complexity for the dynamics that occur in an intercultural work group. Being aware of both the individual and cultural variations will improve your ability to accurately interpret the communication behaviors of fellow group members.

Summary

Japan and the United States are two distinct cultures along the cultural dimensions of individualism-collectivism, power distance, uncertainty avoidance, and face concerns. These cultural dimensions result in different approaches to work group communication. Americans tend to focus more on task communication than on relational communication, to distribute turns unequally, to use low-context communication, to resolve conflicts with either cooperative or competitive approaches, and to use majority decision making. Japanese tend to focus more on relational communication than on task communication, to distribute turns equally, to use high-context communication, to try to avoid conflict, and to use consensus decision making. Three scenarios were presented to help illustrate how these cultural differences result in potential problems when Japanese and Americans interact in the same work group. The challenges and opportunities of intercultural groups are an excellent opportunity to learn more about yourself and your own culture while developing new communication skills. Awareness of cultural and communication differences make it possible to create and maintain a constructive workgroup with positive processes and outcomes for all members.

Notes

1. The term *American* here refers solely to residents of the United States.

2. A *culture* is a population of people with similar attitudes, values, beliefs, and a shared system of knowledge (Triandis, 1995).

3. *Work groups* are groups that perform primarily problem-solving and decision-making tasks. Examples of work group communication include decision-making styles, turn taking, and conflict management.

References

Bales, R. F. (1950). *Interaction Process Analysis: A Method for the Study of Small Groups.* Reading, MA: Addison-Wesley.

Central Intelligence Agency. (2000). *The World Fact Book.* Central Intelligence Agency [On-line]. Available: <http://www.odci.gov/cia/publications/factbook/geos/us.html>

Condon, J. (1984). *With Respect to Japanese.* Yarmouth, ME: Intercultural Press.

Cox, T. H. (1994). *Cultural Diversity in Organizations: Theory, Research, and Practice.* San Francisco: Berret-Koehler.

Duncan, S., and Fiske, D. W. (1977). *Face-to-Face Interaction.* Hillsdale, NJ: Lawrence Erlbaum.

Graham, J. L., Kim, D. K., Lin, C., and Robinson, M. (1988). "Buyer-seller negotiations around the Pacific Rim: Differences in fundamental exchange processes." *Journal of Consumer Research* 15: 48–54.

Gudykunst, W. B., Matsumoto, Y., Ting-Toomey, S., Nishida, T., Kim, K. S., and Heyman, S. (1996). "The influence of cultural individualism-collectivism, self construals, and individual values on communication styles across cultures." *Human Communication Research* 22: 510–543.

Gudykunst, W. B., and Nishida, T. (1994). *Bridging Japanese/North American Differences.* Thousand Oaks, CA: Sage.

Hall, E. T. (1976). *Beyond Culture.* New York: Doubleday.

Hofstede, G. (1991). *Cultures and Organizations: Software of the Mind.* New York: McGraw-Hill.

Japan External Trade Association (2001). *Kunibetsu Gaikyo: Hokubei* [General information: USA] [On-line]. Available: <http://www.jetro.go.jp/re/j/gaikyo>

Ju, Y. (1994). "Supremacy of human relationships: A Japanese organizational model." In B. Kovacic (ed.), *New Approaches to Organizational Communication* (pp. 67–85). Albany, NY: State University of New York Press.

Markus, H. and Kitayama, S. (1991). "Culture and the self: Implications for cognition, emotion, and motivation." *Psychological Review* 2: 224–253.

McLeod, P. L., Lobel, S. A., and Cox, T. H. (1996). "Ethnic diversity and creativity in small groups." *Small Group Research* 27: 248–264.

Nadler, L. B., Keeshan-Nadler, M., and Broome, B. J. (1985). "Culture and the management of conflict situations." In W. Gudykunst, L. Stewart, and S. Ting-Toomey (eds.), *Communication, Culture, and Organizational Processes* (pp. 87–113). Newbury Park, CA: Sage.

NAFSA: Association of International Educators. (2001). *International Education Factsheet.* NAFSA: Association of International Educators [On-line]. Available: <http://www.nafsa.org./advo/facts00. html>

Oetzel, J. G. (1998a). "Culturally homogeneous and heterogeneous groups: Explaining communication processes through individualism-collectivism and self-construal." *International Journal of Intercultural Relations* 22: 135–161.

——. (1988b). "Explaining individual communication processes in homogeneous and heterogeneous groups through individualism-collectivism and self-construal." *Human Communication Research* 25: 202–224.

Oetzel, J. and Bolton-Oetzel, K. (1997). "Exploring the relationship between self-construal and dimensions of group effectiveness." *Management Communication Quarterly* 10: 289–315.

Oetzel, J. G., Ting-Toomey, S., Masumoto, T., Yokochi, Y., Pan, X., Takai, J., Wilcox, R. (2000). Face and facework in conflict: A cross-cultural comparison of China, Germany, Japan, and the United States. Paper presented at the annual meeting of the International Communication Association, Acapulco, Mexico.

Putnam, L. L., and Poole, M. S. (1987). "Conflict and negotiation." In F. M. Jablin, L. L. Putnam, K. H. Roberts, and L. W. Porter (eds.), *Handbook of Organizational Communication* (pp. 549–599). Newbury Park, CA: Sage.

Stewart, L. P. (1993). "Organizational communication in Japan and the United States." In W. B. Gudykunst (ed.), *Communication in Japan and the United States* (pp. 215–248). Albany, NY: State University of New York Press.

Ting-Toomey, S. (1988). "Intercultural conflict style: A face-negotiation theory." In Y. Y. Kim and W. Gudykunst (eds.), *Theories in Intercultural Communication* (pp. 213–235). Newbury Park, CA: Sage.

——. (1997). "Intercultural conflict competence." In W. Cupach and D. Canary (eds.), *Competence in Interpersonal Conflict* (pp. 120–147). New York: McGraw-Hill.

——. (1999). *Communicating Across Cultures.* New York: Guilford Press.

Ting-Toomey, S., Gao, G., Trubisky, P., Yang, Z., Kim, H. S., Lin, S. L., and Nishida, T. (1991). "Culture, face maintenance, and styles of handling interpersonal conflict: A study in five cultures." *International Journal of Conflict Management* 2: 275–296.

Ting-Toomey, S., and Kurogi, A. (1998). "Facework competence in intercultural conflict: An updated face-negotiation theory." *International Journal of Intercultural Relations* 22: 187–225.

Ting-Toomey, S., and Oetzel, J. G. (2001). *Managing Intercultural Conflict Effectively.* Thousand Oaks, CA: Sage.

Triandis, H. (1995). *Individualism and Collectivism.* Boulder, CO: Westview Press.

Watson, W. E., and Michaelson, L. K. (1988). "Group interaction behaviors that affect group performance on an intellective task." *Group and Organizational Studies* 13: 495–516.

Yamada, H. (1990). "Topic management and turn distributions in business meetings: American versus Japanese strategies." *Text* 10: 271–295.

Yoshikawa, M. J. (1982, July). Japanese and American modes of communication and implications for managerial and organizational behavior. A paper presented at the Second International Conference on Communication Theory Eastern and Western Perspectives. Yokohama, Japan.

Part VIII

Analyzing Group Communication

Small group scholars have long recognized the importance of analyzing group communication. Some suggest that the study of group communication can provide an understanding of the relationship between various "input" and "output" variables (Hackman and Morris 1975; Jarboe 1988, 1996; Pavitt 1999). Others maintain that the systematic analysis of group communication can yield important insights about the structure and culture of the group (Bormann 1996; Poole, Seibold, and McPhee 1996), as well as the personality characteristics of its members (Bales 1950, 1970; Bales and Cohen 1979). Perhaps most importantly, the systematic analysis of group communication can provide group members with important information about the effectiveness of their interaction process in group performance outcomes like making a good decision.

While small group scholars acknowledge the importance of analyzing group communication, there is less agreement about how best to go about doing so (Weingart 1997). Some believe that group communication is best analyzed objectively, using trained observers and precisely defined and validated coding schemes. Others advocate the use of discourse analytic methods (such as conversational analysis) to identify the underlying structures and themes embedded in group interaction. Still others believe that ethnomethodological approaches (such as ethnog-

raphy or participant observation) best capture the personal meanings of group members' communicative behaviors.

What Is Method?

Thus far, we have used the term "method" on several occasions but have yet to explain what we mean by it. A *method* is a set of procedures for conducting systematic inquiry (Kaplan 1964). Common methods used to study group communication include observational, experimental, and survey methods. Each of these methods consists of a set of generally accepted procedures for conducting group communication research. The procedures that comprise a particular method are often referred to as "techniques" of the method. A *technique* can thus be seen as the individual steps that constitute a particular method of research. In the context of group communication research, for example, there are techniques for: observing and coding group interaction behaviors, measuring group outcomes, conducting interviews of group members, statistically analyzing group interaction data, and so forth.

Myth of the Correct Method

Before introducing you to the chapters in the last section of this book, we think it important to alert you to a common fallacy of thinking that can hinder the methodological choices of group communication researchers. This error in thinking is what we call the "myth of the correct method." This myth concerns the belief that certain methods of research are inherently better than others because they are more rigorous, precise, accurate, valid, and so forth. While many group communication researchers have succumbed to the allure of this myth, you should resist doing so for several reasons.

While a particular method may be more appropriate or useful than other methods *in a given research context*, it is a mistake to believe that such a method is superior in all research contexts. There simply are no universally superior methods for studying group communication. What makes a particular method "correct" is that it allows the researcher to obtain the data (or information) needed to answer his or her research questions. Thus, there may be several "correct" methods for any study of group communication.

A second reason for resisting the myth of the correct method is that accepting it can limit your command and use of research methods and techniques. Once you believe that a certain method is superior to all other methods, you will naturally concentrate on that method. This specialization may make you an expert in the use of that method, but it will also make you susceptible to what Kaplan (1964) calls the "law of the hammer." Simply stated, this law states: "If you give a small boy a hammer, he will find that everything he encounters needs pounding" (p. 28). In short, if a researcher only knows how to use one method of research, she or he will find that, rightly or wrongly, all research questions can be investigated using that method.

The third reason for rejecting the myth of the correct method is that accepting the myth can cause you to prematurely dismiss studies that do not use the method you regard as inherently superior to other methods. The acceptance or rejection of a study's findings should never be based solely on the type of method (and/or techniques) used in the investigation. Rather, it should be based on a multitude of considerations, including (1) the importance of the question(s) being examined, (2) the theoretical basis for the study, and (3) whether the method employed allows the researcher to satisfactorily answer the study's research question(s).

The analysis of group communication is a complex undertaking, and it is clear that no single method or technique is suitable for the analysis of all facets of group interaction. The challenge facing researchers interested in studying group communication is to possess a comprehensive knowledge of methods and techniques useful for the study of group communication processes. Unfortunately, a presentation of the full spectrum of methods and techniques appropriate for the study of group communication is beyond the scope and intent of this book. The chapters in Part VIII introduce you to the methods that we feel are most useful to the analysis of small group communication.

References

Bales, R. F. (1950). *Interaction Process Analysis: A Method for the Study of Small Groups.* Cambridge, MA: Addison-Wesley.

——. (1970). *Personality and Interpersonal Behavior.* New York: Holt, Rinehart and Winston.

Bales, R. F., and Cohen, S. P. (with Williamson, S. A.). (1979). *SYMLOG: A System for the Multiple Observation of Groups.* New York: Free Press.

Bormann, E. G. (1996). "Symbolic convergence theory and communication in group decision making." In R. Y. Hirokawa and M. S. Poole (eds.), *Communication and Group Decision-Making* 2nd Edition (pp. 81–113). Thousand Oaks, CA: Sage.

Hackman, J. R., and Morris, C. G. (1975). "Group tasks, group interaction process, and group performance effectiveness: A review and proposed integration." In L. Berkowitz (ed.), *Advances in Experimental Social Psychology*, Vol. 8 (pp. 45–99). New York: Academic Press.

Jarboe, S. (1988). "A comparison of input-output, process-output, and input-process-output models of small group problem-solving effectiveness." *Communication Monographs,* 55: 121–142.

——. (1996). "Procedures for enhancing group decision making." In R. Y. Hirokawa and M. S. Poole (eds.), *Communication and Group Decision-Making* 2nd Edition (pp. 345–383). Thousand Oaks, CA: Sage.

Kaplan, A. (1964). *The Conduct of Inquiry.* New York: Chandler Publishing Company.

Pavitt, C. (1999). "Theorizing about the group communication-leadership relationship: Input-process-output and functional models." In L. R. Frey, D. S. Gouran, and M. S. Poole (eds.), *The Handbook of Group Communication Theory and Research* (pp. 313–334). Thousand Oaks, CA: Sage.

Poole, M. S., Seibold, D. R., and McPhee, R. D. (1996). "The structuration of group decisions." In R. Y. Hirokawa and M. S. Poole (eds.), *Communication and Group Decision-Making* (pp. 114—146). Thousand Oaks, CA: Sage.

Weingart, L. R. (1997). "How did they do it? The ways and means of studying group process." *Research in Organizational Behavior.* 19: 198–239. ✦

Chapter 22
Observing Group Interaction

Joann Keyton

Keyton introduces the method of Interaction Process Analysis. This method allows a researcher to engage in the micro-level analysis of group communication. The author identifies the kinds of research questions that the method is designed to address, explains how the method is used, provides examples of the method in operation, and concludes with a brief discussion of the strengths and limitations of the method.

Observing group interaction is fascinating because so much is going on at once. Often several people are talking at the same time. Even if only one group member is talking, others are generating nonverbal behaviors that produce meaning. Even though one stream of the conversation dominates, side conversations may also be occurring. Of course, the more complex the group interaction is, the more challenging it is to observe and capture what is happening in the group. This chapter introduces you to a quantitative method for systematically observing and coding group interaction called Interaction Process Analysis.

Questions to Consider

Before you begin using Interaction Process Analysis (or any method of analysis, for that matter), you should consider five questions. These questions are based on several key characteristics of group communication that challenge group communication researchers (Poole, Keyton, and Frey 1999).

Thinking through these questions will help you develop the most effective method for observing and coding group interaction.

What Am I Observing?

The first question addresses whether a group should be treated as an entity—as an entire group—or as a collection of individuals. Making this decision may not be as easy as you believe. Many concepts observable at the group level of analysis also exist at the individual level of analysis. For example, while group decision making is often thought of as a collective activity of all group members, individuals may also be engaged in their own decision-making processes. Leadership provides another example. Will you observe and analyze leadership as a group construct that requires leading *and* following behaviors, or will you observe and analyze it as an individual-level construct, focusing your observations on the person who is directing the task for the group? Your answer to these types of question will help you distinguish between the individual and group level of analysis. To avoid any confusion, you should develop a clear operationalization of the constructs or variables that are part of your research question or hypothesis.

Generally, group communication researchers are interested in the group level of analysis even though they collect data for each individual in the group. At the group level of analysis, researchers typically study group processes rather than group inputs or group outcomes. This unit of analysis focuses on the *group as an entity*, emphasizing "patterns of intra-group interaction as members exchange information or coordinate their physical efforts as they work" (Guzzo 1995, 6). Because group members interact in a face-to-face (or its technological equivalent) setting, some degree of interdependence is required for group members to satisfy their goal or complete their activity. Because group members, by definition, are interdependent, the communicative behavior of one affects the others. This is precisely the advantage of observing and coding group interaction. No other method allows you to capture and analyze this level of intricacy.

Who Are the Members of the Group?

The second decision you must make before you begin collecting data is to answer the question, "Who are the members of the group?" This may seem relatively easy to answer, but researchers recognize that a group's boundary is not necessarily static or permanent. Rather, bona fide group theory (Putnam and Stohl 1990, 1994, 1996) argues that group boundaries are both fluid and permeable. If you are planning to observe a bona fide group—for example, a project group at your office—the group's meeting may be interrupted by someone who brings critical information to the group. Even though this person spends only a few minutes with the project group, her information changes what the group is talking about. Thus, it would not make sense to exclude her interactions from your observations or analyses.

If you are observing a group over time, new members may join, established members may leave, and other members may be at some meetings and not others. Membership changes may be planned or unplanned, permanent or temporary. Most researchers choose to observe and record the interactions of everyone who is present in the group interaction, whether a group participant is an official member or not, and regardless of the level of their participation in the group.

What Is the Unit of Analysis?

The unit of analysis is the discrete element that is coded. The most common unit of analysis is the message—generally defined as an utterance or idea unit. A message or utterance can be as short as a word or phrase (e.g., "Yeah," "I still don't see how") or as long as several sentences if, together, the sentences express one idea. Using the message as the unit of analysis, a group member can produce one codable unit or several during a speaking turn.

What Behaviors Should I Observe and Code?

Essentially, you observe all of the group's interaction. The coding scheme you select should allow you to categorize everything that was said. Although some coding schemes focus exclusively on interactions that facilitate or inhibit decision making, or look at how persuasive arguments are developed, they should include a code for messages that are not oriented toward decision making or do not develop a persuasive argument. This is a key point. In this type of methodology, you do not select those aspects of the group's conversation that help to prove your point. Rather, you observe and code the entire conversation.

A coding scheme is really a set of carefully defined, pre-established categories. Using the categories, the researcher identifies each segment of a group's interaction as belonging to one of the categories. Although you could create your own coding scheme, there are two advantages to using an existing coding scheme. First, the validity of the categories has already been established. This means that the appropriateness and adequacy of the coding scheme has been developed and tested. Second, the coding scheme is based on some theoretical basis, or communication principles or functions.

How Will I Conduct the Observations and Coding?

Researchers often audiotape or videotape a group's interactions so they have repeated access to the entirety of the group's deliberations. Most researchers find it too difficult to pay attention to the verbal and nonverbal behavior of all group members and simultaneously code the interaction. Having a permanent record of the group's interaction allows the researcher to perform the coding step after the interaction has occurred and allows him to review the interaction as often as necessary. Some researchers rely on the audio or video record of a group's interaction, while others transcribe the interaction into written text, although doing so emphasizes verbal interaction over nonverbal cues. In either case, the researcher will have to review the recording of the interaction because *how* something is said gives additional meaning to *what* is said. Repeated viewing, listening, or reading of the permanent record helps researchers avoid coding mistakes. Sometimes, however, the researcher is restricted to observing the interaction in real-time as it occurs, such as observing your family's dinner conversation. This means that the researcher must code the interaction as he or she observes it.

Can observing a group's interaction change its dynamics? Yes, but you can take a few simple precautions to minimize your influence on the group. For example, you should not sit with the group if you will be observing and coding their interaction as it occurs in real time. Situate yourself so you are close enough to hear everything group members are saying but far enough away as not to be in the direct sight lines of group members. You should avoid shuffling papers and flipping through notebooks, since such behaviors can draw group members' attention away from their interaction. When audio or video recording equipment is used, the equipment should be placed as unobtrusively as possible. Equipment should be set up before the group arrives and tested to verify that the equipment can capture the interaction of all the group members interacting in their typical space (e.g., around a table, seated in easy chairs).

At this point, you might be asking to what degree external observers can make valid assessments of group interaction. This question was answered in a study of support groups for heart patients (Kacen and Rozovski 1998). Social work students either directly watched a support group's interaction or observed the group on videotape. Generally, participants in the support groups, direct observers, and indirect observers made similar evaluations of the progress and outcomes of the groups over a 10-week period. These findings strengthen the argument that observers can make valid and reliable assessments of group interactions.

To achieve this level of reliability and validity, coders must be trained. The coding system should be copied and distributed to all coders so they can be trained from the same materials and so they can return to the coding scheme if they have questions during the coding process. Many researchers prepare a codebook to identify coding units, coding categories, and rules for coding. As part of their training, coders generally practice coding on group interaction similar to that which will be coded as part of the research project. This is an important step as research has demonstrated that training can increase agreement among coders.

This type of methodology requires that two reliability issues be addressed. Both are issues of inter-coder agreement. First, coders must agree upon the unit of analysis being coded. This is known as *unitizing reliability*. If the unit to be coded is a sentence, then agreement should not be too much of a problem, as natural units, like complete sentences, have standardized identifiers for marking their beginning and ending. But speakers do not always talk in complete sentences, which makes identifying the unit of analysis far more difficult. Other coding units, like a message or utterance, are somewhat more abstract, and generally coders need more training time to identify the unit. This first step ensures that coders are coding the same thing. Second, and after the units to be coded have been identified, each coder must independently agree on which category the units will be placed into. The more frequently coders choose the same category, the greater their degree of *categorizing reliability*.

There are several formulas for determining the degree of inter-coder reliability. The coefficient of reliability and Scott's *pi* are commonly used in communication research for establishing unitizing and categorizing reliability, respectively. The formulas and steps for calculating both types of inter-coder reliability are shown at the end of this chapter in Appendix B.

While calculating inter-coder reliability is fairly straightforward, identifying an acceptable level of reliability is more subjective. Generally, researchers make this judgment based upon the research question or hypothesis and the context of the coding. As the number of categories increases or as the coding process becomes more complex, lower levels of reliability may be more acceptable. In communication research, agreement among coders must be at least 70 percent, although 80 percent and 90 percent are more desirable.

IPA—Interaction Process Analysis

Although there are several quantitative coding schemes, Interaction Process Analysis, or IPA for short, is the most widely used coding scheme for group interaction. Developed by Robert Freed Bales (1950, 1953), IPA has long been used as a theory and method to study the task and relational elements of group interaction. It is also the seminal work for distinguishing between a group's task functions and its socioemotional, or relational, communicative functions. The coding scheme identifies each message produced by a group member as either "task" or "relational," based on the function it serves in the group's conversation. Thus, IPA is a micro-level analysis that focuses on the purposes of messages communicated within the group, not on the content of what was said. Because of its functional feature, IPA can be used with nearly any task or work group that engages in group decision making and problem solving. Data from IPA can be used to describe the types of messages used and the patterns of interaction that emerge.

As mentioned earlier, researchers generally use the message or utterance for coding group interaction. In IPA, each utterance or message is treated as a single unit of analysis. All behaviors—verbal statements, facial expressions, hand gestures, bodily movements—can be coded, provided that the observer can assign a meaning to the behavior in terms of the IPA categories (Bales 1950).

Central to the IPA category scheme is a distinction between interaction that is task-oriented—i.e., utterances that emphasize goal completion—and interaction that is socioemotional—i.e., utterances that emphasize the relationships among members. According to the underlying theory, each communicative act can be categorized into one of 12 mutually exclusive categories (see Table 22.1). Six categories describe group members' socioemotional, or relational, communicative acts. Three of these categories represent utterances that promote positive member relations: shows solidarity/seems friendly, dramatizes/releases tension, and agrees. The other three categories represent acts that promote negative member relations: disagrees, shows tension, and shows antagonism/seems unfriendly. Acts not coded into socioemotional categories are coded into one of six task categories. These are: gives suggestion, gives opinion, gives orientation/information, asks for orientation/information, asks for opinion, and asks for suggestion. In the IPA category system, a message would be coded as either a task or socioemotional contribution to the group's interaction, but not both. The IPA system is thus referred to as a "mutually-exclusive" coding scheme.

As a system of functions, the IPA coding categories capture the diversity of message functions that are likely to occur in small groups (Hirokawa and Salazar 1999). This is why IPA has been so popular. It can be applied to almost any type of task or work group, as the 12 communicative functions are presumed to exist in any type of group interaction in which members are making decisions and solving problems. IPA is particularly helpful in identifying how a group's interaction facilitates or inhibits those processes.

There are two drawbacks in using coding schemes like IPA. First, its mutually exclusive categories require that each message or utterance be assigned to only one function. This can be problematic when messages fulfill multiple functions, as they often do in groups. To overcome this challenge, the researcher needs to be very familiar with the group's interaction. Having reviewed it many times, the researcher is more likely to code the message in its primary function.

Table 22.1

IPA Categories

Socioemotional: Positive Reactions	1. Shows Solidarity/Seems Friendly: Shows positive feelings toward another person 2. Shows Tension Release/Dramatizes: Reduces the anxiety that a person or group may be experiencing 3. Agrees: Shows acceptance of what another person has said
Task: Attempted Answers	4. Gives Suggestions: Offers direction/action for how to engage the task 5. Gives Opinions: Advances a belief or value that is relevant to the task 6. Gives Orientation/Information: Reports factual observations or experiences
Task: Questions	7. Asks for Orientation/Information: Requests factual observations or experiences 8. Asks for Opinions: Requests a belief or value that is relevant to the task 9. Asks for Suggestions: Requests direction/action for how to engage the task
Socioemotional: Negative Reactions	10. Disagrees: Shows rejection of what another person has said 11. Shows Tension: Indicates that a person is experiencing anxiety 12. Shows Antagonism/Seems Unfriendly: Shows negative feelings toward another person

The second potential drawback is that observers external to the group are responsible for assigning interaction to the coding categories without asking group members what they intended. One way to overcome this challenge is to take the role of the generalized other by putting yourself in the shoes of the person toward whom that actor is oriented (Bales 1950). By taking the role of the receiver, you will make better choices about coding decisions. Despite these shortcomings, IPA is well accepted as a sound method for identifying the communicative functions of group problem-solving and decision-making interaction, and has a long history in communication research.

Using IPA Methodology

There are three basic steps to coding communication using the 12 IPA categories: (a) obtaining and preparing group discussion for coding, (b) coding the discussion, and (c) interpreting the coding. Each step is discussed below.

Preparing to Code

The first step is to obtain a sample of group discussion and to prepare it for coding. Because IPA is used with task and work groups, it is best to use an extended period of group interaction, or even the interaction of several group meetings. This way you will be sure to capture most of the decision-making and problem-solving processes. If you must use only a portion of a group's interaction, be sure to select a representative sample of it. Appendix A displays the beginning segment of the third meeting of a student group. The group's semester assignment was to develop a proposal on classroom enhancement to be given to the university's vice provost for students. The transcript was developed from an audiotape of the meeting. At this point in the group, members have worked together to identify characteristics of an effective classroom. Between group meetings, some members had been to the library, while others had spoken with university administrators about how classrooms were managed on campus. This third meeting of the project group demonstrates their problem-solving interaction.

Although it is possible to use IPA to code group discussion as it takes place in real time, you must be very familiar with the 12 categories, as you will be required to make instantaneous coding decisions. The best approach is to audiotape or videotape the interaction and prepare a transcript from the recording. The next step would be to read through the transcript while listening/viewing the audio/videotape record of the interaction. This will help you incorporate the nonverbal elements that are not represented in the transcript.

Using both written and visual/audio records of the group's interaction is important because how a message is coded depends on how it is presented. There is a distinction, for example, between asking the question, "Why do you believe that?" in a curious tone (which would be coded as "Asks for Opinion"), and asking it as a challenge by using tone and inflection of voice to dismiss the person (which could be coded as "Disagrees"). Clearly, it is easier to make the most appropriate coding decisions if both audio/video and written records of the group's interaction are available.

Coding the Discussion

Recall that there are two steps in the coding process. First, the coding units have to be identified; then, the units are coded according to the IPA category scheme. A message or utterance is the typical unit of analysis. Read through the transcript to identify complete thoughts and bracket them in pencil. You may change your mind after reading through the transcript a second time, so it is a good idea to view your coding units as tentative at this point. Remember that a message or utterance can be a word, a phrase, or several sentences. It is the completeness of the thought that provides an indication that one message is complete and another message about to begin.

Review the transcript in Appendix A for the brackets that separate each message or utterance. Notice in Adam's first speaking turn how his communication satisfies three different functions for the group. Compare that to Adam's second speaking turn in which his entire speaking turn is devoted to his giving his opinion of what the group decided in a previous meeting. Notice the subtle distinction between him giving his opinion and presenting the information as fact. His words "I thought we had agreed upon" is your clue that this is his opinion. Although Bette's next comment signifies agreement, it is unclear if the other group members agree. Thus, it appears that the Gives Opinion code is more appropriate than Gives Orientation/Information.

After you are satisfied with your bracketing of the transcript, it is time to compare your unitizing to that of the other coders, and then to calculate your unitizing reliability. When reliability is not at an acceptable level, this means that you and the other coders are not consistently identifying what counts as a message or utterance. As a group, all of the coders should discuss the standards for identifying messages or utterances. If reliability is acceptable, you will still need to find and discuss all of the coding unit decisions for which the coders do not agree. Discuss each disagreement until the group of coders can come to a decision. When all coders agree on the unitizing of the transcript, you can move on to the categorizing decisions, using the 12 categories.

As you are coding, you might believe that one message can be coded in multiple categories. But recall that each message can receive only one code. Bales provided some suggestions to help you place a message in the most appropriate category. First, priority should be given to coding a message as category 1 (Shows Solidarity/Seems Friendly) or category 12 (Shows Antagonism/Seems Unfriendly) rather than coding it as another category, especially categories 4 and 5 (Gives Suggestions and Gives Opinions). Second, priority should be given to coding a message in

Table 22.2

Codes by group member and by IPA function.

	ADAM	BETTE	CAM	ZEBO	Total/% of Total
1. Shows Solidarity/ Seems Friendly	2	1	—	—	3/3.95%
2. Shows Tension Release/Dramatizes	—	—	—	—	—
3. Agrees	2	1	—	—	3/3.95%
4. Gives Suggestions	—	1	1	—	2/2.63%
5. Gives Opinions	6	4	2	1	13/17.11%
6. Gives Orientation/ Information	4	12	2	17	35/46.05%
7. Asks for Orientation/ Information	4	6	1	3	14/18.41%
8. Asks for Opinions	—	1	—	—	1/1.32%
9. Asks for Suggestions	—	—	2	1	3/3.95%
10. Disagrees	—	1	—	1	2/2.63%
11. Shows Tension	—	—	—	—	—
12. Shows Antagonism/ Seems Unfriendly	—	—	—	—	—
Total/% of total	18/23.68%	27/35.53%	8/10.53%	23/30.26%	76/100%

category 2 (Dramatizes) and category 11 (Shows Tension), especially when one might otherwise code it as category 6 (Gives Orientation/Gives Information).

Despite these suggestions, there is no single correct coding for any message or utterance. This is why many researchers have two or three observers first code an episode by themselves, then have the coders come together to share their results and reach agreement on those they have coded differently. If you have a question about coding any message, do not hesitate to return to the audio or video recording.

Interpreting the Codes

Several different types of analysis are possible when using IPA. By placing the total number of units for each group member in each category on a spreadsheet (see Table 22.2), you see how each group member communicated relative to the entire interaction sequence. These codes can then be interpreted using two different types of analysis.

The simplest analysis is to calculate the percentage of messages communicated by each group member. This is obtained by adding up the total number of messages coded for an individual and dividing it by the total number of messages coded for all group members (see the bottom row of Table 22.2). This calculation reveals the *percentage of talk time* for each individual and can reveal the equality or inequality of participation that may exist among group members. Generally, all members contribute about evenly to the discussion in effective groups. Conversely, a few members will dominate the group's conversation in ineffective groups.

In our example, group members do not share talk time equally. Bette and Zebo talk most frequently and three times more than Cam does. Although participation is not equal, the group's progress on the goal does not seem adversely affected. However, it will be important to see if later meetings reveal Cam's acceptance of the group's decisions.

A second type of analysis is to calculate the percentage of messages in each of the 12 categories. This is obtained by dividing the total number of messages that all group members contributed to a particular category by the total number of acts for the entire group (see the row totals and percentages in the far right column in Table 22.2). Analyzing the *function percentage* allows you to discover what functions of communication the group uses most frequently. By looking at which categories have the highest and lowest percentages, you can determine to what degree the group spends its time communicating positive socioemotional messages, negative socioemotional messages, or task messages. This type of analysis allows you to make a general assessment of the group's communication climate because you can evaluate the balance of task and relational communication within the group.

In our sample group, there is a predominance of giving orientation/information, followed somewhat distantly by asking for orientation/information and giving opinions. This group's communication clearly is centered in the task functions, as the group spends just above 10 percent of its talk time in the socioemotional functions. Thus, the imbalance between task and relational communication is not a problem—yet. If the group continues to focus primarily on task, relational tensions may rise.

These two analyses give you a general picture, or snapshot, of the group. To understand how communication occurs as a process, however, you will need to have a transcript marked with the coding categories (see Appendix A). One way to approach this type of analysis is to examine the transcript for patterns. Many groups exhibit pattern regularities both in terms of who talks and what type of communication function follows another. Patterns occur because group members react to what another group member says or does. This way you see what communication functions stimulated or inhibited other communication functions.

For example, in our sample group, notice what happens when the group's leader or facilitator tries to facilitate who speaks about what topic. Other than his first and second speaking turn, he does not provide much information for the group. Notice how there are few challenges when group members give information. Generally, other group members accept information given. While this type of pattern may not be a problem in the short term, protracted use of such a pattern could suggest that the group is not engaging in critical inquiry. Also, notice, how Cam's speaking turns are largely ignored by other group members even though the points she raises seem to be important to the group's topic. Thus, a pattern of ignoring Cam may cause relational tension in the group.

Summary

Observing and coding group interaction is a quantitative methodology that allows you to analyze a group's communication by performing micro-level analyses of what members say and do in a group conversation. Before you begin to observe or code, you should think through five fundamental questions. These are: (1) What am I observing? (2) Who are the members of the group? (3) What is the unit of analysis? (4) What behaviors should I observe and code? and (5) How will I conduct the observations and coding?

IPA is an excellent method for observing and coding group interaction because it is a systematic procedure for examining the actual communicative behaviors that take place during group interaction. The theory underlying the method can help you make sense of the data you collect because the theory provides a baseline from which to analyze your data. The data IPA yields can be used to provide a general assessment of how group members communicate or to demonstrate how the communication process unfolds during the group meeting. By coding messages into the 12 categories, you can identify how the group handles both task and relational functions. You can also identify any task and relational imbalances or tensions that exist in a group's conversation, and any attempts group members make to overcome those tensions. The primary advantage of using IPA to code group interaction is that the data it yields will assist you in producing a group-level analysis of a group's interaction; that is, an analysis about the group as a whole based upon what group members actually say and do in the group's conversation.

References

Bales, R. F. (1950). *Interaction Process Analysis: A Method for the Study of Small Groups.* Cambridge, MA: Addison-Wesley.

——. (1953). "The equilibrium problem in small groups." In T. Parson, E. A. Shils, and R. F. Bales (eds.), *Working Papers in the Theory of Action* (p. 111–161). Glencoe, IL: Free Press.

Guzzo, R. A. (1995). "Introduction: At the intersection of team effectiveness and decision making." In R. A. Guzzo and E. Salas (eds.), *Team Effectiveness and Decision Making in Organizations* (pp. 1–8). San Francisco: Jossey-Bass.

Hirokawa, R. Y., and Salazar, A. J. (1999). "Task-group communication and decision-making performance." In L. R. Frey, D. S. Gouran, and M. S. Poole (eds.), *The Handbook of Group Communication Theory and Research* (pp. 167–191). Thousand Oaks, CA: Sage.

Kacen, L., and Rozovski, U. (1998). "Assessing group processes: A comparison among group participants', direct observers', and indirect observers' assessment." *Small Group Research* 29: 179–197.

Poole, M. S., Keyton, J., and Frey, L. R. (1999). "Group communication methodology." In L. R. Frey, D. S. Gouran, and M. S. Poole (eds.), *The Handbook of Group Communication Theory and Research* (pp. 92–112). Thousand Oaks, CA: Sage.

Putnam, L. L., and Stohl, C. (1990). "Bona fide groups: A reconceptualization of groups in context." *Communication Studies* 41: 248–265.

——. (1994). "Group communication in context: Implications for the study of bona fide groups." In L. R. Frey (ed.), *Group Communication in Context: Studies of Natural Groups* (pp. 284–292). Hillsdale, NJ: Lawrence Erlbaum.

——. (1996). "Bona fide groups: An alternative perspective for communication and small group decision making." In R. Y. Hirokawa and M. S. Poole (eds.), *Communication and Group Decision Making* (2nd ed., pp. 147–178). Thousand Oaks, CA: Sage.

Appendix A: Transcript of Group Meeting Taken From Audio Tape

ADAM: [I said earlier we went around the campus and looked at classrooms.[6]] [Here's your camera back.[6]] [I don't want to lose that, that last picture—number thirteen.[5]]

BETTE: [Uh huh,[10]][it's fourteen[6]].

ADAM: [That's the ideal classroom. I liked that classroom in particular. It had everything I thought we decided a good classroom should have—chalk, chalkboards that can be written on, a clock, a pencil sharpener, desks in good conditions, and some left-handed desks.[5]]

BETTE: [Okay.[3]]

ADAM: [Here's the agenda for our next meeting April 24th.[6]]

CAM: [I've already been to the library to look for resources on the perfect classroom.[6]] [An educational expert might have other ideas we should consider.[5]]

ADAM: [Let's talk about the money, the funding.[6]] [Is there any luck on getting that?[7]]

ZEBO: [Would you like for me to give a little information from my meeting?[9]]

ADAM: [Yes.[3]] [You have the floor (with a sweeping gesture as if showing the way.)[1]]

ZEBO: [They, um, do not have central classroom scheduling management.[6]] [This means that each department is responsible for maintaining and scheduling their own classrooms . . . kind of like they owned the classrooms.[6]] [Each department, each college, I'm sorry, I said department, but it's each college.[6]] [But it's really not fair[5]] [because some colleges have more classrooms,[6]] [and other colleges have trouble scheduling things.[6]] [They are thinking about changing to a centralized classroom system.[6]] [This means all the classrooms are pooled together and managed centrally.[6]] [With respect to the budget for classroom maintenance, there is not really a budget specified for the whole university because each college is responsible for their own.[6]] [Does that make sense at all?[7]]

ADAM: [So, like classrooms in the communication building . . . they would get their money from the Communication Department?[7]]

ZEBO: [No,[10]] [from the College of Communication and Fine Arts[6].]

BETTE: [Did that include the painting and everything?[7]]

ZEBO: [He said that was maintenance and everything.[6]] [Last year they allocated one mil- . . . over $1,000,000. He called some lady to make sure. First she said $200,000 but it was really $1,000,000.[6]]

BETTE: [That's a big difference.[5]] [Let me check again with my financial person.[4]] [If it's over $1,000,000. And that was divided up to different colleges.[5]] [The only thing he really told me was that the College of Arts and Sciences was given $400,000 for that,[6]] [I guess, because there are a lot of majors.[5]] [Maybe it's based on number of students in each college?[7]]

CAM: [What else did he tell us (to Zebo)?[9]]

ZEBO: [He's really interested in having this report—what we find[6]] . . . [because, basically, they've never dealt with classroom enhancement before on the university level.[6]] [Each department or college just dealt with their own.[6]]

ADAM: [Yes, that's good information.[1]]

ZEBO: [Cam, didn't he say the registrar's office would be responsible for the scheduling of classes and the instructional equipment as well?[7]] [He was talking a lot about overheads and VCRs as well[6]]. [But he also mentioned chalk,[6]] [and I told him about the pencil sharpeners that we were interested in.[6]]

ADAM : [And what is his name again? Dr. . . .[7]]

BETTE: [Stephen McArvey.[6]] [He's the vice-provost for academic affairs.[6]] [He told me they're going to appoint an advisory committee to work with the classroom scheduling manager on development and implementation of scheduling.[6]] [I think somewhere in our proposal we ought to suggest that students should be on this committee,[5]]

[don't you think,[8]] [because he didn't mention students being on there.[6]]

CAM: [What did they say about the technologies fund?[7]]

BETTE: [That's where they were going to use funds allocated from the technology access fee to provide for instructional classroom equipment.[6]]

CAM: [So we need to check availability of those funds as well, don't you think?[9]]

ADAM: [But you know, I mean, honestly to me, I mean, I think at this point they can find money for the things they want to find money for.[5]] [I mean there is money out there.[5]] [I know they say there's no money here. They really do say that. I know that we're tight on money,[6]] [but if this is their priority,[5]] [they can find the money through these funds to improve our classrooms.[5]]

BETTE: [I told him our group was actually going to do the research to back up what we were going to propose as classroom enhancements.[6]] [He acted really interested.[5]] [So from the meeting with him I kind of feel like we're starting from scratch[5]]—[they really haven't addressed the issues we want to[5]]—[and whatever we say could possibly help.[5]]

CAM: [Because it' s been so decentralized up to this point.[5]]

ADAM: [Right.[3]]

BETTE: [I also went to the budget department to get a copy of the budget before the meeting with McArvey.[6]] [They took my information and said I had to have it approved by someone,[6]] [and, of course, they never called me back.[6]]

CAM: [I think all university records are open.[6]] [Did you try to get the info from another source?[4]]

ADAM: [Isn't that the open meetings law, or public records law, or something?[7]]

ZEBO: [Did you do a follow up call?[7]]

BETTE: [I will, I don't mind at all.[1]]

Appendix B

Calculating Reliability

Establishing reliability is a two-step process. First, you will need to determine the coefficient of reliability (*C.R.*). This formula bases reliability on the ratio of decisions coders agreed upon to the total number of coding decisions made by each coder. This is the only step you will need to determine unitizing reliability.

$$C.R. = \frac{2M}{N_1 + N_2}$$

M = Number of coding decisions agreed upon

N = Total number of coding decisions made by each coder

Step 1: identify the number of coding decisions made by coder number 1
Step 2: identify the number of coding decisions made by coder number 2
Step 3: identify the number of coding decisions agreed upon by the coders
Step 4: compute *C.R.*

$$C.R. = \frac{2M}{N_1 + N_2} \quad C.R. = \frac{2(76)}{79+81} \quad C.R. = \frac{152}{160}$$

$$C.R. = .95 \text{ or } 95\%$$

Now, using the coefficient of reliability from above, you can determine Scott's pi. As an index of categorizing reliability for content coding, Scott's *pi* accounts for the number of categories in the coding scheme and the frequency with which each category is used. This reliability formula can accommodate any number of coders and any number of categories. Moreover, it accounts for the rate of agreement that would occur by chance alone.

$$pi = \frac{\% \text{ observed agreement} - \% \text{ expected agreement}}{1 - \% \text{ expected agreement}}$$

Step 1: determine the coefficient of reliability (*C.R.*), which is the ratio of coding

agreements to the total number of coding decisions, as demonstrated above; this value is the percentage of observed agreement to be used in Scott's *pi*

Step 2: list the frequency with which each category was used in column 1
Step 3: determine the percentage of expected agreement by dividing the frequency for each category by the total number of codings
Step 4: compute the squared percentages of expected agreement for column 3 by squaring the values in column 2
Step 5: sum the values in column 3; this number is the percentage of expected agreement
Step 6. Compute Scott's *pi*

Category	Column 1 Frequency $n = 80$	Column 2 Percentage of Expected Agreement	Column 3 Squared Percentage of Expected Agreement
A	30	.375	.141
B	24	.300	.090
C	17	.213	.045
D	8	.100	.010
			.29

$$pi = \frac{\% \text{ observed agreement} - \% \text{ expected agreement}}{1 - \% \text{ expected agreement}}$$

$$pi = \frac{.95 - .29}{1 - .29}$$

$$pi = \frac{.66}{.71}$$

$$pi = .93$$

Thus, in this example, unitizing reliability was .95 and categorizing reliability was .93.

Chapter 23
Narrative Analysis of Group Communication

Randy Y. Hirokawa
Kathleen M. Clauson
Juliann Dahlberg

The method of narrative analysis focuses on stories told by group members, which are used to identify characteristics of a group's interaction. The authors explain how the survey method is used to obtain narratives, and how the "content analysis" and statistical techniques are used to identify the common "themes" found in the narratives. The chapter concludes with some examples of how narrative analysis can be used to analyze group communication.

> Traditionally conducted social science research has silenced many groups . . . by making them the passive object of inquiry. (Marshall and Rossman 1999, 4)

Quantitative analysis of group communication seeks to reduce human symbolic interaction to numerical data. This works well when aspects of group communication can be observed directly and can be categorized and/or measured objectively. For example, quantitative analysis is appropriate if we are interested in counting the number of contributions each member makes to the overall discussion or in identifying how often each member produces certain types of communicative behaviors. Quantitative analysis is also useful if we are interested in analyzing processual aspects of group interaction—that is, how the communication behaviors of group members change over time.

Unfortunately, not all groups can be directly observed, and not all aspects of group communication can be categorized or measured objectively. Sometimes groups of interest to us are simply unavailable for direct observation. Unarchived historical groups, for example, are difficult to study quantitatively because there is usually not enough reliable data available about their interactions to warrant quantitative measurements. Likewise, laws and public policies make it difficult, if not impossible, to directly observe the deliberations of court juries, organizational groups, health care teams, and the like. Moreover, even when we are able to observe the interactions of groups directly, there are aspects that are resistant to quantitative analysis. Especially difficult to measure quantitatively are aspects of group communication that are highly subjective or individualistic in nature. Personal meanings, understandings, and motives, for example, are too fleeting to be measured quantitatively (Polkinghorne 1988). The 2000 U.S. presidential election provides us with a perfect example. As you may recall, the outcome of the election hinged on the voting outcome in the state of Florida. As the drama unfolded, we learned that there was considerable controversy over how the ballots of Floridians ought to be *counted*. The camp of the eventual winner, George W. Bush, argued that only ballots with clearly indicated votes should be counted, while the camp of Al Gore argued unsuccessfully that ballot counters should also take into account the *intentions* of voters who, for various reasons, did not clearly indicate who they were voting for. The U.S. Supreme Court eventually ruled that only ballots clearly indicating a preference for Bush or Gore should be counted. If the presidential election of 2000 taught us anything, it is that even presumably obvious things like people's intentions are sometimes difficult to measure quantitatively.

Narrative Analysis

What do we do when we are unable to observe the interaction of groups firsthand, or are interested in studying aspects of group communication that are not directly observable or are difficult to quantify? An alternative research technique that can be used in these instances is a qualitative approach called *narrative analysis*. Although narrative analysis can be conducted in different ways (see, e.g., Bass 1985; Carlson 1989; Fisher 1984; Hirokawa, DeGooyer, and Valde 2000; Hollihan and Riley 1987; Mumby 1987), the basic idea is to obtain narrative accounts (stories) from people who had first-hand experience with an event of interest and then to analyze those stories to understand those people's interpretations or understandings of that event.

What Is a Narrative?

A narrative, or story, is a written or oral composition that describes a sequence of events and actions resulting in a particular outcome or ending. Some narratives also attribute motives for the actions of people in the story, as well as reveal what the story's character(s) think, feel, and believe. Narratives can be fictive in that they describe events, actions, and motives that never really happened or are purely hypothetical, or they can be factual in that they recount actual events, actions, and motives.

Walter Fisher (1978) notes that not all stories are equally believable to us. Some stories are so compelling that we believe everything in them, while other stories are so suspect that we are skeptical about everything in them. Fisher argues that there are three qualities or characteristics of a story that influence how much power it has to gain our acceptance and belief: (a) coherence, (b) probability, and (c) fidelity.

Coherence refers to whether we think all parts of the story seem to fit together. For example, when a prosecuting attorney tells the jury that the defendant "left the movie theater, drove home to shoot his wife, then sneaked back into the theater before anyone noticed he was gone," the members of the jury, in assessing the believability of the prosecutor's story, evaluate whether the sequence of events described by the prosecutor follows in a way that makes sense to them. If the sequence of events does not make sense, the story lacks coherence and is less believable.

The believability of a story also hinges on its narrative *probability*. Here the person listening to, or reading, the story assesses how likely is it that the events and actions described in the story actually happened in the way described. In the well-publicized O. J. Simpson murder trial, the prosecution asked the defendant, O. J. Simpson, to try on a black leather glove found at the scene of the crime. When Simpson tried to put on the glove, it was apparent that it did not fit his hand. One of Simpson's defense attorneys, Johnny Cochran, subsequently uttered to the jury one of the most memorable lines of the trial, "If the glove does not fit, you must acquit." In essence, Cochran was telling the jury that the probability or likelihood that O. J. Simpson wore the black glove in question when he allegedly killed his ex-wife and her friend was very small, given the fact that he struggled to get his hand into the glove.

The final influence on the believability of a story is its *fidelity*. Fidelity refers to the extent to which a story corresponds with the reader's or listener's personal experiences and beliefs. In another well-publicized court trial, two brothers were accused of murdering their parents by shooting them repeatedly at point-blank range with 12-gauge shotguns. During the course of the trial, a story unfolded that described the brothers as victims of emotional and sexual abuse by their father. This abuse caused them to fear their parents and ultimately motivated the brothers to kill their parents. Many members of the jury found the story believable because it rang true to the listeners in terms of their personal experiences, attitudes, values, and beliefs. The jury eventually acquitted the brothers of first-degree, premeditated murder largely because they felt that the boys' story possessed fidelity.

In sum, the coherence, probability, and fidelity of a story are of crucial importance to a researcher in deciding whether the story can be depended on to provide an accurate account of the phenomenon of interest. However, on what basis are we justified in accepting the proposition that the analysis of believable stories can help us understand unobservable aspects of group communication?

Justification for Narrative Analysis

A number of authors have provided philosophical and theoretical justifications for the use of narrative analysis as a basis for studying social interaction. Alasdair MacIntyre, in his book *After Virtue: A Study in Moral Theory* (1981) observes that "man is in his actions and practices, as well as in his fictions, essentially a story-telling animal" (201). Fisher (1984) describes the "essential nature" of human beings as *homo narans* (6). He argues that human beings recount and account for human choice and action through "stories we tell ourselves and each other to establish a meaningful life-world . . . relating a 'truth' about the human condition" (6). Donald Polkinghorne (1998), in his book *Narrative Knowing and the Human Sciences* argues that human experience operates in the mental realm and involves personal meanings derived from our direct and indirect interactions with physical aspects of human existence. As mental products, human experience can never be directly observed; it can only be inferred. Polkinghorne goes on to argue that understanding human experience is best accomplished by analyzing the stories people tell us because they

> [retrospectively] sort out the multitude of events and decisions that are connected to [the event in question] . . . [by selecting] those that are significant [to them] . . . and draw together the various episodes and actions into a story that leads through a sequence of events to an ending. (70)

Polkinghorne essentially suggests that stories highlight and convey our basic understanding of what happened, why it happened, and what resulted from what happened (170).

Doing Narrative Analysis

As noted earlier, there are many different forms of narrative analysis. As applied to the study of group communication, the two most common approaches are the *interview* method and the *survey* method. The interview approach is more detailed and time-consuming than the survey method and hence is not used as often in small group communication research. Both approaches are based on the assumption that people's realities are constructed through the act of narrating their stories. In other words, not only is a person's reality unique, but it is not fully experienced by the individual until he or she has talked about it.

Interview Approach

The interview approach utilizes open-ended questions to get group members to elaborate on their group experiences. For example, suppose you want to study conflict communication in groups. You do not need to observe a group engaged in conflict directly. Instead, you can have one or more members of the group tell you about their communication experiences in it. After group members have spent an afternoon in a meeting, ask each group member (separately) to describe their meeting. Prompt each individual to expand on his or her thoughts and feelings about any conflict episodes that may have occurred during the meeting. Write down what you hear and then ask each individual to help you rewrite the account for accuracy. The participation of each group member in this written description is important because it helps to clarify and verify his or her separate perspective. It is important to recognize here that the narratives produced by group members could be different—in some cases, very different. This outcome is appropriate, though, because group members have different realities, and you have worked with each of them to capture his or her separate reality.

Here is where you become a different kind of observer than the traditional social scientist. Had you observed the group and written down your own observations, you would have an "outsider's" (third-person) reality of the event. Instead you have allowed each interviewed group member to understand and articulate his or her own feelings and reactions. You have documented not what you saw or what "really" happened but what that group member saw, felt, thought, and now believes happened. It is important to remember that your observations of the interaction are not as important as the participant's story about the interaction. The purpose of an interview approach to narrative analysis is not to document your own observations but to develop the questions that will help the participant begin to explain his or her reality to you.

Because the participant's narrative is the key to your research, interview questions must be carefully developed. Existing research and participant observation will help you design a schedule of interview questions. To continue our group conflict example, reviewing prior research will help you identify relevant factors such as eye contact, body language, word choice, discussion topics, and so forth. You should develop questions that encourage the participant to reflect on those factors. Brief responses to your questions can be enhanced with prompts, such as "go on," "anything else?" or "can you say more about that?" A good interviewer is not afraid of silence. Deep thoughts take time to come out.

Once you have completed your interviews, transcribe the recorded tape yourself so you can note such details as pauses, voice inflections, laughter, tears, accents and pronunciations, speed of conversation. The mechanics of capturing transcription details contributes significantly to your analysis of group communication. Additional questions will occur to you as you listen. Write them down. Share the transcription with the participant narrator. Ask the questions you wrote when you transcribed the interview. Ask whether the narrator is surprised by anything that he or she reads. Discuss the details and your interpretations to determine whether the transcriptions are accurate and to give the narrator the opportunity to confirm or deny your interpretations.

Once you have verified the interview data, write a thick description of what you heard and saw. "Thick" means having many layers of relevant details. Each time you share an observation and interpretation, you gain a deeper understanding of the participant's reality. Thus, you will again review this narrative together and make changes according to the participant's perceptions. Repeat this process until the participant is satisfied that you have captured his or her reality.

Once you have created the narrative, you can enhance your work by adding your own narrative that identifies your own reflections and observations. A short self-description will help readers understand what biases you may have added to the interpretation process. Compare the participant's story to the research that has already been conducted on your topic, and you have contributed to the general body of knowledge.

Survey Approach

The survey approach to narrative analysis involves the use of an open-ended questionnaire or survey instrument to gather stories of group communication experiences. In the typical study, respondents are asked to recall a memorable group experience, then to provide a narrative account of that experience. Participants are allowed to select their own group experiences and to recount those aspects of the group experience that are significant and meaningful to them. For example, respondents might be asked to:

> Think about your most memorable experience of group decision-making success. In narrative (story) form, please provide a detailed account of that success. In telling your story, describe the kind of group that was involved, what kind of decision was made, how you know the decision was

a good one, and what you think contributed to the group's decision-making success. Please tell your story in as much detail as possible. (Hirokawa et al. 2000)

After the stories are obtained, a procedure is usually employed to analyze the narratives. This analysis usually begins with an identification of the basic *unit of analysis*. The unit of analysis is the aspect of the narrative of greatest interest to the researcher. Units of analysis can be small (micro-units) or large (macro-units), depending on the questions being asked in the study. Examples of micro-units include aspects of the story's characters such as their attitudes, values, beliefs, and motives. Macro-units, on the other hand, include larger components of the narrative such as its themes, episodes, or plot.

Once the basic unit of analysis is identified, at least two research assistants will *independently* read all of the narratives and identify the basic units of analysis found in each of them. For instance, if the unit of analysis is a *theme*, the people reading the stories would identify all the themes found in each story.

After all the stories have been content-analyzed, the research assistants meet to compare the units of analysis found in each story. When discrepancies are found—for example, one reader identifies a theme that was not identified by another reader—the research assistants go back to the story in question and jointly analyze its content to reconcile the discrepancy.

Once the contents of all of the stories have been reconciled, the researcher(s) will organize the content data into a list of *unique* content units. Unique units are those that are qualitatively different from each other such that one cannot be subsumed (or "nested") within the other. For example, "cats" and "dogs" are unique categories of animals because an animal can be categorized *either* as a "cat" *or* a "dog" but not both at the same time. In contrast, "German shepherd" and "dog" are *not* unique categories because it is possible for an animal to be *both* a "German shepherd" *and* a "dog" at the same time. Some researchers refer to unique categories as mutually exclusive ones.

Once the researcher(s) develop a list of unique content units, they may go one step further and organize them into unique *categories* of content units. A *category* is simply a collection of content units that share a common property or characteristic of some kind. For instance, "dog" can serve as the category for individual units like "Dalmatian," "German shepherd," "golden retriever," and the like. Likewise, "fruit" can serve as the category for individual units like "apple," "orange," "peach," and so on. Categorization of content units is often done when comparisons are made among stories—such as when a researcher is interested in knowing if the stories describing successful group experiences differ qualitatively from stories describing unsuccessful group experiences (Hirokawa et al. 2000).

Categorization of content units is usually accomplished through the use of a technique called *Q-sorting*. Q-sorting is a technique used to arrange a large array of data into classification categories. The categories could differentiate data points by class, kind, type, size, shape, color, and so forth (Kerlinger 1986).

The first step in Q-sorting is to write each unique content unit (e.g., "apple") on a 3 × 5 index card. Once a set of cards, each representing a unique content unit, is produced, the researcher will enlist the help of impartial judges to sort the cards into separate piles based on the perceived commonality of the various content units. Thus, for example, a judge would put the cards associated with "apple," "orange," and "peach" in the same pile, but would put the cards associated with "Dalmatian," "German shepherd," and "golden retriever" in a separate pile. After the impartial judges have sorted the cards, the researcher(s) will examine each pile to identify the common characteristic that unifies the content units placed in that pile. Each pile will eventually represent a unique category, and after various adjustments are made (i.e., some cards originally sorted in one pile may be moved to another pile because they share greater commonality with cards in that pile), the researcher(s) will label each category based on its common characteristic(s). For example, the pile containing the cards "apple," "orange," and "peach" will be labeled "fruit" because all three units are different kinds of fruit.

Finally, the researcher(s) report the unique content units and/or unique categories of content units found in their analysis of the narratives and use that data to answer specific research questions guiding their investigation.

Research Example

A recent study by one of the authors of this chapter (Dahlberg 2000) provides an example of the survey approach to narrative analysis we have been discussing. The study focused on the following questions:

1. What are the factors that participants retrospectively believe contribute to successful group decision making?

2. What are the factors that participants retrospectively believe contribute to group decision-making failures?

Method

Undergraduate students in an introductory communication course at a large Midwestern university received extra credit for obtaining written stories of successful or unsuccessful group decision-making experiences.

The survey instrument used in this study contained three parts. The first section asked the narrator to:

Think about your most memorable experience of group decision-making *success*. In narrative (story) form, please provide a detailed account of that success—that is, describe the kind of group that was involved, what kind of decision it was, how you knew the decision was successful, and what you thought contributed to the group's decision-making success. Please tell your story in as much detail as possible.

Section two asked the narrator to:

Think about your most memorable experience of group decision-making *failure*.

In narrative (story) form, please provide a detailed account of that failure—that is, describe the kind of group that was involved, what kind of decision it was, how you knew the decision was a failure, and what you thought contributed to the group's decision-making failure. Please tell your story in as much detail as possible.

The third section, which was optional, asked the narrator to provide demographic information, including sex, age, occupation/profession, years of experience, and the like.

This data-collection procedure yielded 568 stories of group decision-making success and failure from both student and professional populations. These stories represented a wide range of group decision-making experiences, including those coming out of sports, school, and work groups.

Narrative Analysis

The researcher used an inductive approach involving a constant comparative method to analyze the stories. The basic unit of analysis was the explanatory theme—that is, a phrase or statement identifying a single, self-contained, perceived influence on group decision-making success or failure. The analysis proceeded as follows.

First, the researcher read 50 randomly selected stories of success and failure to derive two preliminary lists of perceived influences—one for group decision-making success and the other for group decision-making failure. The focus was on continuously refining the lists so that each included unique perceived influences on success or failure.

Next, the researcher used the two lists to categorize the explanatory themes found in the remainder of the 518 stories. Here the researcher remained open to additional themes not included in the original list. This process enabled the researcher to continually refine the lists of perceived influences on group decision-making success and failure.

After all the stories had been analyzed, 40 undergraduate students were recruited to perform a Q-sort analysis on the two lists of explanatory themes. Each perceived influence was written on a separate index card, resulting in the creation of two decks of cards—perceived influences on group decision-making success and perceived influences on group decision-making failure.

The 40 students, uninformed of the purpose of the study, were asked to independently sort the two sets of cards into common piles based on the perceived similarities of themes. Some sorters began with the cards associated with the group success stories, while the others began with the cards associated with the group failure stories. They then exchanged card sets so that each person sorted both decks of cards. This reverse-order procedure was used to guard against "order bias"—that is, a coder sorting the first deck differently from the second deck.

Finally, general categories of explanatory themes were established from the patterns of sorting resulting from the Q-sort process.

Results

Over a hundred different explanatory themes were found in the stories of group decision-making success and failure. Q-sorting of these varied themes yielded seven general categories of perceived influence on group decision-making performance:

1. *Relational influences*—those having to do with interpersonal relationships among group members (e.g., friendships, conflicts, cohesiveness)

2. *Structural influences*—those having to do with the way the group was organized (e.g., leadership, roles, division of work)

3. *Process influences*—those associated with the procedures and activities of group members (e.g., careful planning, taking short-cuts, coordination of effort)

4. *Emotional influences*—those associated with the feelings and motivations of group members (e.g., disinterest, fear, anger)

5. *Communication influences*—those having to do with the exchange of information and ideas among group members (e.g., arguments, good listening, soliciting feedback)

6. *Individual member influences*—those associated with the knowledge and skills of group members (e.g., experience, intelligence, creativity)

7. *External influences*—those having to do with influences generally beyond the control of the group (e.g., time pressure, unforeseen circumstances, and bad luck)

Direct comparisons of the success and failure stories using these seven general categories revealed that group decision-making *success* was most often attributed to *process* influences, such as "working well together," "coordinating our work," "careful planning," and "cooperation among group members." In contrast, group decision-making *failure* was most often attributed to *communication* influences such as "miscommunication," "poor listening," "constant bickering and arguing," and "failure to share important information with others."

Summary and Conclusions

Studying groups is not easy. As J. Richard Hackman cautions us in his book *Groups That Work (and Those That Don't)* (1990), groups present us with "complex tangles that often are as hard to straighten out as a backlash on a fishing reel" (p. 8). Given the complexity of groups, the challenge facing small group researchers is to devise ways of studying groups that allow us to gain as much insight as possible without being overwhelmed by their complexity and richness. We believe that narrative analysis offers such an approach.

The goal of narrative analysis is to discover and understand what happened in a group from the perspective of group members. Because people naturally interpret, recall, and convey their group experiences narratively (Fisher 1984), we believe that one of the best ways to discover what happens in a group is to ask its members to tell us stories about their experiences in the group. As we demonstrated in our research example, these stories can provide rich and useful insights about groups.

In concluding this chapter, however, we would be remiss if we did not point out some obvious drawbacks to using narrative analysis to study groups and their communication. One obvious limitation is that narrative analysis relies on people's recall abilities, and, unfortunately, individuals' ability to remember things is neither complete nor totally accurate. Most people are able to recall only a fraction of the information presented to them, and what they do recall is often plagued by various degrees of inaccuracy. Our imperfect memory is made even less reliable by *selective memory*. Selective memory refers to our tendency to remember what we *want* to remember, or what is important to us. Unfortunately, what we want to remember, or what is important to us, is usually not all that happened in the group.

Another limitation of narrative analysis is that it depends on personal sense-making, and personal sense-making is inherently *personal*. That is, two people can be presented with the same group situation but will experience it, make sense of it, and narratively recall it in very different ways. The researcher presented with two contrasting stories is thus faced with the daunting task of reconciling those differences in a way that gets as close to what "really happened" as possible.

Finally, cultural beliefs and values influence narrative accounts of group experiences. Thus, accounts of similar group experiences are likely to vary considerably across cultural settings. For example, group members from one culture may attribute their success to hard work and good planning, whereas group members from another culture may attribute their success to having the group proceedings properly blessed by the local shaman (Hirokawa et al. 2000).

Its limitations notwithstanding, we believe that narrative analysis represents a viable, practical, and user-friendly approach to studying groups.

References

Bass, J. D. (1985). "The appeal to efficiency as narrative closure: Lyndon Johnson and the Dominican Crisis, 1965." *Southern Speech Communication Journal* 50: 103–120.

Carlson, A. C. (1989). "Narrative as the philosopher's stone: How Russell H. Conwell changed lead to diamonds." *Western Journal of Speech Communication* 53: 342–355.

Clauson, K. M. (2000). Oral narrative and analysis of one African American woman's struggle for success in higher education. Doctoral dissertation, Iowa State University, Ames.

Dahlberg, J. (2000). Using stories to study group decision-making effectiveness: A test of the functional theory from a narrative perspective. Undergraduate honors thesis, Department of Communication Studies, University of Iowa, Iowa City.

Fisher, W. R. (1978). "Toward a logic of good reasons." *Quarterly Journal of Speech* 64: 376–384.

———. (1984). "Narration as human communication paradigm: The case of public moral argument." *Communication Monographs* 51: 1–22.

Hackman, J. R. (1990). *Groups That Work (and Those That Don't)*. San Francisco: Jossey-Bass.

Hirokawa, R. Y., DeGooyer, D., and Valde, K. (2000). "Using narratives to study task group effectiveness." *Small Group Research* 31: 573–591.

Hollihan, T. A., and Riley, P. (1987). "The rhetorical power of a compelling story: A critique of a 'tough love' parental support group." *Communication Quarterly* 35: 13–25.

Kerlinger, F. N. (1986). *Foundations of Behavioral Research*, (3rd ed.). New York: Holt, Rinehart and Winston.

MacIntyre, A. (1981). *After Virtue: A Study in Moral Theory*. Notre Dame: University of Notre Dame Press.

Marshall, C., and Rossman, G. B. (1999). *Designing Qualitative Research*. Thousand Oaks, CA: Sage.

Mumby, D. K. (1987). "The political function of narrative in organizations." *Communication Monographs* 54: 113–127.

Polkinghorne, D. E. (1988). *Narrative Knowing and the Human Sciences*. Albany: State University of New York Press.

Chapter 24
Evaluating Group Discussion

Steven A. Beebe
J. Kevin Barge

Here, the authors describe an assessment instrument—The Competent Group Communicator *evaluation form—used to help group members determine whether their group is communicating competently. This assessment instrument helps observers of problem-solving groups fine-tune their impressions of group members' communication contributions. Beebe and Barge begin their chapter by discussing the theoretical and research foundations for their assessment instrument. They then discuss the contents of the instrument and explain how to use it properly to analyze group interaction. The chapter concludes with examples of how the assessment instrument can be used to improve group communication in problem-solving groups.*

The primary work of problem-solving groups is to make choices about what solutions will best reduce the gap between some current state of affairs and where the group would like to be. For example, task forces in local, state, and national government address the problem that millions of United States citizens have no health care insurance by choosing among a variety of health care reform plans that may increase the number of citizens receiving access to health care and prescription drugs. Problem-solving groups are charged with the responsibility of overcoming obstacles to achieve a goal; they do this by making choices about potential solutions that are appropriate and effective for the group's unique situation.

Communication scholars have explored several practices that help problem-solving groups make wise choices. Group procedures such as brainstorming and devil's advocacy provide the group with the necessary structure to guide conversations in ways that productively generate and evaluate ideas (Sunwolf and Seibold 1999). Effective leadership can manage the tension between getting the work done and maintaining healthy member relationships, which creates a climate for high-quality problem solving (Barge 1996; Pavitt 1999). Developing group members' abilities in making and analyzing arguments—knowing how to examine the evidence that claims are based on and whether the claims make sense in light of the evidence—enhances the likelihood that groups will make intelligent choices to solve their problems (Meyers and Brashers 1999). Groups have at their disposal a number of practices and structured procedures that can assist their choice making.

The idea that group members need to communicate in ways that facilitate effective problem solving and fit the emerging group context implies that they need to be competent small group communicators. But what is competent small group communication? How do group members know if they have been competent communicators? What standards can be used to assess a person's communication competence? If effective problem solving depends on group members making choices about their communication during group conversations, then it is important to articulate some standards for evaluation that can help group members make wise choices about the messages they select and perform. We begin by exploring what characterizes communication competence and conclude by presenting a practical instrument, *The Competent Group Communicator*, that you can use to assess your own or others' communication competence. We will not only identify the characteristics of communication competence but also discuss specific group communication competencies that research and practice suggest enhances group problem solving.

What Is Small Group Communication Competence?

What counts as communication competence has been vigorously debated. While several definitions of communication competence exist, we choose the following definition: *Communication competence* is an impression of the appropriateness and effectiveness of an individual's behavior in a situation. Let's examine the elements of this definition.

Communication Competence Involves Impressions

Imagine the following set of situations. For each situation, decide whether you perceive the group member to be a competent communicator.

Situation #1: Juan has been selected as a new board member for the Girl Scout Board of Directors. Juan is very excited about being selected. At the first meeting after being selected, Juan interrupts another board member and proposes a new procedure for fund raising. There is silence around the board table and the President of the board finally looks at Juan and says, "We looked at that idea thoroughly about two years ago and rejected it. We also follow Roberts' Rules of Order and what you have suggested falls better under New Business." Has Juan been a competent communicator during the board meeting?

Situation #2: Max, an employee for a manufacturing company, attends a team meeting for the production line. Max has more than 15 years experience on the line and knows all the ins and outs of the machinery, but has a high degree of communication anxiety and gets very nervous when participating in groups. As a result, Max says nothing during the team meeting. Several team members commented afterwards, "I wish he would have said something. I'm pretty new to the production line and don't really understand on how this thing works." Is Max a compe-

tent communicator during the team meeting?

Situation #3: Ann Chinn is President of a service club at her university. She recently returned from a workshop on how to ask good questions that facilitate high-quality problem solving. As she runs the meeting, Ann Chinn consistently follows the guidelines provided in the training and asks good questions. After the meeting, several club members approach her privately and say, "What is with all these questions? I know what you are trying to do, but the stuff you were asking questions about didn't need to be talked about any more." Was Ann Chinn a competent communicator during the club meeting?

Was the group member in each situation communicating in a competent fashion? Your answer to this question, in large part, depends on what model of communication competence you use. Drawing on the work of Brian Spitzberg (Spitzberg 1993; Spitzberg, Canary, and Cupach 1994; Spitzberg and Cupach 1984), we have previously identified four models of communication competence in small groups: (1) communication competence as motivation, (2) communication competence as knowledge, (3) communication competence as skill, and (4) communication competence as impression (Beebe and Barge 1994).

Viewing *communication competence as motivation* assumes that one's level of motivation to participate in groups defines one's communication competence. Motivation is the degree to which a person is moved to approach, engage, and participate in groups. A variety of individual characteristics influence one's level of motivation to participate in groups, for example, cultural orientation, communication apprehension, and interpersonal needs (Haslett and Ruebush 1999). People who are more collectivist in nature, or believe in the importance of collaboration, and are low in communication apprehension tend to participate more in groups. According to this model, Juan in Situation #1 would be considered to be a competent communicator because he is highly motivated to join the group and desperately wants to participate.

Communication competence as knowledge maintains that the defining characteristic of competent communicators is that they have the requisite knowledge about the task at hand as well as the knowledge of how to manage relationships among group members. We call the former task knowledge, that is, knowledge about how to perform a particular activity and how to make decisions, while we call the latter relational knowledge, knowing how to manage group relationships, build positive group climates, and manage conflicts (Morreale, Spitzberg, and Barge 2001). Simply, competent communicators know what needs to be done in terms of task and people. Using this criterion, we would be inclined to say that Max in Situation #2 is a competent communicator. Max had a wealth of experience on the production line and more than likely knew the strengths and weaknesses of the production process.

Communication competence as skill holds that competent communicators can perform repeatable goal-directed behaviors. The notion of repeatable is important because to possess a skill means that you can perform it again and again within particular situations. For example, anyone can get lucky and ask a good question that creates a vibrant discussion, but to genuinely demonstrate mastery of the skill of asking good questions requires a person to do it repeatedly during a group discussion. Goal-directed behavior emphasizes the fact that the behavior must fulfill some function. In small group communication research, functionalist theorists contend that messages must perform four key decision-making functions if a high-quality decision is to be reached: (a) Assess the problem situation, (b) Specify the goals of the decision-making process, (c) Identify a range of alternatives, and (d) Evaluate the alternatives in light of positive/negative consequences (Gouran and Hirokawa 1996; Gouran, Hirokawa, Julian, and Leatham 1993; Gouran 1999).

From a functionalist perspective, a competent communicator is one who can per-form behaviors that meet these four functions on a regular basis. Using this standard, we would say that Ann Chinn, in Situation #3, is a competent communicator because she is skilled at asking good follow-up questions as a result of her training.

We suspect, however, that you may be somewhat uncomfortable in labeling each of these individuals as competent communicators. Why? In Situation #1, even though Juan was highly motivated, he acted in ways that other board members did not appreciate. In Situation #2, even though Max was highly knowledgeable, he did not say anything, which led other team members to be dissatisfied with his behavior. In Situation #3, even though Ann Chinn had mastered the skill of asking good follow-up questions, other group members found her behavior inappropriate. We acknowledge that motivation, knowledge, and skill are important to communication competence, but none of these individual components is sufficient to define competence. In all three instances, the perception of the person's action resulted in a negative judgment of that person's competence. We believe that communication competence is best viewed as an impression.

Viewing *communication competence as an impression* means that people make judgments about another's communication competence. In each of the situations presented previously, other group members made a judgment that the person's behavior did not fit with the requirements of the situation. When we view communication competence as an impression, it allows us to probe what factors contribute to perceptions of communication competence. From this perspective, motivation, knowledge, and skills are factors that influence one's ability to be a competent communicator. The idea of communication competence can be summarized in the following headline: Communication Competence = Motivation × Knowledge × Skills.

A person is most likely to be perceived as a competent communicator when he or she is motivated, has the relevant knowledge, and is skilled at performing the needed behaviors. These three factors interact with one another to produce impressions of communication competence. We do not doubt that there will be times when an unmotivated and unskilled person who lacks knowledge about a situation will accidentally act in ways that are perceived as competent; however, the likelihood of a person being perceived as communicating competently is increased when a person is highly motivated, knowledgeable, and skilled.

Communication Competence Involves Impressions of Appropriateness and Effectiveness

If communication competence is an impression, what are the criteria that we use to form our impressions of competence? There are two major criteria that are typically used when assessing communication competence: (1) appropriateness and (2) effectiveness (Spitzberg and Cupach 1984). *Appropriateness* refers to acting in ways that are perceived as permissible within a given culture. For example, small group members may have negotiated a group culture where it is not permitted to tease one another about their personal lives. A new group member may enter that group and tease another group member about a date he or she had the previous evening. Such an act would be viewed as inappropriate since it violates the norms guiding the group. *Effectiveness* is measured by the degree that an act achieves a particular goal. Sometimes jokes and humor are used to relieve the tension in a group. If the joke relieves the stress of the moment, it would be viewed as effective; if it raised the tension level in the group it would be viewed as ineffective.

Communication needs to be both appropriate and effective if it is to be fully competent. Figure 24.1 illustrates the relationship between these two dimensions (Morreale, Spitzberg, and Barge 2001). *Entirely incompetent communication* is communication that is both inappropriate and ineffective. For example, suppose a group was suffering stress due to the racial diversity present in the group. To relieve the stress, one of the

group members tells a racist joke. Such a joke is not only inappropriate but ineffective as well, because it simply aggravates the situation. *Partially competent communication* can be either appropriate and ineffective or inappropriate and effective. The former is illustrated in groupthink. Groupthink is a phenomenon that occurs when group members making a decision seek premature agreement that often involves members self-censoring their ideas and opinions (Janis and Mann 1977; Janis 1982, 1989; Street and Anthony 1997; Granstrom and Stiwne 1998; Flippen 1999). Members who fall prey to groupthink may conform to the norms of the group (high appropriateness) and not voice doubts or criticism, but such behavior is ineffective at moving the group toward making a high-quality decision. On the other hand, when team leaders verbally abuse other team members, they are acting in ways that violate norms of appropriateness but may be effective at motivating team members. Such behavior may be termed the "Bobby Knight syndrome," after the famed former Indiana University basketball coach who was noted for abusive behavior toward players but who achieved "winning" results.

Highly competent communication is high in both appropriateness and effectiveness. When communicators are very competent, they find ways to achieve their goals that others find acceptable. This form of communication is optimal in that it successfully keeps the tension between achieving one's own goals and self-satisfaction and satisfying others' goals. Competent communicators recognize that others' desires, goals, and expectations directly influence one's ability to act in ways that are communicationally competent. For example, imagine that you are a parent of a middle-school child. Your child's English teacher has told you that your child needs to develop her reading skills. At the same time, you know that your child is fiercely independent and does not want your help. You also know that your child loves to help out with chores around the house. How might a highly competent

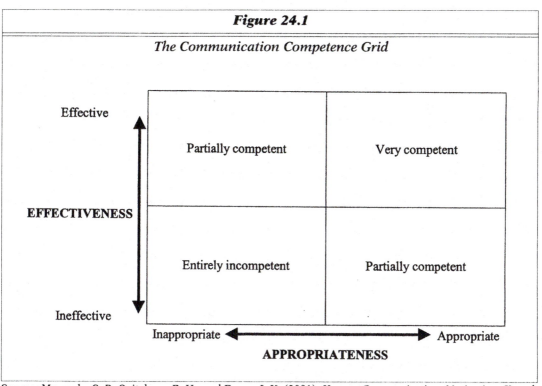

Figure 24.1

The Communication Competence Grid

Source: Morreale, S. P., Spitzberg, B. H., and Barge, J. K. (2001). *Human Communication: Motivation, Knowledge, and Skills*, p. 33. Belmont, CA: Wadsworth/Thomson Learning. Reprinted by permission.

communicator approach this situation? One way would be for you to suggest that the child help you at dinner time. While you are preparing food, it would be helpful for your child to read you the newspaper so you can "catch up" on the day's events. Such a message may be viewed as highly competent because: (1) from the parent's view, it allows you to achieve your goals in a way that keeps the relationship positive, and (2) the child would view it as preserving her independence (appropriateness) and helping the parent (effectiveness). For both parties, appropriateness and effectiveness are high.

Communication Competence Is Situational

How do you know what kinds of communication in a small group will be viewed as appropriate and effective? Are there moments when vigorously challenging ideas, normally an activity that leads to high-quality decisions, can devastate a group? Are there moments when not saying anything and remaining silent is the most competent

thing a group member can do? Are there times when setting goals can be counterproductive and lessen group morale? The short answer is, "Yes." When groups are under high levels of stress and pressures, the continual challenging of ideas may push them over the edge. When a group member has just revealed a personal tragedy in a group, remaining silent and respectful about that person's revelation may be desirable. When a group feels that they have no control over their own fate as a group, a leader setting goals could be harmful. What these examples suggest is that it is difficult to specify what kinds of behaviors are inherently competent or incompetent.

It is tempting to want to specify the behaviors that are viewed as competent or incompetent. However, such a task is impossible, given the situational nature of communication. In particular situations, silence may be an appropriate move to make in a group discussion, while in others it could be harmful. When assessing communication competence, one cannot simply assume that a particular message is either competent or incompetent. Rather, one needs to assess the particular message in terms of its fit with the context.

While several contextual factors may be taken into account, we believe that four contextual factors are most important. We summarize these four factors using the acronym POET, which stands for People, Objectives, Environment, and Time. These four factors focus on distinct aspects of group life:

1. *People:* Who will be affected by my messages? How would they perceive my messages?

2. *Objectives:* What are the key goals or expected outcomes?

3. *Environment:* How would I characterize the climate of the group? Is it supportive or hostile?

4. *Time:* Where is the group in terms of development? Is it still in the forming phase? Has a group culture been established? (Morreale, Spitzberg, and Barge 2001, 316)

Competent group communicators need to take into account how their messages fit with the expectations of others, the goals of the group, the group's environment, and the developmental stage of the group.

The Competent Group Communicator: An Instrument to Assess Problem-Solving Group Discussion

The previous discussion defined communication competence as an impression of the appropriateness and effectiveness of an individual's behavior in a given situation. On the basis of this definition and the assumptions underlying what a competent communicator does, we now turn our attention to presenting a method of assessing problem-solving group competencies. *The Competent Group Communicator* evaluation instrument is a tool to assess the impressions of communication performance during small group problem-solving discussions; it focuses on the messages people use when communicating in a problem-solving small group discussion. When determining whether or not someone is competent, the evaluator bases his or her evaluation on the impression that the group communicator makes. The appropriateness and effectiveness of the impression will depend on a given situation: *The Competent Group Communicator* considers the people involved, the objectives of the group (problem solving), the environment (group climate), as well as factors of time. Specifically, its purpose is to assess nine competencies of an individual group member as well as overall group competency during problem-solving discussions. Although there are a host of existing instruments designed to evaluate group communication (e.g. Chin, Salisbury, Pearson, and Stollak 1999; Davison 1997; Carless and De Paola 2000; Wheelan, Buzaglo, and Tsumura 1998; Anderson, Martin, and Infante 1998; Riddle, Anderson, and Martin 2000), we developed *The Competent Group Communicator* to assess classic communication competencies that are supported by small group communication research and that are typically taught in small group communication classes (Beebe and Barge 1994).

The instrument serves several purposes: (a) evaluating an individual's performance in problem-solving group discussions in an academic class or corporate training session; (b) assessing a person's skills, thus serving as a placement tool for participating in group discussions; (c) measuring pre- and post-test mastery of small group communication skills taught in a small group communication course or seminar; and (d) generating assessment data that could help academic institutions or organizations determine the effectiveness of small group communication instruction and student mastery of group communication competencies.

Small Group Problem-Solving Functions and Competencies

The instrument is designed to assess group communication competencies and is organized around four general problem-solving functions: (a) the *problem-oriented function* focuses on defining and analyzing the problem the group is discussing; (b) the *solution-oriented function* includes identifying the criteria for a solution, identifying possible solutions, and evaluating the solutions; (c) the *discussion management function* consist of those competencies that help the group manage the interaction, such as noting whether group members stay on task and monitoring whether some group members talk too much or too little; and (d) the *relational function* includes such issues as managing conflict and maintaining a positive climate in the group. Each of the four general problem-solving functions includes either two or three specific group communication competencies.

The instrument's development was based upon a series of discussions with speech communication faculty members at several national communication conferences, as well as on a series of pilot tests to confirm the validity and reliability of the instrument (Beebe and Barge 1994; McCormick 1995; Beebe, Barge, and McCormick 1998). The procedures for constructing this instrument were modeled after the successful procedures used to develop *The Competent Speaker* (Morreale, Moore, Taylor, Surges-Tatum, and Hulbert-Johnson 1992). Specifically, we: (1) identified the purpose of the instrument, (2) identified research-based small group communication competencies, (3) identified criteria for assessing the competencies, (4) developed the instrument, and (5) tested the instrument.

One of the biggest challenges in assessing small group communication is to decide which communication behaviors should be assessed. In essence, our question was, what are those behaviors that lead to an impression of competence? To help us identify essential small group problem-solving competencies, we reviewed three areas of research and application (Beebe and Barge 1994). First, we examined the most widely adopted textbooks used to teach small group communication (e.g., Beebe and Masterson 1999; Lumsden and Lumsden 2000; Brilhart, Galanes, and Adams 2001). Our content analysis and review of current textbooks revealed the most typical topics covered in small group communication pedagogy (e.g., group definitions, small group communication theory, types of groups, needs/goals of groups, discussion techniques, roles, norms, status, consensus, cohesiveness, groupthink, conflict, trust, interpersonal communication, problem-solving agendas, preparing for discussion, reasoning, leadership, meetings, and observing and evaluating small groups). Knowing the typical content of small group communication classes helped ensure that our instrument would be useful to students studying small group communication.

A second method of identifying group communication competencies was to review small group communication research. Research that identified specific functions of communication (Hirokawa 1988; Hirokawa and Rost 1992; Orlitzky and Hirokawa 1997; Graham, Papa, and McPherson 1997), and research that sought to test specific problem-solving discussion methods (Brilhart and Jochem 1964; Jurma 1979; Jarboe 1988; VanGundy 1981), were exceptionally useful.

Third, we examined existing small group communication assessment instruments to search for common skills and competencies. We reviewed instruments included in small group textbooks as well as those published in the group communication literature (e.g. Chin, Salisbury, Pearson, and Stollak 1999; Davison 1997; Carless and De Paola 2000; Wheelan, Buzaglo, and Tsumura 1998); Anderson, Martin, and Infante 1998; Riddle, Anderson, and Martin 2000).

On the basis of our review of small group communication texts, research, and existing assessment instruments, we identified nine small group problem-solving competencies organized into four general functions. A group member need not perform all nine competencies to be deemed a competent group communicator. As noted earlier, it is not possible to specify small group competencies that are applicable to every group discussion.

How to Use the *Competent Group Communicator* Evaluation Form

The *Competent Group Communicator* evaluation form is designed to assess the presence or absence of small group communication competencies in a group or team discussion. As we discussed, competencies are specific behaviors that group or team members perform that result in a positive impression, given the people, objectives, environment, and time. Here is how to use the form (which can be found at the end of this chapter).

1. Write the names of group members at the top of the form. (If you have more than six group members, photocopy the form so that each group member can be evaluated).

2. Observe a group or team that is attempting to solve a problem. Sample problem-solving discussion questions include: What should be done to decrease the number of teenagers who smoke cigarettes? What should be done to decrease the spread of AIDS in the United States? What should be done to make a college education affordable to all qualified citizens in the United States?

3. Consider videotaping the discussion. Sometimes it is difficult to make several judgments about group competencies by viewing a group discussion only once, especially if your group includes more than four participants. Many people find it easier to videotape the group discussion so they can observe the group discussion several times. Repeated viewing will enhance both the validity and reliability of the assessment of the nine competencies.

4. When using the form, first decide whether each group member has performed each competency. Circle "NO" if the group member was not observed performing the competency. Circle "YES" if you observed the group member performing the competency at least once (e.g. defining the problem, analyzing the problem, identifying criteria, and so on).

5. For each competency that you circled "YES," determine your impression of how effectively the competency was performed.

   0 = This competency was performed, but it was inappropriately or inadequately performed. For example, the person observed tried to define the problem but did so poorly.
   1 = Overall, there was an adequate performance of this competency.
   2 = Overall, there was a good performance of this competency.
   3 = Overall, there was an excellent performance of this competency.

6. Total the score for each group member in each of the four functions.

7. You can also assess the overall impression of the group's ability to perform these nine competencies. The column marked "Group Assessment" can be used to record your impressions of how effectively the group or team behaved. Circle "NO" if no one in the group performed this competency, and circle "YES" if at least one person in the group performed this competency. After you have judged whether the behavior was or was not performed, then determine the level of effectiveness of how well the entire group performed this competency using the 0 to 3 scale identified in Step 5 above.

The Competent Group Communicator assessment form can help you determine whether individual group members did or did not perform the group problem-solving competencies. If the competencies were performed, you can assess whether the group member left a negative impression (with a rating of "0") or whether the impression was "adequate," "good," or "excellent."

The first function, *Problem-Oriented Function*, includes competencies (items 1 and 2) that help the group or team define and analyze the problem they are trying to solve. Effective group members clearly and appropriately define or describe the problem to be solved. Ineffective group members, however, either inaccurately define the problem or make little or no attempt to clarify the problem or issues confronting the group. Likewise, effective group members offer statements that clearly and appropriately examine the causes, obstacles, history, symptoms, and significance of the problem to be solved, while ineffective members either do not do this or inaccurately or inappropriately analyze the problem. If this first function was performed, the total number of points will range from 0 to 6 (up to 3 points for each competency). The higher the number of points, the better the individual performed this competency.

The second function, *Solution-Oriented Function*, includes competencies (items 3, 4, and 5) that help the group or team develop and evaluate solutions. Effective group members offer clear and appropriate comments that identify the goal the group is attempting to achieve or to identify specific criteria (or standards for an acceptable solution or outcome) for the problem facing the group. Ineffective group members, on the other hand, do not clarify the goal or establish criteria for solving the problem; thus, their groups are not sure what they are looking for in a solution or outcome. Effective group members also offer several possible solutions or strategies to overcome the obstacles or decide upon the issues confronting the group. Ineffective group members, however, offer fewer solutions or they rush to make a decision without considering other options or before defining and analyzing the problem. Finally, effective group members systematically evaluate the pros and the cons of the solutions that are proposed, while ineffective groups members do not examine the positive and negative consequences of the solution.

The third major function, *Discussion Management Function*, includes competencies (items 6 and 7) that help the group or team stay focused on its task and/or help it manage its interaction. Effective group members stay on track and keep their focus on the task at hand. Effective group members also summarize what the group is discussing to keep the group oriented. Ineffective group members have difficulty staying on track and frequently digress from the issues at hand, and they also seldom summarize what the group has done. Similarly, effective group members do not monopolize the conversation, and they actively look for ways to draw quieter members into the discussion. Neither are they too quiet; they contribute their fair share of information and look for ways to keep the discussion from becoming a series of monologues. Ineffective group members, however, either rarely contribute to the discussion, or they monopolize the discussion by talking too much. They also make little effort to draw others into the conversation.

The fourth major function, *Relational Management*, includes competencies (items 8 and 9) that focus on managing conflict and developing a positive, supportive group climate. Effective group members are sensitive to differences of opinion and personal conflict; they actively seek to manage the conflict by focusing on issues, information, and evidence rather than personalities. Ineffective group members, on the other hand, deal with conflict by making it personal; they are insensitive to the feelings of others and generally focus on personalities at the expense of issues. Effective group members look for opportunities to support and encourage other group members. Although they may not agree with all comments made, they actively seek ways to improve the climate and maintain positive relationships with other group members through both verbal and nonverbal expressions of support. In contrast, ineffective group members do just the opposite; they are critical of others. Ineffective members rarely use appropriate humor to lessen any tension between group members (Beebe and Masterson 1999).

Here are examples of specific kinds of comments that a group member might make that illustrates each of the nine competencies we have been talking about. Imagine that the group is a local school board task force trying to determine how to deal with the student overcrowding in their district.

"I think the essence of our problem is we simply have more students in the district than we can comfortably put in existing classrooms . . . somehow we need to provide more class space" (*Defined the problem*).

"As I look at the statistics provided by the superintendent, our overcrowding problem started in the Spring of 2001, which was just about the time the new computer chip manufacturing plant was built" (*Analyzed the problem*).

"I think whatever we recommend should be a solution that will be approved by both the business community and the academic community" (*Identified criteria*).

"Let's consider several possible options. We could add more portable classrooms. We could apply for a federal grant to build a new building. Or we could propose a new 50 million dollar bond package to build the school we really need" (*Generates solution*).

"The advantage of building portable classrooms is that we can do it quickly; the disadvantage is that it will not solve our problem long term" (*Proposes solution*).

"I know it's fun to talk about our winning football team, but I don't think that will help us solve our problem. Could we return to our meeting agenda of discussing the overcrowding at the school?" (*Maintain task focus*).

"Sue, I know you have a lot at stake in this problem because you have two children attending school here. What are your thoughts about building more portable classrooms?" (*Manage group interaction*).

"I think you are each raising a good issue. Let's ask the assistant superintendent to check these figures to make sure that we have accurate information. Would that be agreeable to both of you?" (*Manage conflict*).

"Bea, that is an excellent point. You have a great way of helping us see the big picture" (*Maintain a positive climate*).

These examples demonstrate, for each of the nine competencies, how group members demonstrate their competency through how they communicate with others. The verbal statements and nonverbal expressions of support or discouragement are the means by which you and your group members contribute to the group discussion.

Just because a group member did not perform a specific competency does not mean that the person was incompetent. *It may be appropriate not to perform a specific behavior if performing the behavior would be detrimental to the group's effectiveness.* For example, if the problem has been clearly defined by others and all group members appear to understand the precise nature of the problem, it may not be necessary for each person in the group to chime in with a definition of the problem. Sometimes it is appropriate not to belabor the point if it has been made by others. Evaluating the results in your group will let you see general trends or patterns in the group's discussion. For example, you will be able to track whether the group was weak in the discussion management competencies. Or perhaps they excelled in managing conflict and maintaining a positive climate (relational competencies) but struggled with solution-oriented competencies. This instrument helps you refine your impressions of individual group members as well as those of the entire group by describing whether certain behaviors occurred and also whether those behaviors were effectively performed.

Summary

Group problem solving and decision making is enhanced when group members communicate in a competent manner. Whether it is a business team making a decision about who to hire, a nonprofit board of directors like that of the Red Cross sorting out how to raise additional money, or the student government of a college determining how to improve race relations on campus, when group members act in ways that are appropriate and effective, it is more likely that the group will make wise choices. Communication competence is an impression of the appropriateness of an individual's behavior in a given situation. In this chapter we have described an assessment instrument to help you determine whether your group is communicating competently.

The Competent Group Communicator assessment instrument was designed to help observers of problem-solving discussion fine-tune their impressions of group members' communication contributions. According to small group research and what is typically taught in group communication classes, competent group members should help the group focus on the problem by defining the problem and analyzing issues related to the problem. Group members should also help develop a solution by identifying criteria, generating solutions and appropriately evaluating the pros and cons of possible solutions. Group members should play a role in managing the discussion by helping group members stay on task and facilitating group interaction. Finally, competent group members should do more than focus on getting the job done; they should be sensitive to group relationships by managing conflict and maintaining a positive climate.

The situational nature of communication competence makes it challenging to identify a list of group communication competencies that each member of the group should perform during every group discussion. Although researchers have identified specific communication functions that enhance group performance, it would be unlikely that

each group member would perform each function at every group meeting. The *Competent Group Communicator* assessment instrument provides a tool to help group members formulate impressions of their own participation or to have someone else outside the group assess the presence or absence of group communication competencies. Used effectively, the instrument can help groups identify behaviors that need to be increased or diminished. The purpose of the instrument is to help groups better describe the types of communication behaviors they are performing and to document the impressions that individual members and the entire group make on others.

We encourage you to take the ideas from this instrument and use them to critically examine the communication that occurs in groups in which you participate. If you belong to a hard-charging, sometimes conflict-prone group, it might be useful to take the items relating to relational management and see if your group is meeting the needs of group members. Perhaps you belong to a group that gets along well and has a good time, but you feel that you are spinning your wheels. The task competencies may give you a framework for analyzing what can be done to get the group back on task. When groups are able to take a critical look at their strengths and weaknesses, then their capacity for making positive change is enhanced. This instrument can help you determine which group communication competencies your group can use more of or less of to help you achieve your goal.

The Competent Group Communicator

Problem-Solving Group Communication Competencies	Group Member	Group Member	Group Member	Group Member	Group Member	Group Assessment
Problem-Oriented Competencies						
1. **Defined the problem** the group attempted to solve.	NO YES 0 1 2 3	NO YES 0 1 2 3	NO YES 0 1 2 3	NO YES 0 1 2 3	NO YES 0 1 2 3	NO YES 0 1 2 3
2. **Analyzed the problem** the group attempted to solve. Used relevant information, data, or evidence, discussed the causes, obstacles, history, symptoms, or significance of the problem.	NO YES 0 1 2 3	NO YES 0 1 2 3	NO YES 0 1 2 3	NO YES 0 1 2 3	NO YES 0 1 2 3	NO YES 0 1 2 3
Solution-Oriented Competencies						
3. **Identified criteria** for an appropriate solution to the problem. Explicitly discussed standards by which a solution could be evaluated.	NO YES 0 1 2 3	NO YES 0 1 2 3	NO YES 0 1 2 3	NO YES 0 1 2 3	NO YES 0 1 2 3	NO YES 0 1 2 3
4. **Generated solutions** or alternatives to the problem.	NO YES 0 1 2 3	NO YES 0 1 2 3	NO YES 0 1 2 3	NO YES 0 1 2 3	NO YES 0 1 2 3	NO YES 0 1 2 3
5. **Evaluated solution(s):** Identified positive or negative consequences of the proposed solutions.	NO YES 0 1 2 3	NO YES 0 1 2 3	NO YES 0 1 2 3	NO YES 0 1 2 3	NO YES 0 1 2 3	NO YES 0 1 2 3
Discussion-Management Competencies						
6. **Maintained task focus:** Helped the group stay on or return to the task, issue, or topic the group was discussing.	NO YES 0 1 2 3	NO YES 0 1 2 3	NO YES 0 1 2 3	NO YES 0 1 2 3	NO YES 0 1 2 3	NO YES 0 1 2 3
7. **Managed group interaction:** Appropriately initiated and terminated discussion, contributed to the discussion, or invited others to contribute to the discussion. Didn't dominate or withdraw.	NO YES 0 1 2 3	NO YES 0 1 2 3	NO YES 0 1 2 3	NO YES 0 1 2 3	NO YES 0 1 2 3	NO YES 0 1 2 3
Relational Competencies						
8. **Managed conflict:** Appropriately and constructively helped the group stay focused on issues rather than personalities when conflict occurred.	NO YES 0 1 2 3	NO YES 0 1 2 3	NO YES 0 1 2 3	NO YES 0 1 2 3	NO YES 0 1 2 3	NO YES 0 1 2 3
9. **Maintained climate:** Offered positive verb nonverbal expressions which helped maintain a positive group climate.	NO YES 0 1 2 3	NO YES 0 1 2 3	NO YES 0 1 2 3	NO YES 0 1 2 3	NO YES 0 1 2 3	NO YES 0 1 2 3

Scoring

Problem-Oriented Competencies (0–6)	
Solution-Oriented Competencies (0–9)	
Discussion Management Competencies (0–6)	
Relational Competencies (0–6)	

References

Anderson, C. M., Martin, M. M., and Infante, D. A. (1998). "Decision-making collaboration scale: Tests of validity." *Communication Research Reports* 15: 245–255.

Barge, J. K. (1996). "The dialectics of leadership." In R. Y. Hirokawa and M. S. Poole (eds.), *Small Group Communication and Decision Making* (pp. 301–344). Beverly Hills, CA: Sage.

Beebe, S. A., and Barge, J. K. (1994). "Small group communication." In W. G. Christ (ed.) *Assessing Communication Education*. Hillsdale, NJ: Erlbaum.

Beebe, S. A., Barge, J. K., and McCormick, C. (1988). The Competent Group Communicator: Assessing Small Group Problem Solving. Paper presented at the annual meeting of the National Communication Association, November 1988.

Beebe, S. A., and Masterson, J. T. (1999). *Communicating in Small Groups: Principles and Practices*. New York: Longman.

Brilhart, J. K., and Jochem, L. M. (1964). "Effects of different patterns on outcomes of problem-solving discussion." *Journal of Applied Psychology* 48: 174–179.

Brilhart, J. K., Galanes, G. J., and Adams, K. (2001). *Effective Group Discussion*. New York: McGraw Hill.

Carless, S. A., and De Paola, C. (2000). "The measurement of cohesion in work teams." *Small Group Research* 31(3): 71–88.

Chin, W. W., Salisbury, W. D., Pearson, A. W., and Stollak, M. J. (1999). "Perceived cohesion in small groups: Adapting and testing the perceived cohesion scale in a small group setting." *Small Group Research* 30(6): 751–766.

Davison, R. (1997). "An instrument for measuring meeting success." *Information and Management* 32: 163–176.

Flippen, A. R. (1999). "Understanding groupthink from a self-regulatory perspective." *Small Group Research* 30: 139–165.

Gouran, D. S. (1999). "Communication in groups: The emergence and evolution of a field of study." In L. R. Frey (ed.), D. S. Gouran, and M. S. Poole (assoc. eds.), *The Handbook of Group Communication Theory and Research* (pp. 3–36). Thousand Oaks, CA: Sage.

Gouran, D. S., and Hirokawa, R. Y. (1996). "Functional theory and communication in decision-making and problem-solving groups: An expanded view." In R. Y. Hirokawa and M. S. Poole (eds.), *Communication and Group Decision Making* (2nd ed., pp. 55–80). Thousand Oaks, CA: Sage.

Gouran, D. S., Hirokawa, R. Y., Julian, K. M., and Leatham, G. B. (1993). "The evolution and current status of the functional perspective on communication in decision-making and problem-solving groups." In S. A. Deetz (ed.), *Communication Yearbook 16* (pp. 573–600). Newbury Park, CA: Sage.

Graham, E. E., Papa, M. J., and McPherson, M. B. (1997). "An applied test of the functional communication perspective of small group decision making." *The Southern Communication Journal* 62: 169–279.

Granstrom, K., and Stiwne, D. (1998). "A bipolar model of groupthink: An expansion of Janis's concept." *Small Group Research* 29: 32–56.

Haslett, B. B., and Ruebush, J. (1999). "What differences do individual differences in groups make?" In L.R. Frey (ed.), D. S. Gouran, and M. S. Poole (assoc. eds.), *The Handbook of Group Communication Theory and Research* (pp. 115–138). Thousand Oaks, CA: Sage.

Hirokawa, R. Y., and Rost, K. (1992). "Effective group decision making in organizations: Field test of vigilant interaction theory." *Management Communication Quarterly* 5: 267–288.

Hirokawa, R. Y. (1988). "Group communication and decision-making performance: A continued test of the functional perspective." *Human Communication Research* 14: 487–515.

Janis, I. L. (1982). *Groupthink: Psychological Studies of Policy Decisions and Fiascoes* (2nd ed.). Boston: Houghton Mifflin.

——. (1989). *Crucial Decisions*. New York: Free Press.

Janis, I. L., and Mann, L. (1977). *Decision Making: A Psychological Analysis of Conflict, Choice, and Commitment*. New York: Free Press.

Jarboe, S. (1988). "A comparison of input-output, process-output, and input-process-output models of small group problem-solving effectiveness." *Communication Monographs* 55: 121–142.

Jurma, W. E. (1979). "Effects of leader structuring style and task orientation characteristics of group members." *Communication Monographs* 49: 282–295.

Kacen, L., and Rozovski, U. (1998). "Assessing group processes: A comparison among group participants', direct observers', and indirect observers' assessment." *Small Group Research* 29(2): 179–197.

Kerr, C. (1990) An Analysis of Small Group Communication Texts. Unpublished manuscript, Southwest Texas State University, Department of Speech Communication.

Lumsden, G., and Lumsden, D. (2000). *Communicating in Groups and Teams.* Belmont, CA: Wadsworth/Thomson Learning.

McCormick, C. M. (1995). Testing the Validity and Reliability of the Competent Group Communicator Assessment Test. Unpublished M.A. thesis, University of Colorado, Colorado Springs.

Meyers, R. A., and Brashers, D. E. (1999). "Influence processes in group interaction." In L. R. Frey (ed.), D. S. Gouran, and M. S. Poole (assoc. eds.), *The Handbook of Group Communication Theory and Research* (pp. 288–312). Thousand Oaks, CA: Sage.

Morreale, S. P., Moore, M. R., Taylor, K. P., Surges-Tatum D., and Hulbert-Johnson, R. (1992). *The Competent Speaker: Speech Evaluation Form.* Annandale, VA: Speech Communication Association.

Morreale, S. P., Spitzberg, B. H., and Barge, J. K. (2001). *Human Communication: Motivation, Knowledge, and Skills.* Belmont, CA: Wadsworth/Thomson Learning.

Orlitzky, M. O. and Hirokawa, R. Y. (1997). To Err Is Human, to Correct for It Divine: A Meta-Analysis of Research Testing the Functional Theory of Group Decision-Making Effectiveness. Paper presented to the National Communication Association, Chicago, November, 1997.

Pavitt, C. (1999). "Theorizing about the group communication–leadership relationship: Input-process-output and functional models." In L. R. Frey (ed.), D. S. Gouran, and M. S. Poole (assoc. eds.), *The Handbook of Group Communication Theory and Research* (pp. 313–334). Thousand Oaks, CA: Sage.

Riddle, B. L., Anderson, C. M., and Martin, M. M. (2000). "Small group socialization scale: Development and validity." *Small Group Research* 31: 554–572.

Spitzberg, B. H. (1993). "The dialectics of (in)competence." *Journal of Social and Personal Relationships* 10: 137–158.

Spitzberg, B. H., and Cupach, W. R. (1984). *Interpersonal Communication Competence.* Beverly Hills, CA: Sage.

Spitzberg, B. H., Canary, D. J., and Cupach, W. R. (1994). "A competence-based approach to the study of interpersonal conflict." In D. D. Cahn (ed.), *Conflict in Personal Relationships* (pp. 183–202). Hillsdale, NJ: Erlbaum.

Street, M. D. and Anthony, W. P. (1997). "A conceptual framework establishing the relationship between groupthink and escalating commitment behavior." *Small Group Research* 28: 267–293.

Sunwolf, and Seibold, D. R. (1999). "The impact of formal procedures on group processes, members, and task outcomes." In L. R. Frey (ed.), D. S. Gouran, and M. S. Poole (assoc. eds.), *The Handbook of Group Communication Theory and Research* (pp. 395–431). Thousand Oaks, CA: Sage.

VanGundy, A. B. (1981) *Techniques of Structured Problem Solving.* New York: Van Nostrand Reinhold.

Wheelan, S. A., Buzaglo, G., and Tsumura. E. (1998). "Developing assessment tools for cross-cultural group research." *Small Group Research* 29(3): 359–370.

Subject Index

H

I